The 44th Bomb Group in World War II

The "Flying Eight-Balls" over Europe in the B-24

Also by Ron Mackay

Ridgewell's Flying Fortresses: The 381st Bombardment Group (H) in World War II

The 44th Bomb Group in World War II

The "Flying Eight-Balls" over Europe in the B-24

Ron Mackay & Steve Adams

Schiffer Military History
Atglen, PA

Book design by Robert Biondi.

Library of Congress Catalog Number: 2003105589.

Printed in China.
ISBN: 0-7643-1885-3

We are always looking for people to write books on new and related subjects. If you have an idea for a book, please contact us at the address below.

Published by Schiffer Publishing Ltd.
4880 Lower Valley Road
Atglen, PA 19310
Phone: (610) 593-1777
FAX: (610) 593-2002
E-mail: Info@schifferbooks.com.
Visit our web site at: www.schifferbooks.com
Please write for a free catalog.
This book may be purchased from the publisher.
Please include $3.95 postage.
Try your bookstore first.

In Europe, Schiffer books are distributed by:
Bushwood Books
6 Marksbury Ave.
Kew Gardens
Surrey TW9 4JF
England
Phone: 44 (0)20 8392-8585
FAX: 44 (0)20 8392-9876
E-mail: Bushwd@aol.com.
Free postage in the UK. Europe: air mail at cost.
Try your bookstore first.

Contents

Chapter One

Preamble

The relatively short-term but extremely eventful history of the 8th USAAF during World War II has thrown up some important misnomers ever since. The circumstances surrounding this situation were originally created (inadvertently or otherwise) by the American media of the time. A major example concerns the heavy bomber designs jointly tasked with implementing the daylight precision bombing campaign, namely the B-17 Flying Fortress and the B-24 Liberator.

Both designs carried out their primary function in a solidly efficient manner in the course of a 1000-day Battle against the very best that the Luftwaffe fighter and flak defences system could set out. However, one could be forgiven for believing that it was the Boeing bomber that was the major, if not the sole, participant in the skies over Europe. In the more than fifty years following World War II, both cinema and literary presentations have tended to lean towards magnifying the B-17's presence and influence upon the campaign. Conversely, far less attention in general has been granted the B-24. This imbalance has not only provided real grounds for natural frustration among the surviving combat crew and ground crew veterans who flew and serviced the Consolidated bomber, but

Col. Frank Robinson and HQ 44th BG staff officers at Will Rogers Field in July 1942. This would be the final make up of the 44th's HQ staff prior to leaving for the UK.

is also materially inaccurate in military aviation terms. (The British media is similarly prone to such over-simplifications. Judging by most of its efforts to date, one would think that the Battle of Britain was won by the Spitfire, while the Lancaster was the sole provider of RAF Bomber Command's Night offensive).

Cpl. Quinnie Crews 67th BS armaments section. Photo was taken at Barksdale field.

The seeds for this imbalance in the American public's mind were sown early on during the first parlous months of the 8th USAAF's existence in England. Of the bomb groups on hand during this period, five were operating on the B-17 and two on the B-24. With one notable exception, the bases allocated to these pioneer units were wartime creations, hastily hacked out of the East Anglian countryside. Their living quarters and support structures were largely of 'tin-shack' quality, offering minimal internal comforts and coke-stove heating. Bassingbourn, in contrast, was a pre-war RAF station possessing brick-built and centrally heated facilities, with the 91st BG being the fortunate tenant. It is likely that the superior airfield facilities coupled with its good rail and road access to London attracted the U.S. military correspondents more than did the other USAAF bases. Certainly the 91st BG has a prominent place in post-war circles ranging from the cinema to the aircraft modelling fraternity. In addition, for the duration of the war a large proportion of the B-17 groups were located within reasonable striking distance of London. Contrast this with the 2nd Air Division's B-24 units whose service was conducted from airfields away up in the further reaches of East Anglia – a long way away from 'media country' in the form of Britain's capital city!

Whatever the reason or reasons for the imbalance, the tendency to highlight and even eulogise the B-17's participation in World War II over its B-24 contemporary still persists, and needs to continue to be corrected. In effect, the successful conclusion to the daylight offensive must be viewed in the context of a partnership, not a solo effort.

The 44th Bomb Group minuteman guard. This photo was taken at Barksdale Field, LA.

In the Beginning ...

One of the two B-24 groups on hand as the 8th USAAF commenced its Campaign in an uncertain manner was the 44th BG. The Group already possessed an unofficial title that would immortalise its place in history – 'The Flying Eight Balls' – but this was a title whose origin proved less than complimentary, at least when first taken on board. Almost twenty months had elapsed when the personnel and their aircraft landed in Britain, activation having occurred on 15 January 1941. In that period, the Group had initially been assembled, only to find it subsequently acting as a training unit after an element of its personnel had been hived off to form the basis for no less than five other newly activated groups.

During the first six months of 1942 the desperate situation existing in the Battle of the Atlantic had necessitated the launching of anti-submarine patrols over the Gulf of Mexico by way of combating the U-Boats' severe assaults upon Allied merchant shipping. The combat crews were involved in this duty while serving at Barksdale Field. (A fellow B-24 trainee group, the 93rd BG, not only shared this vital duty, but was also destined to constitute the other half of the 8th USAAF's 'pioneer' strength in Liberators, arriving a few days ahead of the 44th BG). Whereas the 93rd BG was temporarily housed at, and operated from, Alconbury prior to transferring to its permanent home at Hardwick, the initial air echelon of the 44th BG (66th BS) headed for what was to be the Group's permanent base (Shipdham) after an over-night stop at Cheddington. It was largely from these East Anglian bases that each was destined to leave its permanent and richly deserving mark upon the conduct of the air war over Europe.

Gearing up to War

By the end of 1940 the American public's stance upon the growing conflict within Europe was still firmly against military involvement. This was a natural reaction based on several probable factors. Firstly, when viewed in the context of the 1930s and into the 1940s, the continent of Europe was far removed from American shores, so making an Invasion or even encroachment upon the North American continent a highly unlikely prospect. Secondly, many of the current population, or their elders, had emigrated from Europe simply to escape from the despairingly regular occurrence of regional conflicts, as well as the deprivation or persecution that often emanated from such events. The failure of the Versailles Treaty as a successful postscript to 'The War to end all Wars' was yet another likely strong influence against taking any form of military action – why should America bail out Europe for a second time in less than a quarter of a century?

Set against these strands of negative reasoning – at least in some political and military circles – was the growing threat from Germany's Axis partner Japan. Should the latter ever declare War against America, and simultaneously persuade Germany to follow suit, the result would be a twin military assault. This action would not even have to involve an Invasion of America in order to reap its reward. Instead, a naval blockade of America's coastline, coupled with attacks upon her shipping, could be ultimately fatal to her continued independent existence. (The current threat to Britain's trade routes across the Atlantic posed by Germany's U-boat fleet was a grim portent of what could occur to America).

This aerial shot shows how the individual Sites of Station 115 were dispersed into the Norfolk countryside. The main Site in the foreground would later be used as the 14th Combat Wing HQ.

This aerial shot shows Site 3 home for the combat crews of the 67th BS.The 67th was somewhat luckier than the other three squadrons in that all aircrew were on one Site and the ground personal were located on Site 1 in the next field.

The Awakening Giant

As 1941 was entered America's military resources were still alarmingly weak, at least in terms of its Army and Army Air Corps. It was therefore all the more fortunate that positive steps were taken during the course of the year to bring both entities to a point where America could at least prosecute a War. In spite of the nation's geographic isolation from both Europe and Asia, its Air Corps had been pursuing development of the heavy bomber element into a strategic rather than a tactical function. The B-17C and D series' were already in service and were being joined by Groups assigned to operate on the B-24. Just a matter of days after the 1941 New Year's celebrations, orders were cut for the creation of both the 44th BG and 93rd BGs. In the case of the former group it came into being at McDill Field, Florida; however, the initial cadre of four officers and ten enlisted men were from the ranks of the 2nd BG and 29th BG. Four squadrons were to constitute its current strength, being the 66th BS, 67th BS, 68th BS and HQ. Lt.Col. Melvin B. Asp assumed overall command, while squadron command devolved to Capt. Ted Timberlake, Major George R. Acheson and Capt. Samford respectively. This seemingly neat command structure would witness numerous changes before the Group was ready to go into combat, however. This confusing situation was in part to be brought about by the accelerating expansion of the Air Corps. In addition, the Group's progress towards a combat function was to be stultified by the hiving-off of Group personnel to no less than five newly constituted Bomb Groups, and its parallel downgrading to an operational training unit.

There were twin problems facing the squadron cadres of officers and senior enlisted men. Not only were they faced by the prospect of training and disciplining a growing number of new recruits, but also the facilities at McDill were still in the first stages of construction. In fact the first two weeks were spent in tented accommodation at Drew Field before the transfer into permanent barracks from what quickly became known as 'Boom Town' occurred in early February. (The relative luxury of these facilities with their air-conditioning, ample washrooms and screened windows would contrast noticeably with the accommodation experience at Shipdham!)

The experience of the 67th BS was typical regarding the 44th BG as a whole. S/Sgt. Beller assumed the post of 1st Sgt.

The 44th was one of the few 8th Air Force Groups that carried a single Group marking in the form of an eight ball with a yellow bomb and blue wings. Each Squadron was given a color for the bomb nose: red for the 66th, yellow for the 67th, white for the 68th, and green for the 506th when it joined the 44th BG. This example belongs to the 68th BS.

and played an important role in the squadron's establishment by transitioning raw civilians into 'citizen soldiers' as quickly as possible. By April, some 200 personnel were on hand, and individuals were being dispatched to various technical schools for specialised training. At this stage of development, the involvement of the Group with any type of aircraft, let alone the B-24, was at best marginal.

Pvt. Marion Bagley recalled when he arrived on 15 May he was assigned as part of a twenty-man strong ground crew. However, his 'tool-kit' consisted of nothing more than two rags – one to wash the aircraft and one to dry it! The trio of aircraft consisted of a B-18, a PT-17 and a YB-17. Bagley's flights in the latter aircraft were initially varied, albeit mundane, and extended from observing whether or not the tail-wheel vibrated to cranking the landing gear up and down. However, his later detachment to the aeronautical school at Lincoln, Nebraska, was to prove the first stage on the road to full M/Sgt.

Cross-country flights were a regular feature of activities by the autumn of 1941. Local flight activity was similarly being stepped up, providing new pilots with experience in deduced or 'Dead' reckoning pilotage and celestial navigation as well as take-off and landing practice. Gunnery practice was basic, since the 'targets' were no more than oil slicks on the water but a proper bombing range was on hand for this aspect of training. Sgt. Arthur Harvey (66th BS) recalled the primitive oxygen system on the YB-17 he encountered on his first flight. There was no mask; instead a wooden nozzle was held between the teeth and the tip of the tongue regulated the oxygen flow!

Local girls who worked at the Red Cross Club on the base at Shipdham.

2/Lt. David W. Arnold (navigator) 66th BS, and 2/Lt. John Reed (pilot) 66th BS check out the conditions.

At War

Arthur Harvey's reaction to the news of the Japanese assault on Hawaii was probably typical. "I had been in the base theater watching 'Target for Tonight' about an RAF Wellington crew on a mission. When I came out I saw a colleague in the queue for the next showing. He asked if I had heard the news that the Japs had bombed Pearl Harbor. I asked; 'Who's she?' So much for geography lessons. In the days following 7 December nearly all the Groups lost their aircraft to more experienced units. All our aircraft were flown to Savannah, loaded up and parked. We sat about for three days playing cards during a tropical storm before being told the planes were now signed over to the base and we went back to Tampa by train."

The events of 7 December 1941 were just weeks behind the personnel when new orders came in, transferring the 67th BS to Barksdale, a process completed by 10 February. By now the Group's regular involvement with the B-24 had been confirmed. Group personnel strength totalled eighty-one officers and 1135 enlisted men. This figure included twenty-six officers and 221 enlisted men of the 14th Reconnaissance Squadron, which had been amalgamated with the 44th BG. (This subunit would be re-designated the 404th BS on 15 May, and on 6 July, Group records would record its attachment to the 44th BG for administration purposes; its personnel, however, were fated to move to another theater of operations when it transferred to the Aleutians in September as part of the 11th USAAF).

There was natural pleasure at moving to Barksdale, especially when the superior living and mess hall conditions were first sampled. On the other hand, the unit that arrived there had already been stepped down from a combat unit status to serving as an operational training unit. While still at McDill, the decision had been taken for the 44th BG to provide cadres for other Groups now in the procession of formation. Barely had Barksdale been reached when 579 personnel were transferred on the 23rd to the various squadrons of the newly-formed 98th BG. (More enlisted men went to this group during March, while still more were dispatched during the same month to the newly-formed 92nd BG; some of the latter returned when it was discovered that the new Group's 'feeder' unit was other than the 44th BG!).

On 24 February, Lt.Col. Acheson moved up into HQ, 44th BG, his position being filled by Major Don McDonald. This change in squadron CO had by now occurred with sometimes bewildering regularity within all three sub-units of the 44th BG. The 66th BS's Capt. Timberlake was on his second appointment when he handed over the 66th BS to Capt. Posey, prior to moving out to the 98th BG on 25 February, although the gap in between the twin spells of command was but a few days. As for the 68th BS, which had transferred to Barksdale on 7 February, the appointment of Capt. Marion D. Unruth on the 19th was the eighth since the squadron's inception! Finally, the Group command passed from Major Rush to Col. Frank Robinson on 27 March. As April passed, the Group personnel strength was again built-up to 126 officers and 1500 enlisted men – only to be reduced for a third time on 17 May when 656 men went to the 90th BG! That same day the 66th BS records state that personnel were dispatched to the 319th BG, which was a B-26 outfit. (Yet another mass transfer had occurred on 26 March with the 93rd BG's formation when the human 'toll' in Group personnel was 587 enlisted men). It was during May that training concentration was directed towards both day and night flying, while 'blind flying' practice was introduced.

Although the Group's switch over from an OTU function to combat status was still in the future, the fact that its personnel were being trained to fly and service the B-24 was a positive indicator, even if the aircraft were a mix of LB-30s and B-24s, some of which were not in the best of condition. On the other hand, the training emphasis was on bringing pilots, bombardiers and navigators up to the necessary standards – after which they were available for transfer out, with their places taken by raw recruits! The same process affected the enlisted personnel.

Sgt. Marion Bagley one of the 67th's original crew chiefs.

The use of crews flying anti-submarine patrols began in April. This diversion away from training duties was created by the current parlous state of the Battle of the Atlantic. During the first few months after America's entry into World War II, the German U-boats had extended their activities along their adversary's eastern seaboard including the Gulf of Mexico. The scale of destruction wrought upon merchant shipping by what President Roosevelt had described as the 'Rattlesnakes of the Ocean' was horrendous, and the air and naval defences in that period were totally inadequate to stem the attacks, let alone reverse them. The presence of the 44th BG in the region coupled

A mixed group of AAF and RAF men take a break from trying to level off the ground on tech Site near the hangars Note the camouflaged T2 hangar.

44th BG Communications Section – note the two RAF men who were part of a small Section who provided assistance with operational procedure in the early days of combat.

Left: Aerial shot of communal Site A. This site housed the Officers Club, Red Cross Club, Enlisted Men's Club and the Gym/Chapel. Top right is the 67th BS's Site 3. Right: Aerial shot of the sick quarters. The long building in the center is the hospital ward. The small building to the left doubled up as the morgue and garage for the ambulances. Buildings in the background at the top of photograph are part of Site 1 for the 67th BS ground personal.

with the long endurance performance of the B-24 naturally leant itself to providing a much-needed boost to surveillance of the Gulf.

Nothing of positive note was to occur up to the beginning of July at least. In fact the sole recorded incident was of a tragic nature. On the morning of 18 May, nine 66th BS airmen flying in B-24/41-1117 lifted off from Barksdale at 0525. There was a 3000ft. cloud ceiling that provided a visibility of some five miles. A moderate rain was falling and a thunderstorm was located five miles northwest of the airfield. The bomber, heavily laden with fuel, ammunition and depth charges, was barely clear of the airfield when it faltered and fell back to earth. There would have been little or no chance of anyone jumping clear since it would have been at a minimum altitude for baling-out. In the event none of the nine-man crew led by Herbert W. Frawley, Jr. survived the crash and explosion.

Then, on the 10th, Lt. Norsen flying in a 66th BS aircraft set out on yet another patrol. In the bomb bay was a mixed load of 300lb. bombs and a single depth charge, but little was expected to arise from what was seemingly yet another monotonous, if necessary, sortie. The first indication that the flight was to be radically different from all its predecessors came when the bombardier directed the bomber towards a dark patch of water upon which a 300lb. bomb was dropped. Nothing came of this since a large shoal of fish caused the effect. The patrol proceeded and the final leg was being completed when Lt. Norsen picked out a vessel in the distance, followed a few minutes later by a second sighting called in by Lt. Diehl (CP) of a submarine to his right. However, in the time the B-24 had made a turn permitting an approach out of the sun the submarine was virtually submerged. With just a matter of seconds to sight and release the ordnance, the bombardier's second effort was magnificent; the mix of four demolition bombs and one depth charge straddled the vessel's forward length. As the position was being marked in the course of two further passes over the position, a wealth of debris accompanied by a very dark patch of oil was sighted.

Up to July 1942 the 44th BG had consisted of four squadrons with the fourth providing an HQ function. On 1 July, the HQ squadron was disbanded with the majority of its personnel being assigned to one of the three remaining squadrons. Those not so assigned were transferred-out.

The overall flying capabilities of the crews were not being totally ignored by those in authority during the first half of 1942. On 29 May, three 67th BS crews led by Capt. McDonald headed northwards to Bolling Field, Washington D.C. They were attached to the Pentagon's 1st Photo Group, and each consisted of two pilots, one navigator, two engineers and a radio operator. The primary duty was for the aircraft to fly at a fifty-

Pilot Lt. John H. Diehl, Jr. was one of the nine original crew commanders of the 68th BS that arrived at Shipdham. His first mission 6 December 1942 was to Abbeville Airdrome, France. He would fly his final mission as Command Pilot on 21 February 1944 to Handorf airdrome in Germany, by which time he had attained the rank of Lt.Col.

mile parallel spacing in order to photograph eastern Canada between Hudson Bay and the North Pole. The same duty was assigned in respect of the Canadian-United States border zone, Greenland and Iceland. The longest B-24 flight to date was recorded by Lt. Warne; taking off from Manitoba for Hudson Bay, he stayed aloft for just under fifteen hours An interesting diversion from the briefed task was to search and locate no less than eight P-38s along with two 'leader' B-17s, the bombers acting as navigators and taking their charges across the North Atlantic to England. Happily, all ten aircraft were picked out from the icy wastes of Greenland where they had crash-landed, and their crews later rescued.

Mudville heights, another pair of boots swallowed up by the mud of Station 115. A young English lad stands in the doorway of a Nissen hut while watching a crazy Yank fighting a losing battle to save his boots. This was the scene that greeted the men of the 44th when they arrived at Shipdham.

Change of Fortune

The prospect of the Group remaining indefinitely in the OTU 'doldrums' began to disappear during the end of July and the beginning of August. It was then that orders were received for the 44th BG Ground Echelon to transfer to Will Rogers Field outside Oklahoma City. The main ground echelon party shipped out by train on 25 July with the air echelon flying in a few days later; advance parties had gone on ahead as early as the 19th. During the bulk of the next month the art of formation flying as well as the honing of navigational skills on cross-country flights and the perfecting of bombing skills was indulged in, prior to the air echelon making a further transfer over to Grenier Field, NH on 29 August. (The ground echelon had already begun the first stage of overseas shipment around 25 August when its personnel had boarded the trains that would take them to Fort Dix, NJ). The civilian-like regime practised by the Will Rogers hierarchy soon led to major disputes with Col. Robinson. He stood up for his men on a range of issues, in particular the right to go off base without a pass. He also mounted guards on the Group aircraft to ensure only his personnel had access!

The 'Flying Eightballs' title that the Group was destined to bear in perpetuity, has been credited to several sources but the most likely one emanated from Col. Robinson. While at Will Rogers Field he was in conversation one day with Capt. Goodman Griffin. The talk turned onto the matter of overseas deployment. Robinson is reputed to have said that he 'could not understand how the air force could even think he could go into combat with this group of misfits, ninety day wonders and odd balls; he added that, "he had never seen such a bunch of eightballs in his entire military career!" This somewhat harsh snap-judgement on the overall performance of the Group personnel was turned into a positive issue when the B-24s had their noses adorned with a 'Flying Eightball', with different colored noses for each squadron's complement!

The men would leave their over-boots at the entrance to their living Sites, so as not to walk the thick mud into their huts. This was a good idea in principle, but any truck or Jeep churned up the mud into the Sites.

The choice of Grenier Field was hardly a suitable one for a unit wishing to continue to perfect its formation-flying and navigational techniques in the shortest possible time. Not only were weather conditions regularly adverse, but also the available aircraft still on hand from Barksdale were not fully equipped to accommodate high-altitude flying. The base sub-depot was less than adequately furnished to handle the flow of necessary modifications or repairs. Although new B-24s were coming on stream at Grenier Field, these were found to lack certain items of equipment. These deficiencies in turn necessitated the bombers' swift return to Wright Field and Middleton Airport for full updating. Just as great a problem was to be found among the ranks of the combat crews. During its Barksdale spell of duty, the Group was seriously run down in terms of navigators and bombardiers, not to mention engineers and radio operators. Despite the infusion of such essential airmen from arrival at Will Rogers Field onwards, time was still felt to be running short if the Group was to enter a combat zone with the twenty-seven B-24Ds that was its assigned operational strength being flown by equally operationally trained crews.

Whatever doubts might have been expressed on the overall Group performance in the air were put aside in mid-September when the overseas-movement order was issued for an expected date of the 26th. Gandar Lake in Newfoundland was to be the fliers' destination. From here the three squadrons were to head out for England. However, there was to be a period of nearly two weeks spanning the entire Group's arrival within the E.T.O. First to head out from Gandar Lake was the 66th BS, whose nine B-24s set off in the late evening of 30 September, touching down nine hours later at Cheddington.

The diary of Capt. Howard Adams (66th BS) provides a good account of the Atlantic crossing; "I took off from Manchester, NH for Newfoundland's Gandar Lake. A more miserable and bleak place is hard to imagine – no town or roads, few people but much wind and bitter cold. We were held up by weather for two days. My 'Masie' was rather sluggish on take-off, being loaded to capacity with 3145 gallons of gas and a mess of baggage and equipment. On board were my eight crew and T/Sgt. Cotterman. (Cotterman recalled that the delay was due to a 500 mile cold front; also, the men were informed that the first snowfall was over two weeks late and expected at any time, so the rush was on to get away before being snowed-in!)

We took off near midnight on the 29th. It was black as pitch as we pulled up and slowly turned on course, but the full moon soon came out, shining beautifully through the clouds. We levelled off at 500ft. and stayed at this height for several hours to keep below icing level. Then we started climbing through the overcast, picking up a little icing on the wings. It was a little warmer when we reached 7,000ft. and the ice melted to make us feel much better.

Only occasionally did we see the cold Atlantic through the clouds. Every hour Lt. Gotke (N) would call up and give an

The Stars and Strips fly proudly at the HQ building on Station 115.

approx. position and course change. All worked smoothly as our autopilot was doing the work, allowing me to sit and watch the compass and other instruments while making adjustments to maintain a correct course. Finally, the light began to grow light in the east, and one of the most beautiful and breath-taking sunrises I have ever seen followed soon after. The air was crystal clear and as the sun rose out of the water it painted everything a golden color.

Soon thereafter Lt. Gotke called up that we should soon see land and I started a gradual letdown. We hit thick clouds and had to go down to 1,000ft. to get beneath them. The sea looked cold and grey and after fifteen minutes we saw a mountain that seemed to stick out of the water. We climbed back up through the overcast and passed over Dernnacross, changing our course for Prestwick, Scotland.

Here we saw Bob Miller who had taken off a few minutes after us, so we flew in formation until arrival at Prestwick,

A nice shot of the control tower, code name "Pathway." Two of the three T-2 hangars can also be seen; they are #3 far left (68th/506th), and #2 (66th/67th). The third T-2 was used by the 464th sub depot.

where after flying around a bit to orientate ourselves we dipped a wing and landed at 1100 GMT, exhausted but happy. After eating dinner we went to our quarters, a private house, where I fell into bed, not to wake until 0900 next morning!"

T/Sgt. Cotterman recollections included sweating out the take off; "We swung around, revved up those all-important engines and rolled. Slowly at first, as we gathered speed you could sense the terrific tightness in the plane with everyone watching each other. After several seconds that seemed like an eternity the plane shuddered and we knew we were off." Later in the flight, "We were now flying in bright moonlight with soft white clouds below. It is often said that men who fly and make the sky their home can hear music when alone up there. I did not hear music as I looked over that vast expanse of nothing but the steady throb of those engines – our only hope from the icy death in the cold Atlantic below."

The risk of being intercepted by enemy aircraft was ever present, and the guns were slung out on approach to the British Isles. Then; "We got a call over the intercom; "Unidentified aircraft approaching on the left wing." Our attention shifted a mite fast from looking for gulls (a sign of land not too far distant) to this newcomer. We followed his flight until he was well past, but suddenly Sgt. Brewer (TG) called out "Aircraft coming in at three o'clock." As he spoke he swung his guns towards the 'bogey' but this aircraft rocked his wings to show us his RAF markings – he was our escort! He was probably as glad to see us, as we were him. Every bomber reaching England in these dark days meant more power to put against the enemy, and it was sorely needed, as we were to find out."

Lt. William Cameron (co-pilot) left, and Capt. Chester L. Phillips (pilot). Cameron would go on to become 67th BS CO on two different occasions. Chester "George" Phillips was KIA May 14, 1943, while flying the first Kiel mission.

The 66th BS's introduction to the navigational 'hazard' that was the British Isles occurred when the crews took off from Prestwick next day. Howard Adams wrote; "October 1 at noon found us in the air as our squadron of nine B-24s headed for Cheddington. After searching for a field a bit – there being so many others around that it was confusing – we fell into a single trail and peeled off one by one for landing. The ground echelon, whom we had not seen since leaving Oklahoma City on 24 August, gave us a joyous welcome, rushing us off to the officer's club for a good meal."

The progress of the other two squadrons was disrupted by the North Atlantic weather patterns. The 68th BS arrived at Gandar Lake on 2 October but did not depart until six days had elapsed. Their experience during the crossing was less pleasant; thick cloud for much of the flight saw final landings spread between airfields in Scotland, Wales and Northern Ireland. Lts. Holmes and Erwin were grateful for the assistance afforded by a Spitfire pilot whom they encountered, and who led them down into Ballyhalbert, located in the latter-named country. Next morning the eight B-24s headed out for Shipdham. (Lt. Reginald Phillips was still at Gandar Lake awaiting a gas-leak repair to his aircraft, and only arrived at Shipdham in mid-October). Orders dated 5 October that sent the 67th BS on its way were only affected on 9 October. One of the co-pilots barely managing to assist Lt. Chester R Phillips haul their over-laden B-24D off the Canadian airfield runway was Lt. Bill Cameron. He was destined for a long and distinguished combat career with the 44th BG, but held great reservations about his chances of survival on that dark, bleak October evening. As dawn broke the next morning the navigator could not pick up the necessary checkpoints leading the crew to Prestwick. Fortunately the same airfield that had proved to be salvation for Lts. Holmes and Erwin (68th BS) loomed up, upon which the B-24 was set down. (Bill's first contact with Irish Guinness in the RAF Mess to which the American fliers had been later invited was one he would never forget – or repeat!)

Ground Echelon Experiences

Having arrived on 28 August at Fort Dix, NJ preparations for overseas movement were immediately begun. Shortages in individual and unit equipment were made up and War Department ID cards individually processed. A score of other personal details involved allotments, insurance, powers of attorney, and the like. Exchange of all summer clothing for ODs was a firm indication that the men were bound for Europe. All was complete by the morning of 4 September when each airman carted his 'A' bag, rifle, gasmask and overcoat two miles to the railroad station. A combined short journey by train, ferry and truck saw them delivered inside the massive hull of a merchant vessel – none other than the 'Queen Mary'. One anonymous airman gloomily, if naturally, reacted to the sight by muttering "What a big f——— target!!" Any hopes for a luxury crossing of the Atlantic were dashed when the men examined their individual berths; not only was each room to be occupied by eight men, but another eight men would occupy the same room on alternate twenty-four hour spells, with the displaced eight-some having to fend for themselves above deck! There were just two mealtimes per day at 0900 and 1630, and a mandatory boat-drill took place after the early sitting.

The crossing was made in double-quick time, with the liner steaming independently and carrying out zigzag manoeuvres at its maximum speed. The frequent course-alterations made sleeping almost impossible as the men were slung around in their bunks each time the vessel heeled over. Deck sleeping was even more uncomfortable, even with the maximum amount of clothing enclosing their bodies; the combination of the chilled night air and the unyielding deck resulted in many stiff and cramped bodies emerging from a fitful slumber in the dawn light!

Arrival in the Clyde estuary in Scotland in the early hours of 11 September was greeted with universal relief. The process of debarkation took several hours, after which the men boarded the 'Toonerville Trolley' British trains and headed south. An interim stop was made at Crewe in mid-England where the party of nearly 900 officers and men again debarked – this time for a crash session in callisthenics – before the journey was resumed. A few hours more and a final stop was made at Cheddington. By now it was well after midnight, and the barracks into which the men tumbled proved very welcome. They would remain at this airfield close to London until such time as their permanent base at Shipdham was completed. Here the men were lectured on various issues including security, how to behave with the British and the dollar value relative to the Pound. General duties were also carried out, including policing the base, close order drill and study of the manual of arms.

The building seen in this picture was the first to be used as the Post Office at Station 115 Shipdham.

Hollywood came to Shipdham in December 1942. Kay Francis (left) and Martha Raye pose with Col. Frank Robinson 44th BG. The CO was the envy of his men when he found himself with these two beauties. The two stars had made the film 'Four Girls and a Jeep' about the activities of an entertainment party.

The facilities at Cheddington were basic in nature, to the extent that there was no sewage system laid in; the regular emptying of the 'honey buckets' (naturally) was passed down the line to the lower-ranking personnel. The ground echelon was destined to remain here for upwards of a month. In that interval the men had plenty of time to get acquainted with the local population, especially when assembling together at the many pubs in the area. Not so pleasant was the exposure to British food in the mess halls, since normal American supplies were not on hand. (This was a situation that would last well into the winter of 1942-1943 for the 44th BG). The shining exception to this was the availability of that great British culinary dish – fish and chips! Many a 'Sad Sack', disillusioned with mutton, Brussels sprouts and the like, found this meal to be excellent value, particularly when served up in a paper wrapping and also liberally sprinkled with salt and vinegar.

Shipdham-under-Mud (or) Shipdham – 'Home, muddy Home'

The airfield with which the Group's fortunes were to be inextricably bound had not originally been constructed with a view to handling truly 'heavyweight' aircraft. This was particularly the case with the runway surfaces. Therefore the U.S. Corps of Engineers had been deployed to bring the airfield up to the required standard. The consequent disruption to the entire area that was occupied by the Shipdham site meant that the new arrivals would be met by a churned-up mass of soil, made even more glutinous by the winter rain and snow, which they would be forced to negotiate. Mud got in everywhere and the wearing of rubber-boots or overshoes was mandatory.

Sgt. John Wolbarst, 464th sub depot, poses by the base entrance sign. The sign was situated on the mile length that extended from Reymerston to the airfield.

Shipdham was located up in the flat, open reaches of Norfolk. Shipdham village lay just off the western edge of the airfield, and was roughly halfway between the small townships of Watton and Dereham. Some fifteen miles to the east lay the much larger city of Norwich. London was away out of normal social range, except when personnel were granted passes spanning several days.

The airfield layout was of standard format. The main runway was 6000ft. in length and ran in an east-west direction. Two intersecting strips each of 4500ft. ran in an approximate NNE-WSW and WNW-SSE direction. Their lengths commenced several hundred feet to the south side of the main runway's western end and intersected towards their respective northern ends. The enclosing perimeter track created a triangular pattern when viewed from above. The aircraft dispersals numbering fifty-five in total were a mix of 'frying pan' and 'diamond' pattern, and reflected the British and American styles of construction respectively. The control tower, main hangars and support buildings forming the primary technical site were positioned south of the main runway, while the bomb-dump lay marginally to the south west of the NNE-WSW runway (take-off with a fully-laden bomber on this short runway was

Station 115's skeet shooting team. The skeet range was situated near the firing butts on the far side of the field.

even more fraught than usual, given the bomb-dump's location!). The two communal sites and several other technical Sites were scattered around the eastern and southern edges of the airfield, with the furthest up to 1 1/2 miles from the primary technical site. In effect, Shipdham was a typical British World War II airfield with everything dispersed as much as possible to guard against wholesale death or destruction in the event of an aerial assault.

Gearing-up for Combat

The arrival of the 44th BG in England occurred seven weeks after the 8th USAAF had commenced its daylight offensive. In that period, the handful of B-17 Groups on hand had launched around a dozen missions, all to close-range targets in France and the Low Countries while under the escort of RAF Spitfires. The maximum number of aircraft dispatched on any one mission was 108 to Lille on 9 October with seven further bombers making a diversionary sweep. Bombing results had been no more than average even with the availability of the precision Norden bombsight. Losses to date were six bombers, with the Lille mission accounting for four. The Lille mission was also the first occasion that three-figure numbers of bombers had been dispatched upon a mission – a situation that was not to be regularly established until March 1943.

The early fortunes of what developed into the 'Mighty Eighth' were a world away from that Air Force's ultimate status. The operational scenario into which the 44th BG had been thrust was one of uncertainty. Many were the siren voices in Authority (American as well as British) who were already querying the optimism of Generals Arnold and Eaker that their bombers could achieve success in similar circumstances to those that had resulted in apparent failure for the RAF during 1939-1940 and in confirmed failure for the Luftwaffe during the Battle of Britain. Operation Torch (the invasion of NW Africa) was destined to divert the two 'original' B-17 Groups (97th BG and 301st BG) to that Theatre of Operations, so further weakening the already meagre force available to Eaker. Winston Churchill was the most prominent advocate for the 8th USAAF to add their bomber strength to that of the RAF in attacking the Nazi empire by night; his conversion away from this policy was only begun after the Casablanca conference in January 1943. All in all, the 8th USAAF was struggling to hold on to its briefed task of daylight precision bombardment.

On 1 October the Ground Echelon had welcomed the arrival of the nine B-24Ds of the 66th BS at Cheddington. Nine days later, the men were taken to the railroad station, from where they set off for Shipdham. One man recalls that, as the train was approaching the airfield, all eyes strained out of the carriage

Left: Aerial view of the 'Eightballs' nest. The photo shows the unusual set up of three T-2 type hangars: there was provision for a fourth hangar but this option was never taken up. The hangars are: #3 (top left of photo) that served the 68th and 506th B.S, #2 (center) allocated to the 67th and 66th BS, while #1 (right) was used by the 464th sub depot. The control tower was offset to #2 hangar. Right: This aerial shot clearly shows how dispersed Station. 115 was. The technical Site can be clearly seen at the top of the photo, while the living Sites are located at the bottom of the photo.

The tower and the three T-2 hangars can be seen from the 67th BS hardstands on the far side of the field.

windows at the sight overhead – the 67th BS and the 68th BS were flying-in from Prestwick at this point, according to this witness.

A further twenty-seven days was to lapse between the full assembly of the Group at Shipdham and its being placed on operational status. The time was utilised to the maximum in settling in and preparing for active service. The ground crews' physical lot out on the dispersals was poor and not destined to improve until the following spring. Little or no construction material was yet on hand for the men to construct huts within which they could live 'out on the line' as opposed to hiking lengthy distances to and from their current Living Sites. Heating or lighting was non-existent even inside the aircraft, and outside maintenance at night had to be conducted by flashlight. The basically damp climate of East Anglia was alien to the American experience. Hands were soon frozen and stiff, since gloves could not be worn when conducting intricate mechanical checks of the engines, landing gear or similar external fittings. Such work often had to be done by several personnel in successive short spells. Having been relieved, but with no buildings available for shelter, the airman in question would try to bring some warmth into his body frame by any means possible – running, stamping one's feet, thrashing one's arms, etc! All USAAF groundcrew were to experience conditions such as these at some stage, but the support staff of the 44th BG was destined to bear this onerous burden for what seemed an inordinate length of time before seeing a general improvement.

The Air Echelon had been busily involved in refining its techniques for flying a combat mission, particularly as regards formation flying. A tight formation generally reflected the difference between individual and corporate success and failure. Sloppy formation flying would invite Luftwaffe attention, while individual pilot carelessness in holding position all too often resulted in human and material loss. Aircraft becoming detached from the formation were to be regarded as expendable. (Any pilot going down or out of the formation to add his weight of protective firepower to that of an ailing bomber and its crew was likely to face heavy censure or even court-martial – assuming he returned safely!)

Finally, on 6 November came the anticipated clearance for the 44th BG to officially begin combat operations. As the flight personnel went to bed that evening, their thoughts were probably typical of all those faced with an uncertain future fraught with much physical danger. They were a long, long way from home; 'school' was over and they were entering the 'Big League of Sky-fighting' against a skilled and inveterate adversary in the shape of the Jagdwaffe (Fighter Arm) of the Luftwaffe.

Chapter Two

Parlous Beginning

During the 8th USAAF's existence in World War II, it was the custom to ease a Group into combat, whenever possible. One method was for the new unit to fly a short-range mission under regular fighter cover. Such missions were often part of an overall plan, whereby the Luftwaffe was (hopefully) diverted from the main force of bombers attacking a separate target thanks to the 'diversionary' effort flown by the new Group.

The strong fighter cover afforded the 'diversion' effort would be expected to prevent casualties among the bomber formation. For the 44th BG, its first mission on 7 November involved the B-24s in a 'diversionary' function. However, the seven crews who took off did not drop any ordnance. Instead, they headed out for Cap de la Hague, while sixty-eight B-17s of 1st Wing attacked the U-boat pens at Brest.

The local residents had become accustomed to the sight and sound of the American bombers as they practised for their entry into combat. Today's sounds emanating from the airfield were no different, as the initial coughing and spluttering Pratt & Whitney motors came to life and steadily blended into a single sustained roar. Nor did the sight of the seven-strong formation cause much stir as it formed up and headed away. This scenario was to be repeated 343 more times in the thirty months and was destined to bring much closer scrutiny from the civilian population as the air war over Europe reached its crescendo. All too often the proud bomber formation that had departed scant hours before would on its return be scattered and sadly short of numerous B-24s and their crews who had fallen in action. Crash-landings and crashes on take-off, landing or while making practice flights were to bring the material and human cost of the conflict even more directly home to the people.

One bomber returned early from the sortie and one diverted into another airfield. No enemy fighters were actually drawn onto the small formation, which turned for home after approach to the Cape. The absence of the Luftwaffe was fortunate because, according to some Group records, no RAF fighter cover was provided – a very strange situation, especially when given the availability of fighter cover and the short-range nature of the mission! Capt. Howard Adams (66th BS) noted in his diary; "We were supposed to fly within twenty miles of the French coast and then return. Lt. Miller and I trailed the formation in case of dropouts. We flew almost due south up to 18,000ft. I lost the formation going through the overcast and had a hard job catching it again. The formation started leaving vapor trails, which made it look as if they were releasing white smoke. They were very pretty streaming out against the brilliant blue sky. We fired our guns at the English coast while waiting for the Spitfires due to join us there. My top and tail turrets refused to fire so I pulled away for home along with Lt. DuBard, Lt. Miller filling the vacancy. I started to let down and was quickly back in the overcast and rain, flying on instruments. After about forty-five minutes we were at 2,000ft. and to our surprise all we could see below was sea. Quick as a fox I headed west, hitting the English coast in a few minutes; the high winds at 20,000ft. had been faster than anticipated. After searching the countryside for an hour or so we located ourselves and followed a railroad track back to the field. Everybody wanted to know what happened and seemed surprised when we told them nothing." (Capt. Adams had had a second lesson in the

67th BS aircraft were dispatched to Northern Ireland for the necessary modifications to bring them up to combat readiness. The nearest aircraft is B-24D-5-CO 41-23817 L "Suzy Q."

problems of navigating both over Britain and Europe. At this stage of World War II the navigational aids were still few as well as imprecise. It was all too easy to get seriously off track and not all crews having a similar experience to that of Capt. Adams were to be granted the opportunity to redeem the situation).

This very casual entry into combat was not repeated forty-eight hours later, when the target was revealed as the U-boat pens at St. Nazaire. The town was not known as 'Flak City' without reason; the concentration of 88mm artillery sited there was guaranteed to throw up accurate salvoes of shells. As one anonymous airman reportedly stated with feeling; "The Kraut gunners down there (St. Nazaire) are post-graduates at their art!!" Just six crews took part, all from the 68th BS. Bombing was conducted from 17000ft. and all aircraft returned safely. Losses among the other thirty-seven bombers getting over the target were three in total. More might have been suffered because the B-17s had gone in at just 8000ft. as an experiment to achieve better bombing concentration. The experiment was not repeated!

Mission No.3 on 14 November was another 'diversionary' effort. This time four out of the five crews flew to a point off Cherbourg in Normandy. Unlike their baptismal sortie on the 7th the Group was covered by three squadrons of Spitfire

A 67th BS B-24D is surrounded by groundcrews after the aircraft developed some kind of problem while taxing out from the 67th Squadron hardstands. The wooded area was known as the Moat.

fighters. Once again, there was an absence of enemy fighters. Next day involved a full mission briefing, this time for Maupertuis airfield at Cherbourg. One out of the six aircraft 'aborted' but this crew's action might as well been followed by the others. Solid cloud cover was obscuring the target, and since bombing over an Allied country in these circumstances was frowned upon, all five brought their ordnance home. Yet another diversion was flown next day by a mixed formation of six from the 67th BS and 68th BS; the majority of the 66th BS B-24s were still in Northern Ireland having modifications applied. These initially related to the armament, radio and armour provision. The original ventral armament consisted of a remote control fitting that was soon deleted as being impractical. The mounting of a single .50 firing through the rear hatch provided too restricted a range of vision, as well as requiring the hatch to be opened. The next step in ventral armament was a variation of the second but placed further aft and with scanning windows placed in the lower fuselage as a vision aid. The centrally mounted nose gun was raised marginally higher to provide a greater degree of azimuth. A VHF command radio was installed, the trailing aerial gave way to a fixed unit and the IFF system was brought up to date. Armour was placed in the bombardier's area of the nose that also acted as a counterweight to the ventral armament. (Over the next few months, the list of modifications deemed necessary before committing new arrivals to combat would rise to over forty).

The return of the 66th BS aircraft to Shipdham on the 23rd. was a promise of combat operations for the full Group. However, just one more mission (26th) was briefed before the month-end, and this was 'scrubbed' due to bad weather. This cancellation was a foretaste of things to come during the ensuing winter months.

December Blues

The 8th USAAF's first winter of operational existence was destined to be bedevilled by a natural adversary in the form of the weather. Reasonable visibility over the target was a basic perquisite for ensuring accurate bomb strikes. Just as important a factor was for the crews to be able to navigate their way there and back. The onset of winter with an increased incidence of rain, snow and fog was to create insuperable barriers against the launch of a mission, let alone its completion. Between 1 December 1942 and 31 March 1943 the 8th USAAF completed just 26 missions. And so, successive briefings at Shipdham on 1, 2 and 4 December were 'scrubbed' thanks to inclement weather conditions.

An early practice mission being flown over Norfolk depicts three aircraft over Wayland, near Attleborough. The aircraft are approaching Wayland hospital, which can be seen bottom left of the photograph. Closest aircraft is "Hitler's Nightmare' a D-5-CO 41-23774S 67th BS. The lead aircraft is "Black Jack" a D-5-CO 41-23816X of the 68th BS being flown by Lt. John Diehl. The third aircraft is "Suzy Q" a D-5-CO 41-23817S being flown by "Pappy" Moore of the 67th BS.

This is a very early shot of one of the 44th's famous aircraft before her artwork was applied. B-24D-25-CO 41-24225 of the 68th BS, better known as 'Flak Alley' is seen here flying over the Norfolk village of Attleborough. She would fly missions until 24 February 1944 when she was lost on what was her forty-third mission.

The latter briefing had been for Abbeville/Drucat airfield in France, which was put up on the board two days later. This target was exclusively allotted to the 44th BG with the 1st Wing going to Lille, while another Group carried out a 'diversion' sortie. Nineteen B-24s lifted off and headed out; flying lead were six crews from the 68th BS, backed by the same number from the 66th BS and seven from the 67th BS. For whatever reason, the 'recall' signal subsequently sent out was only responded to by the high and low squadron formation elements, leaving the 68th BS to proceed to the target. The dangerously isolated Force made a good drop on the airfield and rallied for the home flight. As it was approaching the Channel coast its luck ran out with the onset of fighter attacks by up to thirty Fw 190s, probably from JG 2.

The recently introduced tactic of head-on approach to the 8th USAAF bombers was to pay huge dividends in the months ahead; the amount of defensive gunfire able to be brought to bear against the 'twelve o'clock' attack-angle by the B-24D and the B-17E and F was minimal. The Luftwaffe attackers swept through the bombers in groups of three and quickly made the effect of their fire evident. Lt. Dubard suffered the total loss of No.4 engine and damage to No.3. on 41-23786/B. The

Left: "Spirit of 76", a B-24D-5-CO 41-23776/W was an original 68th BS aircraft, and was later lost on 27 January 1943. Right: 1/Lt. Maxwell W. Sullivan, Jr. and crew pose in front of 'Spirit of 76.' They were lost on the 27 January 1943 mission while flying in this aircraft after it was hit by Fw 190s and exploded. Bombardier 2/Lt. Albert W. Glass was the only member of the crew to survive.

Lt. James Kahl and crew of the 66th BS are photographed following their return from the 27 January 1943 mission to Wilhelmshaven, Germany.

pilots vainly tried to hold the wallowing bomber in formation but finally fell out to become the main source for assault. The gunners gave of their best and returning crews told of at least three fighters destroyed or listed as 'probables'. Then, a final attack by two fighters from below and behind the B-24 administered the fatal blow. Both top and rear turrets stopped firing and the bomber dropped down towards the Channel waters. The pilots appeared to stabilise the downward angle but as their aircraft hovered above the surface the nose dropped and the B-24 burst into flames upon impact. None of the crew survived the crash, but all were later granted the posthumous award of the Silver Star.

And so the 44th BG had been 'blooded' in combat. Lt. Dubard and his nine crewmen were the first in an all-too-long list of young Americans flying out of Shipdham who would never live to see home or who would languish in a German Stalag for months or years before final liberation; an additional number would experience the 'bonus' of evading capture or of coming down in the neutral territories of Sweden or Switzerland.

An early return to Abbeville/Drucat was the last thing required by the Group fliers, but just four days later (10th) they were dispatched again as a 'diversion' for the main force. This time around, the undercast that prevented bombing was equalised by the absence of enemy fighters. Bombloads were jettisoned over the sea. Two 'scrubbed' missions had occurred on either side of the fore-mentioned mission, but Romilly airfield was in the clear on the 20th. Just over 100 bombers were sent out of which seventy-two bombed. Luftwaffe activity was strong and six crews were MIA, none of who came from the 44th BG, although its gunners fought off continuous assaults by between twenty and thirty fighters.

Capt Adams (68th BS) noted in his diary how the enemy fighters shot past close – so close that the pilots and their aircrafts' camoflage pattern were clearly discernable. He recorded how the waist gunners were 'having a hell of a time' with freezing hands and oxygen masks, the latter problem being solved by utilising the extra masks on hand. The Spitfire escorts gave good support on the way back, but the Capt. felt it was an eternity before the formation crossed out over the Channel. His final comments are worthy of full quotation; "Soon we started losing altitude, and we began to pass the B-17s, feeling very gay at our good luck. We chattered over the interphone like silly schoolboys, everything we said seemed funny, though when our ROG reported wounded on board Major Key's ship we soon sobered up.

After landing we were questioned by Intelligence as we sipped hot coffee. Everyone was polite and the air seemed filled with excitement and endless chatter. Questions; How many planes did you see? – Where did your bombs drop? – Where did you meet flak? – Did you see any bombers go down? We answered the best we could though tired and excited, and food and sleep were all we could think about after our five-hour ordeal. So ended our first real raid." (The reference to 'silly schoolboys' is pertinent, because many of the airmen were barely out of college. Seemingly aimless chatter was far from 'silly'; indeed it was a natural, if not to say necessary, psychological response to the dreadful pressures of combat

The photo shows bombs bursting on the Trystian Lock as well as hits on the inner end of the Eastern jetty and a salvo of at least fifteen bursts across the approach Channel and the Quay to the west.

41-23816 skims low over the Norfolk countryside.

flying). The personnel of the 8th USAAF were boys doing a man's job, all too many of whom were never destined to be around when VE-Day finally arrived. Although the 8th USAAF flew one more mission prior to the year-end, the 44th BG was not called upon to participate.

T/Sgt. Albert W. Emery, engineer on Capt. Arthur V. Cullen's crew. Emery was KIA on a mission to Dunkirk on 15 February 1943.

'Getting to know You ...'

Within the first few weeks of their time at Shipdham, many of the personnel had taken the opportunity to wander further from their immediate surroundings, with Norwich being the centre of attention. The initial experience of one individual in establishing himself with the citizens of East Anglia was proving typical as he recalls; "I caught the Liberty Run whose terminal was the Cattle Market. We wandered down the hill and questioned some civilians; "Where is down-town?" – "Down-town? What's that?" We explained that it was where the main sources of entertainment, etc. were, and they provided an answer. Then we asked, "How many blocks is it?" Came the response "Blocks? ... Blocks?" We were learning our first painful lesson in respect of the, 'common language that keeps us apart'!

The British currency was equally puzzling to most Americans during their initial spell in the country. The multitude of coins going from the farthing to the half-crown, as well as the range of notes, was so involved, not to say arithmetically illogical, when compared to the U.S. coinage and note equivalent. As for that commodity sold in quantity by the pubs – well, beer it might be in name, but to the majority of American servicemen, beer it was not! Of course, the flat and warm nature of the liquid did not prevent its regular consumption by those Trans-Atlantic 'cousins' caring to indulge their thirst in spite of their negative opinions!

Below: A posed photo of a tunnel gunner at his place of work. This gun position was not very effective, and later B-24 models would be fitted with a ball turret in place of this original mounting.

The base personnel had already made acquaintance with their RAF contemporaries detached from No.2 Group HQ at Bylaugh Hall, one of whose number was Cpl. Peter Broadley. He had been on hand when the original USAAF 'tenants' (319th BG) had arrived at Shipdham before departing very soon afterwards for North Africa. The RAF staff was initially billeted on No.1 Site but then transferred to what had been the WAAF dormitory Site according to the intended layout for the airfield before its switch to the USAAF was made. The Enlisted Men's Club running was in the hands of the NAAFI (Navy, Army and Air Force Institute) until early 1943 when the American Red Cross assumed responsibility. The disparity in supplies from British as opposed to American sources, especially in respect of cigarettes and candy, left Peter and his colleagues feeling embarrassed; not only were the available stocks far too small for the numbers involved but the difference in tobacco taste between the respective national brands was noticeable.

On a more positive note, Peter proved to be a sound 'navigator' when the party of airmen waiting in the transports to take them from Norwich one evening were informed by the officer in charge that the descent of fog combined with the blackout regulations had made this impossible. Peter's expert

B-24D-CO. 40-2354/C of the 66th BS was sent to Bovingdon in Hertfordshire for armament modification evaluation. This bomber was lost in a mid-air collision with 41-23818 on 16 February 1943.

knowledge of the route to Shipdham proved invaluable as he guided the driver in the lead transport along the narrow, torturous roads! On a separate occasion he assisted in tracing a route to the nearby airfield at Horsham-St. Faiths where the men remained until next morning when the fog had clear.

Bitter Harvest

Col. Frank Robinson had assumed Group command the previous April and had proved to be a well respected Commander. However, what occurred on the first mission of the New Year was to sadly culminate in dismissal from his post.

At 0830 on 3 January, thirteen bombers led by Major Key (66th BS CO) took off following a briefing for the U-boat pens and support facilities at St. Nazaire. The concrete roofs of the pens within which the U-boats were berthed were impenetrable even for the USAAF's maximum-size ordnance (2000lb. bomb) but the other structures were vulnerable; the 44th BG had been assigned those housing torpedo stocks. A range of technical failures forced five crews to 'abort', but the reduced force held its position behind the B-17s and fought its way through flak and fighter attack to make a strike assessed as 'fair'. So far all had gone well for the Group as it rallied off the target and started for home, but the situation was set to deteriorate, thanks to faulty navigation by the Lead Group. When landfall off the Cornish coast in the extreme southwest of England did not appear on schedule, Lt. Bill Cameron recalled his navigator Lt. Bartmess suggesting that the entire formation was off course and probably heading up the Irish Sea. As time passed by the problem of diminishing fuel supplies loomed up. This was especially serious for the 44th BG since its bombers had taken off with reduced fuel capacity. Finally, the order was given for all crews to turn westward and seek any suitable landing site. Six were fortunate to touch down on airfields, with Lt. Long and his 67th BS crew surviving a heavy crash in 41-23808/P – TEXAN after they lost their last engine as the B-24 settled down. Lt. Hilliard (66th BS) in 41-23771 put down in a field bounded by what were taken to be hedges. In fact these were lichen-covered stone structures against which the bomber was wrecked; Lt. Canfield (CP) was killed and several others seriously injured. Lt. Erwin in 41-23806/Z 'BAT OUT OF

Cannon fire damage sustained by "The Captain and the Kids", a B-24D-5-CO 41-23800/Y of the 68th BS. The photo was taken in the 464th sub depot hangar on 17 February 1943. The damage was sustained on the mission to Dunkirk two days previously. Three of the crew was KIA, one of whom was T/Sgt. John W. Crump the top turret gunner. The plexiglas top turret has been totally destroyed, leaving Crump with no chance of surviving the impact.

Shipdham on the mud.This photo shows an early 1943 mission: if an aircraft happened to stray off the perimeter track and into the mud there was no chance of its being swiftly recovered and permitting any bombers following up behind to get airborne. Consequently, any mission so affected could end up being cancelled.

HELL' (68th BS) was on final approach to an airfield when the B-24 suffered progressive power loss and dived into the ground. Lt. Swanson (CP) was killed outright while Erwin and Lt Davenport (N) later died in hospital. Only two other crew-members escaped injury.

It was several days before the scattered Force was able to wend its way back to Shipdham. Lt. Cameron and his pilot Lt. Chester Phillips were doubtful if they could fly their 'Little Beaver' out of the small grass strip into which they had diverted, but did manage to stagger safely into the air. On getting out at Shipdham, the men were not met by Col. Robinson but by his replacement Col. Leon Johnson. Frank Robinson had seemingly become the 'fall guy' for the mission fiasco, and had been swiftly removed from command. As regards his successor, he must have faced a guarded if not hostile reaction from his new personnel. Johnson was a West Point graduate and more than able to handle this awkward situation for all concerned. He was to earn the full respect of the Group during the ensuing eight months, prior to his elevation as CO of the 14 CBW.

The St. Nazaire mission also proved to be the last flown by Major Algene Key (66th BS CO) although he survived the experience. The Major was a veteran aviator long before World War II erupted. He and his brother Fred had created an endurance record of 653 hours flight-time over their hometown in Mississippi. Both had fought in the Far East during 1942 but following their return States-side Algene was assigned to Barksdale Field and command of the 66th BS. His overall value to the War effort was deemed too great to risk him on combat operations, and so he was 'grounded' and transferred out after what was his fifth mission.

Law of Diminishing Returns

Hard times were looming ahead for the 44th BG and the 67th BS in particular. Over the next few months its original complement of nine B-24s would be relentlessly whittled away along with the vast majority of the 'original' combat crew. This process was not commenced for the bulk of January due to seven out of eight briefings up to the 18th being 'scrubbed' The exception (13th) involved the launch of a 'diversion' mission off the Dutch coast that proved uneventful. The effect of any mission 'scrub' was felt almost as much by the ground crews, as by the combat crews. As regards the fliers, there was a tremendous sense of let-down; after gearing their minds to the grim task in hand, they then had to try to wind down, knowing that they were no nearer the magic 'target' of twenty-five missions that promised a permanent lease on life. A different form of frustration came the way of the support teams. They had probably spent many hours, even the entire night, in readying their bombers for the mission. Now all their dedicated work often carried out under dreadful weather conditions was in vain, with the armourers in particular facing the laborious duty of removing the ordnance.

The month's next full mission went out on the 23rd with Lorient, another prime U-boat base, as the target. Hazy weather caused five bombers to fail Group assembly, while the twelve that did then failed to link up with 1st Wing. A switch to bombing the secondary at Brest was then made, but yet another three B-24s fell out due to malfunctions. Col. Johnson finally decided that his Group formation was too small to risk encountering enemy fighters and turned back. Two more 'scrubbed' missions occurred on the 24/25 January – and then came the 27th.

For the 1st Wing crews attending briefing on 27 January, the magic word 'Germany' was reacted to with quiet satisfaction, mingled with the normal sense of apprehension surrounding any mission. At long last the 8th USAAF was going to hit the enemy in his own industrial backyard. A similar reaction must have arisen among the ranks of the twenty crews over at Shipdham as the briefing staff was outlining the target details for the submarine construction yards at Wilhelmshaven. The bright hopes for a successful strike were to be blunted and finally cancelled out. Solid cloud-banks towering well above operational height coupled to uncertain navigation left the Group floundering over the North Sea and totally adrift of 1st Wing. By the time the ground became visible Col. Johnson, having confirmed the B-24s were over Holland's internal water region the Ijsselmeer, elected to hit a target of opportunity in the form of the Dutch town of Lemmer.

Just as the Group was clearing the area, a number of Bf 109s and Fw 190s attacked. The head-on method of approach was as dangerous for the fighters as for their prey, thanks to the risk of mid-air collision. This was the fate of one Focke-Wulf pilot who, upon completing his run and breaking away rammed the left wing of 41-23690 flown by Lt. Cargile. A progressive disintegration quickly followed the bomber's entry into a flat spin; it began with the rammed wing and a large section of the rear fuselage becoming detached and finished when the right wing broke away. One crewman was reported to have jumped from a waist window with his parachute opening, but nobody – including the Fw 190 pilot – actually survived the incident and only two bodies were later recovered. (The collision was ascribed to the Luftwaffe pilot having already been killed by return fire from another 68th BS bomber).

Ten minutes later the latest head-on thrust by three Focke-Wulfs set No.3 engine on 41-23776/ W – 'SPIRIT OF 76' ablaze. Lt. Sullivan's aircraft dropped out of formation and almost immediately broke up with the remnants scattered in and around Terschelling harbour. Three men did jump clear before the B-24 broke up, but only one of the ten-man crew came through alive. Lt. Glass (B) believed he was blown out into mid-air to come down into the water, from which he was plucked by a Dutch lifeboat. Even then, the severe injury to

On 20 February 1943 tragedy struck the 66th BS with the loss of Captain "Wild" Bill McCoy and part of his crew in a wasteful practice flight accident at Clearmont Hall, near Watton. McCoy was considered to be one of the best pilots in the Group, but even his immense flying skills could not save the situation, when the whole tail section broke off, leaving the aircraft to dive into the ground.

one leg resulted in its amputation, and Glass's ultimate repatriation to the USA after a spell in a POW camp.

There should have been a third 68th BS crew declared MIA from the mission. That this did not occur was at least partially due to the actions of Lt. Diehl flying in 41-23816 BLACK JACK. His fellow squadron pilot Capt. Jim O'Brien's B-24, 41-23819 RUGGED BUGGY sustained an assault from a steep-diving Fw 190 that killed two crew- members as well as knocking out the nose-mounted guns. The tail turret was disabled and the stricken bomber fell down several thousand feet below the formation. The strict rule in such circumstances was for the straggler to be regarded as expendable, and leave the crew to seek their own salvation. What was known as 'Group integrity' was expected to be adhered to, so that every available gun could play its part in protecting the remaining aircraft still within the formation. Any attempt to go down to assist a straggler was deemed a potential court-martial offence, since there was a great risk of the 'protector' crew also being lost in taking this action. In spite of all these restrictions upon individual action, Lt. Diehl dropped down and out to go to O'Brien's aid. The added firepower of the second B-24 then proved sufficient to deter all subsequent assaults. Having cleared the coast but with his navigator seriously injured, O'Brien indicated to Diehl that he take the lead to get both aircraft safely home; this was duly accomplished thanks to precise navigation by Lt. Kelley.

It was a chastened bunch of combat crewmen who landed off that day's mission. Two crews were MIA, a third bomber was badly shot-up and there were several dead or wounded airmen; this was a stiff price to pay for a very uncertain bombing effort. The men then had several days to reflect upon their situation and two 'scrubbed' briefings before the next call to action was set out upon. Even so, the intended attack on the marshalling yards at Hamm was 'aborted' after take off due to so many bombers dropping out through malfunction. One of the primary problems being encountered was the failure of many machine-guns thanks to the type of oil then in use freezing and jamming the weapons. On 2 February, Major Norsen (68th BS) tested a new type of oil upon the machine-guns by flying his B-24 up to 36,000ft. Flight above 10,000ft. generally required the constant use of oxygen equipment. Any failure in the oxygen system would result in the individual or individuals concerned lapsing into an unconscious state within minutes and dying not long afterwards. Such a failure occurred this day and the majority on board passed out. They recovered with one tragic exception; this was Sgt. Krutsch who did not respond to attempts at revival. It was all the more ironic that the oil-tests proved totally satisfactory in maintaining the guns in full working order.

Happy days at Shipdam. Capt. Bill McCoy stands in the doorway with the Group CO Col. Leon Johnson to his right, and Capt. Bob Abernathy to his left. On the far right is Lt. Griffen who would be KIA on 17 July 1943 over Naples.

The 8th USAAF managed one completed mission up to mid-February, but the 44th BG was not called upon to participate. It was a totally different story next day (15th) when the two B-24 Groups provided the entire strike-Force. A large German commerce vessel was reported docked at Dunkirk just across the English Channel and the B-24 Groups were detailed to take the vessel out. (The vessel in question was actually a night fighter-control ship named TOGO converted from its commercial shipping function. It bore both FREYA and WUERZBURG RIESE radar sets with which to report and track incoming RAF bombers and after being refitted in the large dock located in Dunkirk, was transferred up to the Heligoland Bight. Its name was an abbreviation of Togoland, a German protectorate in Africa that was taken away from Germany after World War I). Seventeen 44th BG bombers lifted off and formed

Robert Perkens Post was a civilian war correspondent for the *New York Times* and a member of the 'Writing 69th.' He was killed on 26 February 1943 while flying with the Adams crew.

Aircraft are photographed taxiing out from the 67th Squadron hardstand area.

up with a six-aircraft element from the 93rd BG. In the lead bomber was Capt. Cullen (67th BS) along with Major McDonald as command pilot. Dunkirk, like all the Channel ports, was strongly defended by flak batteries. Consequently the longer than normal bomb-run gave the enemy gunners ample opportunity to accurately bring their firepower to bear. They had the bombers' range zeroed-in as the run was about to be completed.

In the lead B-24 (41-23783/M – BETTY ANNE/GALLOP-IN GHOST) Capt. Cullen saw the 'bomb release' lights go on as Lt. Caldwell (B) operated his bombsight gear. Almost at once there was a massive explosion under the nose that temporarily stunned Cullen. On recovering his senses he found himself in charge of an aircraft with no nose section and cockpit cover! A broken leg hindered his attempt to manipulate the rudders as the B-24 sagged into a steady dive with the inboard engines exuding smoke trails. In the right hand seat Major McDonald with a serious stomach wound motioned Cullen to jump. Instead, the pilot assisted his CO in getting un-strapped and then out through the shattered cockpit. Cullen then followed but broke his leg again as well as an arm through impacting with the tail. Both men reached the ground alive but Major McDonald's wound must have been mortal since he died some hours later while being operated on in a German hospital. (His brother Henry flew many missions with the 305th BG. In addition he was severely wounded by misdirected fire while flying a target-tow A-20. However, he recovered the use of the affected shoulder and arm sufficiently well to continue on combat operations as well as assuming the Group Command late on in World War II).

The other crews gazed in shocked amazement upon the spectacle of the Lead B-24 with its foreshortened forward fuselage. The bomber held position for some time before falling away to the right. In the rear fuselage Sgt. Woo (ROG) had ensured the other gunners had their parachute packs on. Consequently when the bomber was fatally damaged all were in a position to evacuate. However, two of the five crewmen involved did not survive, probably being trapped by the spinning motion of the B-24.

Lt. Oliphant in 41-23794/Q – RAILWAY EXPRESS had suffered flak damage at the same time as Capt. Cullen's bomber. Lt. Diehl then carried out his latest 'protector' role for both Oliphant and a second flak-damaged bomber, 41-23800/Y – CAPTAIN AND HIS KIDS – flown by Capt. Cramer. The Fw 190s that appeared out of the sun almost at once landed their fire upon both cripples. Out over mid-Channel, Lt. Oliphant's B-24 finally succumbed, catching fire in the fuselage as well as Nos.1 and 2 engine, and exploding on contact with the water.

By now, the two surviving bombers were low down and approaching the English coastline. Cramer's lagging machine had suffered damage to the bomb-release mechanism that caused hang-ups as well as affecting the hydraulic and oxygen systems. Now the No.1 engine caught fire just as Lt. Flynn (B) had succeeded in manually jettisoning the ordnance. Then he acted upon his pilot's advice to bale out that was also taken up

Left: Capt. Howard L. Adams was one of the original 66th BS pilots. He would be KIA February 26, 1943, losing his life six days after his best friend and fellow 66th pilot Captain Bill McCoy was killed in a tragic practice flight. Adams was only twenty-five when he died over Bremen. Right: A second shot of Capt. Howard F. Adams (66th BS). The Adams crew included Robert Post, a member of the 'Writing 69th' who was the only reporter choosing to fly with the B-24 crews to Bremen on 26 February 1943. Only two of the eleven men on board survived their bomber's loss.

by Lt. Poole (N) and T/Sgt. Crump (Engineer). Sadly, the low height available resulted in all three men being killed. (Tragically, they would have survived by staying on board. Capt Cramer, realising that his aircraft was failing fast, managed to effect a crash-landing on a beach near Ramsgate from which all emerged with nothing more than slight injuries.). For the second mission running, casualty statistics were two crews MIA, one bomber 'written-off' and several additional crewmen killed or wounded. Before February was out, the same MIA figure would arise twice more.

More Hard Knocks

The grim arithmetic similarity in the February loss record recurred just twenty-four hours after Dunkirk. Major 'Pappy' Moore (67th BS), who was destined to make his mark within the 44th BG in a similar manner to Bill Cameron, was the newly appointed successor to Major McDonald. This day he led the Group to St. Nazaire along with Col. Johnson. Another 67th BS crew taking part was that of Lt. Long, who had survived their crash in Wales on 3 January. Formation flying was never easy and was ever laden with the risk of mid-air collision. The English coast had just slid by when Lt. Billings (66th BS) in 42-40354/C – SNAFU was seen by Lt. Long to drop down sharply to the left. Long's B-24 was positioned behind that of Billings, but he manoeuvred his bomber to bypass the faltering SNAFU by also going underneath rather than above. SNAFU now tragically lived up to its name because as its pilots, upon seeing Long's action, attempted to swing their bomber away to the right, the left wingtip intersected with the lower fuselage of 41-23818/R. Mere seconds later, after tumbling together and then separating, the two aircraft with their volatile ordnance and fuel content disintegrated in two massive balls of smoke and flame; four parachutes were reported but the end result was the post-war addition of nineteen names to the 'Wall of the Missing' at Madingley Military Cemetery outside Cambridge. Of the remaining ten crews, only six actually completed the mission. The formation was not beset by fighter attack until it had delivered its ordnance in a tight, accurate pattern and was heading back. Capt. Clyde Price's gunners in 41-23784 were given credit for five 'destroyed' in the course of a short but intense individual battle; their bomber had been flying in the rear of the formation and had received appropriate treatment from the Luftwaffe.

When this bomber taxied back in at Shipdham the ground crew saw the feathered No.3 engine and various holes, especially in the left wing. Initial checks revealed that numerous fuel cells had been punctured and would need replacement. Then began the tedious task of unscrewing hundreds of screws securing the 35ft. by 3ft. aluminium plates beneath the cells that also formed the wing skinning. The physical effort of

Aircrew can be seen talking over the coming mission that would be a long haul out over the Bay of Biscay to the submarine pens at Bordeaux, France. The mission would subsequently be claimed a massive success. The man responsible for the precise over-water navigation that led the Force to an exact rendezvous over the target was Lt. Edward Mikoloski. Photo was taken at Davidstow Moor in Cornwall.

working the tools at arms length while standing on boxes and ladders was both arduous and prolonged. Screws often fractured, which necessitated drilling out the affected aperture. Then came the releasing of the old fuel cells and their replacement, after which the wing skinning was put back. All in all, the effort took more than twenty-four hours to complete – and then the No.3 engine still had to be attended to. Its removal revealed a damaged supercharger that also had to come out. By the time this latter task had been completed, M/Sgt. Baccash's team had been awake (or rather, by now were reduced to zombie-like status) for well over two days! However, they had fulfilled their basic brief, namely to 'keep em' flying', by returning MISS DIANNE to full operational readiness. It was countless achievements like this that not only kept the 8th USAAF in the air but also enabled it to mount maximum pressure on Germany's industrial and military resources. But anecdotes of this nature were rarely, if ever, deemed worthy of media attention.

Lt. Abernathy and crew pose in front of B-24D-95-CO 41-23779 "4-Q-2." This aircraft would be transferred to the 67th BS after the 14 May mission to Kiel to replace 67th aircraft losses. Lt. Abernathy, is second from the left in the back row. Standing to his right is Lt. Robert E. Kolliner, who would gain the rank of major and become the 67th's CO during March 1944.

The B-24's 'shutter-pattern bomb doors were at times inclined to jam in position. This fault happened to Capt. Chester Phillips in his 41-23807/U – LITTLE BEAVER over St. Nazaire. The flimsy nature of their construction did not prevent Lt. Hill (B) from releasing the ordnance. But what he then achieved was described by Lt. Bartmess (N) as 'the highest trapeze act in history'. Lt. Hill crouched on the very narrow bomb-bay catwalk. Festooned with pieces of wire he secured the flapping door remnants in place to prevent their breaking away and inflicting possible damage on other B-24s in the formation! And so the 67th BS aircraft that was becoming a 44th BG 'character' in its own right came through its tenth mission. The name would be woven into Group annuls along with Major Moore's SUZY-Q, and LEMON DROP from the 68th BS.

Capt McCoy (66th BS) had a deserved reputation as a first-class combat pilot. His massive frame was well known throughout the Group, and he was held in genuine respect by all and sundry. On 20 February, he had made a series of 'touch and go' landings along with his crew and Col. Snavely. Capt. Adams noted in his diary; "After several landings the Col. got out but Bill said he would shoot more landings, with Lt. Brown (B) acting as co-pilot. Twenty minutes after take-off, we heard they had crashed. Bill Brandon and I hoped against hope it wasn't serious, but when we rushed into operations we were crushed by the news that the crew, including Bill, were dead. All the fellows on board were swell, but Bill's loss was perhaps the hardest blow yet suffered by either the 66th BS or the Group. Six foot two, 200lbs., with curly hair and a wide smile, 'Big Bill' or 'Wild Bill' as he was affectionately known was liked by all from Colonel to private. As a flyer he took second to none, as he could put a B-24 through its paces. He led the Group many times and was by far the best at it." It was found the whole tail assembly fell off at around 3000ft. The plane went into a flat spin and dove in at high speed, killing everyone. Bill's loss was felt by the whole Group." Howard Adams had unknowingly made his final diary entry, as his equally young and vibrant life had just a few days to run its course.

Six days later the 8th USAAF struck at Wilhelmshaven, with the 44th BG contributing nine crews. Seven U.S. correspondents of the 'Writing 69th' had elected to take part in

Ground crews of the 68th BS take a welcome coffee and doughnuts break supplied by the Salvation Army wagon parked on the hardstand. The aircraft in the background is B-24D-5-CO 41-23816 "Black Jack" one of the original nine aircraft received by the 68th BS, and the regular mount of Lt. John Diehl.

the mission; only one – Robert P. Post of the *New York Times* – chose to fly on a B-24, in his case that of Capt. Adams (66th BS). Both B-24 Groups were in the trail position to the B-17s with the 44th BG last in line. Fighter assaults developed near Heligoland on the way in but no losses were inflicted until the Group was nearing the target. Then two crews were culled from the formation, both from the 66th BS. In 41-23777/H – MAISEY No.3 and 4 engines were set on fire. The B-24 finally exploded and only two men got out alive – Bob Post was not one of them, and in fact his body was never found. One of the survivors was Lt. Gotke (N) and his last recollection while still inside the B-24 was of somebody pushing his back as all went black. He recovered consciousness only to find his parachute ripcord acting up; he was forced to the desperate act of pulling the chest-pack cover off and feeding the contents into the rushing air. His troubles were not over when he landed, because his canopy snagged the branches of two trees between which he fell – leaving him 20ft. above the ground! He required assistance to rescue him from his still-perilous situation. Later at a First Aid station he was asked about Bob Post, but said nothing in the (vain) hope that the correspondent was still at large.

Just before the I.P. 41-23804/J – SAD SACK became the other victim. Lt. McPhillamey recalled he also had two engines on fire, as well as the bomb bay. All on board (other than Lt. Lippert (N) who was already dead) jumped. Lt. Wockenfuss (CP) had to forcibly remove Sgt. Rudiger (Eng.) from the forward hatch over which he had slumped after passing out. Wockenfuss then dragged his fellow-airman out with him and Rudiger recovered in time to pull his ripcord. The single remaining 66th BS bomber was in deep trouble on the way home. The pilots on 41-23813 and 41-23699, seeing the plight of 41-23811/K – FASCINATING WITCH, swung down and formed a protective screen that sufficed to bring the entire element back to Shipdham.

Left: The dangers of close formation flying and friendly fire are illustrated here: a member of B-24D-5-CO 41-23788D "Avenger's" ground crew holds an ammunition drum with .50 caliber damage as indicated by the white arrow. Right: Major. Dexter Hodge was an original 66th Pilot, who would later become CO of the squadron. Lt. Hodge joined the 44th in the early days of the Group's existence.

Ground crew are busy at work on an engine whose propeller has been 'feathered.' The vast majority of maintenance work was carried out in the open, regardless of the variable and often dreadful English weather conditions.

Capt. Adams had been piloting MAISEY as the Bf 109s from JG 11 had swooped in from ahead. *Leutnant* Heinz Knoke who described the action in his book *I Flew for the Fuehrer* flew one of the fighters. His first approach landed strikes on MAISEY's right wing as he then barrel-rolled and barely missed a collision. His second approach was more deadly as the cannon shells set the B-24's lower fuselage ablaze. His eyes registered the bomber veering right in a wide sweep, as it now became a victim of the 'Heraus-schuss' action. (The term in English basically translates as 'shot out of formation' and was the next best thing to immediate destruction; the bomber in question was even more likely to be dispatched once it had lost the protective fire of the formation). Knoke kept up his assault with two more passes, the last from above and behind, but still in the face of strong defensive fire. Then, he wrote;

"I watch the cannon shells burst and rake the fuselage top and the right wing. Fire spreads along the wing and it suddenly breaks off. The body of the stricken monster plunges vertically, spinning into the depths. A crewmember attempts to bale out but his parachute is in flames; he somersaults and falls like a stone. At 3000ft. there is a tremendous explosion, causing the spinning fuselage to disintegrate. Flaming fragments fall on a farm close to Zwischenahn airfield that set buildings on fire. I land on the runway and run over to the scene where the wreckage lies strewn over the field. The explosion threw the crew out in mid-air and their bodies lie beside the smoking remains. One hundred yards away I find the captain's seat and nose wheel. A little doll, evidently the mascot, sits undamaged between the cabin's shattered windows. This was my fourth victory on my 164th mission. I cannot help thinking about the Americans' bodies. When will our turn come? Those airmen share in common with us the great adventure of flying. Separated for the moment by the barriers of War, we shall be reunited."

The Attrition Continues

Up to the end of February the number of MIA crews totalled ten, with almost equal numbers coming out of the three Squadrons. In addition four aircraft had been declared 'Category E' from a combination of battle damage and forced-landings on return from missions. The prospects for completion of a tour of duty were poor and in the case of the 67th BS personnel were destined to virtually recede to Nil between now and mid-1943.

The last mission in February and the first two in March passed off free of incident although the numbers dispatched were no more than ten on each occasion. The run to Rouen (8th) involved a mixed formation with the 93rd BG of which ten came from the 44th BG. Once again the Group was involved in a 'diversion' role for 1st Wing going onto Rennes. Rouen's marshalling-yards had been the target for the very first 8th USAAF mission on 17 August 1942. That mission had been a 'milk-run' but the experience was not repeated here. Despite a strong Allied fighter escort being on hand, the Luftwaffe succeeded in drawing the Spitfires and P-47s off. The bombers were thus totally exposed when up to forty Fw 190s indulged in their favourite head-on approach. Capt. Phillips was No.3 in the Lead element with Major Clyde Price up front and Lt. Blaine as No.2. The original Group lead had fallen to Capt. O'Brien with Major Posey as Command pilot. O'Brien had been forced to 'abort'; he had landed and taken off in another aircraft but was only able to slot into a rear position by the time he caught up. This situation was to prove fortunate for all on board, since the fighters concentrated on the head of the formation.

1/Lt. James F. Devinney was a senior bombardier of the 67th BS. He was declared MIA on 16 August 1943, but later reported to be a POW.

All the efforts to repair the fuel cells on MISS DIANNE after the 16 February mission were in vain as shells ripped into the fuselage of 41-23784/T. and set it alight. Only Lt. Gross (B) and three gunners out of Major Price's team appeared to have baled out, and Gross died in the arms of Sgt. Erhart, having suffered a severe stomach wound. The same punishing fighter pass took out Lt. Blaine in 41-23988/E – EMMA LOU/DOUBLE PLAYMATE. This aircraft had moved up from a 'Coffin Corner' slot into its forward position that in the event proved to be no less lethal. Lt. Frazier (N) was the sole survivor out of the eleven crewmen on board.

Nose art on B24D-1-CO, 41-23699 P/N "Lemon Drop" of the 68th BS. This aircraft was received 20 September 1942 and was one of the nine original aircraft assigned to the 68th BS. Her combat carrier lasted for forty-seven missions, after which she became the 44th BG Assembly ship. She finally failed her POM inspection test and was ordered to the salvage yard on 1 June 1945.

The double 67th BS loss on 8 March left four out of the nine 'original' crews on hand at Shipdham and added to this was the lack of replacement personnel, as well as the 'grounding' through medical reasons of Capt. Hall. Given these harsh circumstances it is all the more to the remaining airmen's credit that their state of mind remained stable. Most flying personnel were young and spirited; allied to this was the 'it won't happen to me' mind-set that contributed to morale. However, the fortunes of the squadron were to take a continuing dip that culminated in the Kiel strike of 14 May.

A thrust at Vegasack (18th) was preceded by three consecutive 'diversions' off the Dutch coast. The latter mission saw claims from the gunners on the nine Group B-24s for seven 'destroyed' and two 'probable' with several breaking up in the air or striking the sea, while one pilot was reported baling out of his fighter. This tally was achieved at no cost in aircraft but with the loss of S/Sgt. Balsley in a 66th BS bomber; such was the extent of his wounds that he died three days later.

A return to Wilhelmshaven four days later proved to be a bitter introduction into combat for the newly arrived 506th BS, whose inclusion brought the Group up to a full four Squadron establishment. Twelve crews took off, of which ten went over the target. Lt. Fouts piloting 41-24191/X – CACTUS appeared to be having problems in holding his position as the North Sea was being traversed, and finally fell back out of sight. The reason for his B-24's demise would never be known, but the bodies of the entire crew were taken out by the unyielding waters lapping the Dutch coast – ten more names for the 'Wall of the Missing'. The 67th BS suffered its latest loss on the way home. Lt. 'Bucky' Warne's 41-23832/N – 'MAGGIE' had been badly shot up by fighters. A bale-out was finally called even though the lagging bomber was out over the sea. This desperate lottery in a last bid for survival left just two of the ten-man crew alive – and they were very fortunate to be picked up within a short time by a passing vessel. The 67th BS was now down to two 'original' aircraft and three 'original' crews.

The final March mission was to prove an anti-climax for the ten crews participating. A solid undercast that prohibited bombing shrouded the port of Rotterdam. The potentially lethal effect of 'prop-wash' was demonstrated this day when a 68th BS aircraft flown by Lt. Garrett was caught in the turbulent airflow thrown back in the wake of another B-24. The violent change of direction then induced a spin, which took 4000ft. of precious altitude before recovery was thankfully made. This bomber took no further part in the mission, but was in due course to become the supreme survivor from among the original complement of Group aircraft – it was 41-23699 LEMON DROP.

Mud Glorious Mud! Overshoes were initially needed in order to get around the Base, but after the Sites were ultimately cleaned up the overshoes could be left at the entrance to the Living Sites.

The 506th BS Ground Echelon

The Group had commenced operations back in November 1942 with just three squadrons instead of the standard number of four allocated to each bomb group up to this month when the 506th BS complement of bombers joined in the action. The ground echelon for this sub-unit followed on behind and had an unpleasant, not to say potentially lethal, experience before arriving in England. The personnel had left Camp Kilmer on 27 February and boarded their transport in New York harbor.

The 'Chantilly' proved to be at the opposite end of the physical scale compared to the mighty 'Queen' in which the other Sqdns. had crossed the 'Big Pond'. The ship had originally

Major Howard "Pappy" Moore was the CO of the 67th BS. He assumed the Squadron command after Major MacDonauld failed to return from the Dunkirk mission on 15 February 1943.

Major. Dexter Hodge (66th BS CO) hands Crew Chief M/Sgt. Joseph. M. Miller a quart of whiskey for having the best maintained B-24 in the squadron.

Nose art on B-24D-5-CO 41-23819 "Rugged Buggy" of the 68th BS. This bomber was lost on 14 May 1943, one of five fated to go down over Kiel.

been French but had been taken over by the British in 1940. The monotonous food diet comprised chiefly of mutton, when mixed in with the smell of the Indian Lascar crew's quarters, was enough to induce a sense of acute illness, that was soon increased by the turbulent waters of the Atlantic. However, the worst was yet to come as the sixty-ship convoy to which 'Chantilly' was assigned plodded along and right into a U-Boat ambush. In the early evening of the 10th their initial assault sank several vessels steaming to the right of the 'Chantilly'. Capt. Ursel Harvell (Group photo officer) remembered the red lights hoisted by each stricken vessel and the smaller red lights indicating individual merchant sailors as they leapt into storm-tossed water or managed to clamber aboard available life rafts. Next, around midnight the same numbers of merchantmen were culled from left and ahead, and the Capt. later expressd his anger and frustration at the seeming inability of the escorts to stem the tide of assault as well as the stupidity of the U.S. Army at placing skilled personnel on a vessel attached to a snail-paced convoy. Many of the American and Allied military men were seen moving around or sitting in the passageways, scared of being trapped in their room by warped door-frames in the event of the 'Chantilly' suffering the same fate. (Whether or not any more than a small proportion of their number would have survived through getting safely away in the available lifeboats, was very much open to question).

Finally, in the early hours of the next morning, the worst sinking of all involved an oil tanker among the several casualties. There was a massive explosion followed by billowing sheets of flame reaching up thousands of feet to light up the convoy for miles. Now the men on the 'Chantilly' had an understanding of the sheer helplessness of those serving in the Merchant Navy. The latter had to hold position and speed and trust to providence (as well as hoping for a good defensive response from the Naval escorts). Should their ship be sunk, they knew there was little or no chance of being picked up, since the integrity of the convoy was granted unconditional priority – in other words, this scenario was a nautical version of the bomber formation where stragglers were equally regarded as expendable. Thankfully for the 506th BS airmen at least, their vessel survived intact and no further U-boat assaults occurred over the next ten days before anchor was dropped in the Firth of Clyde, Scotland. (Criticism of the naval escorts has to be put in the context of the Battle of the Atlantic at this time. The U-Boat crews were at the peak of their efficiency and operational numbers of vessels, and it would not be until around mid-1943 that the Allied air and sea counter-offensive would turn the tide in its permanent favour).

Although the 506th BS had only commenced operations on 22 March the first decorations awarded to the sub-unit had been earned the previous 23 December during training at Pueblo. A practice bombing flight of three B-24s had just been completed and Lt. Slough in the lead ship instructed the other two crews to fly behind in single file as they headed for the gunnery range. Suddenly, the lead aircraft shuddered, hurling the standing crewmembers off their feet. When Sgt. Caillier (Eng.) was recalled to the cockpit after assisting the navigator back onto the flight deck, he found the co-pilot gone. In addition forward vision had been totally blanked out by a huge mass, indefinable at the time, but later established as part of the tail section from one of the other B-24s. Some degree of forward vision was achieved by 'fish-tailing' the bomber, which was barely airborne due to the aerodynamic imbalance induced by the remnants of the other B-24. Fortunately, the efforts of Lt. Slough assisted by Sgt. Caillier were more than equal to the emergency and they landed in good order. The bombardier had to be cut free due to his leg going through the nose skin to hold him fast. The remaining crewmembers had baled out when Slough had rung the bale-out bell, including the co-pilot who had reportedly beaten everyone out; his career as a flier was subsequently curtailed. And so the 506th won its first two awards long before it entered combat, when both Slough and Caillier received the DFC. (Sadly, none of the seven men on the other B-24 survived).

The installation and maintenance of teleprinter equipment on British airfields was primarily laid to the Post Office engineering department. A combination of increased numbers of teleprinters as ever more airfields were commissioned, and the call-up of engineering staff for military service, resulted in volunteers being sought among the current ranks of the RAF. Cpl. Peter Broadley went on a month-long course in late March. On his return, he became involved in converting the USAAF equipment with units that made them compatible with the British network. A subsequent course for instruction on voice frequency equipment used in connection with teleprinters was completed at the then 2nd BD HQ at Catton Hall by early May. On 11 May the airfield was officially handed over the USAAF

B-24D-25-CO 41-24295 J 506th BS "Wicked Witch" was an original 506th BS aircraft received on 4 March 1943. She was lost on 14 May 1943 (Kiel) on only her third mission along with Capt. Swanson's crew.

Below: Captain. Phillips and crew relax prior to a mission, while their B-24 'The Little Beaver' squats in the background. The Eightball emblem was different to others carried by the Group in that it bore a shark's mouth.

and the RAF numbers were reduced to a level where just one billet on the 14th CBW Site was necessary. In addition the detachment was now titled 2nd BD RAF Substitution Unit. From now on, Peter would not only be 'on call' for the 44th BG but would also assist in equipment-installation at other 2nd BD airfields following their occupation by newly arrived Groups.

Tactical Disadvantage

By this stage of the Offensive the Luftwaffe was fully exploiting the primary defensive weakness in the USAAF 'heavies', namely the poor degree of forward firepower. The nose-mounted machine-guns were all flexible units that were in the charge of the bombardier and navigator. In the case of the B-24 one each was placed high up and directly behind the nose plexiglas, with a third in a central position at the base of the nose frame. Since only two guns could be used at any one time the weight of firepower was not great. The wielding of a sixty-five pound weapon inside a moving platform that was a bomber added to the problems of aiming. Then, too, it was impossible for the side-guns to be manoeuvred into more than an approximate frontal angle, apart from which it was not easy for the two men up front to operate without hustling into each other. The power turret behind the pilots did provide a much better directed and good weight of fire. The main disability for this gunner was out of his hands to correct; an attack from marginally below the bombers line of flight meant that he had great difficulty in bringing his guns to bear upon the swift-moving fighters. The absence of a ball-turret on the current B-24 model was a further serious lapse. Moves were on hand to re-position the central nose gun higher up the frame, as well as mounting twin weapons therein. However, the harsh truth was that the fighters held the overall advantage especially since their opponents had but scant seconds to focus and fire upon their tormentors. The best that could be hoped was for the American gunners to ward off the worst of these aerial assaults. Only the provision of comprehensive Allied fighter cover was likely to change this desperate scenario back to the bomber crews' advantage. (The engineering section of the 67th BS acknowledged the above-mentioned weaknesses; one of its recommendations for the nose armament was for longer ammunition belts to be installed.)

April 1943 proceeded at a similar stuttering operational pace to all previous months, and just four missions were completed, with the 44th BG taking part in all but the final one (17th). Billancourt, France was the primary target (4th) when Shipdham provided a handful of aircraft for a 'diversion' off Holland. The next day eleven out of fourteen crews bombed Antwerp, after which bad weather cancelled all operations up to the 16th. Dock facilities at Brest absorbed the ordnance of eleven bombers on that day; flak was moderate to heavy but the Luftwaffe seemed to have mainly concentrated on the 93rd BG element within 2nd. Wing.

Capt. Chester "George" Phillips of the 67th BS. was KIA on 14 May 1943 over Kiel while flying B24D-5-CO 41-23807U 'The Little Beaver.' Seven of the crew perished, and four became POWs.

By now the bad old days of having to shuffle to and from the living sites to the flight lines were disappearing. The provision of discarded packing crates saw the lumber used for construction of 'on-line' shacks. What began as necessary shelter facilities soon burgeoned into a series of superb accommodation units that far out weighed their equivalent living site locations in comfort. Beds or mattresses and even cooking facilities were the norm. Heating the shacks via the adaptation of thirty or fifty-gallon drums gave a decided edge over the standard pot-bellied' stove – provided the mixture of used engine oil was properly made beforehand! For those who still had the desire to commute, there was now plenty of transport becoming available for this requirement.

Left: B-24D-5-CO 41-23784T "Miss Dianne" of the 67th Bomb Squadron was another of the original nine aircraft assigned to the 67th BS on 20 September 1942. Here, her crew chief Sgt. Baccash poses with 'Miss Dianne' The aircraft was finally MIA on 8 March 1943. Right: 1/Lt. William A. Roach, Jr. and crew were the first replacement crew to arrive at Shipdham and were assigned to the 67th BS. The 14 May mission to Kiel was only their second, and they were lost while flying 42-40126/T "Annie Oakley." Eight were KIA, while 2/Lt. Wyatt S. Kennon (Bombardier) evaded capture but was later KIA: 1/Lt. Louis L. Kissinger (Navigator) was captured and became a POW.

By this stage of the USAAF's presence in England, its personnel had established an overall image that to some of the British population was a little too brash for their liking, and provided the basis for the 'Over-paid, Over-sexed, Over-fed and Over-here' expression. In April 1943 a *Norfolk News* and *Daily Press* reporter Mr. Lee wrote an article on the subject that primarily corrected the image and is well worthy of quotation:

"For some months past the sight of officers and men of the USAAF has been a familiar feature across Norfolk. So familiar that this has long ceased to be a matter of curiosity. Now we accept them – almost, for we are still East Anglian – as part of our community. How did this happen in a country that is seen as traditionally slow at talking to 'foreigners'? Part, I think, because we have been quick to realise these Americans are as much a part of Great Britain. Partly, because an innate hospitality-instinct has been quickened by the thought that they are in a way relations, albeit distantly removed. Mainly, I believe, because so many have proved eager to fit in with our ways and delighted when an 'Englishman' gives the slightest of chances to show what good 'mixers' they are.

"I found this out when I visited a Norfolk base, where the boot was on the other foot. The physical surroundings were familiar. Over the hedge was a farmer drilling barley with his American-built tractor. On this side of the hedge I was in the USA. Where I heard a variety of dialects that made a hardened film fan realise the Hollywood Studio accent I had known so well must seem to Americans just as affected and strange as 'Oxford' does to the blunt Yorkshire-man. However, since none of the men took note of my turns of speech I tried to take things in my stride. I was made to feel very much at home.

B-24D-15-CO 41-24014/P "Scrappy" of the 66th BS was 1/Lt. John Reed's aircraft, and featured as yet another loss on the 14 May 1943 mission to Kiel. It was badly damaged by enemy fighters, but made it back to Shipdham, where it proved to be too badly damaged to land. Reed gave the order for the crew to bail out over the airfield, after which he and Lt. Winger flew their charge toward the coast at Cromer and bailed out. The abandoned B-24 was finally shot down by a Flight of Polish Spitfires.

"I heard much rumour about the Americans lavish life-style, with tales that made a long-rationed Englishman's mouth water. Well, this is surely one item proving the soundness of the old advice to 'believe nothing you hear'. I saw no luxury, and if there is anything in U.S. Army rules corresponding to the Royal Navy's 'hard living' allowance, this USAAF bomber squadrons personnel earn it – they work hard and live just as hard!

"What struck a former World War I soldier was the narrow distinction between the officers and enlisted men's' conditions. They do live up to the democratic idea, with no officer's servants other than for senior members, though I don't quite know about that even. The officer's mess is very spartan, and I understand the combat crews' mess for the enlisted men provides a more lavish food supply in a more comfortable layout by comparison.

"There are no 'passengers', each man having his job, every one of which – outside of the administrative, office and cooking staff – contributes to actual flying operations. I was struck by the independence of the squadron organisation. If a bomber returns shot-up the station has workshops and craftsmen capable of tackling all types of repairs. I saw a new engine fitted to a B-24 after losing one to a fight with a Jerry over Holland.

"One thing particularly pleased me during my tour. I saw one or two RAF airmen and, knowing the station was taken over from the RAF, remarked upon this to my guide. 'Yes' he said, 'But they'll be going soon. We've got to stand on our own feet you know. Those are the last of a grand bunch of fellows. They've taught us a lot. In fact, everything we know about air tactics and operations over here, your boys of the RAF have taught us.'

"I later learned, from the blunt, uncomplimentary comments made by the same man on my first 'flight' in a Link Trainer that Americans like to say what they mean and mean what they say! Therefore, I accepted the compliment to the RAF as one that was completely sincere.

"I came away with a wholesome regard for their efficiency. They may not bother with 'spit and polish' and their military discipline may seem lax to us, but it's their way of bypassing what they regard as unessential. It does not apply to their keenness in the really big job of work they are doing as part of the Allied Air Offensive over Europe."

Extremes in Operational Fortune

May 1943 was to witness the strength of the 8th USAAF being built up to a much more tenable level in crews and equipment. However, the overall increase related to the 1st Wing B-17 units,

'Miss Delores' a B-24D-25-CO 41-24278Q of the 67th BS. with Lt. William Cameron at the controls. 'Miss Delores' was lost 14 May 1943 on the Kiel mission. The aircraft was hit by flak over the target and crashed into the water south of the Island of Ero. 1/Lt. Robert I. Brown and six of his crew were made POW's but sadly the three other crewmen died in the aircraft .

whose number increased from five to nine, and the creation of 4th Wing (later 3rd Bomb Division) with three Groups. The 2nd Wing strength was still maintained at the current level, although the 389th BG were training up and ready to move to England by the end of May. The month was also to witness a swift transition from a nadir in 44th BG Fortunes to Resurrection, all within seventy-two hours.

May commenced with consecutive 'diversion' missions on the 1st and 4th. On 7 May, Capt. O'Brien was promoted to Major and given command of the 68th BS. The previous CO Major Francis H. McDuff had rotated States-side on 13 April, but O'Brien had been absent on other duties during the interim period. Unbeknown to the new appointee was that he would have just seven days in which to enjoy his elevation in rank and post. His future wartime destiny was awaiting him over a northern German city – Kiel.

At this point in World War II the Battle of the Atlantic was still poised on a knife-edge, and any effort to disrupt the U-boat offensive was to be welcomed. The naval base at Kiel was also home to the Krupps submarine-construction yards and was now selected for attack. The 8th USAAF planners arranged that 1st Wing would drop high explosives while 2nd Wing would add to the destruction with incendiaries. At least that was the theory.

The crews who were woken at what was a later than usual hour – 0500 – included Capt. Chester Phillips team flying 41-23807/U – LITTLE BEAVER. In attendance at the briefing but arriving from London too late to be included on the mission roster were Bill Cameron and Howard Moore. Bill now had his own crew, but until recently he and Chester had flown

These four photos show B-24D-5-CO 41-23813V "Victory Ship", Lt. Tommy Holmes's aircraft after returning from the 14 May 1943 mission to Kiel. Lt. Holmes was hit in the head by flak, which ripped through the cockpit roof. The damage to Holmes's aircraft can clearly be seen. In the event Lt. Holmes was not seriously wounded.

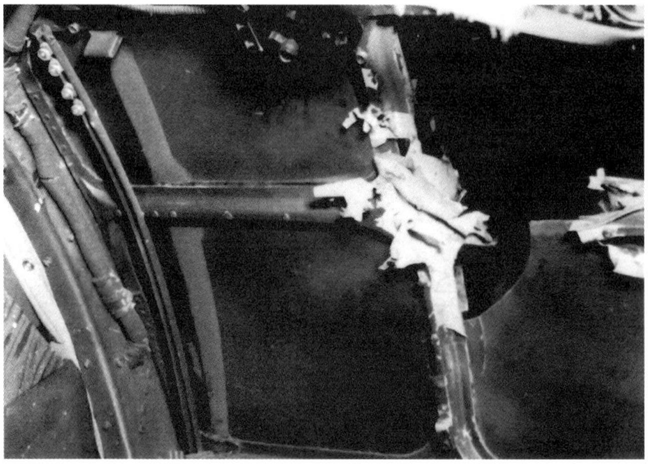

together in LITTLE BEAVER. All three were Group 'originals' but the day's events were to cruelly eclipse that relationship.

Major O'Brien recalled that the inclusion of incendiaries as the bomb-load had only occurred a few hours prior to mission take-off. He and Lt. 'Mac' Howell taxied out in 41-23819/Bar-A – RUGGED BUGGY at the head of eighteen aircraft and lifted off into a clear morning sky. The normal practice of gaining height over England was dispensed with. Instead the Group flew at minimum altitude until well out over the North Sea before climbing to bombing altitude (19,000 ft). The formation was greeted by flak from the Frisian Island chain that should not have been over-flown. The barrage landed strikes on RUGGED BUGGY that caused a serious loss of manifold pressure in No.1 and 2 engines.

The poor trajectory performance of the incendiary weapons meant that the 44th BG was forced to fly an extra two miles beyond normal release-point in order to strike the yards. Flying this additional length through solid flak was bad enough, but a further problem arose at 'bombs away'. The incendiaries not only scattered but also created a 'vertical' spread through which the bombers were forced to fly. The formation had already opened out in order to minimise this anticipated situation and the Luftwaffe took full opportunity in the process.

As the Group turned for home at least three B-24s were straggling. One of these was RUGGED BUGGY whose crew was not only fighting the Fw 190s and Bf 109s but also a severe headwind. The original flak damage had also punctured a fuel tank, whose vapour had pervaded the fuselage interior, with the risk of instant incineration should this be ignited. Sure enough, a fighter attack from behind ended with the bomb-bay area wreathed in flames. Despite this, Sgt. Ernst (ROG) attempted to batter a gap in the forward bomb-bay doors to permit those up front to bale out. His efforts appeared to have succeeded since all the crewmembers up front baled out, as did the gunners in the rear. However there were two fatalities out of the ten-man crew. Once safely down and in custody, a German informed Major O'Brien; "Do you know a little man in a yellow suit? He is Tot (dead)." The basic description fitted 'Mac' Howell whom, it was later believed, had suffered a ripped parachute and was killed upon impact. (O'Brien recalled a

On June 25, 1943 British Foreign Secretary Anthony Eden made a goodwill visit to Shipdham. Here he is seen delivering a speech to crews of the 44th BG. Captain Robert E."Rum Runner" Miller (first at left) and crew stand to attention in front of their aircraft 41-23811/K the "Fascinatin Witch", which was one of the original nine aircraft of the 66th BS.

parachute with a badly torn panel that had plummeting past him as he descended). S/Sgt. Van Oyen was picked up in Kiel Bay but he had already drowned.

The 67th BS had managed to put up three B-24s for the mission. Capt. Phillips had gone over the target and was rallying with the others to head for home when flak got the range on LITTLE BEAVER. Three strikes set the fuselage ablaze and the crippled bomber went into a flat spin. The pilot was killed at his post and Lt. Wilborn (CP) did not jump at the same time as the other survivors. Lt. Bartmess (N), with twenty-two missions in, sadly drowned after baling out over Kiel Bay; his fellow-veteran, Lt. Hill (B) delayed his jump and was fortunate to descend on the shoreline. In all only four men got down alive. The second 67th BS loss occurred around the same time and involved Lt. Roach's crew on their baptismal mission. The circumstances of the bomber's loss were unclear although it did crash on land and six bodies were recovered from the remains. Just Lts. Kissinger (B) and Kennon (B) survived.

1/Lt. Phillip P. Phillips, a 66th BS Navigator receives the Oak Leaf cluster from Col. Leon Johnson. Phillips would be KIA on the 1 August 1943 low-level mission to Ploesti.

The total demise of the 67th BS contingent was completed when Lt. Brown's 41-23278/Q – MISS DELORES was brought down. Flak was again the primary cause, which knocked out one engine and forced the bomber to fall out of formation. The lagging B-24 was then an easy victim for the fighters and Brown called for a bale-out. T/Sgt. Susan (ROG) had manned the top turret after T/Sgt. Wandtke suffered a knee wound. To his frustration he found the guns would not fire directly back between the fins. The intercom was rendered out of action, so Brown's 'abandon' call was not heard. Susan and the others, finally realising their bomber was doomed, did jump. The ROG came down over the water, but after releasing all surplus items and loosening his harness, he misjudged his height for full harness release. The resultant struggle to get out from under the enveloping parachute canopy and its cords could have been fruitless, had it not been for a fisherman in his boat; this individual hooked Susan out by using his gaff-pole. Once in the boat the German uttered the classic expression beloved of all Allied 'POWs; "Fuer Sie ist Der Krieg Fertig" – For you the War is over!!" The three gunners in the rear were lost, with only two bodies recovered.

Fighter attacks from head-on accounted for a fifth Group B-24 that was also out of formation. Lt. Swanson (506th BS) was flying 41-24295/J – WICKED WITCH. The fighter strikes set an engine on fire and shattered cockpit instruments. In truth the aircraft had proved difficult to hold in formation ever since

Left: Combat crew make ready for another mission. The aircraft is "Ruth-Less" a B-24D-25-CO 41-24282/Y of the 506th BS. This bomber was one of the original aircraft received on 4 March 1943. Right: Cleaning up the 66th BS site.

suffering flak damage on the way in. Either way, the end result was that the crew had to bale out. All four officers survived baling out as the aircraft was turned in towards the shoreline, but the five enlisted men perished, either in the aircraft or through exposure after coming down in the sea. Lts. Schieffelbusch (N) and Banks (B) landed well out from the shoreline and were very fortunate to be fished out of the water.

Among the ranks of the battered formation was 41-23014/P – SCRAPPY, which was living up to the name. Lt. Reed (66th BS) recalled that bombs from one of the preceding Groups had actually descended among the 44th BG, fortunately, without lethal effect. Then the top turret canopy was blown clean off by cannon shells that also severely wounded Sgt. Wygonik. First aid was administered by Sgt. Perry who then snapped on Wygonik's parachute pack, ready to bale him out. Temporary dizziness caused by lack of oxygen forced Perry to refresh himself from his mask before returning to his patient – who in that short interval had disappeared! Any concern that Wygonik may have also passed out, fallen through the open bomb-bay and failed to regain consciousness in time to deploy his chest pack was only dispelled much later when news of the Sgt.'s POW status was announced. He had been picked up and swiftly taken to a hospital whose treatment of him was first-class; however, an injury to one eye forced its subsequent removal.

On return to Shipdham, Reed discovered that the landing gear only deployed halfway and then could not be retracted. The risk of either blocking the runway or having the gear 'dig-in' should a grass landing be attempted, left no option but to abandon the bomber. Reed and Lt. Winger baled out the other crew over the airfield and headed for the coast; the Automatic Pilot was applied and both pilot jumped, leaving their charge to fly to its watery fate, but in fact the bomber was dispatched into the sea by Polish fighter pilots. One of the gunners on this crew who was on his first mission, stumped up to the squadron CO, Major Hodges on return to Shipdham; he slapped his flight gear on the table and shouted; "There's your goddam receipt – I quit!!" (The airman in question was later re-assigned to ground duties).

One of the returning 506th BS aircraft, 41-24282/Y – RUTHLESS had suffered heavy damage but was not cleared to land. Instead Lt. Slough was directed to fly westward to Northern Ireland (presumably the depot at Langford Lodge) where repairs could be carried out. Another badly damaged aircraft from the 68th BS (41-24009/W – MARGARET ANN) flown by Lt. Jansen did receive clearance to land, but the presence of four seriously wounded gunners on board was sound

Major Al Key, 66th BS CO (in the dark uniform) is photographed with original members of the 66th BS. (Left to right), Lt. James Barry, Lt. P.P. Phillips (KIA 1-8-43), Lt. Edward Mikoloski, Lt. W. E. Minder, Lt. David Arnold, Lt. Tommy E. Scrivner (KIA 1-8-43), Key, Lt. James W. Kahl, Lt. Rowland M. Gentry (KIA 1-8-43) and Captain. Robert J. Abernethy.

cause for the decision; the fourth gunner S/Sgt. McGrady proved to be beyond all aid and died next day.

The debacle over Kiel was by far the worst blow suffered by the 44th BG to date. The mission also saw the practical elimination of the original 67th BS cadre of aircraft and crews. One B-24 (SUSY-Q) and Bill Cameron and Howard Moore among a mere handful of combat personnel were all that represented the bare remnant of the squadron. Reinforcements of both aircraft and combat personnel for the 8th USAAF as a whole had so far been slow to arrive in England, but it is unlikely the 67th BS experience was remotely duplicated on the other bomber bases. However, a positive and permanent increase in material and human strength was happily on hand. For the 44th BG, the dampening of morale occasioned by the 14 May mission was at least alleviated by what transpired three days later.

Resurrection over Bordeaux

The French port of Bordeaux lay well down on the coastline bordering the Bay of Biscay and close to Spain. The harbour facilities were utilised as a staging post for German blockade-runners and also held a base for U-boat repairs; also on hand was the Matford aero-engine factory. The town had never suffered from the attention of the 8th USAAF up to now, but that cosy situation was to change. The mission to attack Bordeaux was assigned to the 2nd Wing while 1st Wing carried out an attack upon Lorient.

In order to avoid alerting the German defences, the planned route did not extend down over France or along its western coast. Instead, the Force was to make a wide sweep out into the Atlantic and back across the Bay of Biscay. Since the distance from Shipdham to Bordeaux was likely to create critical fuel problems, the participating crews from both B-24 Groups transited to Davidstow Moor in the extreme south west of England on 16 May. Thirty-nine aircraft, with fuel tanks topped off, duly took off next morning with the 44th BG in the lead. Heading the group formation of twenty-one aircraft was Major Moore with Gen. Hodges (2nd Wing CG). The navigational skills of Lt. Mikolowski (N) were tested to the full since there were no physical pinpoints available over the entire 700-mile route to Bordeaux – the technique of Deduced ('dead') Reckoning was all that was to hand. The quality of Mikolowski's work was such that the target loomed up precisely on the briefed ETA.

Lt. DeVinney, Bill Cameron's bombardier now paid his way by a precise sighting and release that culminated in a tight bomb pattern, an act that was repeated by the 93rd BG. Heavy damage to the aero-engine factory was recorded; the harbour lock-gates were shattered and buildings blasted. Very light flak was encountered and hardly any fighters were seen. Just one bomber did not return to England, and even then the pilots managed to divert into neutral Spain. The crew in question was that of Lt. Hilliard (66th BS). 'Runaway' propellers on two engines occurring during the outward route persuaded the pilots that they could not risk flying back over the open sea. They elected to head for Spain and finally landed on a small airfield. The landing proved eventful because not only was the B-24 by then operating on one good engine, ahead of the frantically braking bomber lay a steam-roller positioned just off the runway-end! The crew remained in Spain until early August when they were repatriated by C-47 to England.

Though all other aircraft returned to Shipdham, the crew of Lt. Diehl was short one man, lost in a particularly tragic manner. T/Sgt. Light had been standing by an open waist window when his parachute had somehow opened. The silk umbrella instantly blossomed in the bomber's slipstream, whisking the hapless airman out over the Bay of Biscay and to certain death in the frigid and featureless waters below.

Major Pappy Moore brought "Suzy Q" in for a hard landing on return from the 5 April 1943 mission to Antwerp. A temporary repair was made and she was flown to Langford Lodge, Northern Ireland for major repair work to be done.

The comprehensive success of the Bordeaux mission must have bolstered Group morale. The fact that the Authorities had entrusted a key mission to 2nd Wing alone was an important indicator that the days of the B-24 appearing to be treated in a subsidiary manner to the B-17 were steadily passing away. However, a period of twelve days elapsed until the crews were again called upon. La Pallice was another port on the French Biscay coast housing Naval facilities including U-boat pens. The mission was again entrusted to 2nd Wing and the twenty-one group bombers out of the thirty-eight dispatched did a satisfactory job in the face of light flak.

The 'locust' months for both the 8th USAAF and the 44th BG were at an end. Over the next several months the required function of the two heavy bomber Wings would see a continued common pattern but would involve a geographic separation. In the case of 2nd Wing its Groups were soon to head southward for the Mediterranean. During their time in this new Theatre the crews would be sent to a specific Rumanian target whose legacy was to loom large in the history of the USAAF in Europe.

Chapter Three

Low Road to Ploesti

The possibility of seriously or even fatally crippling key elements of the Nazis' industrial potential was under constant discussion by Washington at this time. Ball bearings and oil were two products that were seen as absolutely vital to sustaining a war. In the case of the former product, Germany's major supply source at Schweinfurt would be the focus of attack by the 8th USAAF during the second half of 1943. As for the question of denying oil to the enemy, there was one huge oilfield complex located within Nazi-occupied Europe, or rather within the boundaries of one of the countries that had thrown its lot in with the Axis Powers, Rumania. Ploesti with its massive complex of production plants lay some miles north of the Rumanian capital Bucharest. The target was away out of range of bombers based in England, but there was a possibility of striking it from Allied bases in North Africa; even so, the allotted task force would be at the full extent of its range.

Back in England, the 2nd Wing's two Groups were joined by the 389th BG (Hethel) during June. However, the strategic air offensive was exclusively prosecuted by 1st Wing in the course of the month. The absence of 2nd Wing at this point was the subject of much discussion within the 8th USAAF, especially among the personnel at the B-24 bases. Ground crews at Shipdham were working on their aircraft one day when a formation of B-24s swept over the airfield at minimum altitude, causing many to duck and even scatter as their ears were swamped by the shocking roar of dozens of Pratt & Whitneys. However, their own Group's aircraft were soon involved in this drastic flight pattern switch. Further confusion as to the purpose behind these flights was added to with the replacement of Norden bombsights by a very basic gun-sight adaptation. In addition the central nose gun was replaced by twin mountings that were retained in a permanent and slightly nose-down position by lengths of bungee cord. The feelings of an anonymous crew chief summed up the situation when he said he didn't know whether he was looking after a B-24 or a 'bloody four-engine Spitfire'!

The low-flying practice extended well into June before its cessation. Orders dated 18 June called for the Group to prepare for departure to Cyrenaica in a staged movement. The first stage involved thirty-nine crews with each aircraft bearing an average of four support staff in addition to its normal crew complement. The aircraft flew from Shipdham down to Portreath in southwest

1/Lt. Curtis S. Griffen, 67th BS pilot KIA 17 July 1943, Naples, Italy.

England (26th). From here next morning the aircraft headed out across the Bay of Biscay and skirted Portugal before landing at Oran in Morocco. Finally on the 28th an easterly heading across North Africa ended with a touchdown at Benina-Main close to Benghazi. The airfield located on the Gulf of Sirte was already occupied by the B-24s of the 98th BG, one of the units originally formed from 44th BG ranks.

The featureless desert plain forming the base was a world away in facilities and comfort, even compared to Shipdham in its worst state. The aircraft were permanently dispersed out in the open where grit and sand thrown up by the regular sandstorms displayed their worst abrasive and clogging effects upon sensitive mechanisms. Accommodation consisted of tents, whose ability to withstand either the extreme heat of day or sub-zero temperatures at night – or even to remain intact in the face of high winds – was extremely poor. The consumption of food was another task fraught with difficulty, given the universal presence of sand. All in all, the crews must have looked upon their normal location in England with some regret; they would have almost two months in which to reflect upon the change.

Invasion Interlude

The presence of no less than five B-24 Groups (the 44th BG, 93rd BG and 389th BG from England and the 98th BG and

Although the photograph is faded it is still worthy of showing, as it is most likely one of the last shots of Major "Pappy" Moore's legendary 'Suzy Q' undergoing maintenance in the desert.

376th BG forming part of the North Africa based 9th USAAF) provided powerful support for the softening-up of Axis defences ahead of the projected invasion of Sicily. Up to now the pace of missions flown had been poor. The beginning of the 44th BG's North Africa spell of duty saw a great upsurge in missions flown, with ten completed between 2-19 July. The average number of Group aircraft sent out was also greatly increased compared to the previous winter, being upwards of thirty for each mission.

The first mission was dispatched to Lecce airfield but only twenty-two of the twenty-four aircraft came home. Major Cramer had taken over from Major O'Brien as 68th BS CO.

44th BG intelligence tent, a far cry from the building at home base.

Group photographic officer Captain Ursel P. Harvell.

Today he was in the right seat of 42-40745 with Lt. Peterson's crew on their first mission. Separate witness reports confirmed that a fighter had landed strikes on the wings and fuselage. Then the B-24 started down and the final crash left nobody alive. Flak damaged 42-40094/E – MISS VIRGINIA in Nos.1 and 2 engines as well as opening gashes in a wing tank. The bomber ran short of fuel and was 'ditched' by Lts. Garrett (P) and Lehnhausen, with both men being thrown through the windshield, after the B-24 broke up in three sections. Despite this, Lehnhausen swam back to the aircraft and released a life raft. The other life raft's securing rope was fouled up in the airframe, so Lehnhausen managed to disconnect it by a non-standard method after all else failed – he simply chewed on it! (Fortunately, the B-24 obliged by staying afloat long enough for this unorthodox action to succeed). The six survivors out of the eleven on board were in a potentially perilous position as they were well away from land where air-sea rescue boats were unlikely to patrol and also had several wounded among their number. The suggestion that they begin paddling was quickly discarded. After several hours a vessel appeared that was steering an angular course westward, and the crew's attention was attracted when flares were fired. Its appearance was very fortuitous since the Royal Navy minelayer had been steaming towards Malta when it picked up the SOS signals sent out by Sgt. Melvin (ROG). (Lt. Lehnhausen was later awarded the Soldiers Medal for his endeavours).

The following seven missions involved strikes upon targets ranging from Messina's harbour and railroad installations in Sicily to airfields at Crotone and Foggia in Italy. All seven resulted in the mainly 500lb. bombs used making good concentrations with no aircraft losses. (The marshalling yards at Reggio di Calabria on 12 July were struck by 1000lb. ordnance). Then the Grim Reaper landed his latest blow over Naples (17th). The flak gunners hit home against 42-63763/F – LADY FIFINELLA causing the B-24 to lose contact with the formation. Several Axis fighters then administered the final blow, setting the right wing on fire, which broke off soon after. Only Capt. Griffen (P) and S/Sgt. Greattinger (LWG) failed to survive the crash although two crewmembers were badly injured; however Italian civilians were reputed to have killed Lt. Potter (CP) after he had landed safely.

The next mission (19th) was the cause of much soul-searching among the American authorities because it involved a target within the city of Rome. The city was world-renowned for its religious significance and had hitherto been declared an 'Open City'. The citizens had accordingly been spared the

Jim Devinney, Bill Cameron, Gola Grett and Bill Dabneny pose in front of the Buzzin Bear.

experience of aerial bombardment. However, the large Littorio rail marshalling yard in the city was a vital cog in Axis transportation of men and materials and could not be permitted to function unscathed. The ground rules for bombing were set out at the briefing; bombing was to be visually conducted and accuracy deemed essential with no near misses to be tolerated. In the case of the 44th BG at least all crewmembers of the Catholic faith were given the option of remaining on the ground, an option that none of them responded to. Capt. Cameron (67th BS) led the Group in SUZY-Q. Weather conditions over Rome were fortunately clear when the Group made its bomb-run and with one small exception involving another Group the explosives and incendiaries dropped by the entire Force descended squarely upon the yards as well as the nearby military airfield.

SUZY-Q and BUZZIN' BEAR were bombers of the 67th BS with their fair share of battle damage. The latter aircraft was involved in action over Naples (17th) that forced her crew

Living quarters, North African style. No more bitching about the living conditions at Shipdham!

Left: "Desert Lilies" was the name given to the open air toilets. These were scattered all round the Sites. Right: Desert conditions were very sparse; here a fire is being lit in order to boil water – an action necessary to avoid stomach problems that would arise should the water be consumed in its original untreated form!

to land away from Benina-Main. As the target was left behind Cameron's aircraft was suffering from very high cylinder-head temperatures and failing oil pressure on No.3 that forced its shutdown. Fuel was thought to be running dangerously low so the pilots decided to divert into Malta. Reaching an island assumed to be their goal, they circled at low altitude while seeking out an airfield. A second engine went temporarily 'out', to leave Cameron with little option but to land on an airstrip that loomed up just in time. The British officer who met the crew after they exited the B-24 confirmed their location not as Malta but as Comiso, Sicily. Then, the bomber had the fuel tanks hastily replenished with sufficient quantity to fly on to Malta, which reached in the late evening. (During their brief time on Sicily the crew had seized the opportunity to obtain a good haul of wine!).

Major Moore had named 41-23817/L after his baby daughter Suzy. After an indifferent combat debut, the B-24 had gone on to record an impressive number of missions. She had spent a prolonged spell at Langford Lodge following one harrowing mission, and returned to Shipdham with a new set of engine and tail section Even so, the scars accruing from regular battle-damage were now evident over her entire airframe. But she was still around, in stark contrast to the majority of her 'original' contemporaries who had been consumed in combat or in crashes in England. Major Moore had flown his twenty-fifth mission in SUZY-Q and it was nearly his last. The B-24's engines failed during landing approach and after touching down short of the runway the pilots were forced to let her run her course through the scrub bush. (It was as well that the incident had not occurred back in England or the result might have been lethal when given the enclosed fields and undulating nature of the countryside).

Build-up to 'The Big One'

The Naples mission was to be the last flown during July. Over the next two weeks the combat crews returned to the low-flying practice procedure begun in England, but with still no real idea of what was to be the end-result in terms of missions. The Authorities had decided not only what the target was to be – it was Ploesti's oil refineries – but also the method of attack-approach. Col. Jacob Smart from Gen. Hap Arnold's advisory council had been handed the primary task of preparing what was now code-named Operation TIDAL WAVE. The normal method of high-level approach to the target was regarded as providing too much leeway in time for the Axis defensive chain to meet the American bombers with a heavy flak and fighter resistance. Col. Smart had therefore proposed that the bomber force would go in at minimum altitude, thereby preserving the element of surprise until the very last moment. The mixture of delayed-action bombs and incendiaries was expected to produce the maximum degree of destruction to the refinery and cracking-plant buildings along with the tank farms in which the finished product was stored. An outline of the entire complex had been created in the North African landscape upon which the B-24 crews were focusing their practice-runs.

Ploesti was still a long way away from current Allied airfield locations; the authorities were of the opinion that with this in mind the Axis military would have become complacent about the possibility of aerial assault and conversely would have dismissed all thought about the necessity to provide a solid defensive cover. Unfortunately, one prominent German by the name of *Oberst* Gerstenburg did not think in this manner. Worse still, he was the military protector for Rumania, and had put his thoughts into operation on the orders of the *Fuehrer*, who had also realised the potentially mortal threat to Ploesti posed by Allied bombers.

The flak defences had been strongly reinforced with both heavy 88mm and 20mm light weaponry. In the case of the latter, many had been disguised in the form of haystacks and farm buildings. The tank farms had been provided with reinforced walls to prevent the spread of burning fuel onto adjacent units. All in all, Ploesti represented a veritable wasps nest against assault instead of still being the site that was deemed wide open to bombing.

The annual production capacity of Ploesti was around nine million tons, of which roughly 40% went to feed Nazi Germany's war machine. The sheer size of the location containing nine major refineries was too large to ensure its total destruction either with the forces available or in the course of a single attack. The alternative was for up to forty selected key installations, such as distilling and cracking plants along with boiler houses, to be struck. These were shared out between three sites. The main one was at Ploesti, the second at Brazi just below Ploesti and the third at Campina to the northwest. Two of the targets were allocated the 44th BG, being Columbia Aquila (Code name WHITE V) and Creditul Minier at Brazi (Code name BLUE). The 66th BS/67th BS elements of the Group were assigned Columbia Aquila while the 68th BS/506th BS took on Creditul Minier, with Col. Posey leading the latter sub-force.

The 376th BG was operating out of North Africa along with the 98th BG; these two Groups were to link up with the three 8th USAAF Groups to form the overall Task Force. The briefed course to the target was northwards across the Mediterranean and up past the island of Corfu. Then a turn made to the northeast crossed Albania, Yugoslavia and Bulgaria and finally led into Ploesti. During the course of the two-week period of training-up the groups had dropped practice bombs on a huge plan-form marked out in the desert; the crew naturally

This photo shows the last briefing for the 44th BG for the Ploesti mission. A great many of these men would not return from the mission.

had no inkling that this represented the actual target layout at Ploesti. The flying conducted at minimum height with some aircraft almost scraping the sandy soil produced the inevitable effect upon the flimsy tents in the area belonging to their fellow-Americans or the local Arab population!

Several defensive modifications were applied to the B-24s. Both pilots' seats were anchored to the flight deck as added security against their tearing loose during a crash landing. Armor plate scavenged from wrecked German aircraft in the region was applied under the pilots' seats and over the navigator's table. An extra machine-gun was fixed in the nose, and a cable extension back to the cockpit would enable the co-pilot to operate the weapon as a basic strafing unit against flak positions.

A total of thirty-nine serviceable B-24s were on hand as the final briefing was conducted on the morning of 1 August. Flying as command pilot with Major Brandon was Col. Johnson; the Group Lead bomber was 41-23817/L – SUZY-Q. Each crew had been reduced to nine since there was no

Left: Captain Bob Miller and Crew 66th BS. Right: 1/Lt. Charles E. Hughes and crew 66th BS interned in Turkey. B-24D-95-CO 42-40777N, "Flossie Flirt."

perceived function for the tunnel gunners. The bomb-loads comprised 139x1000lb. and 48x500lb. weapons along with twenty-two boxes of incendiaries carried in some aircraft. Such were the bare technical facts of the mission. The complete Group would fly to the final turning point at Floresti, when it would split into separate sub-formations assigned to attack Ploesti and Brazi.

Among the personnel due to go were several 'time-expired' men, such as Capt. Cameron (67th BS) and Capt. Houston (68th BS). 'Veterans' within the line-up of bombers were SUZY-Q, BUZZIN' BEAR and LEMON DROP. The feelings of the combat crews were a mix of bravado and apprehension. The distance to be flown promised an extremely wearying length of time aloft as well as a constant battle to harbour fuel reserves as much as possible if a safe return was to be guaranteed.

Lt. Tommy Scrivener (66th BS) was flying 42-40375/G – SCRAPPY II. Two crewmembers from the time when Scrivenor was their pilot were on hand this day. However, they were now both time-expired from having flown as 'spares' on several missions when their own crew was not scheduled. Long before Ploesti was ever thought about one of the duo, Sgt. Walt Patrick (TG) had a dream. This consisted of himself and his fellow gunner Walt Hazelton as the sole survivors who were staring into their crashed B-24 laying in a wheat field; in the background was – a blazing oil refinery! Lt. Scrivenor had asked if Patrick would fly with him to Ploesti. After much hesitation, Walt finally made his decision on the toss of a coin; the side that came down provided a negative response, and thereby saved his life.

1/Lt. Shelby Irby and crew of the 66th BS. Their aircraft for the 1-8-43 mission was B-24D-95-CO, 42-40764/M "Helen B Happy."

1/Lt. Fred H. Jones poses in front of his aircraft: by nightfall of 1-8-43 he and his crew would be POWs.

Heading for Ploesti

There was very nearly a change in the choice of Lead bomber virtually minutes away from mission-start. Overnight SUZY-Q had developed a worrying problem in her No.2 engine that was finally traced to a failed sparkplug in the master cylinder. This was rectified just in time before the crews took up their stations. Engine-start and taxiing culminated with the Brandon/Johnson B-24 lifting off at 0430 in the face of a misty dawn light. A further thirty-six bombers lumbered in to the air and steadily took up their places in the formation.

A low to medium-level crossing of the Mediterranean was made with a view to keeping the 'magic eye' of enemy radar off their track as long as possible. In the event the German monitoring service had already picked up the evidence of heavy aerial traffic around Benghazi and was accordingly on the alert for a probable Allied incursion although not yet aware of its course. Problems began to arise even before the enemy coast was reached when the Task Force started to separate. The situation was caused by the first two groups (376th BG and 93rd BG) who gradually pulled away out of sight. Then, cloud formations were encountered, which further exacerbated the separation factor and ensured there would be two distinct attack phases. The 44th BG was together with the 389th BG with the

98th BG ahead, but as the first of three check-points (Pitesti) was reached the 389th BG banked left to strike at Campina. Unknown to the other two groups was the fact that the leading groups had made a premature turn for Ploesti thanks to mistaking the second check-point (Targoviste) for the final one (Floresti). The error was rectified when Bucharest loomed up ahead, but now the 376th BG and 93rd BG were heading almost due north and were hopelessly adrift from the true approach to their targets. The latter Group's assigned targets were on the eastern and northern outskirts of the town. However, the crews from Hardwick, having sighted a plant complex on the southern approach to Ploesti, decided to strike its facilities – this was Columbia Aquila, due to be attacked by the 44th BG!

This photo was taken back at Shipdham. It seemed like all of the crews who went to North Africa had these photos taken. Sadly, some of the faces wouldn't return to Shipdham.

Into the Jaws of Hell

In the meantime, Col. Johnson's navigator Lt. Selasky had maintained the Group on the briefed route. By now the B-24s were down around 500ft. and heading in towards Ploesti. Running parallel to the course of the Group and the 98th BG was a railroad line. Flak had already been engaging the bombers but what now occurred was a stunning shock. A freight train steaming along in the same direction was seen to drop the sides of the wagons inside which were light flak gun-mounts! The German gunners quickly began to throw up a concentration of fire at the aircraft, whose gunner's frantically returned fire. Ahead of the crews was a second shock – in place of a clear sky and intact target, they were met by flames and black smoke clouds billowing up from Columbia Aquila; in stark contrast, Brazi's Creditul Minier plant was seen to be untouched.

Col. Johnson made the swift decision to press on over his assigned target with his sixteen bombers while Col. Posey eased off right towards Brazi where his sub-force rendered the plant completely out of use for the remainder of its occupation by the Axis Powers. The pilots heading into WHITE V descended even lower in spite of the smoke obscuring the lethal shape of tall chimneys and similar tall obstructions.

Of the seven Group bombers fated to be MIA over Ploesti no less than six came out of the ranks of the 66th BS or 67th BS. None of these losses occurred prior to the formation penetrating what one survivor described as a 'black crematory door'.

The Force was flying in five waves, and by the time the last wave of four bombers emerged out of the smoke it was fully exposed to the flak gunners. Lt. Gentry (66th BS) in 42-40182/A – FORKY II. had two gunners already dead at this point. S/Sgt. Charlie Bridges (RWG) was an RAF veteran with over fifty bombing missions behind him, but his flying career was about to end abruptly. Several fighters latched onto the B-24 and fatally damaged it; a heavy crash-landing left barely enough time for one crewmember – Bridges – to stagger out of the wreckage with a broken back before the aircraft exploded.

Lt. George Winger (66th BS) flying Gentry's right wing was piloting his 41-24015/R – WING DINGER. A flak burst during the bomb run had shunted this B-24 sharply to one side and under Lt. Hunn's B-24 but it still went over the target. By the time the run was completed the shape of the bomber was being enveloped in flames from punctured wing and fuselage tanks. Lt. Hunn (CP) on Gentry's other flank observed the flaming mass pull sharply up several hundred feet, so allowing two gunners to bale out and become POWs. No other parachutes were seen before the bomber bore the remaining six

Lt. Carpenter's crew.

Lt. Felber's crew.

Lt. Tommy Scrivner's ill-fated crew.

crewmembers to their deaths. Tragically, the crew had decided to fly the mission despite having completed their operational 'tour'.

Lt. Worden Weaver (67th BS) was the third wave leader, and his bomber 42-63761/D – LI'L ABNER was fatally crippled through the damage to all but one engine along with shot-away controls. The pilots steered their aircraft nearly forty miles away before they were forced to put her down. Unfortunately a wing dipping during the landing broke up the fuselage. The impact caused the top turret to unhinge, crushing T/Sgt. Schettler in the process. Fire took hold to leave Lts. Weaver, Snyder (CP) and Sorensen (N) trapped up front. The pilot frantically forced open a hole in the windshield and got out; Sorensen's harness snagged on the ragged plexiglas edges, leaving Snyder and him facing an unpleasant death. Fortunately, Lt. Reese (B) managed to scramble back in through the flames to release Sorensen's harness, enabling all three to get clear. The unfortunate engineer proved to be the sole crew fatality.

Two crews were culled from the fourth wave. Lts. Scrivenor and Lasco were flying wingmen to Lt. Miller but had disappeared from the Leader's vision upon traversing the target. Scrivenor's SCRAPPY II was seen to be in flames by several returning witnesses. The pilots' desperate attempt at a crash-landing in a field ended in tragedy, because the aircraft was erased in an explosion before its forward momentum was fully spent. Miller's left wingman was another 66th BS aircraft, 41-24153/L – SAD SACK II flown by Lt. Lasco. One of his gunners S/Sgt. DeCrevel recalled that the fuselage had been riddled by ground fire while the No.2 engine's propeller could not be feathered. Then, several fighters latched onto the B-24 as it emerged from the target area in the company of a group of bombers, and landed further punishment. Lt. Lasco received a horrific wound when a bullet pierced both cheeks and Lt. Stenborn (N) was fatally wounded. Lasco called for the flaps to be lowered as the bomber began to sag downwards; Lt. Kill (CP), getting no response, operated the hand-pump; he then had to turn his attention to levelling off the aircraft on his own because Lasco was now draped across his controls. Somehow the crash-landing succeeded but at the cost of a wholly wrecked machine. The impact had broken both of Lt. Kill's legs and he was tangled up in the mangled cockpit, but his fellow-pilot recovered sufficiently to disengage the co-pilot from his seat and bundle him through a huge fracture in the fuselage. DeCrevel had been thrown against a bulkhead but also recovered and pulled S/Sgt. Shaffer outside after going back to retrieve him. These two gunners and the pilots were the only survivors.

Lt. Reinhart (67th BS) flying in 42-40371/Q – G.I. GAL was one of the last Group pilots to cross over the target, but his

Lt Elmer Rienhart's crew.

B-24 was missing a portion of the left wing. In addition holes behind the Nos.1 and 3 engines were leaking oil and fuel respectively, and the left fin and rudder assembly was damaged. G.I. GAL staggered on for a further fifteen to twenty minutes before it was evident that she was not going to regain friendly shores. The pilots steadily pulled up to around 3000ft. whereupon eight airmen jumped to a safe landing. Lt. Starr (CP) was not so fortunate, since he was killed either by jumping with a faulty parachute or by civilians on the ground.

The seventh total loss over occupied territory constituted the sole Group loss within Col. Posey's formation. The crew's fate proved to be as tragic as that of Lt. Winger's because Capt. Rowland Houston's nine-man team were already 'time-expired'. However, they had elected to fly to Ploesti – a decision that would cost them their lives. Coming off Creditul Minier 42-40995/W – MARGUERITE, which had originally been part of the first attacking wave, was now linking up with other bombers in an effort to provide crossfire protection. *Leutnant* Willi Steinmann flying a Bf 109 selected this B-24 for attack. He closed in steadily in the face of fire from the top and rear turrets before slowly raking his gunfire across his prey's wing-length. The bomber caught fire but so did the fighter. Even worse for Steinmann was the fact that his greater speed had brought him almost under the B-24, which was dropping down from its altitude of less than 200ft.! The German pilot's reaction was to loosen his seat harness, jettison the canopy and literally fly the Bf 109 into the ground. Amazingly, he survived the experience although he had no further recollection of events until he was sitting on the ground near the burning fighter. Close by was the burning wreckage of his victim, but none of its crew had enjoyed the same good fortune.

Lt.'s Dave Arnold and Phillip P. Phillips. Phillips was the navigator on the Scrivner crew for the Ploesti mission and was lost and listed as KIA.

The Return Leg

So far the Group toll in lost B-24s and their crews was seven, but this figure was to be added to as the scattered remnants of the TIDAL WAVE Force battled their way back to North Africa. Two crews ended up 'ditching' in the Mediterranean and two more staggered their way to neutral Turkey. The first-mentioned pair, those of Lts. Carpenter and Jones, both came from the 67th BS. The Carpenter crew were flying in 41-24024 – BEWITCHIN' WITCH and their bomber had suffered fractured fuel lines during the target run. They managed to clear the European coastline but were then involved along with other straggling B-24s in what was the final fighter assault. Damage to two engines was later followed by a third engine going 'out'; as the bomber lost height the sole remaining option to 'ditch' was taken up. The other seven men were in their 'ditching' positions up front as Carpenter and Lt. Rumsey set their charge down on the water. The initial impact bounced the still intact aircraft back into the air, and it promptly broke in two on coming back down. All but two managed to scramble out and into their dinghies, in which they spent an uncertain night. Next morning an RAF Wellington from an air-sea rescue squadron came across the miniscule shapes of the life rafts and dropped both water and supply containers. The fliers then proceeded to circle for anything up to five hours before being relieved by a second Wellington. Finally, an RAF ASR launch hove into sight and plucked the undoubtedly relieved Americans out of the sea.

Above: Lt. George Winger was a 66th BS pilot who was KIA on 1-8-43, another victim of the formidable defenses at Ploesti. Right: Sgt. Howard F. Gotts (Radio Operator) and Sgt. Elvin L. Phillips (Tail Turret) on Lt. Wingers ill-fated crew. Both were listed as MIA, and their names are entered on the Wall of the Missing at Florida and Cambridge.

Lt. Jones's 42-40780/H AVAILABLE JONES managed to remain intact up to the point where the Columbia Aquila plant was being left behind. Then the constant ground fire knocked out No.4 engine while the waist gunners were wounded by another burst. A collision with a barrage balloon cable left the bomber in the air but all too soon it was losing speed and out on its own as well as suffering sever drag from the static No.4 propeller that refused to 'feather'. The fighter attacks did their worst but at their conclusion AVAILABLE JONES was still there. The jettisoning of all unnecessary equipment served to gain enough altitude to clear the land, but by this stage No.3 engine's pressure was failing, and it was switched off. An inexorable loss of altitude then ensued that culminated in 'ditching' action being taken.

All survived the experience and floated in the life rafts overnight. Next morning they were sighted by a U-boat whose Captain did not pick them up. The ugly possibility of drifting around indefinitely was happily cancelled out a few hours later when an Italian floatplane (probably part of an air-sea rescue unit) flew over, landed and took the crew to Brindisi. (Five crewmembers ended up in a monastery out of which Lt. Dukate (CP) and S/Sgt. Sigle (TG) escaped back to Allied lines around October!).

One of the two crews making a diversion into Turkey was that headed by Lt. Mitchell. His B-24 42-40267/N HORSE FLY had been seriously damaged but he and Lt. Decker steered their crippled bomber safely into neutral territory, from where

Above: 'Horse Fly' a B-24D-45-CO 42-40267/N of the 67th BS. This bomber was seriously damaged and barely made it to Turkey where it was interned along with 1/Lt. Edward R. Mitchell's crew.

Right: T/Sgt. Harold Kretzer the Engineer on George Winger's crew was MIA 1-8-43 and has his name listed on the Wall of the Missing at Cambridge, England.

Below: B-24D-35-CO 42-40182/A of the 66th BS. This aircraft crashed into a cornfield on leaving the target at Ploesti. Eight of the crew were KIA and one made POW.

all nine men were repatriated. Sadly, Mitchell's lease on life had but a matter of months to run. Lt. Hughes joined Mitchell in Turkey. He and Lt. Hunn pulled 42-40777/ N – FLOSSIE FLIRT through the target with minimal damage other than a shot-up fuselage. The two other B-24s in their wave had been shot down; two successive attempts to link up with other stragglers had swiftly resulted in each of their 'companions' being downed! Then they were assailed by a fighter but not only survived the experience – they had the satisfaction of seeing their pursuer fly into the ground. Damage to a stabiliser, and loss of fuel, as well as two wounded gunners, persuaded Hughes to turn southeast to seek the neutral sanctuary afforded by the Turks.

Capt. Miller (66th BS) had gone over Columbia Aquila as the Leader of the fourth wave only to emerge on his own in 41-23811/K – FASCINATIN' WITCH. On the run into the target the B-24 had lost the base of the left fin, had suffered a large gash in the left aileron, as well as sustaining supercharger, oil-line and induction system damage to three engines. Bullets, one of which nearly tore Rowland's left leg off, then struck S/Sgts. McDonnell (ROG) and Rowland (WG). It was some time before assistance could be rendered to Rowland because all other crewmembers were busy fighting off attacks. The condition of Rowland in particular persuaded Miller to head for Malta as the closest available hospital facility. The pilots' task was not made easier when the electrical system went 'out' leaving them to fly with the barest form of instrumentation; the navigator also had to rely on the 'dead reckoning' method of course calculation. All three performed well and the ailing B-24 finally deposited its crew safely on the Island.

One further crew came down on Cyprus hours ahead of the other Group bombers. Lt. Whitlock (506th BS) flying in 42-40370/V – HEAVEN CAN WAIT had been forced to 'abort' on the way in over Rumania. Engine problems, coupled to their position at the rear of the formation ultimately forced him to head back for the nearest available friendly airfield – in this case, Cyprus. The bomber limped southward for nearly five hours with No.1 engine switched off. A short distance away from the Island the B-24 began to drop when it suffered the loss of more power. The crew were fortunate that not only did Cyprus appear in time but that the heading was directly towards the runway end!

Back at Benina-Main the personnel had gathered to await the Group's return. Any hopes that they would gaze upon neat formations of aircraft entering the circuit were soon dispelled as the bombers began to straggle in over the airfield at well-dispersed intervals during the late afternoon and into the

Right: Captain Rowland M. Gentry 66th BS, KIA 1-8-43. He flew the ill-fated 'Forky II' 42-40182/A. The target was the "White Five" designated refinery over which Gentry led a V-Flight.

Below: T/Sgt. John F. Cox stands at the right waist gun position. The silver patches to his left cover the damage made by a 37mm shell exploding in the waist area. Cox was peppered by fragments that embedded in his back. The incident happened over the target at Ploesti. He was part of Shelby Irby's crew on B24D-95-CO 42-40764 M "Helen B Happy."

Below: Two horrific shots of 1/Lt. Henry A. Lasco, Jr. a 66th BS pilot. They show the full measure of the wounds he sustained on 1-8-43. He would make a full recovery and be returned to duty after release from a POW camp.

Right: This photo of 1/Lt. Lasco after return to duty with the 446th BG: note the faint scar on his cheek, all that remains of the original massive wound.

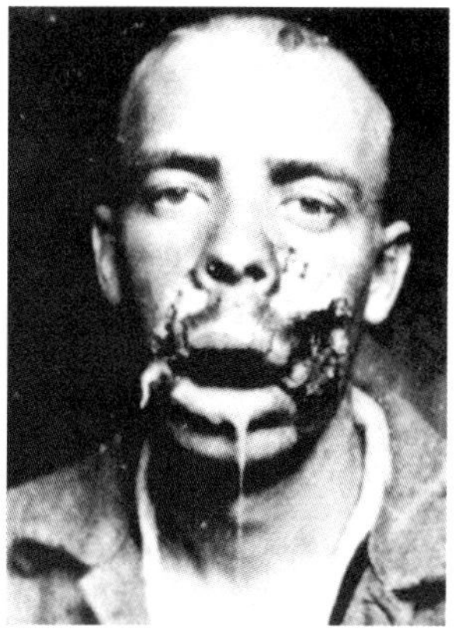

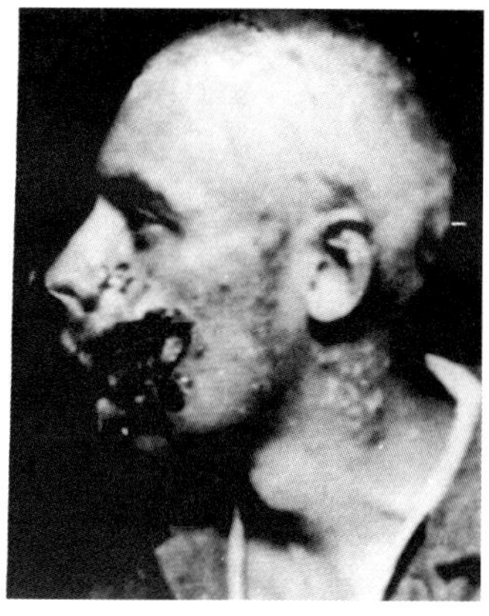

Pages 58-60: Aerial Strike photos of Ploesti 1-8-43.

Top: The debriefing of the crews who made it back from the Hell called Ploesti – their faces say it all. Col. Johnson can be seen on the right of the photo.

Above: General Ent (left) shakes hands with Col. Leon Johnson.

Above: Stand down and a seventy-two hour pass in Tel Aviv for these three lucky men after the Ploesti mission. They are all members of Lt. Martin's crew, being (left to right) T/Sgt. Jack Shelton, T/Sgt. Harry Snead and S/Sgt. William gaffney. 68th BS.

evening. Only twenty-four of the thirty-seven crews that had departed so hopefully in the early morning light came back on 1 August. Their time in flight averaged between thirteen and fourteen hours. The experience of the Brandon/Johnson crew was typical; the pilots landed back at 1804, which meant they had been in the air for thirteen hours thirty-four minutes!

Ploesti had been a qualified disaster. Eleven of the absent aircraft were either smouldering heaps in Rumania that had consumed many of their crews, or were lying on the Mediterranean seabed, or were sitting on airfields in Turkey. The remaining pair of absentees was safe on Cyprus or Malta. The Group MIA losses were in almost exact proportion to the overall task force figure that stood at fifty-four out of the 177 dispatched by the five Groups. A great deal of destruction had been visited upon the bulk of the Ploesti complex but the overall result was not the 'knockout' blow that had been predicted. It would take the concerted efforts of the entire 15th USAAF extending over many months of 1944 for this to be achieved.

Chapter Four

More Hard Knocks

The presence of the 44th BG in North Africa did not finish immediately following the mission to Ploesti. The Group along with its fellow Groups from the 8th USAAF was retained with a view to supporting further Land operations in Sicily and latterly into Italy. The missions to be flown were to extend as far as Austria in one case but were generally concentrated on the island and southern Italian mainland.

The severe burden placed upon the shoulders of the crews involved in Ploesti was to be recognised in mid-September. Five Congressional Medals of Honor were granted, three of them posthumous. One of the living recipients was Col. Johnson, the other being Col. 'Killer' Kane of the 98th BG. Three Distinguished Service Crosses went to Capts. Bill Cameron (67th BS), John Diehl (Squadron CO), and Reginald Phillips (both 68th BS), along with three Silver Stars; the latter decoration involved Capt. Holmes and Lts. Klekar (B) and Stine (N), also members of the 68th BS. In addition, dozens of Distinguished Flying Crosses were awarded across the ranks of the Group, many of them posthumous.

A period of almost two weeks went by before the Group flew its latest mission. This was another lengthy haul to strike at the aircraft production factory in Wiener-Neustadt up in Austria. A total of twenty-three crews participated and were faced with nearly twelve hours in the air. Enemy reaction to the invaders was surprisingly poor despite having more than enough warning of the bombers' normal high-level approach. Bombing results were assessed as 'good' and the aircraft returned, albeit not all to Benina-Main. Two crews diverted into airfields on Sicily, one of which was led by Lt. Lehnhausen (68th BS). He had already survived a 'ditching' when flying as co-pilot to Lt. Garrett on the 2 July mission to Lecce. Now in charge of his own crew for the first time and flying 41-24211/ U – WING AND A PRAYER he found the aircraft was running dangerously short of fuel and made for Sicily. The aircraft was virtually running on fumes when a small airstrip was sighted. To the crew's dismay the site was not only very small but was liberally pockmarked from the effect of bombs and shells. As he orbited this airfield a second airstrip was sighted and headed for. The situation this time round appeared no better as the area was equally pock-marked with craters. However, a grass-covered section seemed to provide a suitable but very limited length and width on which to safely put down a big bomber. Lehnhausen managed with some difficulty to persuade the others that a landing could be safely executed, especially since No.3 engine had just gone 'out' and a second was faltering (and would fail during the landing approach). There would be just the one landing attempt because of rising foothills encroaching on the far end of the airfield. Unknown to the pilots was the fact that the nose wheel had just been replaced but not flight-tested. Sure enough, the unit folded upon contact and the B-24 skidded to an undignified but intact halt.

Foggia possessed a large marshalling yard as well as an airfield. The airfield had already been attacked by the Group on 15 July and had proved to be a 'milk-run' in terms of opposition, as had similar targets attacked within the same far southern region of Italy during the same period. It was probably with this previous experience in mind that the opportunity was taken for a number of new crews to be 'blooded' in combat. The 67th BS dispatched Lt. Leighton Smith in one of its 'experienced' B-24s BUZZIN' BEAR while Lt. Bateman took the controls of another veteran bomber SUZY-Q. Four of Lt.

Whitlock's 506th BS crew were down with dysentery and were naturally replaced. The normally unspoken feeling among combat personnel was that 'milk-runs' were never guaranteed, and this sombre statement was tragically borne out today.

Once again twenty-three aircraft were dispatched and headed across the Mediterranean towards the heel of Italy before making their approach to the Foggia plain region. Although flak was present as ever during the bombing run no aircraft appears to have been more than slightly damaged by the gunfire. This easy-paced situation altered drastically not long after coming off the target and rallying for the run back to North Africa. A pack of Bf 109s and Fw 190s suddenly loomed up and quickly began to land punishing strikes on the formation.

Lt. Curelli was leading one of the new crews in 41-23778/F LADY LUCK but the aircraft cruelly denied its positive title to nine of the ten airmen aboard. Having lost the No.3 engine the bomber dropped out of formation and was promptly assailed by the fighters. Attempts to open the bomb bay doors with a view to jumping were manually made by Sgt. Grinde (Eng.) but the aircraft went into a spin and the sliding door giving access to the bomb-bay was jammed into position. S/Sgt. Wesley Zimmerman (ROG) recalled that a few seconds later the B-24 exploded and he was blown out from the flight deck to become the sole survivor. (Two witnesses claimed to have seen several parachutes descending, but none of their human burdens reached the ground alive; Zimmerman came across the body of his pilot).

Up to now the 506th BS has been free of any aircraft casualties during the 44th BG's North African detachment, which included the costly strike on Ploesti. This spell of immunity was now broken over Foggia to the tune of two crews. Lt. Whitlock in 42-40606/X – TIMBA-A-AH! was flying in a 'Tail-end Charlie' position. His aircraft survived the first two fighter passes almost intact but the third proved fatal. Sgt. Dunajesz (WG) was killed as well as Sgt. Bonham (TG). Fire in the bomb-bay was tackled by Lt. Wilson (CP) and S/Sgt. Stewart (Eng.); the bomb-bay doors were jammed and Wilson's attempt to break through one side by jumping down resulted in his death; Stewart also failed to survive, having apparently resumed firing his guns. The interphone system had been disabled and Whitlock managed to scramble out through the cockpit hatch as the B-24 went into a terminal dive. Back in the waist S/Sgts. Knox and Kosch wrestled with the tunnel-gun hatch; their efforts were in vain and so Knox literally threw his fellow-gunner out of a waist window before following suit; sadly, Kosch did not survive the descent. The physical effort

Walter Bunker 506th BS, photographed shortly after returning from the first tour in North Africa.

A V formation shot of three B-24Ds of the 66th BS: the nearest aircraft is 'Sure Shot', in the center is 'Avenger', and 'Facinatin'Witch' is the remaining bomber.

required of Knox at this point was severe because of wounds to his legs that had left them almost paralysed, and it took all the strength in his arms to clamber over the waist windowsill and out. (The subsequent hospital experience when the surgeons removed shell fragments from his legs without the benefit of an anaesthetic was long remembered by Knox!). T/Sgt. Mundell (ROG) was the fifth man out of the ten to bale out and survive.

The other 506th BS bomber culled from the formation was that of Lt. Austin, whose B-24 was 42-40778/T – SOUTHERN COMFORT. Strikes on Nos.2 and 3 engines set both on fire, and the bomb bay was soon a mass of flames, cutting off the men in the rear from those up front. The bale-out bell was still functioning and so the four gunners quickly made their exit either by the waist windows of the camera hatch. S/Sgt. Joe Warth observed his aircraft erupting against a hillside as he floated down. All ten men baled out, but Lts. Singer (N) and Finder (B) were killed, through their parachutes having suffered battle damage and not opening properly as a result.

A single aircraft was lost from the 68th BS, being 42-40373/Z – NATCHEZ BELLE. Lt. Shannon's bomber had fallen well behind the Group formation and became the focus for heavy fighter attacks. Lt. Temple (N) recalled that Sgts. Heller (WG) and Smith (G) were killed as their aircraft with two engines on fire went into a glide. Bale out was called for and all surviving crewmembers bar Lt. Hersh (CP) jumped clear. Hersh had come down with Shannon to the bomb-bay ready to jump but had forgotten to bring his chest-pack. Fire in the radio compartment prevented his return to the cockpit. He then refused his pilot's offer to share the one available chest-pack, saying that this would jeopardize Shannon's chances of survival.

Sgt. Strandberg (ROG) was standing between the pilots as the attacks developed. A 20mm shell impacting with the fuselage left side of his compartment ripped a massive hole in the aircraft's skin and threw him bodily across to the other side. A temporary paralysis in his legs fortunately subsided quickly

Sgt. James Caillier, a gunner on Frank Slough's crew, smiles for the camera shortly after returning from the first period of detached service to North Africa. The aircraft is "Ruth-Less" of the 506th BS.

B-24D-5-CO 41-23811/K 'Facinatin' Witch' of the 66th BS. This B-24 was lost on 1-10-43 along with Lt. Bridge's crew.

Below: 1/Lt. Frank Slough and Flying officer Raymond Lacombe shut 'Ruth-Less' down after the flight from North Africa that completed the 44th BG's first spell of detached service with the 9th AF.

enough for the Sgt. to grab his parachute-pack and head for the bomb bay from where he baled out. He, along with three fellow-gunners and Lt. Temple subsequently managed to escape from Italian custody and regain Allied lines; Shannon and Lt. Collins (B) were not so fortunate and ended up as POWs for the duration of World War II.

This mission was to prove another solid blow for the 67th BS with no less than three crews MIA along with two 'veteran' B-24s. Lt. Smith was flying BUZZIN'BEAR and among his crew was Lt. Jim DeVinney, Bill Cameron's experienced bombardier. Returning crews said he appeared to be having problems in holding position in the formation before the fighter attacks came in. The last sight of the B-24 as it fell away with the gunners firing desperately at the Bf 109s and Fw 190s was of the aircraft breaking in two and four parachutes issuing from the front section. In fact all four officers, the engineer and ROG managed to bale out successfully; the four other gunners were probably already dead thanks to cannon shell or bullet strikes.

Bill Cameron's pride and joy was joined in her fiery fate by SUZY-Q, the sole surviving 'original' B-24 in the 67th BS, and equally the pride of Major Howard Moore. However, the exact circumstances in which this bomber met her fate remained uncertain, especially since none of Lt. Bateman's crew survived the experience. However, the burning wreck of the B-24 was reported as lying on a beach.

The trio of 67th BS losses was completed by 42-41021/T, BLACK SHEEP, flown by Lt. Piemental. Under regular attack by fighters, the pilots were attempting to take up a course for Sicily. S/Sgt. Blakeney (Asst. ROG) recalled that No.3 engine was set on fire and subsequent fighter attacks fired up No.2. The gunners put up a sustained defence of their bomber even though the tail turret was immobilised but the sustained punishment handed out later disabled a third engine. The B-24 was miraculously still aloft but steadily descending when the fighters gave up. A bulk jettisoning of equipment could not halt the descent and the B-24 was somewhere approaching the Toe of Italy (over one hours flying time from the target) when Lt. Pimental and Lt. Hager (CP) were finally forced into a crash-landing on a beach at Reggio Calabria. By then three engines were on fire and the lack of operable flaps meant that the landing was made at a much higher speed than normal. The impact tore off the bomb-bay doors, causing injuries to some of those in the rear fuselage. Sadly, half the crew were killed when the bomber blew up in the center section shortly after coming to a halt, after which fire rapidly took hold and swept forward. Lt. Hager suffered serious burns to his face, arms and hands but managed to scramble out of his cockpit window. The other three officers and T/Sgt. Curry (Eng.) remained trapped and their screams could be heard as the other members of the crew vainly tried to break through. Hager joined the four gunners in the rear that had also got clear, and all were rounded up by the Italians and taken to Bari. S/Sgts. Blakeney and Hess later broke out of their POW camp along with two other crewmembers and ultimately ran into units of the Canadian 5th Army.

Butlers 67th BS B-24D-160-CO 42-72860 N 'Miss Emmy Lou' after he had to make a crash landing on return from Wiener Neustadt in Austria on 10 October 1943.

Open air briefing for the 44th.

Of the remaining sixteen crews completing the mission, at least one – Lt. Henderson (67th BS) – diverted into Malta. The loss of nearly one third of the Force was a clear remainder that there would never be any guarantee of a 'milk-run' in the ETO during World War II. The award of a Silver Star to Col. Posey for his efforts to hold the formation together was scant consolation.

Three days later the Group was again briefed for Foggia but in the meantime the number of serviceable B-24s had fallen greatly. In fact only the 66th BS and 68th BS could meet this available total. Even then four of the ten crews dispatched had to 'abort', the primary culprit being engine oil leaks. Any foreboding felt by the six crews who made the ten-hour haul to Foggia was thankfully groundless; this time round the target was bombed with virtually no interference from the Luftwaffe being recorded.

What was to be the last mission during its detachment to North Africa (but not the last ever from the Mediterranean Theater of Operations) was flown on the 21st to Cancello, Italy. Once again the continuing problem of serviceability resulted in just eight bombers taking off, out of which one 'aborted'. The other seven all made it back to Benina-Main, having made a good strike and receiving little or no attention from the reported fighter Force (approximately thirty) engaging the overall Force.

Home for Good?

Late in August, orders were received for the three 8th USAAF Groups to transfer back to their bases in England. The aircraft making the flight flew in three stages via Tunis and Marrakesh in Morocco, and were down at Shipdham by the 31st. All the aircraft arrived safely but there were three personnel fatalities, all occurring another Group. S/Sgt. Haaf and Sgts. Weems and Woolfe were coming back with the 389th BG after having been 'loaned out' from the 44th BG. Their B-24 went MIA and it was only later that the bodies of Weems and Woolfe were swept up onto the Brest peninsula.

The combat crews were greeted with enthusiasm by the ground crews in particular. The majority of these specialists had had to be left behind when the Group decamped overseas and had had nothing much to occupy themselves with between the end of June and now. One way in which to restore general

The Liberators kick up a dust storm as they taxi out for a mission during the second detachment to Oudna #1, Tunis, North Africa.

spirits was through the medium of sport. Softball proved to be the most suitable game for the ground conditions to be found in the East Anglian soil on which Shipdham stood. The four squadrons along with the medical section and the 464th sub-depot produced teams, and it fell to the 67th BS outfit to finally be crowned undisputed champions of the league, as they were undefeated during the entire mini-season!

On a more sombre note, a serious injury to one man had been incurred through enemy action. One night in July an unidentified Luftwaffe aircraft swept over the airfield in the dark but no explosions occurred to indicate that a bomb-load of any standard type had been dropped. In fact the crew had released their ordnance in the form of small anti-personnel bombs. These were intended to lay dormant until handled, stood on or driven over when they would activate. The task of finding and rendering the weapons harmless began next morning. Until this was done, all British civilians working at Shipdham were advised to stay off the airfield. When this request was addressed to Mr. Brown (clerk of works) he rounded on the two officers in question – as far as he was concerned the airfield was British and his staff must have unfettered access! Brown's assistant later sent out on an inspection visit in his Morris van now paid a heavy price for this obdurate stance – his foot was blown off when his vehicle ran over one of the bombs!

Cpl. Broadley (RAF Substitution Unit) recalled that although Major Hammer and Capt. Neri ran 44th BG communications, it was RAF Signals personnel who handled the SBA (Standard Beam Approach) equipment. He also remembered that 'call outs' to handle problems at Wendling (392nd BG) for example always required the use of USAAF transport, even though Peter had his own driving licence. The minimum rank for USAAF drivers was sergeant, and the likely, but ever unspoken, reaction to chauffeuring around an airman of lower rank was one that intrigued their British cousin! (Not only that, but the driver in question had to hang around until the task in hand was complete, however long it might take). On one occasion he was 'called out' in the night only to find one of his bicycle wheels punctured. He set off for the long trudge from his Site to Group HQ to do his duty; on the way back a car stopped and a quiet voice said, "Wanna' lift, Corporal" – it was none other than Col. Leon Johnson, who duly delivered his passenger to his billet!

Short Interlude

On 2 September 1943, Col. Leon Johnson stepped down as Group commander to be officially succeeded next day by Lt.Col. James Posey. Johnson's subsequent promotion to CO of the 14th Combat Bomb Wing did not result in much of a physical change of location – the 14th CBW HQ was destined to be located between the flight lines and main sites at Shipdham! By now the 67th BS also had a new CO because Major Moore had been posted back to the United States. In his place stood the equally efficient and respected Bill Cameron who held the same rank. The difference between this officer's tenure as commander and his contemporaries throughout the 44th BG during World War II was that he was destined to serve two terms in this function.

Maj./Gen. Hodges Commander of the 2nd Bomb Wing.

Below: B-24D-95-CO 42-40764M 66th BS "Helen B Happy" crashed shortly after take off on the first leg of the return flight to Shipdham 11 October 1943.

The return to England for all three Groups operating the B-24 was to last barely two weeks. In that brief period the 44th BG would fly just four missions, the first of which saw a return to the 'diversion' type of operation. On 6 September the crews flew out over the North Sea while the B-17s headed in force for Stuttgart – a mission that would cost fully forty-five of 1st Wing's total force. Next day, the Group along with the 389th BG were assigned the Dutch airfield at Leeuwarden, which was a key night fighter base. Almost solid cloud at the target forced a switch to a secondary target, which also proved to be 'socked in'. This unsatisfactory scenario was redeemed as the bombers re-crossed the Dutch Coast. Clearer conditions and the presence of a convoy close to the island of Texel resulted in a tight bombing pattern landing in among, and in several cases upon, the vessels. Two days later a second airfield at Abbeville-Drucat in France was struck with only 'fair' results by seventeen of the nineteen aircraft sent out.

The weather was still proving as formidable a foe as ever, and no operations were launched for five days. Then, on the 15th the bombers were dispatched to France to bomb another airfield near Chartres (Conches). The mission went off well, with sound bombing results, little flak and no fighter opposition, although just twelve out of twenty two crews managed group assembly and went over. This mission was launched much later than normal, so that the formations not only landed in the dark but were also still over France as darkness was descending. The returning crews stated among their recommendations that this operational factor should be avoided in future, since fighter attacks had been difficult to detect in the gloom, and had led to the loss of at least one B-24 from another Group. This incident in turn made gunners on other bombers nervous and led to fire being opened up on any object deemed to be hostile, although the bulk of the ammunition was apparently directed at several straggling B-24s. (This was a lesson that was not apparently taken on board prior to the Hamm mission of 22 April 1944. The mission timing was such that the bombers' return occurred after night had fallen. Luftwaffe fighters infiltrated the 2nd BD ranks and created chaos over the bomber bases in the process).

However, what sense of satisfaction the returning crews might have gained from today's action was forgotten on landing. The bald fact was that the Group was required to return to North Africa! Barely twenty-four hours after landing off the Chartres mission, with all necessary preparations rushed through, the first crews took off and headed southwest for their jumping-off airfield in Cornwall. (Some aircraft and crews were retained at Shipdham and several 'diversion' missions were flown in between 26 September and 4 October; in the same period a number of replacement crews were assigned).

Second Taste of the Desert

The reputed rationale behind the re-deployment of the 2nd Wing Groups to North Africa was due to stiffening Axis resistance against the initial Anglo-American Invasion of southern Italy. The landing at Salerno had certainly faced seeming disaster during the first two days but the likelihood of a second 'Dunkirk-style' evacuation was averted; this was due to a combination of concerted bombing and shelling by heavy units of the Royal and U.S. Navies. By mid-September the overall ground battle was going in full favour of the Allies, with no real need for any aerial reinforcements to be dispatched from England.

Col. James Posey took over command of the 44th BG from Col. Johnson, on 3 September 1943.

This time around the assigned airfields were somewhat closer to England, with the 44th BG operating out of Oudna in Tunisia. Tented accommodation was still the order of the day and the heat was in unpleasant contrast to the late summer weather in England. By the 21st operations were ready to commence, and the crews were briefed for the docks at Leghorn. The 44th BG was Lead Group to the other two Groups but neither managed to make Wing assembly, so leaving the Shipdham formation to head north alone. Light flak concentrations did not have any effect on the bombing effort, which was 'excellent' in accuracy and concentration. Two crews 'aborted' with the pilots of 42-72877 (67th BS) reporting oil leaks from two of its R-1830-43 engines. The fault was traced to leakage via the engine breathers, which was a recurring problem with this engine type in desert operational conditions.

The other crew in 41-23699 (also 67th BS) suffered loss of supercharger boost on two engines; no leaks upon check of the induction system threw suspicion on the supercharger regulators being faulty.

Targets in the northern reaches of Italy and into Austria were to be the focus of attack during this spell of detachment that would culminate in a final, horrendous run to Weiner-Neustadt. Pisa's marshalling yards bore the brunt of the B-24s' ordnance on the 24th. Weather conditions were perfect from halfway up the Italian peninsula. The central and eastern sections of the yards were well plastered by twenty of the twenty-two crews dispatched, loss of manifold pressure and a leaking fuel cap being the reasons for the duo of 'aborting' bombers. Next day turned out to be a total failure when eighteen aircraft took off to bomb Lucca airfield near Pisa, but subsequently responded to a 'recall' signal. And then came Wiener-Neustadt.

A Reverse over Austria

The B-24s' airfields in northern Tunisia brought them somewhat closer to their targets in Europe compared to Benina-Main and Berka. However, the crews still faced lengthy flight-times when dispatched to targets such as Pisa, Leghorn and now Wiener-Neustadt. The previous run to the latter source on 13 August had resulted in a twelve-hour slog, but at least no casualties were suffered by the 44th BG. A major Messerschmitt aircraft production factory was located at Wiener-Neustadt. Since fighters were currently proving a mortal stumbling block to USAAF heavy bomber operations, any diminution in the strength of the *Jagdwaffe* (Luftwaffe Fighter Command) was desirable. The 8th USAAF had already struck at the company's Regensburg plant during the 'Anniversary' mission dispatched on 17 August, and this was a second effort at major disruption.

The briefing for the mission on 1 October was made in the knowledge that weather conditions might prove variable. Twenty-six aircraft took off from 0700 onward as a part of the attacking force. In the Lead Group's Lead bomber as Command Pilot was Brig.Gen. Hodges. The B-24s traced a route up along the Adriatic, but began to encounter increasingly solid cloud formations once over land. Finally, on approach to the target the bombardiers were forced to bomb through what was an inadequate envelope of clear air, and which caused bombing results to be assessed as 'poor'. All of this was conducted in the face of prolonged flak barrages as well as sizeable numbers of fighters.

Two of the canisters that contained the butterfly bombs: note several de-activated bombs laying on the floor of the truck.

Sgt. John Walbarst 464th sub depot with a German bomb after it had been disarmed by a bomb disposal team from the Chemical Company.

The 67th BS had dispatched eight crews out of the twenty-five that went over Wiener-Neustadt. As the ground crews scanned the skies to the north for first sight of the returning Group later that day they were undoubtedly feeling uneasy on seeing the far-reduced number of B-24s (ten) that now comprised the formation. Once all the aircraft were landed, it was the 67th BS personnel who received the greatest shock – only one of their number dispatched had come back! The accounts of the mission as told at de-briefing were of an aerial ambush that had cost no less than seven bombers along with their crews.

The initial fighter assaults began as the bombers were tracking in from the I.P. to the target. The first of the three losses suffered by the 67th BS occurred at this point. The left turn at the I.P. had caused the Low squadron to be forced out of position and just in time to receive a full-scale attack from directly ahead. Lt. Henderson's bomber (42-72853) took the full brunt of the gunfire on the right wing, knocking out both engines and inducing a steep spiral action. Henderson gave the order to bale out. Of the two officers to get out alive, Lt. Greyhosky (CP) was very fortunate to do so. He was knocked out as he went to jump and somehow recovered in time to get clear. He had no subsequent recollection of how he did so, since by the time his senses had been restored, he was already on the ground! Just one other crewmember was able to survive.

Also downed as the bomb-run was about to be completed was 42-41017/L-bar. Its 67th BS crew was led by Lt. Carpenter, and included S/Sgt. Paliga (Eng.). Paliga was on his twenty-fifth mission but his regular crew had already finished up and so he had flown as a 'spare' in order to complete his 'tour'. It was Paliga's opinion that the sheer weight of Luftwaffe firepower was swamping all defensive efforts by the American gunners. His B-24 absorbed strikes from one of the fighters, and all too soon two engines burst into flames followed by a third. S/Sgt. Irwin (ROG) handed him a chest-pack before stepping down into the bomb bay. When the engineer followed down he found Irwin draped across the catwalk with the parachute canopy deployed and out in the slipstream. Irwin had previously told Paliga he was afraid he would pass out after jumping and not be able to operate his parachute. The alternative was for him to prepare to jump, and pull the ripcord while holding his hand over the pack; should he pass out after jumping the natural action of his hand falling away would permit the parachute to operate. Sadly, his plan had gone wrong and now he was 'snared' through the canopy lines getting tangled with the auxiliary fuel tank in the bomb bay. Paliga's attempts to free his fellow crewmember were unsuccessful, and as the onset of anoxia began to take effect he was forced to abandon his action and bale out. (Lt. Pratt (CP) physically dragged Irwin out with him as he was baling out, but the hapless airman was pulled free due to the tremendous air pressure, and fell to his death.) S/Sgt. Brady (LW) recalled S/Sgt. Bryl, an RAF veteran with upwards of sixty 'operations' (RAF for missions) before joining the USAAF, being blown out of the tail turret into the fuselage. His death was quickly followed by that of the other waist-gunner, and the ball-turret gunner. The two surviving gunners got clear as did the co-pilot and navigator before the B-24 exploded. Amazingly Lt. Carpenter survived as well although believed to have still been at the controls when the B-24 disintegrated.

The third 67th BS loss was believed to have occurred at the start of the air battle. However, the circumstances surrounding the demise of 41-23918/O – BELA remained unclear. Two gunners from Lt. Bronstein's crew did manage to bale out however.

Lt. Bridges (66th BS) had taken off in 41-23811/K – FASCINATIN' WITCH, a 44th BG 'original'. The inboard engines of this veteran B-24 had gradually been consuming so much oil that the Squadron Engineering officer had 'grounded' it. Bridges had persuaded his fellow-officer to release the aircraft for this mission on the rather tenuous grounds that it was not expected to extend over more than ten hours. When up somewhere over the Italian/Yugoslavian border the same inboard engines lost power as the Group began its second stage of ascending to bombing altitude. Bridges continued on at the present altitude and somehow managed to subsequently nurse his ailing bomber back into formation. The bombs had just been dropped when fighters swooped in to inflict strikes that knocked out both of the malfunctioning engines as well as firing the pair of bomb-bay fuel tanks within the forward section. Three gunners were killed during these strikes but the remainder of the crew baled out successfully. Bridges was more fortunate than the others; he was imprisoned first in Hungary and Yugoslavia before escaping in May 1944 and making contact with Tito's partisans. He was finally flown back to Italy the following August.

A second 66th BS bomber 42-72877/A was being flown by Lt. Hobson. The intercom system was disabled during the first fighter attack, a fire developed behind the No.4 engine; further damage probably affected the elevators and rudders because the pilots immediately felt the controls go slack. An uncontrolled climb to the right occurred almost at once, and even more damage was inflicted by the persistent fighter attacks. The B-24 finally stalled and went into a spin, an action that was only partially corrected by feathering all functioning engines and lowering the flaps. The easing of centrifugal force that resulted from this permitted the six surviving crewmembers to bale out through the bomb bay and nose-wheel door. (Hobson landed close enough to the crashed bomber to see that the control surfaces had been almost totally excised from the right side of the tail, so confirming the impression of loss of control during the first stage of the fighter assault.)

Although the unfortunate 67th BS suffered the highest percentage of losses on this mission the overall loss factor was shared across the Group's strength, with one crew going MIA from both the 68th BS and 506th BS. Lt. Whittaker's 41-23816/X – BLACK JACK had been around for marginally over one year following assignment on 20 September 1942. Eyewitnesses stated that the bomber fell back and down to the left just after the target with a burning bomb-bay and several parachutes issuing forth. Further erratic movements ended with the aircraft splitting in two after all other crewmembers had jumped. Unfortunately, the likelihood that all ten airmen had at least got clear was not borne out by the facts. Lt. Whittaker was killed while Sgt. Reasoner (TG) alone among the ROG and the four gunners actually survived after the bomber exploded, and he was so badly burnt about the head and face that he was later repatriated.

The final Group victim was 42-72857/X-Bar whose 506th BS crew was that of Lt. Olson, who was to be the sole fatality. This bomber was subject to attack by a *Schwarm* of Bf 109s whose gunfire ignited the bomb-bay fuel tank The bomb-load was jettisoned as the B-24 peeled off to the right and the crew began to bale out. Of the nine airmen landing safely, only S/Sgt. Bugyie (BT) was not promptly captured, but his bid for possible freedom ended just four days later.

One of the many anti-personnel bombs dropped on the airfield.This nasty little weapon was known as a butterfly bomb because of the small wings that would deploy when making contact with the ground – it could inflict bad wounds when activated.

Captain Nathanson stands in the crater made by a fifty kilogram high explosive bomb that was dropped on Shipdham airfield during the night of the 23-24 August 1943.

The Stragglers Return

Seven other B-24s suffered serious damage as well as having crew- members wounded. F/O Taylor brought back 41-23699 – LEMON DROP (a 68th BS bomber) as far as Bari, having had the No.3 engine and radio and electrical systems disabled. The cripple remained here for upwards of a week before repairs were completed and the onward flight made to Oudna. Lt. Butler diverted into Catania, Sicily in 42-72860/N – MISS EMMY LOU where a crash-landing was made; transfer of this B-24 out of the Group occurred nine days later, followed by salvage action on 30 November. Another long-serving B-24 was 41-23235 – EARTH-QUAKE MCGOON, which had originally served with the 506th BS from 4 March, but was now with the 67th BS. The bomber was brought down on a beach near Salerno by Lt. Aldrige but was struck off Group records and finally salvaged the same day as MISS EMMY LOU (30 November).

Lt. Butler had been flying his B-24 as No.2 within the Low Left Squadron, but moved his charge up into the Lead when Lt. Carpenter was downed. A call to S/Sgt. Kooken (TG) enquiring if the other B-24s were closing up to their aircraft was tersely answered to the effect that they were all going down! Lt. Butler therefore pulled up under the Group Lead ship; apparently when Lt. Lenhhausen witnessed this action he commented to his crew; "That Butler's a goner!"

MISS EMMY LOU (named for Lt. Butler's baby, Emily) was heavily damaged during the combat, having suffered hydraulic system failure as well as fuel loss and the latter problem dictated a diversion towards Sicily. Once at Catania, Neeper cranked down the landing gear. He also remarked that one of the flap cables was shot out but that the remaining one should hold half flap. Full flap was applied and the landing approach commenced. Then when a few hundred feet up a drastic aerodynamic imbalance occurred when the right flap popped up and the left went full down! The pilot fully advanced the throttles and with the help of Lt. Tenney (CP) attempted to correct the position with full right rudder. The errant B-24 touched down in a skid and at high speed but the landing gear held up – at least until the bomber over-shot the runway and ploughed into sandy soil, when the nose wheel collapsed. One of the gunners had been badly wounded so he was removed and taken to a nearby hospital.

The 66th BS had three aircraft landing elsewhere than Oudna. Lt. Oakley (66th BS), having had Lts. McKenney (CP) and Young (N) seriously wounded, also brought off a crash-landing at Foggia. In fact McKenney was an airplane commander who had taken the right seat this day. Between the I.P. and the target a cannon shell burst through the windshield, causing him head injuries that left fragments in his skull and cost him his right eye. One engine had gone 'out' under the battering and following 'bombs away' Oakley had pushed the bale-out bell, in response to which two men jumped. McKenney was about to follow suit when he saw his pilot indicate that he could bring the aircraft under control again, so he crawled back up from the bomb-bay and rested by the top turret-base. The target was safely cleared but two hours later a second engine went 'out' and the pilot had no option but to make a forced-landing in what turned out to be a ploughed field. In spite of this, the landing was brought off in good order, although the nose-wheel on 41-23936/J – QUEEN ANNE dug in and caused a skidding motion. Two of the gunners had received wounds of lesser degree and all four men were taken to a British Field Hospital for treatment. Lt. Irby flying 42-40764/M – HELEN B HAPPY and Lt. Comey in 41-23769/B went into airfields at Palermo and Salerno respectively. (The latter aircraft was also struck off Group records on 15 October and salvaged on 30 November).

The seventh 'straggler' was Lt. Kessler (68th BS) flying 41-24009/W – MARGARET ANN. Three gunners were wounded, with S/Sgt. Storovich (TG) bearing a flak fragment in his spine. This B-24's radio equipment was shot-up as was the hydraulic system and No.1 engine was exuding heavy smoke. The landing gear and flaps were hand-cranked, leaving the residual amount of hydraulic fluid for the brakes as the bomber circled a small Canadian airfield at Bari. The ground controller fired flares to warn off the crew, since he regarded the grass strip as too short for a safe landing. No response could be made in order to inform him of the emergency situation, thanks to the shot-up radio system. The result was an over-shoot that tore up a fence but left the strip otherwise intact. This bomber's service with the 44th BG was over and she was transferred out to the 98th BG in mid-October.

The grim comparison of today's mission with the Group experience over Ploesti was all too evident. In each instance, seven crews had been declared MIA and to these negative human and material statistics had been added almost the same total of diversions as well as B-24s lost through the act of 'ditching' off the 1 August mission. North Africa was proving as much of a trial for Group morale as the ETO had hitherto been. However, the Group's tenure of combat service in the MTO was effectively over. On 3 October, orders were received transferring the crews back to their operational 'home', and effective next day.

Back at Palermo HELEN B HAPPY was under repair with her crew blissfully ignorant that they were about to be 'orphaned'. By the time aircraft and crew arrived back at Oudna, their fellow-airmen were departed. On 10 October, the Irby crew took off in their B-24, ready to take the same route back to Shipdham via Marrakech. The aircraft was just a few hundred feet up when it lost all power. In the nose Lt. Rendall (N) was trying vainly to dissuade Lt. Saenger (B) not to bale out. The bombardier had previously 'ditched' and was unwilling to risk another crash-landing. He did jump as the bomber passed over a shallow valley but the vertical drop was still too short to allow the parachute to properly deploy, and he was killed. His action was to prove all the more tragic since the crew all survived the crash-landing, although several sustained minor injuries.

A second 'orphaned' crew was that of Lt. Butler. The airmen had been stranded for two days at Catania, before their pilot fortuitously ran into an old high school acquaintance, now a C-47 pilot. He accordingly arranged for the crew to be flown back to Oudna, where the fact of the 44th BG departure for home was confirmed. No one in authority appeared either willing or able to arrange the necessary transport to England.

The friend did fly his fellow-airmen as far as Algiers but from here they were on their own. It was several days more before they could get on board an ATC Flight going to Prestwick, Scotland. Once there, rail passes were obtained for the final leg of the journey to Shipdham via Norwich.

It was during October that S/Sgt. Blakeney (LW) on Lt. Piemental's crew got back to the Allied lines in Italy. He had been captured and held in a building in Reggio, Calabria along with four surviving crewmembers. This included Lt. Hager (CP) who had been critically burnt escaping from the crash-landed B-24. Proper medical attention was denied the Lt. for several days, but the roll of bandages and a lotion salve provided did at least ease the worst of his shocking condition that might otherwise have proved fatal. Following this initial period during which a transfer to a dungeon-like room took place, the men were moved on to Bari. The walk to a German HQ for questioning was fraught with danger from an infuriated civilian mob that was barely kept at bay by the Italian guards. After interrogation the airmen were taken to a temporary POW camp. Here, officers and enlisted men were split up, with the latter being taken by train to Sulmona, north of Rome.

The monotonous diet of macaroni and hard tack was rarely relieved by the arrival of Red Cross parcels. During this time the number of Italian guards steadily went down after Italy surrendered, so raising the prospect of a breakout. One day in October, around twenty POWs took the chance (and the risk of being shot) by charging the main gate and dispersing into the countryside. S/Sgt. Hess paired off with Blakeney while S/Sgt. Dones (Eng.) and Farley (TG) did likewise. Over the ensuing four days the two escapees lived on raw potatoes, tomatoes and even figs, a nutritional combination guaranteed to induce – diarrhoea! After one week, desperation drove them to seek food and shelter from a farmer. He took them in, but was later seen to leave and head towards a nearby village; fearful that he was about to betray them to the military, the pair reluctantly left their refuge.

The sun was used as a crude 'compass' for a southerly heading, but recurring hunger as well as exhaustion induced a second approach to a farmer's house, where they received bread and goats milk cheese. Thus replenished they plodded on as far as Campobasso, around sixty miles north of Naples, which was now in Allied hands. They were aware of being near the front lines, doubtless due to hearing the exchanges of artillery fire. On one occasion they were receiving water from a farmhouse when the farmer's wife yelled out "Tedeschi!," having spotted a German patrol; the resultant race across several hundreds of yards of open space to a wood was one neither man would forget, but they got away. Noticing another farmhouse, close by which was a group of soldiers minus their helmets, the airmen got near. When a woman emerged from the property Blakeneny approached and asked her in French what nationality the soldiers were; the answer was Canadians! Blakeney advanced after telling his companion to remain concealed, calling out in French to the men "Je Suis American", and all was over. (Hess's blond looks were the reason why he was told to stay put for fear of being identified and shot at as a German; one of the Canadians later remarked it was as well Hess had taken Blakeney's advice!). Three days later, they were back in American hands, and in the town that their crew had bombed on 16 August when they were shot down – Foggia! Both were back in London by the month-end or early November, where they were decorated by Gen. Eaker and granted a twenty-day leave period.

Lt. Robert C. Peterson navigator and 'Pilot officer Rusty.' 'Rusty' reputedly flew the low-level mission to Ploesti on board 'the Avenger' (41-23788) of the 68th BS.

Chapter Five

Autumn Build Up

The 44th BG's unconditional return to England occurred as the 8th USAAF was in the process of the next stage in its build-up. On 13 September, the 'Wing' title had been superseded by 'Bomb Division' with subsidiary Combat Bombardment Wings contained within each Division. In the case of 2nd Wing, to the 'original' 44th BG and 93rd BG was now added the 389th BG and 392nd BG, with four more Groups due to arrive before the year-end. The 44th BG and 392nd BG linked up under the 14th CBW, but the 93rd BG and 389th BG were assigned to the 2nd CBW and 20th CBW. In time all four CBWs were to build up to their full strength of three Groups but this situation would not occur until 1944. (The third Group to join the 14th CBW in April 1944 was the 492nd BG. Between 11 May and 7 August it lost fifty-six B-24s MIA during just sixty-four missions, and was disbanded; its CBW place was then taken by the 491st BG who moved over from the 95th CBW on 14 August).

Although the main body of the Group had been detached to North Africa, there was still ample opportunity for combat missions to be flown from Shipdham at that time. A sufficient number of replacement crews had been assigned to do so with the available bombers on hand. The bulk of these missions were diversionary in nature with one notable exception on 9 October, and the numbers of crews participating were small. On 26 and 27 September the Group contingent linked up with the 392nd BG; in the case of the former mission just three aircraft were dispatched. By the beginning of October Shipdham's personnal and aircraft reserves were sufficient to send out much larger numbers. The second monthly mission (4th) was the latest 'diversion' run. The intention of the joint-Group force of thirty-six B-24s in flying out towards Wilhelmshaven and Emden was to draw the Luftwaffe away from the B-17s going to Frankfurt. The 'milk-run' nature of the previous three missions was not repeated here, because the tactic worked only too well. Between thirty and fifty fighters rose to intercept the B-24s in the region of Heligoland and pressed their attacks home almost fanatically – probably too fanatically in one instance. A 506th BS crew led by Lt. Johnston were flying in 42-40989 – HOLIDAY MESS. One of the Bf 109s shot through the formation but then collided with this B-24. The shattered remains of both aircraft tumbled down into the North Sea bearing all eleven airmen to their deaths. This was the sole Group loss in aircraft but not in crewmembers. Head-on attacks upon 42-72873 –RAGGEDY ANN (67th BS) sent the bomber into a spin. Lt. Stamos called for a bale out, and sadly for Lts. Must (N) and Campbell (B) they responded, only to float down into the pitiless wastes of the sea. The pilots recovered from the spin through use of the automatic pilot and returned to Shipdham.

Full Stride

The North African contingent were back on site by 5-6 October but the first mission flown after this had occurred involved just eight crews. The 8th USAAF had begun a series of four missions on 8 October that would culminate in the infamous 'Black Thursday' attack upon Schweinfurt and its ball-bearing factory complex six days later. The second mission of 'Black Week' went out on 9 October when targets in Poland and Prussia were singled out. Danzig's shipyards were the Primary for the 2nd BD with similar facilities at Gydnia briefed as the Secondary. Unfortunately, the Lead Bombardier mistook the latter target for the Primary and toggled his load; what then compounded

Back to North Africa: note the newly applied Group markings of a Circle A on the tails. The furthermost aircraft has not yet had the A applied.

the error was the fact that the bombs fell far short of the shipyards.

This mission entailed some ten hours flight time, which was a hard enough physical slog for an experienced crew, never mind a 'rookie' team such as that of Lt. Insley, especially as their B-24 (42-72879/G) was placed in the formation's 'Coffin Corner'. The pilot recalled how the first sight of flak had his feet dancing all over the rudder pedals, while a flak shell bursting on the bomb-run was close enough to be heard. The twin-engine fighters encountered, although regarded as not too aggressive, seemed to turn their main attention on the Low Squadron. No losses were incurred in this fashion but as the formation coursed out over the North Sea Lt. Insley's crew nearly joined the MIA list.

The bomber suddenly yawed as No.4 engine's fuel pressure dropped to zero, so the propeller was 'feathered'. In very short time fuel pressure on all remaining engines was totally gone and the B-24 converted into the next thing to a 'flying brick'. The bale-out bell was rung but the situation was fortunately stabilised by the engineer. Earlier in the mission the engineer had been transferring fuel when the latest bout of fighter attacks had him called back to his top turret. As the fighter attacks finally ceased the radio-operator had been requested to close the transfer pumps behind the bomb bay – instead of which he closed the fuel shut-off valves in the front of the bomb bay! The correct action was now taken and the undoubtedly shaken crew resumed course for Shipdham, from where they later successfully completed their combat tour – of no less than forty-eight missions!

The Danzig mission was destined to be the sole positive one sent out during October. On the 10th nineteen aircraft crossed out to a point in the middle of the North Sea, with the intention of diverting fighters away from the 1st BD and 3rd BD assault on Muenster. The bomb-loads carried were for use against possible enemy convoy movements, but these were all returned to Shipdham. Three more Alerts on the 11th, 12th and 14th ended in 'scrubbings'. This set a pattern for the rest of the month with six more similar failures, although diversionary 'sweeps' on the 18th and 20th were completed. November was to prove to be much more involved in terms of missions.

Over-fed?

The image of the U.S. serviceman in Britain as being 'over-fed' (among others criticisms) was not always thanks to his government's efforts to provide him with a palatable and comprehensive range of food. This included supplies of ice

Pilot Officer 'Rusty' was Lt. Peterson's pet dog and came to England with his master. It is believed he flew on several missions including the Ploesti mission. Here he sits on 500lb. bombs.

cream, a deficiency that was often solved by personal initiative, as the following example demonstrates;

One day a member of the 14th CBW HQ staff, Major Barrett Taylor, stopped by a small tobacco, candy and newspaper shop just off the base. He noticed a Frigidaire emblem mounted on a cabinet that was smothered under piles of newspapers. In response to his query, the owner said that, yes, this was an ice cream manufacturing and storage unit whose motor had long burnt out. The Wartime restrictions on 'luxury' products meant that it now served as a basic storage facility. Therefore, when he was asked if it could be loaned to the 44th BG for the duration of the war, having been repaired and operated in the meantime, he readily agreed.

Sgt. Backman (mess Sgt.) was tasked with arranging for the Base shop to bring the unit back to operational condition. Then came his direct involvement in matters; the desired ice cream mix was arrived at after various experiments using powdered milk, powdered eggs, cocoa, vanilla extract and sugar. And so the 14th CBW Staff was to enjoy this sought-after product until the HQ's transfer to Bury St. Edmunds, whereupon the owner received back his hitherto redundant cabinet!

The Salvation Army tea wagon staff is serving hot tea and coffee to the ground crews. This was a welcome and necessary break for the ground crews working outside in the elements.

Retrenchment

The gradual failure of the 'unescorted bomber' theory, whereby the B-17s and B-24s were expected to gain their targets and return with minimal losses in aircraft and crews, was finally recognised during the 'Black Week' missions of 8-14 October. Although deep-penetration missions were destined to be launched during the winter of 1943-1944, the regularity of such thrusts would not become established until the advent of long-range escort fighters. The arrival of the first P-51 Group was imminent but the 8th USAAF Command could not be sure of the likely benefit this would grant the bombers crews until the fighter's overall performance was put to the test in combat. Attacks were launched along the European coast and into western Germany during the final two months of 1943. In the case of the 44th BG its crews were granted credit for seven missions; on the other hand there were as many occasions when planned missions were 'scrubbed'. The weather in wintertime was even more unpredictable then usual while the ever-shortening hours of daylight applied a further limitation upon the duration of missions.

One target in particular would crop up over November and December. The city of Bremen was a major shipbuilding source and also contained a Junkers production plant among other industrial sites. However, the first mission involved the naval port of Wilhelmshaven. This attack involved the 8th USAAF's first experience with the British radar equipment known as H2S and named H2X by the Americans. This was a plan position indicator that displayed a basic outline of the geographic area over which the bomber was flying on a screen. The Lead B-17s and B-24s could continue to sight their targets even if these were cloud-shrouded. However, the desired 'precision bombing' effect was sacrificed for an 'area' pattern of strikes extending anything up to several miles in diameter. The main benefit accruing from the introduction of H2X was that some form of pressure was from now on heaped upon the Nazi war machine under weather conditions that previously would not have permitted mission completion or even the dispatch of a Strike Force. Twenty-two of the thirty crews taking off went over the target to drop their loads on smoke markers. Only one bomber was damaged when a flak shell took out its oxygen system, forcing Lt. Dick O'Neill to drop down some 10,000ft. and come home alone. A hung-up bomb caused further temporary concern but was later jettisoned by Lt. Carver, an armament officer flying as a 'supernumerary', and a man thought eminently suitable for this task! (The O'Neill crew were to be lost on 11 December in a rather needless and self-imposed manner).

Muenster north of the Ruhr Valley was a key rail junction and was the focus of 8th USAAF attention on the 5th. The possibility of having to use H2X again proved unnecessary since clear weather was encountered in place of the expected cloud cover. However, a strong crosswind made the accurate aiming of incendiaries difficult, although the explosive bombs

Above: Lt. Bickerstaff limped back to England, but would get no further than the North Norfolk coast, before he "bellied" the aircraft in a field at the top of Hungry Hill, Northrepps.

Right: Lt. Bickerstaff, walked out of the hole in the side of the cockpit, but Lt. Jope was pinned by his legs in the nose section. Locals tried for at least two hours to dig him out. Eventually a Coles heavy lift mobile crane arrived from RAF Coltishall and preceeded to raise the aircraft frame enough to effect the Lt.'s release.

did land with reasonable accuracy. Flak was moderate to heavy but failed to bring down any of the twenty-six Group B-24s. However, 42-7535 – PEEP SIGHT (506th BS) – was heavily damaged, but was brought back safely by Lt. Parker.

It was several weeks since death had last claimed a crew along with their bomber, but its malign influence was never far away, and arose again on 13 November. The mission was the first in a string of four runs to Bremen, each of which would cost the Group in terms of crews declared MIA or killed over England. Although the P-47 escorts were unable to take the 'Big Friends' deep into Germany, they could range as far as the north western region of the Third Reich, thanks to the improved quality of drop-tanks now on hand. The bad old days when the 44th BG could barely scrape enough operational aircraft to exceed double figures were totally gone. Today's run saw thirty-three crews going out, although only twenty were on hand over Bremen. The Luftwaffe was present in numbers and handed out punishment. The persistent con-trails thrown back in the frigid atmosphere were skilfully used to close in upon the bombers and simultaneously avoid attention from the P-38s and P-47s.

Lt. Hansen and his 67th BS crew were flying their first combat mission but had been used for crew training ever since their arrival at Shipdham. Their B-24 was 42-7650/ J-Bar, – OLE MISS, which had No.4 engine disabled by rockets discharged from a Me 410. Formation was nevertheless held until the turn for home was being made. It was then that a flak strike totally destroyed No.4 as a power source and crippled No.2. The Dutch coast was by-passed but by then the chances of reaching England were felt to be zero; the grim option of 'ditching' so far from help was an even less inviting prospect, so the pilot turned back for a landing somewhere in the flat Friesian countryside. The fates still appeared to be conspiring against their survival, when just the left main gear descended and worse still then refused to fully retract. Hansen knew that the B-24 was too low for baling out the crew and now took drastic action. He headed for the far bank of a canal, dipped the left wing just before reaching it, and achieved his (risky) intention of tearing off the entire gear structure through impact with the canal bank! He and Lt. Hanson (CP) then succeeded in pulling their charge up sufficiently to complete a crash-landing that inflicted no serious injury upon any of the crew. Personnel from a nearby flak battery soon rounded up the airmen for ultimate delivery to a POW camp.

The good fortune enjoyed by the Hansen crew was in stark contrast to the nine men flying with Lt. Almlie in 42-40973/D BATTLEAXE. The 66th BS bomber and crew were last observed with smoke issuing from an engine as the B-24 was going down under seeming control. The final demise of BATTLEAXE and the ten souls aboard was not witnessed, but there were no survivors to report on what happened. A second 66th BS bomber 42-7647/R – SABRINA flown by Lt. Hart crashed near the Base; S/Sgt. Hurst (LW) and Sgt. Olsen (TG) were killed in the incident, while several others had already suffered combat wounds. In addition, S/Sgt. Procyszyn (Eng.) had baled out over Germany.

One more 66th BS aircraft flown by Lt. Bickerstaff staggered back to a crash-landing inland from the coast and close to Cromer, but the incident left just one crewmember injured. The No.3 engine on 41-29168/F had been disabled during the bomb-run, and fuel was seen to stream off both wings as the turn for home was made. The formation was left and all possible gear jettisoned over the sea. The fuel standpipes finally recorded 'zero' levels as the English coast was approached but the engines still kept going. Lt. Jope (N) had insisted on staying at his post, in the hope of guiding the pilots to an airfield but this proved an unwise action after all power failed just as the coast was crossed. The flaps could not be lowered as the now defunct No.3 engine operated the hydraulic pump; then just before touching down in a field the right wing caught on a tree, causing the bomber to slide sideways, an action that put undue stress on the fuselage, tearing off the nose and the No.4 engine. Lt. Summers (CP) recalled literally stepping out of his side window that had been ripped off by the No.4 engine and directly onto the ground. The crew got out but only when the pilot took a head count was it realised Lt. Jope was not present. He was in fact trapped in the nose section, having failed to get back to the flight deck before the crash-landing occurred. All attempts to free the airman by digging out the soil were foiled by the twisted metal pinning the Lt. in place. It was not until the pilot had gone to summon assistance in the form of a British mobile crane from RAF Coltishall, which hoisted the nose up, that Jope was got safely out. (Local people had dug for at least two hours, and later received commendations for their efforts from HQ, 8th USAAF and the RAF). Lt. Jope had broken both legs, and his obvious discomfort was immediately relieved by a shot of morphine prior to his being removed to hospital. Several other men bore lesser injuries from items tumbling around during the landing.

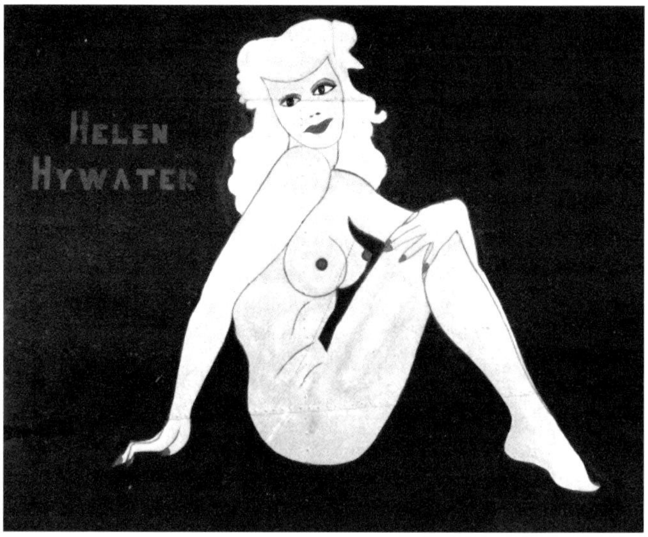

"Helen Hywater", a 68th BS B-24D-15-CF 42-63971/W, was lost on 18 November 1943.

The list of injured crewmembers was completed by the 68th BS. Three gunners on Lt. Anderson's 42-7551/Y were wounded during the height of the fighter attacks. All three refused first aid and defended their heavily damaged B-24 until clear of the coast. The landing at Shipdham was fraught with danger because just one engine was running normally by then while one main gear tire was flat. In spite of these disabilities the pilots brought off a smooth touchdown, but the degree of

The elephant train moves along the perimeter track past the tower towards the west end of the main runway for another mission.The aircraft seen here are mainly B-24H models.

Lt. George Insley's crew.

damage suffered merited the bomber's transfer to 3rd Strategic Air Depot (S.A.D.).

Bad Day over Norway for the 67th BS

The 67th BS had arguably absorbed more than its fair share of losses within the Group ever since arrival in England, and the latest instance in this litany of disaster occurred five days after the Bremen mission, and two days after an 'aborted' run to Oslo. A re-run of the mission sent out on the 16th was made and thirty-four crews were dispatched to attack the airfield at Jkeller near Oslo, Norway. Before it was completed three crews and six B-24s would be struck-off Squadron records. The distance was too far for constant escort cover, so the gunners had to fend for themselves. The Luftwaffe intervened both during the approach run and during the withdrawal phase. The three 67th BS MIA losses occurred after the fighter attacks had long ceased but the English coast was still a distance away.

Lt. Houle's 41-29164/I had suffered severe damage and finally 'ditched' some minutes flying time away from Norfolk. Capt. Butler recalled circling the B-24 after it had broken in two on impact, while his crew threw out several one-man dinghies. No survivors were seen and the pilots reluctantly turned for home after radioing for A.S.R. assistance, and then confirming that their own B-24's fuel situation was critical. All ten airmen were later confirmed lost. Twenty more names were fated to be entered on the Wall of the Missing at Madingley Military Cemetery. Lt. Dobson's crew in 42-7603/L-Bar and Lt. Johnson's team flying in 42-7545/D – TOUCH OF VENUS were the unfortunate crews swallowed up in the dark maw of the North Sea. All three losses were later ascribed to a combination of battle damage along with fuel shortage.

One more crew joined their fellow-airmen under the waves. Capt. Mitchell had diverted into Turkey on 1 August, but his luck now finally ran out. He had been re-assigned from the 67th BS to the 68th BS since Ploesti, but was flying in 41-29139/E from the 67th BS. A second 68th BS crew had much better fortune Capt. Weant's 42-63971/W – HELEN HYWATER was so seriously damaged that her pilots elected

Left: Crew Chief Sgt. Richard William's ground crew is working on 'Flak Alley.' A full engine check usually involved a time-consuming element of their work. Right: Col. Fred Dent and George Rebich: the photo was taken shortly after the nose wheel collapsed. The aircraft concerned is 41-24234/E, 'Mr. 5x5', a D-25-CO of the 66th BS. The incident happened 11 September 1943 and it took thirty-four days to repair the damaged nose area and nose wheel.

to head into nearby neutral Sweden. The airfield at Trollhutten received its latest unscheduled 'arrival' of an Allied aircraft, but the crew's attempts to destroy their crash-landed B-24 proved to be only partially successful. The crew were subsequently repatriated to England. One crewmember on a 68th BS aircraft was killed at his post; S/Sgt. Merrigan (WG) in 41-23788 – AVENGER was hit by a bullet and killed instantly.

Five B-24s from the 44th BG had been lost in action but the sixth was 'written off' in a dramatic way at Shipdham. Lt. Griffith' s 41-29161/H-Bar was another 67th BS bomber that had been shot-up. In spite of this Griffith had circled a 'ditched' B-24 while notifying the air sea rescue service. Then, on entering the airfield circuit and lowering his landing gear he found to his dismay that the right main wheel only partially lowered, and defied all attempts to bring it back into the wing. All the crew, apart from Sgt. Kuban (BT) who was seriously injured and in no condition to jump, made their exit over the airfield. Griffith and Lt. Grono (CP) now attempted the hazardous task of bringing themselves and their wounded gunner down safely. However, instead of belly-landing the B-24 it was brought in for a landing, using the two available wheels. The film recording of the incident shows how the bulky bomber was held level until the last possible moment. Then, the aircraft swung inexorably to the right onto the grass as a ground loop began to develop. Before the ground loop was completed the right wing had ground along the runway surface with sparks flying from the propeller-tips, the left main gear had collapsed, and the aircraft had halted with the nose almost facing back in the direction it had touched down. The Nos.1 and 2 engines were shaken from their mountings but the aircraft was otherwise in one piece. Sgt. Kuban was given medical attention on the spot before removal to hospital. S/Sgt. Forrest Clark broke his ankle on landing at Park Farm. The award of the Silver Star was later made to Lt. Griffith.

The dull overcast conditions prevailing on the 22nd could not dampen the special event that took place in front of the control tower. Brigadier General Leon Johnson had been awarded the Congressional Medal of Honor for his leadership on the Ploesti mission, and today Gen. Devers presented him with the Nation's supreme decoration. The General, ever a man to conduct himself modestly but firmly, later spoke of his reac-

Opposite

Top: The waist gunners inspect the flak damage to B-24H-1-FO 42-7535 'Peep Sight' of the 506th BS. Note the damage next to the waist window, and further damage to the roof of the fuselage. The small window above the "Star and Bar" has been blown out.

Bottom: A wounded gunner is photographed being removed from 42-7535 'Peep Sight.' This aircraft was struck by flak over the target at Muenster.

Left: Nose art on 42-7535: 'Peep Sight' was transferred to 3rd S.A.D for use as a transport after all turrets were removed.

tions to both the award and the mission. On 1 August, when faced with the fact that the assigned target had already been bombed he said; "I personally think that our losses would have been greater if we had not been forced to fly through the fires of the other group's bombing. While we were flying under the cover of the smoke and fire we were comparatively safe from flak. It was after we got clear that the ground fire intensified." As regards his feelings about flying the mission (having been aware of a loss-rate of at least 50% having been regarded as reasonable provided success was achieved!); "I did not ever think about getting back because I just felt that I would. Of course a lot of men had that feeling and it didn't do them any good. I scare as easily as anyone, and I don't know if I'd want to do it again, but it is easier to take fifteen minutes as we did in the target area than hours of fighter opposition. We flew for over fourteen hours, and I had to assure Sgt. Ray (WG) flying his first mission that they weren't all like that!" Finally, he summed up his overall feelings by saying; "I have no exclusive ownership on this medal, but accept it for every man who took part. I didn't do anything that every man behind me didn't do – the higher the rank the easier it is to get a medal."

Two mission 'scrubs' between the 22nd and 25th, included one each to Bremen and Berlin. Over three full months would elapse before the 8th USAAF was to 'Beard the Nazis in their Den' by assaulting their capital, but not so with Bremen. Next day Bremen was again briefed and this time the mission went ahead. A combination of smokescreens and intermittent cloud made photographic confirmation of what was regarded as a good bomb pattern very difficult. While heading in towards the target, the danger of flying close formation was tragically exposed. Lt. Trolese's 41-24234/N – MR. 5x5 probably flew into prop-wash and rose up beneath and to the right of Lt. Cary's 42-7501. The propellers on the latter B-24 instantly acted like giant buzz-saw blades as they bit their way through the tail section of MR. 5x5.The truncated remains of the 66th BS aircraft tumbled away to smash into the ground, leaving nobody alive, even though several parachutes were seen to come out. The other B-24 was also thrown out of control by the impact but the pilots managed to arrest the subsequent spinning action and head back to Shipdham, though not before dropping from 24,000 to 10,000ft. Bombs were salvoed and although flak was encountered at the coast, Lts. Cary and Lee brought their crew safely back over the North Sea.

The 67th BS 'original' B-24D, LEMON DROP, was viewed with mixed feelings by some who flew in her. Her original pattern 'needle blade' pattern propellers and constant-flow oxygen system were two of the primary technical deficiencies regularly commented on by such individuals. She had had her share of incidents but kept coming home, and indeed would outlast many of her contemporary B-24s. Over Bremen her nose frame absorbed the slicing effect of a trailing cable that remained embedded for the duration of the mission. It was believed to have been the support for a bomb dropped by a Luftwaffe fighter; the Germans had already indulged in air-to-air bombing against the USAAF bombers, and this device was a variant in attempting to bring them down in this manner.

Lt. Hansen's 'Ol'e Miss Bad Penny's' is seen in its final resting place at Schoterzijl in the Nettherlands. The aircraft was a B-24H-1-FO, 42-7850 /J.

Sgt. Richard William's (left) crew chief and Pvt. Laurence (Slick) Villermez, pose in front of their Charge "Flak Alley" of the 68th BS.

All crews returned from Bremen but one was reduced to nine living members. The insidious danger of anoxia had struck to claim the life of S/Sgt. Semons, the ROG on Lt. Heskett's 68th BS crew; his oxygen mask had collected enough moisture to cause the bladder to freeze and cut off the oxygen flow. Several personnel had been wounded while the sub-zero temperature had laid others open to frostbite. Lt. O'Neill and his

67th BS crew added a second hair-raising chapter to their combat career during November. Damage to the right main gear on 42-7521/B – POOP DECK PAPPY led to a risky crash-landing at Shipdham that was fortunately successful. The degree of fuselage damage was repairable but the B-24H was later transferred-out to the 392nd BG.

The last day of November was scheduled for a mission to Solingen in the Ruhr. The Group took off and headed out through constant heavy cloud-layers. Failure to link-up with the bomber stream resulted in a turn for home over Holland. (As it so happened Solingen had been spared the attention of the 8th USAAF for a mere twenty-four hours). The weather was no better on 1 December when Solingen was again briefed, but this time around the B-17s and B-24s got through to bomb using H2X to pick out the otherwise obscured target. Both flak and fighter reaction was sluggish and very dispersed, so the absence of one 67th BS crew on return to England was a matter of surprise if not concern. What had actually caused Lt. Taylor's team to land up inside Belgium was seemingly a case of operational 'self-injury'. On the way back Sgt. McCue (RW) overheard a conversation between the pilot and S/Sgt. Wojcik (Eng.) regarding whether or not the necessary switching procedure for the fuel tanks had been completed. A short time later, just as the coastline of Europe was being left behind, Lt. Taylor announced he was turning back and the bale-out order was given as soon as land was again below 42-7544/C-Bar – SEED OF SATAN. All ten airmen exited in good order, of which five ended up in captivity. The other five enjoyed varying degrees of freedom. Lt. Taylor and S/Sgt. Dzwonkowski (BT) both got back to England, while Lts. Akins (CP) and Dolgin (B) along with their ball-turret gunner were able to evade until 25 March 1944 when they were apprehended.

By now the regular supply of B-24H aircraft to the 8th USAAF was supplementing the 44th BG's cadre of B-24Ds. The new Model incorporated defensive improvements among several other refinements. The framed nose structure of the D Model with its flexible guns gave way to a twin-gun power turret in the upper nose. The Emerson Company provided the turret, which was a flat-fronted unit given the designation A-15. The B-24H also featured a ball-turret in place of the B-24D's tunnel-gun. The latter fitting was relatively inflexible and provided greatly inferior vision-scan compared to the new installation. There was a price to be paid particularly by the navigator and bombardier as regards physical comfort. The flexible nature of the nose turret meant that all efforts to prevent slipstream effect from entering the forward fuselage proved to

Lt. Rockford Griffith made a spectacular two wheel landing at Shipdham on returning from the mission to Kjeller, Norway, 18 November 1943. Aircraft 41-29161/H was a B-24 H-1-CF originally serving with the 392nd BG. Bomber was salvaged on 19 November 1943.

be difficult. This compared badly with the B-24D's solid structure up front. Back at the waist gunner positions the exposure to temperatures recorded as low as -50 or -60 degrees was as bad as ever. It would be some months yet before all B-24s would enter service with fixed Plexiglas frames incorporating flexible gun-mounts. On the other hand, the fitting of electrically actuated engine superchargers to the B-24H was a solid advance over the original hydraulic-operated units. The fluid was liable to be adversely affected by the sub-zero temperature and lead to uncertain supercharger performance, compared to the constant power function of the new system.

Solingen was the first of nine completed December missions, more than half of which were completed using H2X. In that time a further seven B-24s would be 'written off' Group records along with the majority of their crews. A further ten days elapsed, during which a mission to Cognac-Chateaubernard airfield (5th) was recalled over France. Emden was attacked on the 11th but heavy smokescreens and an approach made into the sun were the joint reasons for bombing results assessed as 'poor'. Adding to the sense of frustration was the latest aircraft loss that was all the more tragic since it was self-inflicted. Lt. O'Neill had been observed taking evasive action during previous missions while on the bomb-run. This action was fraught with danger as it created the risk of being struck by bombs from higher-flying B-24s. Sure enough, just as 41-23232/M – CALABAN was releasing its load during a swing to one side, its path coincided with bombs that snapped off the right wing outboard of No.4 engine as well as cutting off the tail section. The shattered bomber slumped into a spin and was seen to crash somewhere along the Emden estuary, killing all but one on board after they were probably pinned in place by the centrifugal forces. (This was the same crew that had survived two serious incidents in November, but sadly there was to be no chance of 'third time lucky'). The fortunate exception was S/Sgt. McAdams (Eng.).

Targets in northwest Germany continued to appear on the mission schedule, but on the 13th the announcement that the Group's latest target was Kiel must have brought a reaction of muted apprehension, especially to those still around who had been involved with the expensive May attack to that city. The reality turned out to be an extremely easy-paced experience for the twenty-four crews involved. Flak and fighters were dispersed and few respectively while overall 8th USAAF losses were around 1%, none of which involved the 44th BG.

Bremen, in contrast, was proving a much tougher target with between 6% and 8% 8th USAAF losses occurring on the two November missions. Nor was this grim statistic destined to materially slump during December, especially on the 20th. Before then, the city was selected for assault on the 16th when more than 500 out of the 600 bombers dispatched completed the mission. The 2nd BD was now able to send out up to six Groups, including the 446th BG whose combat debut this was. Only twenty of the twenty-two crews going out landed back at Shipdham. Lt. Insley (66th BS) had diverted into Rackheath in 42-7335/M – THE BANSHEE, this B-24H being one of a number of bombers to be transferred-in from the 392nd BG in early October.

Lt. Jones (68th BS) had also suffered battle damage to his bomber, but the conclusion to the mission for the bulk of his crew flying in 41-23788/D – AVENGER was lethal by comparison to Lt. Insley's team. The B-24 had lost No.4 engine and suffered bomb-bay damage from flak strikes on the way in. Lt. Griffin (CP) recalled how after he and Jones had struggled for some time to hold their bomber aloft the bale-out order was finally given. Griffen was one of just four crewmembers responding to this order, which was just as well for these men,

Left: The twisted and burnt nose section of 'Helen Hywater' after the crew set her on fire at Trollhatten in Sweden on 18 November 1943. Right: The burnt out tail section of 'Helen Hywater' at Trollhatten, Sweden.

Gen. Leon Johnson, receives his nation's supreme award, the Congressional Medal of Honor, for his courage and Leadership on the 1 August 1943 low-level mission to the Ploesti oil refineries. This was the sole ceremony of its kind staged by the USAAF in Norfolk.

since they were to be the only survivors. Lt. Jones stayed at the controls, even though all power on the right was observed by Group witnesses to be gone, and steered his erratic bomber back to the Humber Estuary. A beach area seemed a good place to crash-land, but the choice was a tragic one – it was part of a mine-field, several of whose weapons exploded on contact with the B-24 after it was set down, killing all six airmen.

It was back to Bremen on the 20th when twenty-seven bombers were culled from the 472 bombers granted mission credit. Flak was plentiful and caused substantial damage to eight out of the nineteen B-24s. Fighters were also present and it was from this source that one Group aircraft was lost. The eleventh mission for Lt. Maynor's crew was their last. Fighter gunfire forced 42-7630/Bar-P out of formation before the target but the crew made their bomb-run and were on the way home when again shot-up. By now the aircraft was well down and proving difficult to handle as well as running out of fuel. Naturally, fearful of the survival chances from a 'ditching', the pilots turned back towards the German coast and baled the crew out. Only Sgt. Aho manning the nose turret and S/Sgt. Stoffel (RW) failed to survive, having probably landed in the sea and died of exposure. Two other gunners were very fortunate to be spared this fate since a seaplane reportedly picked them up. (The North Sea was unforgiving at any time, but especially during the winter months).

Gen. Leon Johnson 14th CBW CO and Col. Frederick Dent 44th BG CO hold the 2nd Distinguished Unit Citation ribbon awarded for the Ploesti mission. The first DUC was for the 14 May 1943 mission (Kiel)

Capt. Butler's current 67th BS aircraft was 41-23878/A – MISS EMMY LOU II, named after his daughter, and was a replacement for the original EMMY LOU that was 'written off' in Sicily on 1 October. Battle damage five days before over Bremen had been repaired and the crew were making the required test flight, as well as participating in a formation practice sortie. On board was Lt. Grell (CP) who had just transferred-in from the Anti-Submarine Command.

The flight was proceeding uneventfully until the aircraft were coming back in around 800ft. when disaster struck. An explosion occurred in No.3 engine and this was coupled with total power-loss in the remaining Pratt & Whitneys. There was no option but to attempt a crash-landing at West Bradenham just northwest of the base, Capt. Butler straining on the controls while his co-pilot was vainly attempting to start the engines. The left wing impacted with a tree seconds before the ailing B-24 thumped onto the ground and broke apart; miraculously, all twelve men on board were left alive although some suffered varying degrees of injury.

One so affected was the pilot who discovered when attempting to release his seat harness that his left hand was

B-24D-25-CO, 41-24234 'Mr. 5x5' was a 66th BS. Aircraft was finally lost 26 November 1943 as a result of a mid-air collision with 42-7501.

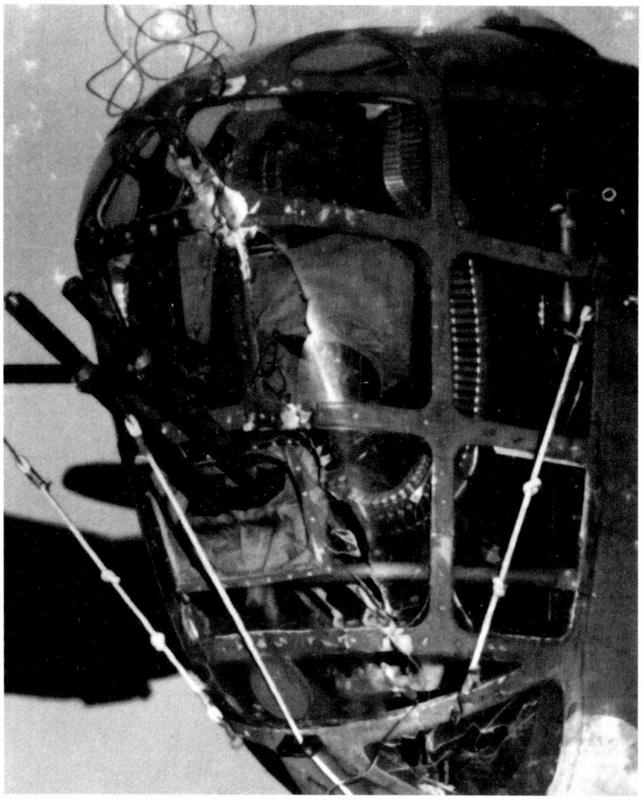

Left: Head-on shot of the damage to 'Lemon Drop' of the 68th BS, caused by a cable bomb drawn along behind a German fighter. Right: The damaged Plexiglas nose can be seen at the top with cable still wrapped round the nose. The incendiary attached to the cable missed the props, but went into the forward bomb bay and thankfully did not ignite. Note the bungee cables fixed to the guns: these were fitted to the aircraft for the Ploesti mission in order to keep the guns at a depressed angle.

now at right angles to the arm! Having completed this action with his right hand he got out through a convenient fracture in the fuselage, but then found that he could not stand due to an injury to his left leg. By now fire was catching hold and ammunition 'cooking off' in the blaze.

The personnel were out and assembled before it was realised Lt. Nicholson (B) was not on hand. In an act of great courage, T/Sgt. Neeper (Eng.) clambered back on board via the top hatch, and then reappeared, dragging the unconscious officer behind him.

The airmen ran or crawled away from the wrecked bomber to be met by a staff car bearing Gen. Johnson who had seen the crash and had raced ahead of the rescue services. A gate was removed from a fence and used as a makeshift litter on which to transport Capt. Butler to an ambulance for later transfer to Wymondham Hospital. (One of the 'walking wounded' was calmly carrying one of his ears that had been sliced off by fragments from the exploding engine; S/Sgt. Mason (ROG) handed the item to the medical staff, one of whose surgeons sewed it back on!).

The incident was to see the end of Capt. Butler's combat career with the 44th BG. Col. Dent (Group CO) wanted to retain his immediate services as 67th BS Operations officer. However, he ultimately acceded to the wishes both of Capt. Allison (Medical Officer) and Major Cameron (67th BS CO), since it was the doctor's opinion that upwards of six months would elapse before the Capt.'s injuries would fully heal.

Gen. Johnson's innate sense of humanity once again surfaced at this time. Capt. Mikoloski was currently on Johnson's staff as Group navigator, having completed his combat tour with the 67th BS in June. The Capt. was a married man with a baby son who suddenly died during the month. The prospect of gaining the necessary emergency transport back to the States was poor, in addition to which the job at hand had to be seen through. However, the General arranged for his key member of staff to act as courier for the delivery of his (Johnson's) Medal of Honor back to his family in America! The question of emergency leave was neatly solved in this manner.

Christmas was looming up but the pitiless demands of combat did not allow for any halt in its conduct. This was total war, and goodwill was to be in short quantity until hostilities

Below: B-24H-1-FO 42-7521B. 'Poop Deck Pappy.' Lt. Richard F. O'Niell brought her in for a crash landing on return from the 26-11-43 mission to Bremen. The aircraft sustained damage to fuselage stations five & six. The aircraft was subsequently repaired and transferred to the 448th BG at Seething.

Right: Ground crews have attached cables to lift the wing of 'Poop Deck Pappy' before lowering the main gear and towing it from the runway. Lt. O'Neill and most of his crew would be KIA a scant sixteen days after this crash landing.

Bottom: Mission return: the ground crews sweat out their charges.

P-38 Lightning coded CG-A of the 38th FS, 55th FG flopped into Shipdham.

were over. So it was that nearly 200 bombers went over Muenster on the 22nd of which just five were MIA. However, nearly half of this figure came from the 44th BG. Weather conditions were particularly unpleasant and featured clouds up to 20,000ft. as well as thunderstorms. Bombing was conducted by PFF method with bomb-loads released through the solid undercast. The flak over Muenster was not heavy but did succeed in bracketing the Group formation, and was probably the prime reason for two B-24s from the 66th BS failing to return.

The B-24H being flown by F/O Miller was 42-7638 that had been under repair at Rackheath since returning off the costly 18 November mission and had only come back onto combat status on 17 December. Now Miller and Lt. Charles Taylor were desperately trying to hold formation. Their efforts gradually tapered off as the ailing bomber slipped ever further behind and below the Group. It was last seen as the German-Dutch border was reached.

The aircraft was still in cloud and faltering along on less than half-power when the bale-out order was given, but this was hastily cancelled when Miller saw water through a gap; his action was not quick enough to stop two crewmembers jumping however. The remaining six took up their positions and the act of 'ditching' was completed in the southern reaches of the Ijisselmeer (now Holland's completely enclosed inland water region). Unfortunately, only three crewmembers at most actually seem to have got out of the largely submerged aircraft, including Lt. Taylor, who recollected seeing two fellow-airmen floating in their "Mae Wests." He managed to get a life raft out of its housing above the wing but the effort required to inflate it exhausted him to the point where he could not even climb inside. Instead, he clung to the side until assistance came his way. The other two airmen were less fortunate and passed away from exposure before they could also be pulled out. (Charles Taylor returned to the scene in the early 1970s to participate in a television programme 'Some of our Airmen are no longer

Crash site of Capt. Richard Butlers 'Miss Emmy Lou II' at Richard's farm, West Bradenham, Norfolk.

Missing'. This primarily dealt with World War II aircraft hitherto declared MIA along with their crews and discovered during land-reclamation operations in the Ijisselmeer. In this way, the MIA tag attached to the unfortunate airmen – a situation generally causing even more anguish to their relatives than knowing they were dead – could be finally removed and their remains granted a Christian burial).

The other MIA bomber had already gone down at this time. Lt. Oakley's 42-7533 had first suffered flak damage and then sustained heavy damage from fighter attacks. Three of the engine superchargers were disabled, making formation holding hard. The bomb-load could not be released, which put extra strain upon the already labouring engines, two of which eventually went 'out'. A few minutes before Lt. Miller was last seen, witnesses saw Oakley's B-24 begin to spiral down. The pilots' efforts to correct this action probably took precedence over thoughts of sounding the bale-out bell, although T/Sgt. Byers (Eng.) and Sgt. Fleischmann (ROG) did jump as the spiral began to tighten. Only Lt. Powers (N) got out alive from the remaining men on board and he had scant seconds to spare between his exit, pulling the ripcord and landing safely. The pilots appear to have pulled the B-24 into a shallow dive just before striking the ground hard, since this was the scene witnessed by a Dutch farmer whose barn was just missed by the plunging aircraft. Then what turned out to be Lt. Powers came running towards him yelling a warning to lie down. Almost at once the bomber disintegrated in a massive explosion that deeply cratered the site, and expunged the lives of any crewmember that might have survived the crash itself. Only Byers managed to evade immediate capture, having been hidden under hay in a barn. His bid for freedom lasted some time, as the local Resistance moved him around, but he was ultimately betrayed to the Germans. (Sgt. Fleischmann had a double stroke of luck this day, because he had originally trained as part of F/O Miller's crew).

A short-range mission to the Pas de Calais on Xmas Eve resulted in the two twelve-plane Flights reporting bombing results as 'poor' and 'excellent' by each sub-formation. The region under attack was to become known as the 'Rocket Gun Coast' by the Americans, but what was being attacked were the 'ski-sites' for the forthcoming V-1 Offensive against southern England. A stand-down was granted just for Christmas Day and many men took the opportunity at attend the airfield chapels, while others visited with the local population.

1/Lt. Arthur Marcoullier brought 'Heaven Can Wait' back to Shipdham with battle damage received over Emden on 11 December 1943. 'Heaven Can Wait' was B-24H-1-FO 42-7507/X of the 68th BS.

"Calaban" was 41-24232/M a B-24D-25-CO of the 67th BS. It was received on 2 March 1943 and lost on 11-12-43 after being struck by bombs released from another aircraft.

Lt. Kent Miller's crew. Lt. Charles Taylor, co-pilot (front row left), was the sole survivor from the crew when they 'ditched' in the Ijisselmeer on 22 December 1943. Lt. Kent Miller the pilot is in the front row and third from the left.

Mission return: a 44th BG ship passes the ground crews near the tower.

B-24H-1-FO 42-7501/P 'Bings Big Box' of the 68th BS, was a former 392nd BG aircraft but had flown no missions with that Group before transfer to the 44th BG. It is seen here after returning from a mission with a propeller blown off. Aircraft would be shot down on the 21 January 1944 mission.

On the 22 December mission, Lt. Heskett (66th BS) had pulled alongside Lt. Oakley to try to determine why his fellow-pilot was not keeping up, but had been waved forward by Oakley. Now eight days later he was to taste the bitter seeds of combat failure, although the ultimate outcome for him was far better than for Lt. Oakley. The mission was to bomb the chemical works of I.G. Farben-Industrie at Ludwigshafen. Fighters struck over northeast France on the way in, and selected 42-7548/T – BULL O' THE WOODS among others. Lt. Heskett was then in the act of moving across to fill a spot vacated by a B-24 that had 'aborted' and was now totally exposed to these attacks. Lt. Billings (CP) and two gunners were killed as the bomber developed a steady turn in a downward direction. The bale-out bell was rung, but as Lt. Rendall (N) moved back to get up onto the flight deck his clothing snagged one snap of the dinghy stowed in the passage that connected the nose with the deck. He hastily disengaged the other snap from the stowage point and then jumped through the nose wheel door. Opening his parachute got rid of the dinghy but also resulted in the loss of his escape kit. This was held in the pocket onto which the first snap had engaged, which had been ripped off by the departure of the dinghy! (In fact Rendall got into Resistance hands but was utilised by his guardians to assist in the movement of fellow-evaders, this service being requested in view of his passable French. The following June he was either caught by, or betrayed to, the Germans). Lt. Heskett not only evaded capture but was back in England within a very short period of time. The other six survivors shared his good fortune, although their pace of movement in the quest to get back into Allied hands did not appear to be as swift.

"Bull of the Woods" 42-7548 a B-24H-1-FO of the 66th BS was formerly a 392nd BG bomber and was lost 30 December 1943.

Chapter Six

Build-up to 'Big Week'

Preparations for the projected invasion of western Europe had included the establishment of a first-class body of senior Allied commanders headed by General Eisenhower. As far as the Air Force was concerned the change of title from 8th USAAF to USSTAF announced on 1 January 1944 also brought changes in command, with Gen. Eaker transferring to the Mediterranean, and Gen. Doolittle taking his place. The basic brief of the RAF and U.S. Strategic Bomber Forces was two-fold. First was the continuation of operations to destroy German industrial potential. Second was the need to neutralise the Luftwaffe to the point of impotence before the Invasion could be regarded as feasible. The latter situation depended as much on shooting its fighters out of the sky as striking at aircraft production and storage capacity; the ever-expanding strength in P-51s along with the P-47 and P-38 groups currently available was expected to handle the aerial aspect of the second brief.

All of this was ahead of the bomber crews at Shipdham and elsewhere in East Anglia as they filled into the briefing-rooms on 4 January for what was the first of the month's missions. Five would be completed but at least nine more would be 'scrubbed' before or after take-off. The Group also sought out targets of opportunity on two further occasions when unable to strike at the Primary or Secondary. Kiel proved to be a positive start to 1944 with a seven-hour run that resulted in an unobserved bomb-drop by nineteen bombers. Although no losses were incurred, several crewmembers fell victim to frostbite. Kiel again felt the weight of the Group's ordnance the very next day when a visual run produced good results. The crew on 42-7476/H 'NICE N' NAUGHTY' (68th BS) had the very good fortune to survive the crash of their bomber during take-off on the 5th when the aircraft's impetus was stopped just short of – the bomb dump!

The first of the 'abortive' missions occurred on the 7th when bad weather intruded so badly upon assembly of the entire Force that a 'recall' was sent out after the bombers had crossed into Europe. The first target of opportunity mission was on the 11th when heading for Brunswick. A recall signal had just been responded to when Capt. Lehnhausen, flying as the 14th CBW lead sighted a factory complex at Meppen close to the Dutch border, and the resultant bomb pattern struck home. On board the Lead bomber was Col. Fred Dent acting as Command Pilot. The Col. was now the latest 44th BG Group commander, having taken over from Col. Posey on 4 December.

Any lingering thoughts that the odds against combat survival were appearing to get better were tossed aside on the 14th. This day the latest run to the 'Rocket Coast' produced a poor set of bombing results even in the face of little flak. The handful of fighters engaging the Group was generally fended off, but at the cost of Lt. Goodwin in 41-23779/G – 4-Q-2. This 'original' B-24D from the 66th BS took a direct strike on No.2 engine, which caught fire. As the bomber went into a glide the pilot called for a bale-out. S/Sgt. Capo (RW) suffered severe facial burns in the process of getting out through the bomb-bay, but was still more fortunate than his fellow-airmen; all but S/Sgt. Monks (who had also baled out) were killed when an explosion ripped the bomber apart, with the wreckage falling near Rouen.

Flying aircraft in World War II was ever a potentially lethal business from the moment of take-off to that of landing, and whether engaged in combat or non-operational flights. Lt. Hovey (68th BS) had recently joined the Group and his crew

Aerial shot of the 'Victory ship' a B-24D-5-CO 41-23813/V and a 68th BS veteran of forty-nine combat missions, one of which was to Ploesti.

were engaging in a practice flight on the 13th. Capt. Kuch (also 68th BS) was flying another B-24 along with Major Jansen on a 'slow-time' test check and was on his final approach, with what was Hovey's aircraft ahead of him. Kuch noted that the No.1 engine propeller was stationery as the bomber began an over-shoot. A strict operational principle was always to bank away from a 'dead' engine or engines; turning into 'dead' engines almost always dragged the aircraft down in that direction. This is what now transpired as Hovey banked left and started an inexorable slide towards the ground. The pilots appeared to have regained temporary control when the B-24 levelled off before it again slumped, striking the left wing against an oak tree before cartwheeling into a spinney and promptly exploding. Capt. Kuch circled the crash-site and directed the emergency vehicles towards the location, albeit with no real chance that the rescuers would find anybody alive. In fact, Lt. Sowers (B) had been thrown clear but his lease on life ran out scant hours later in the Base hospital. (42-7551/Y had borne the name 'The Jinx'. A young local boy Brian Peel working in a nearby field had witnessed the foregoing details of the bomber's demise).

'Milk-run' Myth

An almost daily series of 'scrubbed' missions occurred up to the 21st when the Group again set out for the 'Rocket Coast'. Two sub-formations attacked sites at Escalles-sur-Buchy in the Pas de Calais but paid a very heavy price in completing this short-range mission. Five crews were MIA and a sixth came back to a hard crash-landing in Kent. Four of the MIA losses were borne by the 68th BS with the fifth suffered by the 66th BS. These two Squadrons had made no less than five or six bomb-runs before succeeding in accurately striking their target. All this was done in the face of regular fighter attacks, while the flak gunners had gradually closed their sights upon the circling formation.

During the second target run-up S/Sgt. Mayhew (TG) called in several fighters. His bomber was 42-72813/L – QUEEN MARLENE of the 66th BS, which was thoroughly shot-up during the fighters' pass. Lt. Spelts (P) never completed his call to abandon the aircraft, but Mayhew acted upon it by opening his turret doors, falling backwards and grabbing his chest-pack. He managed to prise open the lower escape hatch and tumbled out – to discover his pack was only hooked up to the harness on one side! Pulling the ripcord did not result in the pack fully opening, so he had to physically pull the parachute out. Fortunately, the air pressure finally acted to deploy the canopy and Mayhew floated down safely; he recalled seeing scattered parts of what was his B-24 cascading down around him. On the ground, he immediately cleared the scene since he had seen German vehicles racing to the nearby crash-site. Coming across a farmer with a log-filled cart, he induced the Frenchman to allow him concealment under the wood. So began

67th BS armament section. Left to right: Kodem, McCreery, Crews and Henry.

B-24H-1-FO 42-7549 K "The Shark" was yet another aircraft transferred from the 392nd BG, which joined the 44th BG prior to 9 October 1943.

"Nice and Naughty" a B-24H-1-FO 42-7476 H of the 67th BS had flown ten missions before being written off after crash landing on the 4 January 1944.

a bid for freedom that ended successfully with his return to England during May.

The third bomb-run attempt was in progress when Lt. Howington's 42-7635/Q – RAM IT – DAM IT! took the brunt of 20mm strikes from a head-on pass that killed or fatally injured all up front in the bomber, as well as firing the nose area. T/Sgt. Barlow (Eng.) suffered shrapnel wounds when his turret plexiglas was shattered. He immediately dropped out of his seat and snapped on his chest-pack, and got out safely along with the other six enlisted men. Sadly, Lt. Howington was one of the fatalities among the eleven airmen on board. (The extra man was Sgt. Reeves; he was a ROG currently flying as a temporary cameraman while in the process of recovering from nose and ear problems caused during his combat tour).

T/Sgt. Barlow was one of the five airmen who became a successful evader, the other two men being captured. Having landed near a village he was quickly hustled into a wood by a Frenchwoman where he met up with S/Sgt. Blakely. The subsequent German search did not uncover the pair of airmen, and later that evening T/Sgt. Rosenblatt (ROG) and Sgt. Klein (LW) linked up, to begin their evasion attempt. Sgt. Reeves got back to England around the same time as Barlow. He had barely escaped detection by the Germans while being moved through Paris by the Resistance, but finally completed his train and bus journey as far as the Pyrenees. He was fortunate to survive the mountain crossing because his guide abandoned him, and he was left to struggle through the snowfields whose frigid temperatures nearly claimed his life.

Lt. Mathisen's crew were on their sixth run according to the MAC Report. This states that at 1526, 42-7514/O was seen to nose up and over with flames issuing from the waist, and fall away to crash at Bruay; only Lts. Cleary (N) and Hoeltke (B) as well as T/Sgt. Allen (Eng.) escaped with their lives. This was an experienced crew with eighteen missions. Lt. Starring's crew was flying their first mission in 41-23813/V – VICTORY SHIP. The contrast between crew and aircraft could hardly be greater because this B-24D was a Group 'original' bomber. The MAC Report put its loss at 1516, which seemed to indicate that this occurred during the early or middle stage of the mission. Fighter gunfire initially knocked out two engines and killed Lt. Rhodes (CP), but Lt. Starring still managed to hold

Col. Frederick Dent Group CO. 4 December 1943 to 29 March 1944.

formation. Then a third engine was disabled and the aircraft slumped earthward. Just half the crew survived after the bomber went into a spin.

Lt. Sobotka's 42-7501/P was shot up by Bf 109s around the same time as Lt. Mathesin, and while in a banking attitude. The Nos.1 and 2 engines were knocked out, whereupon the bomber went over on its back. The pilots managed to bring their charge back upright but could not arrest the flat spin motion, especially with the rudder controls gone. Lt. Rosenblatt (CP) recalled having to hunt for his and Sobotka's chest-packs, before clipping his on and handing over the other pack to his pilot. Six out of the ten-man crew survived; Rosenblatt and Lt. Teitel (B) evaded capture and succeeded in returning to England.

"The Jinx" was transferred from the 392nd BG, before October 7, 1943, and was B-24H-1-FO (42-7551).

The second sub-formation involved the other two Squadrons. The efforts of Lt. Cookus (67th BS) to lead the others on a clear bomb-run were thwarted no less than five times by the solid cloud cover. So it was that Major Anderson (506th BS) flying with Cookus as Command Pilot (and due to complete his 25th. and final mission today) elected to 'abort' the mission. Suddenly, a flak barrage of fierce proportions erupted around the B-24s, which were operating at the much lower altitude of 12,000ft. compared to normal practice. The Lead bomber in particular took a terrible beating from at least six or seven strikes. The No.1 and 2 engines were mangled or

Col. Frederick Dent and his staff, 29 February 1944.

blown off, No.3 engine was set ablaze and the bomb-bay catwalk was ripped apart. The right main gear was also torn off and the hydraulic system went 'out'. Major Anderson was fatally wounded and S/Sgt. Trechel (ROG) was blown out into mid-air but amazingly managed to survive to become a POW. Two further men – Capt. Weiser (Group bombardier) and Lt. Ager (Gunnery officer) – baled out to also end up as POWs.

The natural instinct to switch off the burning engine had to be resisted as long as possible; otherwise the aircraft would never remain in the air. The cockpit began to fill with smoke as the pilots finally stabilised 42-299970/M-Bar – LIBERTY BELLE around 8000ft. England was less than ten minutes flying distance away but 'ditching' was even more out of the question, given the bomber's state and the presence of wounded aboard. In addition the bombs were still in position, but Lt. Cole (B) literally ripped his hands to shreds in his bid to free at least part of the ordnance, before collapsing back on the flight deck. In the rear compartment Sgt. Fong (BT) had miraculously survived the virtual destruction of his turret as well as the blazing hydraulic fluid in that part of the fuselage that sprayed his clothing, and left all three gunners with bad facial burns before running out.

The crippled bomber was just within sight of friendly soil when No.3 engine finally blew up. Lts. Cookus and Holladay now desperately looked for a clear stretch of land on which to settle, but just after switching off the remaining engine they spotted a house directly ahead. A final swing to one side prevented a certain fatal collision, and the flying 'wreck' touched down, tobogganed across the firm surface of a field and ended up with the nose embedded in a ditch.

No.3 engine continued to burn despite operation of the extinguisher equipment and the able crewmembers frantically tore off cowling sections and stuffed soil into the gaps to control the flames. It was all the more urgent to prevent the fire spreading since three men were trapped in the nose section and it was at least three hours before they were extracted. Two were got out alive but Lt. Cole was the tragic exception since he died of suffocation before he could be released. Civilians rushing to the site gave general assistance; they included a car driver who transported Sgts. Fong, Kowalski and Boyd to a local hospital where their burns were attended. (It was suggested that the formation had strayed too close to Calais with its dense flak concentration, so accounting for the punishment handed out. Several other B-24s were heavily damaged, with the hole-count reaching over 300 as regards Lt. Thornton's bomber! Thankfully there were no recorded fatalities or serious wounds among the crews concerned).

'Nice and Naughty' sits on the road at the west end of the main runway after returning from the 4 January 1944 mission to Kiel. She over-ran the end of the runway, crashed through the fence and ended up on the road outside the airfield perimeter, tearing off her undercarriage in the process. The pilot was Lt. Richard E. Harleman.

Nose art of 'Victory Ship', which was lost on 21 January 1944, going down near Auffay in France.

LIBERTY BELLE was one of the first batch of B-24J-55 models to arrive at Shipdham during late 1943. One huge advantage enjoyed by this Consolidated-built model over previous B-24s was the provision of electrically operated engine superchargers. Their hydraulically operated predecessors were liable to suffer malfunction leading to partial or total failure. This potentially disastrous condition was, in turn, due to the flow of fluid being adversely affected by the sub-zero temperature levels encountered at normal combat altitude.

A further week went by in which the Group recovered from this latest blow and which also involved four 'scrubbed'

Above: B-24D-25-CO, 41-24225/T of the 68th BS completed forty-one missions but was lost on its forty-second mission to Gotha, 22 February 1944.

Below: Ground crew from the 68th BS ham it up next to 'Flak Alley.' The art work, which related to the ladies of the night in London and the attendant VD risk, was altered slightly with the addition of knickers.

Right: Another hash mark is being added to 'Flak Alley's' tally.

Left: B-24-J-55-CO 42-99970 'Lib-erty Belle' of the 67th BS. Lt. Cookus brought her back to a heavy crash-landing after the bomber was badly shot up over France on 21 January 1944. Right: A second shot showing the twisted nose section of 'Lib-erty Belle' seen at Brambling Down, Wingham, Kent on 21 January 1944.

missions. Then, the third briefing for Frankfurt in that period proved to be positive on the 29th. Some three hours after take-off the Group was crossing over France when fighters latched onto B-24H/41-29157 and shot out No.4 engine as well as the controls to the tail section. Lt. Maynard (66th BS), after dropping out and being seen to join another Group, elected to head for Switzerland. The MAC Report stating that the bomber was last seen with two parachutes coming out and the bomb-bay on fire was not accurate. All ten airmen were still on board as the bomber flew a descending route to Switzerland. On the approach to the French/Swiss border, and by now down to a mere 1000ft., they were met by gunfire that disabled No.2 engine. The pilots circled back to begin baling out the crew but only three managed to do so before the B-24 crashed.

A second crew was culled from Group ranks just before the I.P. An Fw 190 scored hits on Lt. Pinder's 42-7547/X-Bar – SKY QUEEN, which was also a B-24H (both 67th BS). The pilot was later to recall that this occurred on the third pass, knocking out No.4 engine and firing the wing, as well as severing vital control cables under the flight deck. The various fates suffered by some of this crew were to typify the unpredictable nature of combat flying. Lt. Stubbs (B) was killed in the nose turret. S/Sgt. Green was in shock from serious wounds to both legs; his fellow-gunner S/Sgt. Robinson helped him on with his chest-pack and pulled his rip-cord as he was pushed out, but failed to get out after probably giving up his own pack. T/Sgt. Sofferman (Eng.) managed to evade capture and was at large along with Lt. Pinder until 1 April. Then, both men were intercepted by German police, but not before a gun-battle that left Sofferman dead. Lt. Grono (CP) had earlier partnered Lt. Griffith in the spectacular but successful crash-landing on return from the Kjeller mission of 18 November. Now, he was able to bale out and get down safely before being captured. His prospects of living a full life were to be cruelly cut short however. During the next six months, he developed tuberculosis and was repatriated, only to die from this condition in August. Lt. Boomer (N) and T/Sgt. Hall (ROG) were the remaining survivors from the crew.

Lt. Duffy's 42-7509/Bar-V (506th BS) lost one engine and had his rear turret shattered among other damage to the fuselage and wings. S/Sgt. Chopp (TG) suffered facial injuries that later resulted in one eye being removed, but bravely said nothing about his condition until Duffy landed back at Shipdham. The landing itself was eventful because it was made without brakes, with one flat main gear tire – and with the ball turret in the lowered position!

February 1944

The sustained action that evolved over German soil during the latter part of February was to witness the start of a decisive stage in the daylight bombing Offensive. Up to that point the Luftwaffe had given as good as it had got – sometimes even better – but from then on in its USAAF Fighter Command ad-

'Queen Marlene' a 66th BS B-24D-155-CO 42-72813/L was lost on the 21 January 1944 mission to Escalles in France. The bomber was attacked by Fw 190s and shot down after 'bombs away.'

versary began to inexorably turn the tide of this key air battle in the Allies favour.

However, the B-17 and B-24 crews commenced the month with missions whose targets were spread through western Europe. The Pas de Calais received heavy Group ordnance in the shape of 2000-lb bombs (the largest capable of internal stowage). Bombing was made blind with the use of another British device known as G-H. The fact that the normal rule of not bombing in this manner over occupied Europe was waived depicts how urgently the Allies regarded the need to counter this latest military threat posed by Nazi technology. Icing levels were high and moderate flak was encountered but the Group cleared the target without loss. However, one crew were missing when Shipdham was reached, being that of the 506th BS'es Lt. Bolin flying 41-24282/Bar-V – RUTH-LESS. Not long afterwards came the chilling information that the bomber was laying a crumpled wreck near Eastbourne on the south coast. Bolin had been seeking a landing site in very poor visibility and had flown into a hill. One of the ten airmen did survive for a few hours but expired during the night.

Death or injury was an airman's constant companions when anywhere near a bomber. This grim factor was demonstrated next day, as the bombers were winding up for a mission. Sgt. Hantober (ROG) of the 67th BS leapt out of his aircraft's bomb bay in order to gain order-copies he was missing from an adjacent aircraft. He then impacted with the No.3 propeller and was instantly killed. His immediate replacement T/Sgt. Scott had not been scheduled for the mission. He was hustled out of bed, dressed and was rushed out to the aircraft. He then recalled that the crew were shaken up by the incident, but still took off, albeit nearly thirty minutes behind the other crews who were now airborne. Lt. Thom's crew were on their first mission and keen to participate. However, the Group was never sighted before the 'recall' signal was issued. The mission cancellation made Sgt. Hantober's death appear all the more needless.

Tours airfield in central France was visited on the 5th when the virtual absence of flak was made up for by the hostile attentions of the Luftwaffe. The enemy fighters damaged one B-24 (67th BS) out of the fifteen-strong Group formation, whose pilots diverted into an airfield in Kent with two wounded crewmembers. This crew was much more fortunate than one of the 68th BS contingent flown by Lt. Bohnisch. His bomber was 42-100181/Z – STAR VALLEY, which reportedly lost part of one wing and went into a spin, killing all but S/Sgt. Klein (RW).

The first of four short-range missions to the Pas de Calais was made on the 8th. The 66th BS had one crew divert into

'The Shark' flying over Wayland, near Attleborough, Norfolk.

The veteran B-24-D 'Lemon Drop' taxies out for another mission. She would eventually become the Group 'Judas Goat' after being stripped of all armament and painted in Yellow and Black stripes.

Manston with sufficient damage to retain the B-24 there until 13 March, with all four engines being changed. (This was 41-29208/D – SHOO SHOO BABY).

Gotha was briefed on the 9th, but was then 'scrubbed' shortly after take-off. Sgt. D.V. Chase's (67th BS) comment on this issue was very pertinent; "For every mission flown there was, or seemed to be, a mission 'scrubbed' or cancelled for reasons ranging from icing, dense and very high cloud-layers or hurricane winds aloft, to a planning change at Bomber Command. Naturally a 'scrub' or early call-back did not count towards an airman's mission tally – but it did raise his anxiety level!"

A succession of daily runs to the 'Rocket Coast' was made between the 11th and 13th. On the latter occasion the ground and Intelligence staff had just three hours spanning the time from the Group receiving the Field Order to take-off. It was to the full credit of all ground-support personnel that every operationally fit B-24 was fully loaded and ready to roll. PFF bombing was made on all but the 13th. Also, two separate targets were bombed on the 13th. One fatal casualty was recorded on the 11th when flak struck to take the life of S/Sgt. Myers flying in a 68th BS bomber. However, all aircraft returned from the trio of missions, although 42-7535/U – PEEP SIGHT (506th BS) landed at Hawkinge in Kent without proper control over the brakes and flaps, having been well shot-up. According to Lt. Golubock (CP), an RAF amphibian – probably a Walrus of the air sea rescue squadron based there – was about to take off as the bomber approached at high speed, but the pilot became aware of the situation in time to taxi out of the way! After touching down the pilots locked the brakes and the B-24 finally slid to a halt in a revetment. Three men were wounded, but the third, Sgt. John (RW) had expired from his injury, one of his legs having been blown off. The scale of damage was sufficient to merit the aircraft's transfer to 3rd SAD where she was used as a transport following removal of the turrets.

The winter weather was continuing to play havoc with 8th USAAF operations, as the 44th BG crews found out to their frustration, when three 'scrubs' occurred over the ensuing six days. So, on the morning of the 20th, and with the overall weather pattern no more than indifferent, personnel attending the briefing for an aircraft factory at Halberstadt could have been excused for anticipating yet another cancellation. This eventuality did not occur, leaving thirty-seven aircraft to head out over the North Sea. 'Big Week' was on!

'Big Week'

The USSTAF planners had set their bomber crews the primary duty of disrupting the Nazi aeroplane and aero-engine industry through a continuous series of attacks upon major sources of production. The weathermen had predicted a high-pressure system likely to track across Europe from the northwest for upwards of a week. Operation ARGUMENT, which was forever after better known under its colloquial title of 'Big Week', was accordingly laid on and initiated on the 20th. Over the next six days the heavy Groups based both in England and Italy would record more than 3000 individual bomber sorties. (The estimated loss-factor for the first day alone was some 200, in view of the Luftwaffe's still-potent presence and the location of the targets within central Germany. This forecast was thankfully well out of line with the true overall figure for the whole period of 137 B-17s and B-24s).

Bombing was due to be conducted by PFF in view of the projected cloud cover over the target but this specialist equipment malfunctioned. Fortunately two visual targets of opportunity then presented themselves in Oschersleben and Helmstedt; the former location contained a major Fw 190 production factory. Both targets were struck with fair result from 13,000ft. at the cost of two crews. All ten men on Lt. Decker's 42-64166/A – BIG FAT BUTTERFLY were lost on the way back, having fallen out of formation and into another Group. The 506th BS crew were joined on the MIA list by Lt. Rawson and his 506th BS team flying in a 68th BS bomber 42-100373/Y and on their first mission. A series of passes by one specific fighter was reported as the target area had been cleared. One engine was damaged, and left insufficient power for the bomber to climb to the briefed return altitude of 18,000ft. Fire in the tail section partially destroyed Sgt. Wapensky's (TG) chute-pack and he was injured by gunfire. His search for a spare pack proved fruitless, and a last desperate bid to assist him out and down was made by Lt. Lewis (CP); Wapensky held onto his back as both jumped out but the opening force created by Lewis'es parachute inevitably shook the hapless gunner off and he fell to his death. Lt. Rawson was fortunate that his co-pilot noticed the release mechanism of his flak suit had jammed; Lewis tore the equipment off before retrieving the pilot's chute-pack and passing it over. Three gunners had been wounded or killed by the fighter's fire, and exactly half the crew ultimately survived baling out. Lt. Johnston (N) was one of the all-too-many airmen who were killed when their parachute failed to open. Two crews had gone down in action but the Group suffered three aircraft losses. The third occurred near Ipswich as 42-100285/J of the 66th BS was right down on the deck. All power was suddenly lost and the crew were very fortunate to escape death after the B-24J struck a copse of trees and crashed in a field.

The physical and psychological energy of the crews were due to be tested to the full over the next five days, when all but one would involve missions similar in duration to the 20th. The second 'Big Week' sortie for the Group was to Handorf airfield close to Brunswick. In fact thirty-five of the thirty-seven dispatched aircraft laid their ordnance upon a target of opportunity, which was another airfield at Diepholz. Enemy opposition proved to be much less of a problem than the fierce cold; there was still a shortage in stocks of electric flying-suits,

"The Impatient Virgin" a B-24H-5-CF 41-29231 over-flies Shipdham airfield. Her structure clearly shows the wear and tear of combat.

Nose art for the 'Impatient Virgin' a B-24H model 41-29231 of the 67th BS.

and the personnel not so kitted out were even more prone to frostbite.

Next day the first of what would be two briefings for Gotha during 'Big Week' was laid on. Assembly proved difficult in the face of poor weather conditions but after completion the bombers crossed out over the North Sea and Holland. Then, a 'recall' signal was sent just as the Luftwaffe was beginning to intervene in numbers close to the Dutch/German border. Lt. Mercer (67th BS) was an Element Leader up to the stage where the Group passed through a solid cloudbank but this was no longer the case upon emerging on the other side, both of his wingmen having gone. The B-24D of Lt. Evans (42-72865/F-

B-24H 42-7551/Y "The Jinx" lived up to her name when she clipped a oak tree and cart- wheeled into a spinney at Letton Hall, Cranworth, Norfolk two miles short of the runway on 13 January 1944. Lt. Hovey and his crew was a replacement crew with no combat time and who were completing a training flight when Fate took a hand and claimed them. Lt. Sowers was thrown clear but would lose his fight for life early the next day.

Bar – F FOR FREDDIE) was a definite victim of the fighters, with nine crewmembers finally forced to vacate their doomed aircraft near Wesel. Lt. Flaugh (B) was the sole fatality and his body was never found, so his name is inscribed upon the Wall of the Missing at Margraten Military Cemetery. The third mission for Lt. Fish and crew in 42-100402/M-Bar was to prove fatal for all ten men, but the circumstances of their loss was never established. The likelihood was that their B-24 had got as far as the North Sea before crashing or being 'ditched', and so their names joined that of Lt. Flaugh on the Wall of the Missing.

A twenty-four hour respite from combat was granted on the 23rd but this was only due to the planned mission to Stuttgart being 'scrubbed' before the aircraft had taken off. No such cancellation occurred early next morning when Gotha was again marked up on the Briefing Room map, with the Group slated to fly as the 14th CBW Lead. Consistent fighter attacks came in along the approach route to the Gotharwaggonfabrik aircraft production plant. The complex was thoroughly plastered by the bombs of the 14th CBW as well as other Wings of the 2nd BD; in the case of the 44th BG its contribution was in the form of 52 x 100-lb incendiary loads.

During the bomb-run 41-29148/B was struck by flak. Nos.1 and 2 engines were knocked out, and the bombs could not be released even by manual means. The inevitable then happened as the straggling bomber came under heavy fighter assault. Lt. Etheridge (P) took what evasive action was possible; in so doing part of the bomb-load broke free. With power reduced by

This was the scene of total destruction on top of Butts Brow, Willingden, Sussex on the afternoon of 2 February 1944. Lt. Bolins and crew in B-24D 'Ruth-Less.' had bombed the V-1 sites at Watten in France, but lost their lives in the crash. A memorial to the crew now sits on the top of the ridge where the bomber crashed that fateful afternoon.

half, it was equally inevitable that altitude was being rapidly lost. Part of the right stabiliser was shot off and when it finally became clear that the aircraft was not going to get over a line of hills looming up the pilot ordered a bale-out; only Lt. Buechsenstein (N) did not survive, but the reason for his death remained unclear. (After the war, a female eyewitness of the incident claimed that she had seen an injured American airman with one arm and one leg almost severed; this man died shortly afterwards, and may well have been the unlucky navigator). S/Sgt. Hawkins (BT) was captured by armed *Hitlerjugend*, one of who hit the airman's face with his rifle butt, an act that dislodged most of his teeth.

B-24J-100-CO, 42-100402/M of the 67th BS. This bomber was fated to be MIA on the 22 February 1944 mission to Gotha in Germany. None of Lt. George E. Fish's crew would survive their aircraft 's loss.

Left: On 9 February 1944, luck for Lt. Winchester's crew ran out when their aircraft failed to lift off and crashed at the end of the runway. The Chemical Company is removing the bombs from the aircraft. It would prove to be a long day for these personnel since the mission was recalled. Right: 'Hells Kitten', 41-29236 of the 66th BS crashed on takeoff on the morning of 9 February 1944. Lt. Winchester's crew was on board.

The propeller wash thrown back by each bomber added to the difficulty of holding formation should any aircraft veer enough to fly through this turbulent air flow. Lt. Bell (68th BS) flying in the veteran 41-24225/T – FLAK ALLEY was thrown out of formation when his B-24 was caught in this manner as the turn for home was being made. The fighters promptly pounced upon the straggler and dispatched the bomber on what was her 42nd and final mission. Six airmen in all did not survive. Lt. King (CP) had been wounded by a 20mm shell and although landing safely, expired a few minutes later. S/Sgt. Milillo (ROG) was reportedly killed when his parachute did not open, while S/Sgt. Sullivan (LW) and Sgt. Haynes (RW) died of their wounds soon after landing. Sgts. Hammontree (BT) and Gleason (TG) also died, but whether they were trapped when the B-24 exploded or not was never confirmed. Lt. Schroeder (N) was so badly wounded that he was repatriated in September.

'Big Week' drew to a close next day when the 2nd BD's specific target was Fuerth. The 44th BG was in the Division Lead slot, and Lt. Saylor flew with Col. Hodge as the Com-

Crew chief and flight engineer check out the nose wheel on "Sack Artist" a J-65-CO 42-100073 H of the 67th BS. This aircraft had a short combat career of seventy-two days and twelve combat missions with different crews.

Above: Lt. Keith Cookus and crew pose beside the wreck of 'The Impatient Virgin' shortly after Lt. Cookus had brought the battle damaged aircraft in for a wheels-up landing. He made the landing with one engine "feathered" and one not producing full power. Right: B-24H-5-CF, 41-29231 lies broken and beyond repair at Lympne airfield in Kent. Lt. Cookus brought 'The Impatient Virgin' back with battle damage from the 25 February 1944 mission to Furth in Germany, but the bomber broke its back during the resulting crash landing.

mand Pilot at the head of thirty-three Group bombers. Fighter opposition was not met but flak harried the force from the I.P. to the target. The clear conditions allowed for a good concentration of bombs but no Shipdham aircraft was lost during the actual mission. However, fuel shortage caused several crews to divert from Shipdham. One B-24 (41-29231/J – IMPATIENT VIRGIN) was crash-landed at Lymnpe in Kent after all but the pilots had been ordered to jump. The bomber was so badly damaged that it was declared 'Category E'.

Just as with the hoped-for dislocation of Nazi industry by the destruction of its ball-bearing factories did not basically happen, so a roughly similar situation was now to exist as regards the enemy's aero-industry resources. True, very heavy damage was visited upon many of the production factories and storage depots. However, the limited calibre of USAAF explosive ordnance was generally deemed not to have destroyed the solid structures of much of the plant machinery. In addition the Germans swiftly dispersed their aviation resources in the wake of 'Big Week', and actual fighter production increased in the following months.

If this proved disappointing in immediate terms, then the events of March-April 1944 in particular were to swing this specific issue back in the Allies favour. This would be due to the depredations wrought among the ranks of the Luftwaffe fighter pilot strength by the 8th Fighter Command's P-47s and P-51s. No amount of increased production could balance out the loss of experienced pilots suffered by the Luftwaffe from early 1944 onwards. This human haemorrhage was one that would never be staunched in the future – the GAF would, in effect, literally bleed to death!

To the undoubtedly exhausted bomber crews at Shipdham the lack of completed missions for the remainder of February probably came as more of a relief than the usual frustration-feeling at not getting on with their mandatory twenty-five mission 'tour'. As it so happened their energies would be again fully tested over an even longer period in March as the daylight Offensive reached and sustained a decisive peak of activity.

Chapter Seven

'Big B'

For a number of months the thoughts of the 8th USAAF combat fliers had been much taken up with the prospect of striking at the Nazi capital city Berlin, or as it was colloquially known, 'Big B'. The city was a key industrial center and was worthy of full-scale assault on this basis alone. In addition, the American authorities reasoning was that the Luftwaffe would certainly be drawn into full-scale defence of the city. It was hoped that, in this way, the 8th. Fighter Command would then be able to inflict insupportable losses upon the German fighter pilots by drawing them into the Battle for supremacy of the skies over Berlin and by extension over central Europe. Once the back of the *Jadgwaffe* had been broken the 'Big Friends' could go about their business in an even more effective manner.

The bomber crews were under no illusion as to the hard task facing them before this ideal situation had been attained. However, the month of March opened with a mission to Frankfurt (2nd) that produced mixed bombing results for the attackers. Marshalling-yards appeared to be the primary target, but wholesale PFF failures meant that only a proportion of the 375 crews did strike this target-category, among which were ten from the 44th BG. Fierce headwinds on the return leg caused much concern over dwindling fuel reserves. Lt. Rose did in fact lose power on all four engines but this was due to a problem with the fuel-transfer system. None of the crew was injured and the B-24 was later brought back to combat status.

Next morning the reaction when the briefing officer stepped up to the Target Map, removed the cover, and said; "Gentlemen, your target for today is Berlin" was surely greeted with a mix of profanity, cheers and reflective silence. The specific target listed at Shipdham was located in Oranienburg. However, the entire mission proved to be fruitless thanks to the bad weather conditions, and a 'recall' signal was finally issued with bombs jettisoned in the North Sea. This action very nearly resulted in one 68th BS aircraft loss, that being flown by Lt. Townsend. His altimeter was frozen up and his estimated height upon jettisoning was far lower than was safe; the bomb-blast from the exploding ordnance severely damaged the underside of his B-24.

Twenty-four hours later, the same target was briefed, but once again the weather intervened. This time the Group did not even get off the ground thanks to the combined effect of snow and ice. In fact just a handful of bombers did get through to 'Big B' from the formations getting into the air, and this was only after ignoring the general 'recall' signal that had again been issued.

Bordeaux was located in southwest France and entailed lengthy hours of flying. The primary target for the 2nd BD, the sole participating Division, was Bordeaux/Merignac and two other airfield. None of these were in fact bombed, and the 44th BG for example dropped on similar type alternatives at Cognac and Bergerac. No crews were lost, but the aircraft bearing Col. Dent as Command pilot swerved off the runway and crabbed along on its side before coming to a fortunately intact halt.

It was a case of 'third time lucky' for the 8th USAAF's prospect of striking full-scale at Berlin as over 700 B-17s and B-24s lifted off into the dawn light to course out eastward over the North Sea. Industrial plants at Genshagen were the Primary with Tempelhof airfield the Secondary. The Luftwaffe duly responded in full and its pilots along with the formidable flak batteries downed sixty-nine bombers, none of which were from the 44th BG. However, the cost to the *Jadgwaffe* was even more severe. The Group's primary target was over-flown twice in vain attempts to bomb visually, after which Col. Culbertson turned the Group towards Berlin in hopes of a visual sighting. A suitable industrial and rail complex came into sight, but seconds away from bomb-release he yelled for the bomb-run to be abandoned as Tempelhof became visible. The Norden bombsight system could not be reversed and so the bombs went down on their target of opportunity.

There was a period of twenty-four hours respite from combat on the 7th after a mission to Lippstadt was 'scrubbed'. During the day a practice formation was flown by several crews, among who was Lt. Folsom (66th BS) in 42-7582 – ICE COLD KATY, along with a reduced crew of five and S/Sgt. Barber, a crew chief. As the formation was approaching the airfield from the west eyewitnesses sighted a P-47 coming in from above and ahead. The sun was by quite low on the horizon and may have been a contributory factor in what now transpired. The bulky fighter swept in among the bombers to impact with ICE COLD KATY and rip off the entire right wing, before disintegrating. The few seconds that the B-24 remained level before spinning down and crashing just off the northwest edge of Shipdham gave little or no scope for any of the crew to escape. Nor did Lt. Schreiber the P-47 pilot from the 65th FW HQ Flight fare any better, since his truncated remains were located several hours later.

Col. Frederick Dent 44th BG CO (left) talks with Gen. Leon Johnson the 14th CBW Commander on the balcony of the control tower.

Berlin beckoned for the second time on the 8th and the Group, with Col. Dent in overall charge of the 14th CBW, dumped its ordnance on the key ball-bearings factory at Erkner. Flak was as fierce as ever, but the enemy fighters were kept at bay by the escorts. Otherwise, the 8 1/2 hour mission was noted more for its physical stress than for hostile interference with

'The Shark' sits on the hardstand in the 67th BS area: she was formerly with the 392nd BG but had flown no missions with that Group prior to her transfer.

On 2 March 1944, Lt. Rose managed to put B-24J-85-CO, 42-100295/V of the 68th BS, down at Thorpe Abbotts airfield on four 'dead' engines. This total power failure was traced to the fuel transfer system.

crews or aircraft. What was significant about the day's mission was its number – 100. This milestone had taken fully sixteen months to achieve, as the 8th USAAF had survived its initial spell of failures and delays to be built up to its current level of operational strength and efficiency.

There was no respite for the Nazi capital on the 9th as a rather lesser Force of just over 520 bombers coursed selected industrial targets, that were cloud-covered and as a result were mainly bombed by PFF method. For the third successive mission no aircraft were yielded up to the enemy defences but one airman did pay a heavy price. This was Lt. Jewell (66th BS) who was flying 42-99980/D – E.Z.DUZIT. Just as the bombs were released a shell burst upon the aircraft's nose, wrecking the nose wheel, knocking out the forward oxygen system and the radio system, and disabling No.3 engine that contained the hydraulic pump. A shell fragment struck the pilot's left leg to leave the limb hanging by a shred. Seeing this, and Lt. Jewell's attempt to cut the remnants free caused his co-pilot to vomit and pass out. He was helped to recover, which was just as well, since the onus on making a safe landing was now his alone. This was his first mission, so his pilot had to explain how the landing should be made, while maintaining current control via the autopilot. In the event the landing at Shipdham was pulled off almost perfectly by the novice co-pilot. Two parachutes were attached to, and then deployed from, the waist windows to act as substitute brakes due to the normal system being inoperable. The B-24's skidding nose-down landing was recorded for posterity by a Movietone cameraman and Jewell was transported to hospital. (The following February, and fitted with an artificial leg, he was restored to flying status!).

For almost a week the Group was virtually non-operational thanks to 'scrubbed' missions or not being called upon. The single mission flown in that time (12th) involved only the 14th CBW and was a short hop to the 'Rocket Coast' when bombing was conducted through overcast by PFF method. This was a departure from the requirement to only bomb visual targets in

On 5 March 1944 Lt. Duffy of the 506th BS was flying B-24D-15-CF, 42-63965, with Col. Dent as his co-pilot. The aircraft could not gain enough lift and crashed at the far end of the field.

The burning wreckage of Lt. Glen Folsom's B-24 lies scattered over the airfield, after a mid-air collision with a P-47 from the 65th FW HQ Flight. Incident occurred on 7 March 1944.

The tail section of F/O Charles H. Schreiber's P-47 lays in a twisted pile on the west end of the airfield at Shipdam. The major part of the fighter's wreckage was located just off the airfield.

Nazi-Occupied countries, but indicated the serious nature of the enemy scientists' suspected threat to deploy un-manned weaponry. The Group was short one aircraft on return but its crew at least were safe. Not so the B-24H (42-7507/X – HEAVEN CAN WAIT) of the 68th BS. It was crash-landed near Friston, Sussex by Lt. Bowman, when it was consumed by fire. A number of other crews were forced by bad weather over Norfolk to divert into other airfields on the south coast.

The brief departure from longer-duration missions ended on the 15th when air-industry targets at Brunswick were attacked through almost solid cloud. Flying with the 66th BS was Lt. Talbott in 42-52332/K – MY ASS'AM DRAGON. On the way over problems with the superchargers were only partially solved by manipulating the supercharger and throttle controls, and formation position was finally lost on the way back. Fw 190s approached from behind and below, to catch the lagging bomber with its ball turret out of action. Fuel leaked into the bomb-bay and the hydraulic pump was out of action due to the No.3 engine being struck. Sgt. Gasser (LW) was struck by some of the gunfire that riddled his side of the fuselage but he was saved from serious injury by his flak-vest. The fire in the bomb-bay grew in intensity as altitude was lost and the crewmembers finally began to jump out. However, Lts. Goldman (N) and Moriarty (B) were still on board when the pilot went to bale out, only to be knocked unconscious when the aircraft went out of control and the nose wheel snapped down. Somehow, Lt. Talbott was thrown clear and regained enough consciousness – or his chest-pack was activated through ripping or some other form of contact – to come to on the ground near Nieuw Leusen, Holland. He released his harness and was just starting to walk when a Dutchman approached him; this was the first of three individuals whose advice over the next few hours culminated with the pilot being concealed in a house. It was the start of months of evasion before Allied troops liberated the region. All but the navigator and bombardier baled out safely with T/Sgt. Swick (ROG) also becoming an evader.

The loss of MY ASS'AM DRAGON was the start of a bad run of losses with nine more B-24s lost over the ensuing three days. Frederichshafen was way down by the Swiss border and the distance flown was normally a guarantee of strong fighter resistance. Surprisingly, this did not materialise on the 16th while what flak was available had its effect weakened by the dropping of 'Chaff' aluminum strips that disrupted the gun-laying radar. No aircraft were downed but 42-7549/K-Bar – SHARK FACE was tailing the formation, having lost one engine before the target and then experiencing difficulties with a second. Lts. Scarborough (P) and Bean (CP) kept on course for England and finally made an approach to Woodchurch, Kent. Sgt. Landells (BT) noted that the functioning engines suddenly stopped, after which he found himself staring vertically down out of the waist window when the left wing dropped. He was then thrown bodily forward when the bomber struck the ground and disintegrated into sections. Apart from Landells, only the two waist gunners and tail gunner survived the crash, and Sgt. Stickel (waist gunner) died some weeks later.

Nose art shot of 'E Z Duzit' a B-24J-55-CO, 42-99980/H of the 66th BS aircraft.

Frederichshafen was scheduled two days later, and this time around its defences took more than a full measure of the 44th BG by culling eight bombers from out of the formation. An Fw 190 components factory was attacked and well smothered in bombs, but all four squadrons were to mourn the loss of crews. The 66th BS was least affected in that just the single B-24 was MIA; this was 42-7618/C in the hands of Lt. Telford, whose crew were due to rotate home after today's mission. Shortly after bombing flak ruptured fuel cells in the left wing, after which oil pressure on Nos.1 and 2 engines was lost. T/Sgt. Culler had transferred fuel over to the right wing, but recalled that on return to the flight deck he saw a posse of Swiss Bf 109s surrounding the bomber! The American 'guest' aircraft was duly escorted to a landing at Dubendorf. The fact of internment, however pleasant and free of risk, played upon Culler's mind to the extent that he resolved to escape. His first bid ended near the Swiss/Italian border, after which he and his fellow crewmember (S/Sgt. Melson) were sent to a regular prison camp. Here, they were visited by the American Military Attaché who informed them that they were now common prisoners, and whose release would not be guaranteed even at the war's conclusion! This spurred on the duo to subsequently repeat their bid, which was successful

A single loss was also experienced by the 67th BS, when flak crippled 42-100073/H-Bar – SACK ARTISTS in the course

Major Hodges talks with Gen. Johnson the 14th CBW Commander after the second Berlin mission. Major Cuthbertson, who led the 44th on the first Berlin mission, stands directly behind Hodges.

Lt. Kenneth G. Jewell, 66th BS pilot of 'E Z Duzit' being carried away from the aircraft. Jewell had been hit by flak over Berlin on the 9 March 1944 mission. The flak burst nearly tore his leg off at the knee.

Below: Dramatic shot shows Lt. Harold L. Koontz (co-pilot) landing 42-99980/H back at Shipdham off the 9 March 1944 Berlin mission, after his pilot Lt. Jewell had been very badly injured by flak. This was Koontz's first combat mission.

of the Group's second run into the target. The right wing was forced upwards at a dangerously sharp angle by a strike and two engines were set on fire. This critical situation left the pilots with little alternative but to bale out immediately or head for neutral territory right across the Bodensee (Lake Constance) and do so there. This latter option was taken up and all twelve airmen (including Capt. Cardenas acting as Command pilot) got out and down intact.

Two B-24s were crossed off 68th BS records. The first was 42-109800/T which followed Lt. Telford's example and was landed at Dubendorf by Lt. Dyer. His squadron companion in ill luck was Lt. Nichols. His aircraft was 42-100112/Q that had developed engine problems on the way over. Flak took out a second engine on the individual bomb-run made by the pilots before attempting to get back into formation. Nichols got over Switzerland and baled his crew out. Then he started to follow them, only to consider the possibility of landing what was a much-lightened aircraft; just as he was about to resume his seat the No.2 propeller came unstuck and crashed through the fuselage into his seat! That act made his mind up, and he baled out in double-quick time. The entire crew survived to be interned.

It was the 506th BS who suffered the most both in terms of aircraft and personnel losses. Two crews got through to Switzerland. Lt. Irwin's entire crew were interned and his bombardier Lt. Libell recalled that the reason for a second bomb-run was due to a single straggling B-17 cutting across the 44th BG's course and forcing its eighteen crews to go round again on the lead aircraft's order. The second run was made at the same height and airspeed. Two engines were disabled while fuel streamed from a hole between Nos.3 and 4 engines, but miraculously only caught fire at a point level with the tail! Switzerland remained the sole viable option and so Dubendorf received yet another Group B-24 this day in the shape of 41-29431/Q-Bar.

The second interned crew was headed by Lt. Lucas flying 42-100400/Bar-Y – SHOO SHOO BABY. No details other than that the bomber was last seen under control and heading over Lake Constance, after which it became the last of the Group's interned aircraft to land at Dubendorf this day.

The remaining pair of 506th BS crews did not enjoy similar good fortune, nor did all individual members even survive. The

Above right: 'Heaven Can Wait' a B-24H-1-FO, 42-7507/X of the 68th BS. Bomber was received from the 392nd BG prior to 18 October 1943. Right: 'Heaven Can Wait' burns itself out on the runway at Friston, Sussex. Lt. Bowman and crew were uninjured. Below: This is all that remains of 'Heaven Can Wait' after the fire had finally burnt itself out. Below right: Nose-on shot of 42-7507: note the 'feathered' propeller on the No.3 engine.

worse afflicted team in this respect was that of Lt. Frank flying in 42-52305/P – I'LL BE BACK. The No.4 engine was set ablaze during the second bomb-run and Lt. Donnelly (N) last saw the pilot hunched over his controls, with fuel spewing out into the bomb-bay and the right wing on fire. (The MACR states that the bomber was struck, after which it slid down and to the right. Two parachutes emerged and then the left wing tore off and the aircraft exploded.). Donnelly was the sole surviving officer, along with three enlisted personnel. The fourth crew fared somewhat better after their B-24 (41-29172/T) suffered ruptured fuel tanks. Despite the proximity of Switzerland Lt. Houghby decided to try to regain English shores. However, the need to conserve fuel meant flying on minimum power and therefore alone. The lone bomber struggled up as far as the Pas de Calais area at around 11,000ft. but decided against dropping to low altitude in an evasion attempt; the pilots preferred to utilise their available height to try a power-glide across the Channel. Sadly, the first bursts of flak removed part of one wing and also damaged the controls to force the bomber into a shallow right turn. Lowering of the landing gear had the effect of halting the flak but Lt. Houghby realised this was but a reprieve from the inevitable and ordered his crew out. He himself broke a foot on landing and was soon rounded up by a Wehrmacht motorcycle patrol.

The sight of barely half of the aircraft dispatched coming back into the Shipdham circuit must have shocked and dampened the spirits of all watching personnel. It would be some time before the true facts emerged, but at the time the disappearance of eight aircraft along with some eighty combat crew was a sickening reminder of the continuing cost of the daylight Offensive.

The ensuing two days involved no operations, but did see a change in command of the 67th BS. Major Bill Cameron stepped down to be replaced by Major Robert Kollinor, and was assigned to HQ, 44th BG. A mission on the 21st involved four Groups of the 2nd BD attacking V-Sites in the Pas de Calais. Short-range missions of this nature drew the following pertinent comment from Sgt. D.V. Chase; "Some missions were of shorter duration and proved less difficult than others ... but anytime anyone is shooting 88s and 110s at you 'meager flak' is a term that can only be applied when the final shell explodes near your ship, and your name is not upon it!" These heart-felt words highlighted the fact that 'milk-runs' were no guarantee of survival; in the case of the Pas de Calais, this was a region with flak defences that were probably as, if not more, concentrated compared to many of Germany's major cities.

B-24H-15-FO, 42-52332 'My Ass'am Dragon' was a 66th BS, which was MIA on 5 March 1944. Aircraft was one of four losses borne by the 2nd. BD this day while attacking targets in southwest France.

The fourth battering of the Nazi capital during March took place on the 22nd and revealed the dramatic downturn in bomber losses compared to the first mission – twelve B-17s and B-24s compared to sixty-nine on the 6th. This was a direct result of the depredations wrought among the Luftwaffe fighters by the 8th Fighter Command. No longer could the German pilots dictate where, when and in what numbers the bomber stream could be assailed The general physical discomfort of another eight to nine hour haul could be borne by the Americans in these circumstances, although there was ever the risk of individual injury or even death when ploughing through the comprehensive flak barrage thrown up by 'Big B's' defenders. The Shipdham fliers returned in good order from Berlin after bombing through a solid undercast.

Change of Group Command

Col. Fred R. Dent had served as Group Commander since 4 December 1943 when he had relieved Col. James T Posey. Now he in turn was to step down from this post on 29 March. He was replaced by a combat veteran from the 95th BG based at Horham. He was Col. John H. Gibson, who had joined the B-17 equipped Group in August 1942 where he served as the

Group S-3 (Operations Officer) and completed twenty-five missions.

Four more missions were completed in March with all but one involving a similar time-span in the air to the 22nd. An airfield at Bramsche was attacked with unobserved results (23rd). Next day clear conditions over St. Dizier/Robinson airfield permitted the target to be saturated while the inaccurate flak did no material damage and the escorts ensured the Luftwaffe was kept at bay. However, any sense of satisfaction among the crews on completing the mission was surely dampened by the news that the requirement for completing a combat tour had been increased from twenty-five to thirty missions! (In fact a sliding scale was also introduced to cater for how many missions an individual might have flown by this stage. For example, if he had flown twenty missions, the extra demand on his services might only extend to two extra missions. On the other hand, an airman with just a few missions completed could well be faced with the full quota of five).

A recent transfer-in from the 392nd BG was 41-29538/X, which was assigned to the 68th BS around the mid-period of March. On the 23rd, Lt. Barry's crew, still un-tried in combat, were due to make a flight in this bomber along with Lt. Davido. Sgt. Whitworth recalled that earlier in the day the crew had practiced getting out of a B-24 in an emergency. That same afternoon, the aircraft had reached take-off speed when it lifted into the air and touched down on the left side. The main gear on that side folded up and the resultant skid ended with the bomber still intact but with both left-side propellers torn off. The morning's 'dry-run' was put to good (and undoubtedly grateful) use as all eleven airmen sprang out and away from the scene!

16 March 1944 at Woodchurch, near Kingsnorth, Kent. 'The Shark' makes her final landing, an end result that spelt disaster for Lt. John I Scarborough's crew, with six men of the 67th BS crew killed instantly. Four of the gunners would be pulled clear, but Sgt. Stickel would later die of his injuries. Bomber was B-24H-1-FO, 42-7549/K.

The latest run to the northeast region of France occurred on the 26th when Oschersleben was 'scrubbed' and substituted by Petit-Bois-Tillencourt near Abbeville. The flak as ever was of the 'intense and accurate' type although no aircraft were brought down. Then it was back to the 'long-haul' business, which this time entailed an attack upon Mont de Marsan airfield, nestling close to the French/Spanish border. Enemy fighters were again conspicuous by their absence but the flak batteries made up for this by culling two crews from the 44th BG whose bomb-run was made at around 12,000ft.

The crew of Lt. Hess (67th BS) fared much better than that led by Lt. Harleman (68th BS). Heavy damage to the fuel tanks induced the pilots to head for Spain. Once over the coast Lt. Hess baled out his crew before trimming the B-24 (41-29554/J-Bar – TEXAS ROSE), directing its course out over the Bay of Biscay and baling out. However, the bomber had a

Left: Lt. George D. Telford and crew were interned in Switzerland on 18 March 1944, following the 2nd. BD assault on targets at Friederichshafen in southern Germany. Right: B-24J-65-CO 42-100073/H 'Sack Artist' of the 67th. BS crashed at Fehraltdorf, Switzerland on 18 March 1944: while being flown by 1/Lt. Raymond J. LaCombe and crew. It was on fire but the pilots made it to the Swiss border where the crew bailed out, and the aircraft exploded at such a low altitude that it sheared the tops off some trees.

Above: Lt. Irwin's 'Shoo Shoo Baby' down at Zurich canton, Dubendorf in Switzerland. This 506th aircraft was a B-24H-15-CF, 41-29431/Q. Incident occurred on 18 March 1944 when a number of 44th crews diverted into the neutral country. Right: The tail of Lt. Irwin's aircraft seen on 18 March 1944.

mind of its own and circled back, just missing the pilot as he descended before striking the ground and skidding to a halt, still basically intact!

Lt. Harleman also directed his damaged bomber towards Spain, but elected to fly his course at low level. This proved to be a fatal choice because 42-109836/B came under fire as it skirted the French coastline. Fire started in the bomb-bay and 'ditching' action was initiated. However, the bomber split just aft of the wing trailing edge, throwing the four gunners in the rear fuselage out into the sea. All four survived with varying degrees of injury, but their six companions up front were less fortunate and perished; Lt. Baum (B) was spotted very briefly swimming clear of the wreckage before sinking.

This was a sad manner in which to complete operations in March. Missions were planned to Berlin and then Landsberg and Lech (30th) while Ludwigshafen was lined up for the 31st. All three were 'scrubbed' at different stages. A seed-change in operational requirements was about to begin as April was entered that would basically span the next few months. This was to be linked to a prime reason for the bombers' function, namely the successful Invasion of Western Europe.

On a happier note, three of Lt. Howington's 68th BS crew left Casablanca for England in late March, this being the final stage of a successful evasion attempt; they were S/Sgt. Blakely, Sgt. Klein and T/Sgt. Rosenblatt. Blakely had landed near a wood after baling out of his doomed B-24, and shortly after concealing himself had seen T/Sgt. Barlow (Eng.) coming along a trail accompanied by a woman; his whisper to attract attention obviously shocked the Frenchwoman but she quickly recovered and told them to hide in the wood until she returned. In that interval the Germans searched the area, but the fliers were still undiscovered when the woman returned to escort them to her house.

Here they linked up with Klein and Rosenblatt, and were provided with civilian clothing. Three days later, all four were taken to Poix for a rail journey to Paris, where they were then split up. Blakley shared his room with an RAF evader for the next two weeks before transfer to another house. New photographs were taken to replace their Service-issue items and by 1 March 'Gaston Louis Humbert' (Blakely) was ready to depart Paris for the south. However, the party evacuated the train as it slowed down near the village of Foix south of Toulouse and some thirty miles distant from the French/Spanish border. Five guides were gathered here, ready to escort the fourteen evaders. The first stage of the trek ended at a barn where the party languished for five days, held up by snowstorms. The party set off again, but T/Sgt. Barlow began to show signs of physical distress, and he was reluctantly left

Lt. Lucas landed 42-100400Y a B24J-100-CO of the 506th BS. He made this landing at Zurich canton, Dubendorf in Switzerland on 18 March 1944. The nose wheel collapsed during the landing.

Lt. Nichols 'Paper Doll' on the side of a hill at Dietschwell, St. Gallen, Switzerland on 18 March 1944. 'Paper Doll' was a B-24J-70-CO, 42-100112/Q of the 68th BS. 'Paper Doll' came to rest on the side of the hill after narrowly missing a barn, and after the crew had all bailed out. Just prior to bailing out Hollis Nichols (pilot) went back to his seat with the intention of making a crash landing. As he was about to get in his seat once more a propeller broke free and slashed through the cockpit and into his seat, and this made his mind up to promptly get out!

behind, as he was slowing down the others progress. (Barlow would get back to England in a protracted and almost incredible manner, the details of which will be recounted later).

The airmen were forced to regularly wade through the snowdrifts, and on one occasion were very fortunate to evade a German patrol that passed along the road shortly after the men had crossed over and climbed up the adjoining slope. Finally, on 13 March the guides located the door to an aqueduct tunnel that permitted access to the other side of the rugged terrain that would otherwise have had to be scaled. The men had won through to the small Principality of Andorra, where they rested for two days before making a final nighttime walk across into Spain. Once in that neutral country, a British Embassy Staff member in a car met and then transported them to Barcelona. After receiving medical checks and proper civilian clothes, the men were on their way first to Madrid and then via Gibraltar (where the clothes were exchanged for full uniform) to Casablanca. A nine-hour flight in a C-87 two days later brought the airmen back to England, and ultimate return home in mid-April. (Blakely's brief visit to Shipdham on the 12th saw him awarded his T/Sgt. stripes).

The arrival of the Group at Shipdham in late 1942 had encountered an airfield literally swimming in mud, where even the 'main roads' were badly affected. In addition the Line Crews in particular had to wait until the late winter period until sufficient building material (whether or not legally acquired) became available for the construction of 'line shacks', a number of which were of good enough quality for the personnel to use them as much for accommodation as for shelter.

One enterprising 67th BS crew went further by adapting a bomb shelter. These structures were open to the skies and normally well waterlogged, but this particular example located by the squadron sheet metal shop was somehow unaffected by the East Anglian elements. A wooden cover was placed round the entrance to which was attached a modified door. The lighting consisted of an electrical line extended from the sheet metal shop, while a modified 'heater' was built. A fifty-gallon drum was placed on the vent end of the shelter. Heater fuel consisted of 100 octane mixed with motor oil. In addition hot water was available from an aluminium tubing coil placed around the stove jacket. The heat would induce spurts of hot water to surge up into an old oxygen tank where it would be stored for general use! The stove fuel line was fitted with a hand-regulated valve and the adjusted flow maintained a good temperature. On hand was a radio and even a toaster. Here was a self-contained team who could work as it were 'on site' and not have to make the protracted round-trip to their normal living quarters. (The living Sites were becoming badly over-crowded by 1944 as the Group complement of aircraft increased; with it went a corresponding upsurge in personnel required to maintain them).

Left: Major. William Cameron relinquished command of the 67th BS to Major Robert Kolliner and moved up to HQ, 44th BG. Maj. Cameron was destined to hold the position of 67th BS CO twice. He was part of the original 67th squadron that came to England in 1942 and went home with the Group in 1945. His first mission was 17 November 1942, and his last came on 10 April 1945 as Command Pilot with the rank of Lt.Col. Right: Major Robert Kolliner was Bill Cameron's replacement as CO for the 67th BS.

Left: B-24H-15-CF 41-29538/X of the 68th BS. Lt. Davido lost power on the take off run for the 23 March 1944 mission to Osnabrueck while piloting this bomber. Right: Lt Davido was a 68th BS pilot who finally finished his tour of combat duty in November 1944.

Chapter Eight

The Transportation Plan

One of the basic problems facing the D-Day planners was how to stem, if not totally cut off, the reinforcement of Wehrmacht strength in the Normandy region in the immediate aftermath of the 'Overlord' landings. The method finally agreed upon was for the Battlefield to be isolated through the bombing of the road and rail network feeding into northwest France. The availability of both the 9th USAAF and its RAF contemporary (2nd Tactical Air Force) for this vital duty was timely. However, Gen. Eisenhower had previously requested that the Strategic Air Forces be put at his disposal as well. This switch in basic function in the weeks prior to and beyond D-Day, did not sit well with either Gen. Spaatz or Air Chief Marshal Harris, but both these senior airmen were persuaded to agree. (As events were to cast up, both of these heavy bomber Forces would still carry out a degree of operations relating to their basic brief).

Although Eisenhower's control was effective from April, the switchover to a tactical function for the B-17s and B-24s was tardy at least during this month. Certainly, the 44th BG's mission list was to display a predominance for targets within Germany, although that pattern would be more balanced out between the two separate requirements in May.

April did not start out well for the 2nd BD, whose Groups were briefed to attack Grafenhausen. This southern German town was located down towards Switzerland and not too far away from Schaffhausen, with the latter located on a spit of Swiss land surrounded by German territory. The ingredients for a military (and by extension a diplomatic) blunder arose on, of all days, 1st April. The weather conditions were none too good but this in itself was not the root cause of the incident, since navigational errors were regarded as a contributory factor. The majority of the 44th BG did strike their Primary target, but the remaining element sought a target of opportunity that turned out to be Schaffhausen. The bombs dropped by these crews impacted south east of the town but other Groups struck locations within the unfortunate town.

Lt. Milton Rosenblatt made a surprise but welcome return to Shipdham on the 2nd. He had been flying as co-pilot to Lt. Sobotka on 21 January when their 68th BS aircraft had been shot down. He remembered that the fighters latched onto his B-24 flying the 'Tail end Charlie' position. Top and tail turrets were knocked out, control cables severed and two engines set on fire. His bale-out was so close to the ground that the parachute swung just the once before depositing him in a clearing within a wood. He hid out for around thirty minutes before then breaking out and starting to walk. The first person he met was a Frenchwoman whose quick talking was incomprehensible, although Milt felt that she was aware of his status. He was sheltered in her farmhouse overnight and provided with clothes before setting out again. Two days later, having eaten little or nothing and hidden-up in any available cover, he decided to take a chance. He displayed his shirt with the wings to the man who responded to the airman's knock at the door, and was promptly pulled inside. Food and a mattress were provided, and later that day he was collected by a schoolteacher. They cycled to another house where a trio of individuals interrogated Milt in order to dispel any suspicion that he was a German 'stooge' trying to infiltrate the local Resistance network. The test was passed, whereupon one man drove him to his farm at which he stayed for a week.

The next move was to the home of a Resistance leader. Here Milt was used to establish the 'bona fides' of fellow evaders, as well as forging identity cards and travel permits, including his own. A full month later he was alerted to the need to move again, because his 'host' was under suspicion by the Germans and would have to flee France. The two men planned their escape via the Pyrenees, but then came word that Milt was to be spirited out by boat through Brittany.

His most hair-raising moment came at the Paris railroad station where he and two other evaders had been told to wait; then they were to follow three Frenchmen standing at a specified point over to and through the relevant platform barrier. A German officer approached Milt and asked (in French) for a light from the flier's cigarette. The evaders had been instructed never to respond verbally, but thankfully Milt had grasped enough of the language since his arrival to be able to respond appropriately but silently! The subsequent movement onto the platform, and I.D. check by German soldiers passed off without further incident, as did the journey to Brittany, where a truck collected the men for delivery to yet another house. The adjoining barn had a concealed trapdoor under which was a room holding around thirty evaders.

Two nights later the group was on its way to the coast. The second incident of note occurred as the men were walking in single file along a hedge-enclosed path. One of their guides came running back, instructing them to clamber over the hedge and hide; the pair of German soldiers who strolled by a minute or so later fortunately did not pick up the resultant commotion! Once reassembled, the group got to a point high above a beach. From here they moved forward and down the cliff face in twos and threes, this act occurring as the pair of patrolling sentries were at the extremities of their 'beat'. The Royal Naval vessel assigned to pick them up sent small boats to within wading distance of the shore, but the evaders were still waist-high in water at the pick-up point. From then on, it was plain sailing and crew and 'passengers' were back across the Channel in a matter of hours. (Milt's 1960s visit to the beach made him gasp in shock when he saw the precipitous nature of his descent in 1944 – a descent that he explained would never have been attempted by him in the light of day!).

The ensuing four days left the Group firmly stranded with no missions scheduled at all, while the 6th saw a very marginal increase in combat activity. In this case, just two crews went out to bomb Watten in the Pas de Calais – Lt. Sidney Paul in 42-100423 THE WASP NEST, (506th BS) and Lt. Dale Benadom in 41-29544 FLAK ALLEY II (68th BS), along with a B-24 from another unit that was equipped with G-H. The entire 2nd BD Force consisted of just twelve bombers from

D-Barfly a B-24J-60-CO 42-99986/D of the 67th BS was received at Shipdham during January 1944.

five Groups and the bombing results were judged good, even in the absence of visual sighting. Meanwhile the Group flew practice missions or indulged in ground training up to the 8th when the second completed mission for April was flown – and a shockingly eventful action this proved to be.

The Group was allocated the lead for the 2nd BD that in turn was leading the other Divisions. The region around the city of Brunswick was thought to bring up the worst in Luftwaffe resistance, and the fighter pilots were labelled the 'Battlin' Bastards of Brunswick'. The fact that this central area was on the main approach to Berlin was probably as good a reason for such activity. Industrial locations within the city formed the briefed target but when this and the Secondary were found to be obscured by smoke-screens a target of opportunity in the form of Langenhagen airfield was attacked with excellent effect.

The positive outcome to the mission palled in the light of what happened in a matter of minutes when eleven crews were

S/Sgt. Will Lundy was an asst. crewchief who subsequently became an instruments specialist within the 67th BS.

downed, so making this the worst loss-scale suffered by the Group during its entire combat career. Once again the losses were spread between the four squadrons and once again the 506th BS absorbed the lion's share. The Group had crossed over the distinctive shape of the Dummersee (Dummer Lake) and was turning right for the Primary when dozens of enemy fighters swept in from ahead and out of the sun. Just one single attack was made by this mass formation but in those few seconds it had handed out a heavy degree of punishment among the B-24s.

To Lt Pino flying as co-pilot on the 67th BS bomber 42-52293/G-Bar – JUDY'S BUGGY the effect of the weapons being fired was likened to winking light bulbs. His bomber suffered hits on Nos.3 and 4 engines that caused the former to fail totally but did not prevent Lt. Wahler from holding formation to bomb before No.4 also went 'out'. Full rudder and trim tab adjustment barely enabled the pilots to keep their aircraft on course for England but the effort was ultimately successful as the Suffolk coast loomed up. Just inland was an airfield at Beccles upon which Wahler decided to set down. Before he did so, five of the crew were baled out. This number included Sgt. Meskinis (TG) whose turret had been demolished around him but whose injuries were felt not serious enough for him to jump. (Tragically, he was later found on the ground with his heated suit cord instead of the ripcord in his hand.) The remaining five airmen included two who were felt to be incapable of jumping due to their injuries. The flaps were manually pumped down in the absence of the hydraulic pump that was powered by the now defunct No.3 engine, and the landing passed off in order.

Wahler's crew had made it back home, but fully eleven other crews had gone down over Germany. The 66th BS was the least affected in this respect with just Lt. Richardson's 42-99996/I lost – little consolation for the ten airmen on board, not one of whom survived. The survival rate on the first of the two 67th BS bombers MIA was hardly better, with Sgt. Thomas (RW) getting clear scant seconds before the spinning B-24 flown by Lt. Mayes (42-110083/X-Bar) erupted into the ground near Langenhagen. Lt. Thorn flying 42-7767/C-Bar had lost his ROG in gruesome manner before the crew's first mission when the hapless airman ran into a propeller. On this day the pilots were having problems in holding position according to Lt. Gille (N) who was one mission behind his regular 506th BS crew and who had volunteered to fly with Thorn as a 'replacement'. When the fighters struck the bomber was straggling and caught particular hostile attention. Two engines were crippled and as the B-24 lagged ever further behind the Group a second assault inflicted further destruction. The aircraft steadily descended from 21,000ft. on less than half power as the crew began to evacuate the doomed machine. All ten crewmembers landed in good physical condition apart from Lt. Gille who had sprained an ankle. Their bomber crashed within the city of Hannover.

A trio of crews from the 68th BS were lost with thirteen out of the thirty-one airmen killed. The worst affected crew was that of Lt. Altemus flying 42-110020/Z. According to T/Sgt. Baker (Eng.) the bomber burst into flames that shot from the bomb-bay forward to the flight deck. Baker quickly opened the hatch in the cockpit roof, an action that ducted the worst of the fire out into the slipstream, but not before the engineer had been badly burnt around his head and lost consciousness for a short time. He snapped on his chest-pack upon recovering and exited via the forward-right bomb-bay door that had somehow been forced open. Lt. Phelan (CP) did the same after the pilot indicated that he bale out, but although Lt. Altemus had said he would follow he sadly became one of the seven fatalities among the eleven on board. Lt. Barry lost the Nos.2 and 3 engines on 42-99987/S – PIZZ AND MOAN in the course of

B-24H-1-FO, 42-7522/S 'Southern Comfort' was the second aircraft to carry this name. She is photographed sitting on the ground at Thurleigh, home for the 306th BG.

the attack that also claimed S/Sgt. McKenna (Eng.). Barry and the other eight crewmembers baled out in good order.

The third MIA squadron bomber was 42-109822/O – TOWNSEND'S TERRIBLE TEN. On an earlier 'aborted' mission the crew had been fortunate to survive the jettisoning of their bombs after descending to too low a level before release. That degree of good fortune was to desert five of the ten on board this time around. The bomber suffered three separate attacks, the first of which knocked it out of formation as well as destroying an engine, and the second just as the pilots were almost back in position. Two further engines were disabled at this stage to leave the crippled B-24 sagging relentlessly downwards and wide open to the final assault. Lt. Paul (N) had his helmet blown off and thought he was blind when he could not open his eyes. In fact blood had sealed the lids, which he managed to prise apart, much to his relief. He then assisted T/Sgt. Nealon (Enlisted Bombardier) to clip on his chest-pack and jumped out through the nose door aperture. Nealon's pack had been inadvertently clipped on upside down, and in his dazed state of mind (due to a serious head wound) he literally tore the canvas cover off instead of searching for the ripcord that was now positioned on the left side instead of the right! Three others baled out safely but Lt. Townsend was not among this number after the bomber tore itself apart in mid-air.

Nose art of 42-52293/G "Judy's Buggy" of the 67th BS.

Although the 506th BS absorbed nearly half the Group losses in aircraft the proportion of deaths among the fifty participating crewmembers (seven) was low, albeit tragic for the unlucky exceptions. Lt. Herzing's 42-110023/T – RUBBER CHECK was thoroughly shot-up with Nos.1 and 2 engines smoking and No.3 set on fire. Momentary hesitation between the pilots about what to do was ended when it was decided to 'get the Hell out'. The bomb-bay doors were hanging down and swinging wildly in the slipstream to make the act of jumping out very hazardous. In spite of this all ten airmen baled out in the Hannover region and got down to become POWs.

Major. Kahl the 66th BS CO, photographed with his HQ staff.

Above: 'Shack Rabbit', 42-7767S is a Ford-built B-24H-5 of the 67th BS. The ground crew is running up one of the bomber's engines. Right: Nose art of "Shack Rabbit" 42-7767/C, which was downed on 8 April 1944 with Lt. Thom's crew. Note the rabbit mission 'hash marks.'

This good fortune was shared by Lt. Marx's crew in 41-29153/Z-Bar – GREENWICH. Following release of the bombs the flak-afflicted bomber with its No.3 engine out of commission went into a spin that was only corrected when within several thousand feet of the ground. As an aid to re-stabilising the aircraft, T/Sgt. Franklin (Eng.) threw the hydraulic switch by way of gaining the necessary pressure to activate the flaps as well as the bomb-bay doors, so providing the crew with a better chance of escape. Bale out was then called for as Lt. Marx said that he and Lt. Brockman (CP) could not hold level flight for more than a few seconds. Their gallant action was sufficient for all ten personnel to jump and float down around Herford. The third crew to be totally spared was headed by Lt. Winn who was one mission ahead of the others – who were all on their first! They were positioned behind the Deputy Lead and had both engines on the left wing set on fire, shortly after which all baled out, leaving 42-100423/A to fall to her destruction.

Lt. Johnson flying in 42-73506/Bar-X got through to bomb with his B-24 relatively intact but no sooner had 'bombs away' been confirmed, and Lt. Baumann (N) reached for his logbook to record the fact, that flak struck home. Baumann was badly burnt by the flames that erupted around the forward interior, but before jumping out he opened the nose turret doors thereby allowing Lt. Wiest (B) to get out; the latter airman would have otherwise been trapped due to the absence of an internal emergency release handle. The crew all baled out after the bomber had detached itself from the formation. As the men were nearing the ground Lt. Williamson (CP) heard the sound of small arms fire being directed at the parachutes. On landing he then heard Lt. Johnson shouting to the effect that he was giving up and for his captors not to shoot. Almost immediately a volley of shots rang out and the pilot was killed.

Lt. Sprinkle's 42-109827/Bar-Q at the rear of the formation was shot-up by the fighters as they struck around the time the I.P. was reached. The cannon shells smashed into the top of the fuselage/wing area to ignite the fuel and oxygen systems; the flames were further spread by the slipstream sluicing in through the open bomb-bay doors. The bale-out signal was given and Sgt. Freeman (TG) scrambled out of his turret and followed both waist gunners out through the camera hatch. Only one of the waist gunners survived, as did Lt. Sprinkle and S/Sgt. Winn (ROG). The pilot was actually blasted through the cockpit roof when the aircraft exploded and the majority of the six fatalities probably occurred at this point. S/Sgt. Radu (Eng.), whose body was lying in the vicinity of the crash-site, was identified by Sgt. Freeman next day, who noted that his parachute had not opened.

The 506th BS actually had eight crewmembers killed on 8 April. The crew of Lt. McCaslin had not flown together very long, having previously flown with other crews. Lt. Bartol (CP) had already put in a good number of missions and was already checked out for an Airplane Commander post. Their B-24H (42-7509/V-Bar) was left wingman to Col. Gibson (Group CO in place of Col. Dent from 28 March, after the latter officer was wounded in action). The bomber took cannon strikes that did surprisingly little damage. McCaslin recollected that the Group took up course for Hannover as the Secondary target and commenced what seemed an inordinately long bomb-run. Flak was bursting all around and one shell made its lethal effect felt just as the bombs were released. Fragments of the casing penetrated through the windshield and struck Lt. Bartol in the head. (His remains were later incarcerated at the Madingley Military Cemetery, to which his father made an annual visit for many years after World War II).

The good fortune attending Lt. Wahler's crew (or rather for those members returning to Shipdham), was paralleled by all on board Lt. Wind's 506th BS bomber. The pilot was taking his crew on their first mission after flying his own first run a few days previous. On that occasion he had informed his crew on return that 'There was nothing to it. We just flew there, dropped our bombs, and came home'. What occurred today swiftly disillusioned him on this matter! Cannon shell hits had knocked out the No.2 engine, while flak hitting home threw fragment of Plexiglas in the pilot's face and hands. Then, while on the landing approach the B-24 ahead ground-looped and blocked the runway. With two engines 'red-lined' and liable to fail at any moment a frantic diversion was made to touch down on the cross runway. One main gear tire was punctured and the drag caused the aircraft to slew off the runway before its momentum was spent. Latter on, holes in the oil-tanks of Nos.3 and 4 engines were among the many holes within the airframe. Despite this, the ground crew worked overtime to return their charge to combat status by the 11th. (Sadly, their efforts were in vain because the B-24 was declared MIA over Bernberg on this date).

Lt. Wind's physical problems received attention from a doctor at a nearby military hospital to which Dr. Allison (Flight Surgeon) had dispatched him. However, over six hours went by before the Lt.'s condition was cleared, and during this time the doctor performing the task was busy lecturing a fellow practitioner about his technique. This was the first example of several 'administrative' hurdles due to face the pilot over the next day or so.

Frank Seigilinsky, a 68th BS carpenter, is snapped on top of 'Any Gum Chum.'

He was assigned to an otherwise empty ward where a hard-nosed nurse received him. She tossed him a pair of pyjamas and told him to take a shower before assigning him a bed. Upon donning the pyjamas, they were found to be too small, whereupon he explained the problem to the nurse. Her surly response was to point him towards the clothing store from where he should sort out the problem! This was finally done, and he took to his bed having been on his feet for more than twenty-four hours.

Less than six hours later he was awakened and informed that the bed was to be made up within thirty minutes, and he should seek another bed. However, he was barely settled into the new sleeping unit when he was again awakened, this time to face an un-appetising breakfast.

He was not categorised as a 'bed patient' and was still in his flight clothing. His status meant that he had to eat in the Mess Hall – only, on arriving there he was informed that he should have brought his Mess kit. The mordant expression now uttered by the thoroughly frustrated airman shook the staff into issuing the top of a Mess kit and a spoon!

The fact of not being a 'bed patient' meant that Lt. Wind could not return to the ward prior to 7.00 pm, so he sought to pass the time at the Officers Club – only to be barred entry, on the grounds that he was not in 'Class A' uniform. This was the last straw for him. Consequently, when his face bandage was removed next day, but he was informed that his release was dependent upon paper work that usually took at least two weeks, he decided upon instant action. Two of his crew arrived with an ambulance twenty-four hours later, into which he scrambled; what he said to the surly nurse who informed him that he could not leave without the necessary paper work being on hand was never recorded but it was surely plainly, if bluntly, stated!

Above: 'Pizz and Moan' leads a Group formation to bomb the target at Cognac in France. Right: Nose art of B-24 J-60-CO, 42-99987/S lost 8 April 1944 along with Lt. Barry's crew. The Group was leading the 2nd. BD this day and paid an extremely high price for the 'Honor' with eleven B-24s and their crews declared MIA!

It was bad enough to be instantly transferred from the relative security of a bomber to being faced with a descent into a hostile enemy environment; worse still, was to find oneself thrown alone into this harsh scenario, following the loss of all his fellow crewmembers, as happened to Sgt. Archie Thomas (RW) on Lt. Mayes 67th BS bomber. He later recalled how four of his fellow enlisted men had expressed the view that "If it is my time to die, I am ready to die for my Country", to which he retorted "I am not ready to die for my Country,' but rather I am ready to LIVE for my Country!" – a tragic prophecy in the circumstances.

His B-24 was hit during the first fighter pass, caught fire and began to spin. On hearing the bale-out order he pulled off his flak vest, grabbed his chute pack and reached the escape hatch. The combined attempts of three of the gunners to fully release the hatch failed, but Thomas still managed to force his way through the gap. He was in the air scant seconds before hitting the ground a mere 100 yards distant from the smashed wreckage.

His freedom lasted just sixty minutes before two German soldiers intercepted him as he tried to hide in a wood, after which he was temporarily incarcerated in a nearby village in the company of another B-24 airman. Both men began the journey to Dulag Luft north of Frankfurt. Here they came across their first taste of civilian hostility during the short tram ride from Frankfurt railroad station to the camp, when their guards had to hold a mob at bay.

His facial burns and abrasions to one foot were given scant medical attention, and next morning Thomas was visited in his small cell by a German officer who presented the airman with

Entrance to the 506th BS area.This is Site 2, which was the furthest Site from the airfield.

Each Site was made up of a mixture of different types of buildings, including metal Nissen huts and Maycrete structures.This is Site 2, home for the 506th BS.

the usual 'simple' form. His reaction to Thomas entering the bare details of name, rank and serial number brought the standard one of sharp anger and a demand for the document's comprehensive completion. Thomas reminded his captor of the Geneva Convention requirements for POWs, upon which the German modified his tone to a more persuasive pitch. He finally departed and this proved to be the sole occasion Thomas would be questioned prior to his departure several days later for Stalag 17B in Austria.

The chastened but relieved crews returning from the 8 April mission were not to know that almost the same number (eight) from among the Group ranks would not see out the month at Shipdham as their B-24s were similarly claimed in combat or through operational failure. For Lt. Palmer (68th BS) and his crew this reprieve lasted a mere twenty-four hours, as they headed out the following day for Tutow airfield, up towards the Baltic coast. This was yet another deep-penetration mission that gave the Luftwaffe ample time to marshal its fighter defences. The deterioration in the weather forced a 'recall' signal to be sent but not before a proportion of the bombers, including part of the 44th BG, had reached the target and bombed through heavy flak and regular fighter assaults.

It was Palmer's 42-72858/U – PISTOL PACKIN' MAMA that proved to be the unfortunate exception when cannon fire severely damaged the center of the right wing. The resultant exposure of the surrounding metal to the slipstream seriously impeded forward motion even on maximum power and an inevitable loss of contact with the formation then developed. Sgt. Kruse (Eng.) later noted that the bombers' route was then close to Hamburg and therefore not too distant from the Baltic coastline. The decision was taken to head northward for Sweden and although several fighters did intercept the aircraft, none of these seem to have closed to firing range or if so to have opened fire upon their prey, according to Kruse. Once over Swedish airspace a flight of Reggiane 2001 fighters took up position and led their 'guest' into an airfield at Malmo. The nose-wheel could not be deployed so four crew in the back acted as a counter-weight and moved slowly forward on Sgt. Kruse's visual signal from his position ahead of the bomb-bay as the B-24 slowly settled. The landing on the airfield's grass surface went off all right although some earth from the 'digging' action created by the nose was scooped up into the bomb bay. (Ninety more Allied airmen found a safe sanctuary this day when nine other USAAF bombers joined PISTOL PACKIN' MAMA in diverting into Sweden).

The target choice for 9 April was the first of six consecutive Group missions involving either airfields or aircraft production factories. The Junkers plant at Bernberg had been one of the key locations involved in the 'Big Week' assaults and was revisited on the 11th. Lt. Mercer (67th BS) 'aborted' when well into Germany. First the landing gear had tended to creep down, and then two engine superchargers failed. The isolated bomber was fortunate to be picked up by a P-47 whose pilot shepherded his charge back to England. This degree of fortune was not visited upon seven of Lt. Money's 506th BS crew or their bomber 42-7522/Bar-S – SOUTHERN COMFORT. The bomb-bay doors would not open as the tracks were frozen according to Sgt. Kirschner; he had no sooner informed Lt. Money than he recalled a flak burst striking the bomb bay. (According to the MACR report, the right side doors were not raised, and the fire was caused by the bombs striking the door surface upon release). Whatever the circumstances were in creating this situation, the fact was the B-24 was doomed as fire swept through the fuselage. In one of those many sacrificial acts of gallantry, S/Sgt. Roop (TG) took his own chest-pack and clipped it onto Sgt. Young (RW) whose hands were too badly burnt for him to do so. S/Sgt. Kirschner could not release his oxygen mask hose from its regulator, and was badly burnt around the head when forced to remove the mask. Lt. Money was very lucky to get out alive, with fire erupting all around to leave just the cockpit side windows as a possible avenue of escape. Lt. Stamos (CP) was already dead, so Money braced himself and succeeded in kicking out the right window. Then, he held the co-pilot's wheel in order to keep the aircraft steady as he torturously worked himself outside, before attempting to tilt the machine up to the right. This latter action was done in order to clear the No.3 engine whose propeller was still revolving! Although he was apparently knocked out after finally releasing his grip (in Lt. Money's opinion by a propeller tip clipping his head) he recovered in time to pull his ripcord, and become the third survivor out of his crew, S/Sgt. Roop being one of the seven fatalities. S/Sgt. Kirschner's burns were treated both by German and British POW doctors, but he was later repatriated home in February 1945.

Zwickau was briefed along with the ball-bearing facilities at Schweinfurt. The latter target was then selected but reversed in favour of Zwickau, when the formations were already dispatched and about to cross into Europe. In the event, the mission was recalled, but not before two Group crews had an unnerving experience. In turning for home Lt. Mueller's B-24 collided with that of Lt. Mercer (67th BS); fortunately the contact was marginal and the damaged rudder on the latter B-24 did not hinder the pilots in making a sound if nervous landing.

Lechfeld down in southern Germany was an experimental base for the Luftwaffe, as well as having an adjoining Messerschmitt production factory, and was the subject of a pounding by the sixteen B-24s reaching there. The reduced size of the formation was indicative of the fact that the Group was still rebuilding its human and logistical strength following the events of 8 April. Lt. Mercer recorded his third incident in twenty-four hours when the engine superchargers failed on his regular aircraft 'L'IL COOKIE; fortunately, this occurred as the enemy coast was reached, otherwise the result could have been potentially lethal for both bomber and crew.

Lt. Griffith, who along with Lt.Grono had brought off a spectacular two-wheel crash-landing on 18 November, led another 67th BS crew on today's mission. An over-heating of all four engines between the coast and the target proved irreversible despite opening the cowl flaps and placing the fuel mixture levers into the 'full rich' position. The resultant drain on the fuel reverses made the chances of a safe return virtually nil. Therefore, once the bombs had been dropped, a course for Switzerland was taken up, after confirmation of the hopeless fuel situation was made. Low oil pressure forced the shutdown of No.2 engine but the pilots managed to stagger into Switzerland. Even then, the crew was fortunate to evade the several bursts of Swiss flak fired at their B-24 before making a landing at Dubendorf.; three of the shells burst around the waist area of the bomber, and Sgt. Forrest Clark was wounded in the

Site 3 was allocated to the 67th BS aircrew for their living quarters.

hand. (Lt. Griffith, along with S/Sgt. Bartay, did manage to escape and return to England during the following winter).

All military aircraft were stressed to a maximum all-up weight for operations, which in the case of the B-24 was assessed at 62,000lbs. in theory but was recommended to be restricted to 56,000lbs. for combat purposes. In fact the former figure was often well exceeded, which in turn, placed a truly tremendous burden upon the pilots, many of whom had never been exposed to operating aircraft in this critical manner. When, to the inherent problems of flying tight formation in grossly over-laden bombers, was added the vagaries of the weather, the stage was set for disaster as occurred on 21 April. The Group was slated to return to Zwickau and among the formation was 41-29418/U – TURNIP TERMITE, a B-24H that had arrived just a few days prior to this day. The Group encountered bad icing conditions during the course of making assembly north of Norwich. Suddenly the bombers shuddered and bore sharply right and then back before canting over into a spin. Nothing could be done to recover from this vicious action that saw the tail and right wing finally twist off. Lts. Havens (P) and Del Grande (CP) were initially tossed into the cockpit roof and then cast out into mid-air when the fuselage disintegrated. None of the other eight airmen emerged alive from the incident.

Mother Nature had once again made a contribution to aerial disaster and had proved to be as unforgiving an adversary as her human counterpart. (Lt. Hawkins (506th BS) had a similar experience this day but managed to recover from the spin when still several thousands of feet up). The subsequent recall of the Group due to inclement weather conditions added to the cruel irony of the bomber's loss. Lt. Mercer's run of 'incidents' continued when, after landing at Shipdham, smoke began to issue from what was believed to be the bomb bay, still packed with fragmentation bombs. Sgt. Kipnes grabbed a fire extinguisher but while heading down for the suspected source of the fire he tripped. The dropped fire extinguisher went off and defied all attempts to halt its flow. As it so happened the smoke had issued from the navigator's shorted 'Gee' Box and had been channelled via the connecting passageway into the central fuselage, so the Sgt.'s actions proved unnecessary!

B-24H-15-FO 42-52618/B "Chief Wapello" of the 506th BS. This bomber subsequently transferred to the 66th BS and was coded V+.

Dusk falls on yet another day at Shipdham. The aircraft are back from another mission, the aircrew's job is done, but the ground crews job is just commencing, repairing and replacing damaged parts.

Prior to this latest mission the Group had gone out to Brandenburg airfield (18th), Gutersloh airfield (19th) and finally to Marquise/Mimoyecques in the Pas de Calais (20th), but the latter mission was recalled due to the overcast. A seed change in Group operations occurred on the 20th. Major Kahl held a meeting with all 66th BS combat personnel and informed them that from now on the squadron would function as a permanent PFF unit; their current B-24s were to be relocated among the other three Sqdns. The 20th was also notable for the rare interdiction Force dispatched by the Luftwaffe to attack locations in East Anglia. Shipdham received some attention when bombs were dropped along with strafing runs that narrowly missed a 67th BS bomber and its ground crew but otherwise did no material damage.

The mission to Hamm on the 22nd was sent out late in the day, so that the participating Group returned to a darkened countryside. Unknown to the crews was the presence of a small Force of Me 410s from II./KG 51 that had infiltrated the 2nd BD element of the bomber stream and commenced to hand out punishment to the bewildered formations they were flying within as the Groups were on final approach to their airfields. Shipdham appears to have escaped the Luftwaffe's attention as regards both its twenty-five participating crews and the airfield itself.

A number of casualties were inflicted on the officer cadre of the Group's combat crews over the ensuing three or four days that had nothing to do with the Germans. On the 23rd after partaking of the evening meal numerous individuals began complaining of stomach pains, the cause of which was then traced to Ptomaine poisoning. The situation became so severe that missions planned for the 24th and 25th had to exclude the 44th BG due to this form of culinary attrition among the pilots, navigators and bombardiers. The Germans had won a tiny reprieve from aerial assault through no direct involvement of their selves! But it was back to business on the 26th when the Group headed out to bomb Guterloh airfield; however a solid undercast prevented bombing. Then next day the Group hit another milestone by flying its first double-header mission.

The first mission on the 27th went to Moyenneville in France as did the afternoon sortie when the marshalling yards at Chalons-sur-Marne were hit. A total of forty-five crews participated over the day's activities, and they saw nothing of the Luftwaffe. The intensity of flak varied from moderate to intense particularly during the morning mission when one bomber was taken down. Lt. Clarey was flying in his 67th BS aircraft 41-29467/X. A flak shell impacted with the forward section of the right wing, which fell off and induced the B-24 to drop away in a tight spin as flames consumed the airframe. Shortly after, the aircraft exploded killing seven of the crew. Only S/Sgts. Shirley (Eng.) and Chagnon (ROG) managed to bale out and survive; their pilot was adjudged to have also got out but never had time to deploy his parachute. And so once again the adage 'There are no easy missions' came to mind.

Sgt. Harry Steele crew chief of J-125-CO, 42-110024 "Ole Cock" of the 506th BS. Bomber was received in March 1944.

S/Sgt. Earl R. McArtur, 67th Crew Chief.

Berlin closed off the Group's mission account for April. The cost of the four missions to 'Big B' during March had been just two crews, but the defences would demand a rather higher price from the 44th BG this time around, as well as leaving the 8th USAAF short of sixty-two bombers.

Fighter cover was present in reasonable strength on the way in but was absent as the bombers turned for home. This was a situation capitalised upon by the Luftwaffe who successfully sniped at the exposed B-17 and B-24 formations.

The flak gunners also added to their score in particular over the Big City while the *Sturmgruppen* struck very hard at elements of the 3rd BD.

Lt. Schuyler (67th BS) was leading his crew on their tenth mission in 42-100279/I-Bar. He recalled the 'Little Friends' weaving their patterns above and around the bomber stream. Then, this pleasant scenario was brutally interrupted with the approach of a swarm of 'bandits' directly ahead. His aircraft survived the onslaught and after 'bombs away' was still in formation. Just north of Berlin a series of successive flak patterns closed inexorably from the left, the third of which struck home and caused No.2 propeller to run away. This was followed shortly after by the No.4 engine losing manifold pressure. The double disability now proved too much for the B-24, which steadily lost pace with the Group.

A check of fuel reserves confirmed the pilot's suspicion that there was insufficient to get back to England and probably enough to get the B-24 as far as the enemy coastline. Not long after this a group of six Fw 190s that had been harassing another Group took up a course that took them on a left hand angle towards the single bomber. Schuyler waited until the pack were within firing range before turning his aircraft in a diving turn in their direction. The effect of scattering the fighters worked as the speeding B-24 hurtled downwards; all but one of the attackers failed to take up the chase but this exception closed inexorably in upon his desperately weaving prey. The encounter went on for a matter of minutes before reaching its lethal climax. Sgt. Schow (TG) engaged the Focke-Wulf as it swooped in from behind but his bullets had no apparent effect even though seen to strike home. In contrast the 20mm cannon shells set the fuselage on fire as well as shattering Schow's turret. The end had come for his B-24 so Lt. Schuyler turned the bomber back in the direction of Germany and set the autopilot prior to following his entire crew out and into captivity.

B24J-100-CO 42-100429 "Consolidated Mess" of the 506th BS, was received 18 February 1944. The name is a play on the aircraft manufacturer Consolidated's name. By the end of the war this aircraft had clocked up a significant total of sixty-nine combat missions.

'Greenwich' 41-29153/Z was a B-24H-1-CF of the 506th BS. She was received at Shipdham during October 1943, and was ultimately lost on 8 April 1944 along with the Marx crew during a costly mission to Brunswick.

A very early photograph of 'Glory Bee' of the 67th BS. The aircraft was a Ford built H-15 42-52616 and was received during April 1944. By war's end she had amassed no less than 101 combat missions.

An RAF Halifax heavy bomber is snapped being towed to a hardstand in the 68th BS area. 'Heaven Can Wait' is also seen as she squats on her hardstand.

The second Group bomber declared MIA came from the 68th BS. This was 41-29471/X, which was bearing Lt. Sweigart's crew. Loss of oil pressure on No.3 engine began a process that ended many thousands of feet lower down with the pilots fighting to hold what was a very uneven, curving course while staggering along at minimum speed. The concealing cloud cover finally gave out and the ailing bomber was quickly engaged and struck by flak. One burst threw Lt. Turocy (N) out through the nose wheel aperture and killed Lt. Roberts (B); Turocy was lucky that his chest-pack was already clipped on and he was one of the three survivors along with the pilot and Lt. Greene (CP). Lt. Sweigart made an eventful descent due to his leg straps not being buckled and he nearly hung himself in his harness! Fortunately the bale-out height was no more than several thousand feet and the Lt. was safely delivered into a field.

A third Group crew were granted a reprieve from death or captivity in circumstances that were generally very unfavourable in respect of the B-24. The 'art' of 'ditching' was one that was even more incapable of being practiced than the act of baling out safely. In addition to this, the 'ditching' qualities of the B-24 were arguably much worse than any other Allied heavy bomber. The bomb-bay catwalk was really incapable of absorbing the shock of impact without collapsing, after which the fuselage was liable to split. Even if this action did not occur the 'shoulder' position of the wings ensured that the bulk of the fuselage was under water and liable to be swamped by the onrush of the water, making the chances of getting out extremely hard.

Lt. Hruby's 506th BS bomber 41-29513/Z had taken flak strikes over Berlin that were believed to have adversely affected the fuel tanks. In addition the No.2 engine was suffering a power 'surge'. Although Sgt. Clark (Eng.) responded to his pilot's request for fuel status as the Dutch coast was passed by saying that the instrument gauges were almost at zero, Lt. Hruby still headed for England. Engine RPM was reduced to a minimum tolerable level and all surplus equipment thrown overboard. Amazingly, the bomber stayed aloft until within sight of friendly soil. By the time the engines finally cut out in unison, the remaining crew had assumed 'ditching' positions. The pilots eased down from their height of around 6,000ft. at 125 mph and with a twenty degree flap setting. S/Sgt. Blanchard (ROG) had barely lowered the trailing aerial preparatory to sending a distress signal when a flak jacket being thrown out chopped it off! An alternative message was hastily sent using the fixed aerial and the I.F.F. switched to the emergency band before screwing down the transmission key. (It was later established that his efforts proved to be in vain). The pilots donned their steel helmets, which action proved to be necessary. The bomber was levelled off in a nose-high attitude above the sea, which was displaying a slight swell.

The touchdown was carried off so smoothly that the bomber's onrush stopped with the entire airframe intact. The impact had thrown both pilots against the windshield but their helmets absorbed the force. The cockpit rapidly filled up almost to the roof while the rear fuselage was similarly swamped. The six men up front scrambled desperately out via the cockpit hatch and all ten airmen emerged relatively unscathed to find just one of the life rafts could be partially inflated. Four men clung on to one, with a fifth inside to stabilise it, while four were similarly involved with the other raft pack. The tenth man (Sgts. Fount and Tom Bartley were twins, one of which had swum after the emergency equipment that had drifted away) was gradually being pulled further away from his fellow-crew-members who were trying to paddle in his direction.

It was all the more fortunate that a Royal Navy minesweeper was in the vicinity, whose Captain duly steered in the downed crew's direction and plucked them out of the water after some forty minutes. The thoroughly numbed airmen had their flight suits replaced by heavy clothing and blankets as well as a tot of rum. (This was one group of B-24 aviators at least who would hear little or no criticism of the aircraft's 'ditching' qualities! In addition the crew were almost certainly the sole complete team to survive a B-24 'ditching' in the E.T.O. at least).

May 1944

May 1944 was, with the exception of June and July, destined to herald the start of ever-lower monthly MIA figures at Shipdham. Never again would the Group suffer double-figure losses, although there would be several occasions when three or four crews would fail to return off the same mission. This month also witnessed a continuing upsurge in missions with twenty- one recorded. Three of these involved raids upon what would prove to be the Nazi industrial 'Achilles Heel' – oil. Nearly half of the remaining missions were directly involved with the Transportation Plan while several of the sorties into Germany were also directed at similar facilities to those outlined in the Plan.

May commenced with a relatively short run to Liege, Belgium and involved fifteen crews whose 8,000lb. bomb-loads provided a solid concentration on one end of the city's marshalling yards. Two days later a second 'short' mission to Wizernes in the Pas de Calais struck at what were probably sites for Hitler's range of rocketry weapons. The third mission (4th) was much longer in duration and intended to hit an aircraft factory at Waggum. The Group with Col. Gibson in charge led the 2nd BD but extremely poor weather at the enemy coast caused the mission to be recalled. However, several crews did proceed on their own initiative to tag onto those formations that did gain mission 'credit'.

A practice mission (5th) involved a very early take-off in the dark, but assembly of the Group proved almost impossible even in the full moonlight, and was only completed in the full light of day; at least one near-collision was averted at the last moment. It was back to business on the 7th with the 2nd BD going to Muenster and Osnabrueck while the B-17 divisions struck at Berlin. The 44th BG was assigned to the latter target with bombing conducted with PFF help. The eight-hour mission was completed with little fighter opposition and moderate target flak but the -40 degree temperature provided an uncomfortable physical backcloth to what was an otherwise positive outcome.

Sgt. F. Chowanski 67th BS was the crew chief for B-24H-1-FO 42-7552/A. 'Lil' Cookie.' This aircraft would be transferred to the 489th BG where it became the Group 'Assembly Ship.'

Lt. George J. Thom and crew went MIA on 8 April 1944 but all on board survived to become POWs. The 2nd. BD suffered nearly 10% losses this day while assaulting targets around Brunswick and Hannover.

B-24H-1-FO, 42-7522S 'Southern Comfort' of the 506th BS was lost on 11 April 1944 along with Lt. Money and crew. Just three of the crewmen on board, including Lt. Money, survived the incident.

44th ground crew shelter from the sheeting rain under a RAF Halifax that landed at Shipdham.

Osnabrueck was to commence a run of seven daily missions, the majority of which were 'deep penetration' in nature. Brunswick was the target assigned the 2nd BD (8th) although the 44th BG records indicate that the Group was initially briefed for Gutersloh airfield. Strong Luftwaffe resistance was encountered that took out a proportion of the eleven MIA crews, but none of these was from the 44th BG, whose gunners were credited with at least three of their assailants. The mission was notable for being the inaugural run of the 66th BS in its new PFF function.

Back over England a new 66th BS crew was making a practice sortie in 41-28795/D with the intention of test-operating the PFF equipment along the coast. The reduced eight-man crew included two bombardiers and two navigators but no gunners apart from T/Sgt. Russell (Eng.). A simulated bomb-run upon Yarmouth was in progress when two explosions were felt one after the other. The B-24 nosed into a dive that defied all the pilots' and Engineer's efforts to fully control and finally ended with the bomber assuming an equally dangerous nose-up attitude. The personnel then began to bale out but T/Sgt. Cargill (ROG) was still on board when the aircraft slammed into the ground near Halvergate. Lt. Musgrave (P) did get out but plummeted down with an unopened chest-pack. Although the crew sighted no enemy aircraft, examination of the burnt-out wreckage exposed several cannon strikes to confirm that the bomber's demise was directly due to this source. This incident once again brought to light the necessity of having all gun positions manned, whether or not the sortie was to do with a combat mission.

The bombing of St. Trond airfield in Belgium was reportedly carried out at the request of the RAF. This airfield was the hub centre for NJG 1, the original Luftwaffe night fighter unit that was founded back in late 1940, and a prime source for the defence of Germany's night skies.

The danger of flak to the USAAF bombers over any target was further heightened by the risk of the bomb loads being detonated even after release. This was the probable cause for what happened to Lt. Larson's 42-100110/P – NORTHERN LASS. The load of fifty-two M47 100lb. incendiaries were flowing out in a close-packed line when the bottom one exploded, probably as a result of a shell burst. Its blast set off a series of sympathetic explosions that swept upwards and reached almost to the bomber's gaping bomb bay. The propeller on No.4 engine became detached while No.2 emitted smoke, in addition to which the intercom system went 'out'. The crewmember sent aft to inform the others of what was happening found nobody there. Five of this very experienced crew now on their 28th mission (nineteen of which had been flown with the Italian-based 449th BG) had taken to their parachutes as the aircraft dropped out of formation. Four ended up as POWs while the fifth, S/Sgt. Ferguson (RW) evaded capture. The five remaining on board were to prove more

The B-24 flown by Lt. Rockford Griffiths is photographed at Dubendorf in Switzerland on 13 April 1944. On 18 November 1943 Griffiths along with Lt. Grono (co-pilot) had brought off a spectacular crash-landing on two wheels at Shipdham.

fortunate in that they managed to extinguish the fires created by the blast and the pilots steered their crippled B-24 back to Shipdham.

The Diepholz mission (10th) proved to be a failure thanks to the weather, whose cloud formations stretching up to 30,000ft. finally forced a recall signal to be issued, in addition to which no mission 'credit' was granted. The following morning saw a better, if not perfect result at Mulhouse in France. This time round the cloud cover over the city's marshalling yards intruded upon accurate bombing so targets of opportunity were sought and hit; at Orleans/Bricey airfield the bombs struck hangars and other support buildings, while the marshalling yards at Belfort were also squarely struck. Lt. Walsh (506th BS) was flying in a rear part of the sub-formation attacking Orleans/Bricey. One out of the small force of Bf 109s engaging the Group closed in on 42-94999/Bar-B and riddled the right wing and fuselage with cannon shells as well as setting No.2 engine ablaze. Two men were wounded but all ten baled out near the village of Patay west of Orleans. S/Sgt. Peloquin (Eng.) had the unnerving experience of his ripcord failing to operate, and passed the bulk of an estimated 15,000ft. fall by tearing open the pack cover and feeding the pilot-parachute out, which in turn deployed the main canopy. Just a few seconds lapsed before it deposited its human burden on the ground! (S/Sgt. Peloquin met up with Sgt. Richards (LW) several weeks later as both were being transported by the Resistance to a camp in the Foret de Freteval that would ultimately hold hundreds of Allied evaders. They would remain there until mid-August when the U.S. Third Army arrived to liberate the region). Lt. Walsh also evaded capture but was not apparently involved with the above-mentioned concealment. Lts. Mercer and Wahler (67th BS) diverted into the same RAF airfield on the south coast after running short of fuel. Both aircraft and crews were well fuelled-up – the latter with that great British culinary offering, fish and chips – after which they took off and returned at low-level to Shipdham!

The Group's involvement in the oil campaign that commenced on the 12th saw seventeen of the nineteen aircraft dispatched making an excellent bomb-pattern on the refineries at Zeitz. Of the other two crews, one had 'aborted' and the other was MIA. Lt. Vance (67th BS) was flying a replacement for his original B-24; the latter machine had developed engine problems. So Vance had hurriedly landed and grabbed a second

Nose art of the ill-fated lt. Havens aircraft that broke up due to icing during assembly for the 21 April 1944 mission to Zwickau, Germany. Aircraft previously served with the 486th BG and transferred to the 44th BG in April 1944. The aircraft was a H-15-CF 41-29418/U of the 68th BS.

bomber (42-100042/J-Bar). Although the MACR report stated that fighters had caught the bomber as it was straggling, it was flak that caused this loss according to the pilot. Two shells burst under the nose to set the right wing on fire, cut control cables and caused a hole in the rear fuselage that proved big enough for the men to bale out through! Lt. Davidowitz (B) was so badly wounded he could not move and went down in the blazing bomber, to become the sole fatality among the ten on board. (The crew had been due for R and R but decided to fly the mission; as it was, their 'R and R' session lasted a lot longer than normal as well as being spent in a much less pleasant location!).

The pace of combat dropped noticeably over the intervening eleven days at least. Tutow airfield was bombed through solid cloud on the 13th while installations at Siracourt in the Pas de Calais took a pounding two days later. Then followed two mission 'scrubs' and a third day where the Group

Lt. Haven's 68th BS crew poses for a photograph at the start of their combat tour. Sadly, eight would lose their lives during assembly for the 21 April 1944 Zwickau mission when the aircraft iced up and disintegrated in mid-air. The main body of the wreckage still lies in a lake at Taverham Mills, just outside Norwich.

were 'stood down' from operations before the crews were alerted for yet another attack on Brunswick (19th) and aviation facilities within the city. Flak was intense as was the scale of fighter opposition but all crews returned with most of their aircraft suffering no damage. Another 'stand-down' occurred on the 20th when the fourth of a succession of 68th BS 'evaders' from the mission of 21 January 1944 turned up. He was Sgt. Chandler (Eng.) from Lt. Starring's aircraft VICTORY SHIP. The other three all came from Lt. Howington's RAM IT-DAM IT (also 68th BS) and were T/Sgt. Rosenblatt (ROG), S/Sgt. Blakely and Sgt. Klein (LW). A fifth evader was reported to be in London; this was Lt. Teitel (B) from Lt. Sobotka's 42-7501/P. (It is ironic that none of the three-named pilots survived the loss of their aircraft).

Crew chief Pappy Hill and his 'Northern Lass.'

Four missions were put in over the ensuing five days, but only one was what could be termed a long-range effort. Siracourt and St. Pol were struck on the 21st followed by two daily sorties somewhat deeper into France to bomb airfields at St. Avord and Melun. The Group was forced to salvo into the smoke column that obliterated the latter-named target. The first of two exceptions to this pattern of operations occurred on the 25th when the bulk of the 2nd BD struck at several marshalling yards. The 44th BG added its ordnance to the destruction heaped upon the facility at Belfort as well as the locomotive repair yards sited there.

It was now two weeks since death had stayed its hand among the personnel and their aircraft but this was just the latest temporary reprieve for numerous hapless souls as the War ground remorselessly onwards. Lt. Tomer's 68th BS crew incurred the Group's seven latest casualties. Their bomber 42-94962/X-Bar was reported to have gone into a steep dive with one inboard engine smoking and the other having a 'feathered' propeller. When last seen it was heading towards the Swiss border that was very close to Belfort. In fact the aircraft had been turned for home but before doing so its bomb-load was jettisoned on the first available open area. The pilots were unable to gain height above 10,000ft. and their B-24 became an inviting target for any flak positions that their path took them. Sgt. Anderson (TG) was of the opinion that all six men up front were killed or fatally wounded by a direct hit, following which the bomber lurched downwards to crash west of Paris. Anderson, along with Sgts. Steburg (BT) and Brose (RW) quickly donned their chest-packs and jumped; Brose was the only one to escape capture.

Then on the 27th a 'double-header' mission was completed. The first sortie involved twenty-four crews hitting marshalling-yards at Saarbruecken while the second involved just eight B-

'Pathway' was the radio call sign for the control tower at Shipdham. The tower structure was not the standard USAAF control tower pattern but was rather a design for standard RAF bomber airfields.

The ground crew are changing an engine on B-24J-125-CO, 42-11031/H, 'Phyllis' which was taken on charge at Shipdham during March 1944.

Lt. Menzil walks down the wing of 42-50326 after he had brought her back for a crash landing on 29 March 1944.

Flak damage on 42-50326 can be discerned, while hydraulic oil from the shattered oil lines streaks all down the fuselage.

24s split among all four squadrons to bomb military installations at Fecamp in the Pas de Calais. Both efforts were regarded as eligible for the 'milk-run' category since overall enemy opposition was sparse in nature.

It would be oil targets that would account for the three remaining crews declared MIA during May, starting with a return visit to Zeitz on the 28th. Twenty-six crews took off after having experienced a disturbed night. This was caused by a snap Luftwaffe raid that landed its ordnance near to the 506th BS Site. Among the nine B-24s of the 68th BS was 42-110045/F piloted by Lt. Gurman. Flak near the Dummersee knocked out No.2 engine and the pilots turned back. Not long after doing so Lt. Gurman announced that he could not maintain altitude and advised the crew to jump. This they did with all ten getting out and parachuting. However, Sgt. Wiitala (Nose gunner) was shot at and wounded in his back by a farmer after he had landed but he managed to hobble away and out of range, to be later apprehended by soldiers.

Poelitz was located northeast of Berlin and possessed a large synthetic-oil refinery. Although the 8th Fighter Command had largely wrested control of the skies from the *Jadgwaffe*, there were still occasions when the German fighters got through to the bomber stream in numbers. An estimated fifty Fw 190s were reported by the Shipdham gunners, to which the Group lost a single B-24. This occurred as the formation was tracking in over the Stettinersee (Lake Stettin) to pick up the I.P. Fighter attacks were coming in on formations ahead and shortly after Lt. Foy's 42-73500/F took strikes that knocked out No.4 engine and inflicted damage upon the controls. The pilot had suffered a head wound from a bullet that fortunately was not serious enough to hinder his continued function in flying the B-24. For upwards of half an hour the now-straggling bomber crept back towards England before the decision was taken to swing north towards Sweden. As much as possible was then jettisoned, including the radar-blinding 'Carpet' equipment. At this stage up to eight P-38s flew cover as a course up past the Danish coast was maintained. A final, safe landing was made at Soeve near Gothenburg with Swedish fighters acting as a second 'escort'.

The second Group bomber culled from the formation was crippled by flak and was bearing the very experienced 506th BS crew of Lt. Golubock; their B-24 was no less 'experienced' as it was a Group 'original', 42/63962/Bar-W. Its name was now PRINC-ESS although it had previously borne a more sharp-toned variation (PRINC-ASS!). The pilot recollected that while the crew were on a week's leave at the 'Flak Farm' (rest home) a radar-jamming device had been installed. (This was almost certainly 'Carpet' that possessed an apparent ability to jam German radar-guidance systems for the flak guns for anything up to a mile in circumference). The crew appreciated the superior flight characteristics of their B-24D compared to later variants.

The mission to Poelitz passed off in order up to the stage where the Group formation was heading back after crossing the Baltic coastline. Then, a single Me 410 swooped through the bombers while hastily spraying his fire. It was Lt. Golubock's aircraft that was struck by the wildly directed spray of cannon shells. His No.1 engine was disabled and the left wing tanks were punctured to release a flow of gas. Luck was still with the crew to the extent that the gas stream kept clear of the engine superchargers, otherwise the result would have been instant ignition.

The crippled engine's propeller refused to 'feather', thus placing a tremendous sideways drag upon the airframe that could barely be countered through full winding-in of the rudder and aileron trim-tabs. The bale-out bell was rung, but just as a warning to the crew to prepare for possible bale-out; Sgt. Jones (TG) was already gone, after probably having his mind made up about the bomber's terminal condition on sighting the stream of gas! The other nine airmen stayed at their posts as course was taken up for Sweden and equipment was jettisoned. It was at this point that an even greater, if inexplicable, stroke of luck happened. A group of fighters approached from ahead but just flew straight past! It was Lt. Golubock's later opinion that the German pilots probably regarded the bomber as being already doomed and not worthy of wasting their ammunition upon. However, it was still airborne and theoretically capable of getting all the way back to England, so should have been dispatched. (A second more likely explanation for this conduct was that the fighters had expended their ammunition and were heading back to their airfield).

Whatever the explanation the ailing B-24 was steered out over the Baltic, past the Danish Island of Bornholm and up to Malmo. It was here that the crew experienced its third stroke of luck. One of the Swedish P-35 pilots approached from underneath to inspect the bomb bay whose doors had been knocked open by the Me 410's cannon shells. He came too close and ripped off his antenna mast on the bomber's left wing! It must have been a very thankful crew that touched down on a grass-covered airfield a few minutes later.

Twenty airmen were MIA but had received the continued gift of life either as internees or as POWs. This was sadly not the case for the twenty-first casualty, S/Sgt. Williams (68th BS) who was the engineer on Lt. Joy Smith's FLAK MAGNET (42-50381/D). A cannon shell from a Bf 109 struck the top turret and the fragments caused a deep wound in the Sgt.'s back. He fell onto the flight deck and expired shortly afterwards, despite the application of sulphanilamide powder and compresses. One of those attending Williams was Sgt. Sprowl who had received shell fragments in his scalp and who was in turn treated by a fellow-crewmember. A third airman was also wounded.

One of the returning bombers had been damaged on its left wing and fuselage; this was the 506th BS's 550328/Bar-D – PREGNANT PEG. When it was decided to deliver the B-24H to the 3rd Strategic Air Depot (SAD) at Watton, the catwalk was strengthened by the addition of a telegraph pole. This was inserted along the catwalk's length and braced by a jack, as well as being lashed in position by cables. The repaired machine was returned to Shipdham on 9 June and continued operations over the next two months.

The telegraph pole fixed through the center of the bomb bay is intended to strengthen the back of 42-50328. This was how it got its name the 'Flying Log' or 'Pregnant Peg.'

The 2nd BD's penultimate May mission was directed at Air Depots in northwest Germany. Very effective escort cover was provided by P-51s and P-38s; this situation was in direct contrast to the previous day over Poelitz when escort provision was reported as 'very poor' at the de-briefing session. The moderate flak over Rotenburg left several aircraft damaged but did not otherwise intrude upon an excellent bomb-pattern being achieved by the twenty-six crews led by Capt. Gildart and Major Lehnhausen (Command pilot). The same number of crews were sent out to strike marshalling-yards at Brussels on the 31st but were recalled due to bad weather conditions when just minutes away; however, mission 'credit' was granted. As May was exited the main event whose success was dependent upon a similar positive result for the Transportation Plan was just six days away – D-Day!

Chapter Nine

'And Morning shall Come ...'

In the autumn of 1940 after France had been forced to surrender to Germany Winston Churchill had broadcast to that subjugated nation's people in their own language. His quality of expression in that tongue was notoriously indifferent to poor, but his magnificent rallying call to emerge out of the darkness in which they were currently steeped, was particularly relevant to what was to transpire a full four years later. The final sentence was to the effect that the French should 'sleep well and gather your strength for the morning – for the morning will come, and its kindly light will shine on the brave and true'. Now in June 1944, Churchill's reassuring prophecy was on the point of being fulfilled, almost upon the fourth anniversary of his telling speech.

Such prophecies, however grandly expressed, were reflected upon in a much more diminished fashion by the personnel of the Allied military forces prosecuting the conflict in the west. However, there was a sense that the situation was building up to a climax in mid-1944. Rumours abounded as to the date and location of Operation OVERLORD, but in the meantime the Air Forces proceeded with their operational Brief by conducting a systematic battering of German defensive positions along the channel coast as well as striking at airfields.

It was only on 2 June that the 8th USAAF first ventured over the Continent when just over 800 out of the total dispatched Force of 926 bombers from all three Divisions dropped around 2400 tons of ordnance on V-1 locations within the Pas de Calais. Twenty-eight crews from the 44th BG went to Berck-sur-Mer and bombed through a solid undercast. (Official records are at variance with those at Shipdham, since the latter records clearly state coastal defences as the source of attack). The fliers were undoubtedly mystified by the requirement to fly a complicated series of 'dog-legs' over England that lasted for most of the mission-duration prior to actually heading out across the channel. The reason for this apparent senseless action would only become clear four days later. During the afternoon, missions to railroad and airfield targets between Paris and Normandy were mainly launched by the 1st and 3rd BDs.

Coastal defences in the Pas de Calais were the focus of attention for a lesser-sized 8th USAAF Force whose effort was again split between morning and afternoon sorties. The heavy cloud cover encountered forced the use of PFF methods upon the attackers so results were unobserved. The Group was fully involved in the morning assault, and dropped its bombs on gun batteries at St. Albins and Point de St. Quintine. The latter was visually attacked but was struck by mistake; this was of no consequence either tactically or in the broader strategic terms, because the Pas de Calais was not to be the focus for the actual Invasion. Four 66th BS crews went out with the 446th BG and 467th BG to provide PFF facilities during the afternoon.

Around this date an incident involving another Group's B-24 occurred at Shipdham. The personnel were watching several bombers straggling overhead, when one from the ill-fated 492nd BG operating out of North Pickenham was seen to drop out of the sky. The bombs were still on board due to the mission having been 'aborted' on account of poor weather. One of the fire-crews, including Sgt. Atchley and Pvt. Bunalski were off-duty and eating supper when the call came, and the crew responded by dashing to the crash-site in order to extinguish the blazing remnants. Suddenly one of the fragmentation bombs 'cooked off' in the heat and exploded, killing the two named personnel. The survivors recovered from being thrown to the ground by the blast. They continued to extinguish the fire

'Any Gum Chum' was B24J-125-CO, 42-110035/Y of the 68th BS, which operated out of Shipdham between its arrival on 27 March 1944 and its loss in combat on 7 July 1944.

despite the fact that the bulk of the bomb-load was still intact until ordered to move back by the Officer-in-charge. Also on hand were the Medics, who were expected to retrieve the crew's bodies in the face of the ammunition and oxygen bottles that were going off. Sgt. Mastradone (67th BS) recalled he and a fellow medic crawling along with a stretcher to and from the wreckage with at least two bodies, there being no survivors from among the B-24 crew. (Posthumous awards of the Soldiers Medal went to Archley and Bunmalski, while the Bronze Star went to S/Sgt. Provenzano, Sgt. Sulprizio, PFC Lazarewicz and T/S Schrack). This incident highlighted the fact that danger was often attendant upon numerous aspects of the ground echelon's work.

The bulk of the 2nd BD, including the 44th BG, was not called upon on the morning of the 4th but the Shipdham crews were also left out of proceedings for the afternoon sortie when railroad bridges around Paris were assaulted along with several airfields. The same exclusion scenario recurred on the 5th for all but six PFF crews all of whom were assigned to operate with the 95th CBW. The 489th BG was Lead Group, to whom 41-28690/B+ MISSOURI SUE, flown by Capt. Mazure, was attached. Also on board was the Deputy CO of the 489th BG, Col. Leon Vance, serving as Command Pilot. The initial bomb-run was non-productive due to faulty PFF equipment, whereupon Col. Vance ordered a second run with no alteration in height and speed. The flak gunners were zeroed-in by the time 'bombs away' was about to be signalled, and strikes on the lead B-24 killed Capt. Mazure as well as virtually amputating one of Col. Vance's feet. The hydraulic and electrical systems were shot out, the radio compartment destroyed and the right rudder and elevator shredded.

The bombs were still on board as Lt. Carper (CP) cut off power to the engines and held the damaged B-24 in a shallow glide back across the Channel. Lt. Bail (radar navigator) applied a tourniquet to Vance's thigh and then ordered the crew to bale out as the English coast was crossed. Vance refused Bail's suggestion, and the latter was finally forced to get out of the aircraft on his own. What happened then is primarily conjecture; opinions subsequently expressed felt that the Col. believed at least one crewmember remained who was too badly wounded to bale out. He therefore returned to the cockpit in a bid to 'ditch' the bomber and so provide a chance of survival for the individual or individuals concerned. His action was probably done with a view to avoiding the bomber crashing onto friendly soil and causing death or destruction.

During the brief crossing all but one of the bombs had been got rid of, but the single weapon's explosion was the probable cause for the aircraft disintegrating upon impact with the water. It was all the more amazing that Col. Vance not only survived, but furthermore, managed to swim towards the nearby shoreline. A vessel in the vicinity actually picked him up in the course of this latter effort. Leon Vance's perceived gallantry and devotion to duty was subsequently acknowledged when he was awarded the Medal of Honor. He was also the sole recipient of America's supreme military decoration earned by a B-24 crewmember of the 8th USAAF. (Tragically, he survived this horrendous mission, only to be one of the passengers declared 'missing' over the North Atlantic in the C-54 Evacuation aircraft taking them back to the United States).

On the late afternoon of the 5th a state of full security was established but the fact was not immediately circulated; for example, several 68th BS personnel who had just been granted passes were turned back by the gate-guards. The ground crews had already prepared their aircraft for operations that had already been 'scrubbed' on two separate occasions, so the restriction to base clearly suggested that something significant was looming up. Later in the evening Sgt. Kipnes was due to fly his thirtieth and last mission and remembered how the film the audience was viewing in the base cinema was turned off and the lights switched on. Then, Col. Hodges stepped up onto the stage and instructed all combat crews present to report for briefing while ground crews were also to proceed to their aircraft.

Those crews filing into the briefing room during what was still the dead of night, and who still had no inkling of what was about to unfold, were hardly surprised at being aroused so early. What did give them a charge was the reason for the mission – D-Day was on. The months of softening up the enemy's strategic and tactical strength was about to pay off. First, the Wehrmacht's ability to reinforce the intended Allied bridgehead was to be severely blunted by the shattering of both the road and rail communications into Normandy. Second, the virtual absence of the Luftwaffe over the region this day was in no small measure due to the depredations brought upon its fliers by the 8th Fighter Command in particular.

The reason for the seemingly pointless flight over England prior to completing the mission of 2 June now became clear. The 8th USAAF 'heavies' were to bomb coastal defensive positions ahead of the initial landings. In order to ensure an uninterrupted pattern of attack over what was a relatively congested airspace that would also be compressed in time, the Groups would have to fly protracted courses over the English countryside before slotting into their positions within the bomber stream. The case of the 44th BG was probably typical in this respect. Six separate sections each consisting of six led by a 66th BS PFF ship began to take off at around 0200 and the Group assembly completed at 10,000ft. at 0323 before the formation took up a north westward course to a second point east of Manchester. This was reached at 0402 (16,000 ft) where a looping right-hand orbit was made before swinging almost due south to a point south of Birmingham at 0505. The final stretch over England was slightly east of south and out over the coast to the east of the Isle of Wight at 0535. The T.O.T. (Time Over Target) for the bombing of locations at St. Laurent-sur-Mer and Colleville-sur-Mer was 0600, but in fact bombs were released at 0557.

The pitch-black skies combined with a solid overcast did not make for swift and easy assembly and contributed to one collision involving the B-24s of Sgt. Tom Parsons. and John McClane (both 68th BS). Parsons later remembered how his aircraft crossed too close under another and was forced upwards by the turbulent air. Thankfully the damage was confined to a mangled top section on one fin and rudder, and the crew continued onwards. (Parsons completed the last of his thirty-one missions on 17 October). Lt. McClane also recollected how his tail gunner had yelled out a warning about an encroaching bomber from below and the thump of the contact that damaged the underside of the tail. Up front in the Lead bomber was a familiar figure to most Shipdham personnel – this was their former Group Commander, Leon Johnson, who today was flying as Command Pilot.

The 44th BG was destined to have the honor of opening the entire bombing assault but the persisting undercast ensured that the results would remain unobserved. The six sub-formations, each consisting of six B-24s and headed by a PFF B-24 dropped on locations at St. Laurent-sur-Mer and

RAF Lancasters line up near the control tower. Their bases were 'socked in' and Station 115 proved to be the only available airfield open into which the crews could divert.

Colleville-sur-Mer east of Caen. The crews did at least have the satisfaction of seeing the vast shipping armada steaming across the Channel thanks to breaks in the clouds at this stage of the mission, although their impression of action on the beaches was limited to gun flashes thrown up from the Naval bombardment.

The Parsons crew slid thankfully onto their bunks after landing around noon, but their slumber was broken several hours later as they and other 68th BS crews were rousted out to fly a second sortie. The target this time was further inland at Vire but the bombs were not dropped even after repeated runs over the area by the twenty-four bombers that had been dispatched. Sgt. Parsons also noted that in the short period spanning the pair of missions, his B-24H (42-94892/U) had its damaged fin and rudder repaired. He also noted that after landing back and getting to his barracks well after midnight "I was more tired than I have been for a long time!" Combat flying was very much a young man's game but everyone was liable to reach a point of utter exhaustion that was no less mental as physical.

A third mission had earlier been flown by twelve aircraft to attack a defensive position at Foret de Cerisy, but once again the bombing results were unobserved thanks to the solid undercast; no PFF support was provided for this sortie.

J.T. Elias was a 68th BS gunner who later wrote a fine, under-stated account of the D-Day operation as seen through the eyes of a typical bomber crew:

"The 'Alert' had been posted on the bulletin board the previous evening but no crew caller had interrupted the sleepers in Hut 7. Still, with nerves on edge, all the guys had one eye open during the damp cold night, twisting and turning under their scratchy blankets. But the door had not suddenly opened, cruel lights turned on and an abrasive yell of "Up and at em'" had waked the heavy sleepers.

"Most were up by 8 am, and I turned on the radio as my first daily act. Soon after the music stopped and an announcer came on – it was the Big One. "Today, 6 June, Allied forces stormed onto the Normandy shores for the long awaited attack upon Hitler's Europe." Complete silence reigned for a minute, after which the day's routine resumed – we had expected this for weeks and shrugged off the news, although surprised we had not flown in support.

"Some of us went for breakfast, while several others roused the dormant fire in the tiny hut stove. Bread, jam and margarine was brought out, and Bob Keegan put on a pot of water for the coffee. (we preferred this to the powdered eggs or 'S… on a

The scene of utter devastation at Holland Hall, Garverston, Norfolk. 2/Lt. Raymond J. Sachtleben's 856th BS/492nd BG, B-24H-25-FO 42-95160S fell from the sky after pulling a tight turn to avoid a collision. The B-24 then spun onto her back and went into the clouds inverted to make violent contact with the ground at 17:30. Two fire crew members from Shipdham, tried to pull out some bodies but the fragmentation bombs on board 'cooked off', killing both men, who were awarded posthumous Soldier's Medals (Sgt. Atchley and Pvt. Bunalski). Incident occurred during June 1944.

shingle' put up in the Mess Hall). An overcast sky, damp air, cold wind – a typical Norfolk day greeted us as we tramped to the Aero Club for morning tea, toast, sandwiches, scones. Our two pretty English girls took our orders and smiled at our flirtations; they had months of experience fending off all kinds of offers from the woman-hungry GIs but still liked us. The Club's tables and chairs were a great improvement over the mess hall's equivalent facilities. Most talk was the normal – girls, passes to London, bikes, happenings at the local Higham pub. Yet in the back of our minds was the thought of men hitting the beaches, of friends in the paratroops, infantry, artillery – brothers and cousins facing bullets and cold steel.

"Back in the hut an hour later we were still on 'Alert' and shortly the crew caller came in with solemn eyes and subdued voice. "Your turn to go, men. Briefing at 1.30." All twelve airmen from the two crews sharing the hut now got ready, then got onto our bikes and headed for the Briefing room.

"We were going to Normandy, but would go in at 12,000ft. to make sure we hit the target and not our men. We made our preparations to fly, picking up flying clothes, escape kits, pistol, seeing our chaplain. Then on the truck for the ride out to 'Flak Magnet' where we threw jackets and 'chutes on board and sat down outside with the officers to await the control tower flare whether or not we were operational. 'Skipper' Smith conferred with Al Bogdonas (crew chief) who was so efficient, all 'Skipper' had to do was ask if all was OK. It always was, and we were never to 'abort' due to mechanical failure.

"This was the time to work off some of our tenseness and fear. Bobby Burns (TG) and 'Gino' began to wrestle while we egged them on. When they stopped, Kenny Sprowl (ROG) grabbed Johnny Shelton's (WG) hat and was chased round the plane, but as they rounded the tail the green flare went up. We boarded, all smiles gone, all was now business.

"The Group assembly went well once we broke through the first layer of clouds. We watched London slide by, its barrage balloons looking like little pearls, the suburban developments like tiny toy houses, and wondered if we would have the luck to go there on pass again. Then the coast, and the broad expanse of sea. The sun glinted on the restless water, which seemed to be painted with ships, large and small – ships everywhere, with one lane going to France, the other to England. We listened as 'Skipper' told about his amorous exploits in London, Powner (N) and Barlow (B) breaking in to tell of the women they had. Were they boasting? When men are facing Death, are facts the only things that matter?

"From the nose turret I saw the gaggles of planes, the vast shipping armada, and soon the dark land ahead, from which smoke columns were rising. We would be easy targets for the flak gunners at 12.000ft. As we moved inland I could see black bursts with dead red centers surrounding the Sqdns. up front. Seconds later, came the bumps that told us on the toggle to drop the bombs – I was to switch them out when the Lead Bombardier dropped.

"Sweat poured down my brow as I focused on the planes ahead. When, Oh when, would he drop? The ship shook and stumbled and wriggled as flak burst around. At last, the bombs fell. I flicked the switch, the plane rose momentarily as our bombs went out. We turned right. Then the plane shook almost out of control but 'Skipper' managed to right it. 'Gino's' voice said "No.4 is smoking." I could not turn around as I had to scan for 'bandits'. Moments later, 'Gino' had the fire under control and soon it was out. Now with three engines we were out of formation, but in mere minutes we were over the coast and away from harm.

"I looked down upon the smoking coast. Down there were my friends from home. Had they survived? Were they prisoners? Were they wounded and bleeding to death? Were they making progress or were they surrounded? Were they able to make progress? Were they wet and cold? Were they hungry? All these questions entered my mind. Here I was, up out of harms way, going back to a dry bed and hot food, and down there were my friends and relatives – and I did not know how they were faring.

"We flew back alone. We were leaving the action, but down there they would be in the thick of action for days, weeks. All the way back I prayed silently for those poor men down below, for those who had died in the assault, and for the living."

Lt. James Wright stands next to 'Corky' a B-24H-20-DT, 42-51101 of the 68th BS. 'Corky' was a veteran of sixty-five missions but would be lost on her sixty-sixth Mission on 28 January 1945.

The die was now cast for a decisive land campaign in western Europe that together with the other Allied 'pincer' offensive coming up through Italy and the relentless Soviet advance in the east was to throttle the life out of the Nazi threat to liberty.

The USAAF heavy bomber Force was by now built up to a level unheard of until late 1943. Then the dispatch of more than 300 aircraft was an event of note; now in mid-1944 a total of well over 1000 could be regularly quoted, while there were to be occasions when that figure was brought up to the 2000 level. An added bonus from this logistical advance was the splitting of the already pressurised Luftwaffe fighter strength by making attacks on several geographically distant targets.

Between 7-14 June, the 8th USAAF's bombing effort was concentrated over France and Belgium, with over 7000 individual bombers dispatched to pound marshalling-yards, rail and road bridges, airfields and similar tactical targets likely to disrupt the flow of reinforcements with which to counter the invasion armies. Eisenhower's promise to his soldiers, "when you look up and see aircraft they will be ours" was bearing its full fruit as the Luftwaffe's response was initially almost nil and indeed was never to gain any form of coherent strength in the weeks ahead

The pace of operations at Shipdham remained at a constant high pitch during June, with few breaks experienced by either the combat or ground crews other than when the weather intervened to cancel a mission. A road and rail 'choke-point' at Lisieux, a marshalling-yard at Angers, a return to Orleans/ Bricey airfield and bridges located at Montfort and La Passioniere formed the targets up to the 11th. The sole day's rest occurred on the 9th thanks to poor weather conditions. The latter date was also the first time the crews received the attentions of the Luftwaffe since D-Day. However, the Bf 109s and Fw 190s were few in number and inflicted no material damage. All these missions entailed no more than five hours flight time and progressed with little or no flak interference, although the bulk of bombing results were unobserved due to the cloud formations.

Next day (12th) was the first mission for Lt. H.C. Henry's 67th BS crew and they duly participated in a thirty-six strong assault dropping fragmentation bombs upon an airfield at Illiers L'Eveque. Lt. Jones (B) had decided to ride in the nose turret but his large frame, which was further expanded by his flying clothes, made this act impossible; he therefore swapped places with Sgt. Moore (RW). Just past Caen Sgt. Tillner (LW) opened up on a 'bogie' adjudged to be making an attack curve on the B-24. Neither he nor Jones was able to identify the aircraft but the incident proved that Tillner was correct to apply the basic principle of 'fire first and identify later'. (Bombers were ever at a basic disadvantage against fighters even when in formation, apart from which Allied pilots had it drilled into their minds that they were never to point their noses towards an Allied 'heavy' – to do so invited an inevitable 'gunner's greeting'!).

Concentration upon the tactical aspect of operations continued for most of the next week at Shipdham, although an Alert called on the 13th for the Merseburg/Leuna oil refinery in Germany was later 'scrubbed', as was a scheduled mission to the same target (16th). Chateaudun airfield (14th) was attacked but a second day's sortie to another airfield was cancelled. Bridges at La Frilliers and Tours and Melun airfield were hammered on the 15th and 17th respectively with a good concentration of ordnance seen on the first mission but with no similar confirmation over Melun due to solid cloud cover.

The use of Lead Bombardiers on whose B-24 the other bombardiers released their bombs dictated some form of instantaneous signal other than visual conformation. Smoke-flares and signal lights in the tail of the Lead ship were two technical aids. At Shipdham the 464th Sub-Depot staff created a third method, although the first 'test run' proved to be potentially lethal. T/Sgt. Wolbarst, the Group senior NCO I/C bombsight and autopilot maintenance, was involved along with S/Sgt. Goucher (68th BS armourer) and S/Sgt. Piela and a team from the sheet-metal shop. In Piela's possession was an aluminium plate, a foot square, onto which was secured four Verey-Pistols whose barrels were cut-down. The firing mechanism consisted to two modified bomb-rack releases; when cocked with a powerful spring and fired electrically, the effect was to activate the actuating arms that in turn hit the Pistol firing pins.

A 68th BS bomber was selected and the work begun during the evening. A slot was cut in the roof, followed by the riveting of the plate's top edge to a longitudinal stringer with the pistol barrels just protruding outside. T/Sgts. Wolbarst's expressed

B-24, 42-95142 was the third of four aircraft to carry the name 'Southern Comfort' and is seen here landing back at Shipdham.

feeling that the attachment arrangement was too flimsy brought a tart response from Piela. This was to the effect that he (Piela) wouldn't tell Wolbarst how to fix bombsights! S/Sgt. Goucher and Wolbarst then got on with their work of stringing wire back from the intervalometer to the waist location of the flare-tray, after which the pistols were loaded and cocked.

The control tower had been warned of what was to happen, and T/Sgt. Wolbarst returned to the nose and commenced the test. A loud bang, a crash of rending metal followed by sounds of hammering on the fuselage were all mixed up with blood-curdling yells from S/Sgt. Goucher by then standing outside. Smoke poured out of the waist window and the interior lit up by ricocheting balls of fire. It transpired that the recoil had pushed the pistol barrels below the roof, causing the flares to discharge inside! A large section of the roof was torn off, but the smouldering remnants had gone out before the fire truck arrived. S/Sgt. Piela's team were none too happy at having to start all over again. Worse still, was the fact that those airmen out on the roof began to get intermittent shocks from their electrical equipment, this being due to the late evening rain! By midnight the apparatus was re-installed and this time round the test went off perfectly. Later, as T/Sgt. Wolbarst was dropping off to sleep, he recalled with a start that the bomber had been fully laden with ordnance and fuel. The prospect of even one flare landing in an ammunition box would probably have seen not only an end to the test but also to the aircraft and its two attending airmen! (Had this happened, it would have made the fact that the mission on which the equipment was to be used was 'scrubbed' all the more tragic).

The first diversion from tactical operations in June occurred on the 18th when oil refineries in the Hamburg area were slated for assault by the 1st BD and 3rd BD, while the 2nd BD went for Luftwaffe control centers. In the case of the 44th BG both the Primary and Secondary was obscured and what ordnance was dropped was directed at Targets of Opportunity. A single squadron (68th BS) went out next day to Antheaux in the Pas de Calais but a second projected mission involving just the 67th BS was 'scrubbed'.

T/Sgt. Barlow, Lt. Howington's engineer, had last been mentioned during his original attempt to cross the Pyrenees in mid-March along with three of his crew when he had fallen ill and had to be left behind. What then transpired proved to be a combination of determination and good fortune, given that he was now isolated and possessed out-of-date ID papers for the border zone. He had decided to make his way back first to Toulouse and then Paris and this he achieved, but not without two slices of luck. The first came when he was stopped by two French policemen while waiting for a train at a station near Toulouse. Their hostility towards this individual who could not answer their questions turned positive when he explained whom he was, and they let him go. Next day, having failed to make any Resistance contact in Toulouse, he decided to make his way back to Paris. The presence of Germans in the ticket queue made him hesitate to speak French at the ticket desk. He finally moved away and approached another French policeman who duly obliged by purchasing the necessary item!

Back in Paris he made contact with his helpers and was later questioned on his failed attempt. The decision was taken to assist him again but it was three monotonous weeks before the bid was started. In the meantime he had been practicing callisthenics in order to ensure a more reliable physical state for what would be a gruelling journey.

Sgt. Hughlette H. Salter crew chief with his aircraft 'Channel Hopper.' This aircraft was fated to be lost on 21 July 1944.

Lt. Raymond Craig and crew. This photo was taken on the morning of 6 June 1944, 'D-Day', on return from the mission.

By mid-April Barlow was back in Toulouse along with several other evaders as well as Resistance members under threat of arrest. The party of forty-six was split into groups of six and given enough food for three days. However, the trek was fated to extend over a much longer period and food had run out by the fifth day. It was then, while resting in a barn that the crisis broke out. A guide ran up to say that a German patrol was fast approaching. Gunfire sounded out even as the evaders were scattering while their guides attempted desperately to at least delay the soldier's advance by returning the fire.

Barlow and two other American airmen, one of whom had a map of the area, had got together and decided to head east rather than south, on the assumption the Germans would be looking out for evaders taking the latter direction. An RAF evader was run into during the day, and all four staggered along until they came across a small cabin in which they stayed overnight.

Next morning they started up an extended slope whose crest (hopefully) marked the start of neutral Spanish territory. The group had found the initial going very difficult, and towards mid-morning noted a German patrol with dogs leaving the vicinity of the cabin. Now began a race to out-distance the soldiers – an unlikely act in view of the airmen's weakened physical state. Barlow was forced to leave his companion behind as he had collapsed; the other two were further ahead up the slope. All three managed to reach the crest and into its free-lined edge, but shortly after shots were heard.

Barlow's emotions were a mix of happiness at getting into Spain and sadness at what he thought was his companion's lethal fate. The latter emotion vanished a day or so later when Lt. Lyles walked into the hotel where his companions were staying. He explained that on recovering consciousness, and seeing the spurts of snow thrown up by the bullets, it had acted as a spur for him to struggle up the remaining distance onto the crest!

Two weeks now elapsed before the snow-blocked roads were cleared and the six airmen – two more had evaded capture after the ambush – were first moved down to Zaragoza and on to Gibraltar, the latter destination being reached in late May. Barlow was back in London on 1 June, and now was ready to depart for the States by aircraft.

The oil offensive was slowly winding up to its ultimate climax, and featured in the operational plan for the 20th. Nearly 2000 bombers were dispatched to industrial points in Germany, with the 2nd BD being assigned the refinery at Poelitz. (Several of the Division's Group also flew separate missions to strike at V-1 sites in the Pas de Calais). The crews were aloft for well over eight hours and encountered steady fighter attacks. By now the flak defences at Poelitz were large enough to provide a barrage that in the grim expression of the time was 'thick enough to walk on'. The M.P.I. was smothered in strikes in spite of the gunners' attention, but they left their mark upon a number of the B-24s – no less than twenty crews were fated to divert into Sweden off this single mission!

One of the Germans' victims in this respect was 42-94892/U – BATTLIN' BABY. This 68th BS B-24H had been involved in a mid-air collision on D-Day but had returned to Shipdham with a damaged fin and rudder. Its luck was out the second time around although it would still survive total destruction. Sgt. Ferrara (Eng.) recalled that flak disabled the electronic control for the engine turbo-superchargers. The waste gates stuck in the open position, so placing the units in the 'low blower' position and bereft of power. The bomb-run was not yet completed and the double disability provided by full weight and no superchargers left the aircraft as a straggler. Attempts after 'bombs away' to close the waste gates using a spare amplifier failed and so Lt. Keller called up the Group leader to say he was heading for Sweden 'with one engine out'. Fortune was on the crew's side as they managed to cross northern Germany and the Baltic with no further enemy attention before landing at Bulltofta airfield. (Ferrara's specific engineering skill saw him retained in Sweden to assist in repair of the B-24s on hand, whereas the other crewmembers were returned to England within weeks. He acted as co-pilot on several transit flights of the bombers back to England after World War II, one of which involved BATTLIN' BABY).

Berlin was on the target-list next day, and proved to be as tough a target as ever, with forty-five bombers taken down out of the formations. Genshagen in 'Big B's' southeastern suburbs contained the Daimler-Benz motor factory. Take-off at 0500 had Lt. Jones, bombardier on H.C. Henry's 67th BS crew noting "up again at midnight – how I wish they'd give us a rest!" The formations were routed to fly to the south east of the target before turning on the bomb-run. Cloud cover disappeared a few minutes before the bombs were released and the intensive flak barrage could be seen making its deadly effect upon preceding formations.

Lt. Howe's 506th BS crew were a well-seasoned team on their fourteenth mission and were able to handle the flak burst shortly before 'bombs away' that caused 42-100411 /E-Bar (67th BS) to fall out of formation. With the bomb-load jettisoned and no apparent serious damage inflicted the pilots decided

De-briefing on the run. This crew is being de-briefed after the first mission of D-Day; while this is going on the ground crews re-fuel and re-arm this 67th aircraft.

upon a heading for Sweden. The arrival of Bf 109s on the scene sadly put an end to this inviting prospect as their cannon fire riddled the left stabiliser and wing. S/Sgt. McConnaughhay (Eng.) watched one burst of fire trace a path up along the aircraft's spine and end by shattering his turret's Plexiglas. A blow to his neck and a sticky feeling within his flight suit convinced him he had been hit but he kept firing. He then recalled having a short panic attack at the prospect of bleeding to death from his suspected neck wound, followed by a complete reaction- reversal to one of fatalistic calm. The bale-out order was given and he got out of the turret and started to look for his chest-pack. This was finally found, but as he started to undo his heated jacket prior to donning the pack he noticed pieces of plastic falling out. Furthermore, the 'sticky feeling' then turned out to be sweat. So it was that his 'neck wound' was nothing more than the plastic striking him, with the 'blood' coming from his own sweat!

The Sgt's bale-out displayed his still confused state of mind, because his parachute did not open as he was expecting. It was only when he realised that his left hand was clasped over the ripcord hand and firmly preventing the latter from functioning that he eased up and took the necessary action! He landed safely, released his harness and ran over to a tree-shrouded pond; there he concealed himself by wading into the water. This ploy succeeded in keeping any search party from finding him, and he got clear of the area later that day. Then began his attempt to get through to Sweden, a stratagem that extended over ten to twelve days, but almost inevitably ended with his capture, and ultimate transfer to Stalag Luft 1, Barth. All but one of the other crewmembers was captured at the crash-scene. The unlucky exception was Lt. Henderson (CP) who was later adjudged to have been killed by civilians.

On board 42-95349/S – FLAK MAGNET, Lt. Barlow (B) and S/Sgt. Elias (LW) were frantically attending to a deep flak wound inflicted on Sgt. Shelton's neck. The blood-loss was so great at one stage that the gunner's survival was in doubt, but the basic medical attention bestowed by his fellow-crewmembers was sufficient to ensure his safe return and transport to hospital. (After release from hospital and while visiting London he suffered further (equally non-fatal) injury from the blast of a V-1 flying bomb!)

Tactical targets dominated the remainder of the month, although Bremen was attacked by the 1st and 3rd BDs on the 24th, and a wholesale assault on targets located in Central Germany was conducted five days later. The 44th BG made a 'double-header' effort on the 22nd when V-1 sites and St. Cyr airfield were struck. Laon/Athies airfield was hit next day followed forty-eight hours later by a precision strike at a

1/Lt. John W. McClane, Jr. Navigator 68th BS, stands next to his much beloved 'Lili Marlene', 260/P. He flew with another crew on the first mission of 6 June 1944. This flight nearly cost him his life when the aircraft he was in was involved in a mid-air collision. The quick thinking gunner called out the shadow approaching and only a glancing blow was made, after which McClane's B-24 went onto the target. John flew the second mission of the day with his own crew and in 'Lili Marlene.' (His pilot was not impressed with John's flying with another crew!).

powerhouse near Doullens. This latter target was bombed from 25,000ft. so it was all the more to the credit of the Lead Bombardier that the bombs landed accurately. Separate twelve-plane formations dropped on similar facilities at Abbeville and Amiens with greatly variable results – the latter target was completely missed! The 25th should have seen a mission to strike an airfield near Munich. Lt. Jones (67th BS) remembered the briefing being at 0230 and his crew later settled in their B-24 when the red-red flares signalling a 'scrub' were fired from the control tower.

Creil lay north of Paris and possessed a rail junction that was to become notorious as the most bombed example to emerge from the Transportation Plan assaults. A good-sized 2nd BD Force was dispatched but the results were almost nil according to official records. The 44th BG bombed using G-H in the face of intense and accurate flak. The damage so inflicted led to one MIA loss and at least five other aircraft diverting into other airfields in England, while the majority of the B-24s landing back at Shipdham bore evidence of strikes.

The 506th BS sustained the single MIA bomber and crew. Lt. Scudday was in charge of 41-29496/Bar-Q – TUFFY and Lt. McCormack (N) noted that the bomb-run was unusually long, while the G-H bomber was in his opinion 'all over the place'. Scudday was Deputy Lead in his sub-formation that had fallen well behind the Lead Squadron and his friend and fellow-pilot Lt. Winn remembered him yelling to the G-H aircraft to change altitude, otherwise the flak gunners would zero-in on the smoke marker dropped by the Lead squadron. The Squadron was bare seconds away from releasing its loads when the B-24 was struck. McCormack and S/Sgt.Tepe manning the nose turret managed to scramble out through the nose wheel doors while S/Sgt. Acuff (LW) was blown out of the rear fuselage, and only managed to clip on his chest-pack in mid-air. Another gunner also baled out but had the cruel luck for his canopy to be run into by another B-24's propeller; the shredded mass trailed the unfortunate airman to his death. Nobody on the flight deck could have survived its total destruction that blew out the roof and the side windows, after which the B-24 was seen to fall away into a spin.

Lt. Tucker was piloting 42-50339/Bar-C – FEUDIN' WAGON, which took direct hits on Nos.2 and 4 engines. Further damage was inflicted by fighters that affected the hydraulic and oxygen systems. Despite this, the crippled 506th BS bomber was kept aloft but began to experience problems with the remaining two functioning engines as it swept in over the north Kent coast and approached an airfield at Kingsnorth The main landing gear could not even be manually cranked down. T/Sgt. Romeo (nose gunner) was down in the nose trying to lower and lock it in position. He was alerted to the imminent crash-landing but for whatever reason did not move back before the impact. This had the effect of snapping the wheel back up into the compartment, whereupon the hapless airman was crushed to death. The crew were on their twenty-seventh mission, so the Sgt.'s death was all the more tragic, given that nobody else was even injured in the incident. (However, S/Sgt. Breakey (TG) was fated to die with another crew on what was to have been his last mission).

Lt. Anderson (68th BS) had a similar experience to Lt. Tucker in that two engines were disabled and the hydraulic system was not functioning. P-38s escorted the bomber to Manston, one of three emergency airfields on England's east coast with extra-long runways. There, the aircraft was eased into a smooth landing on the main landing gear; the nose ploughed into the ground thanks to the absence of the nose wheel, but the pilots brought their errant machine to a safe, if eventful, halt.

Ten airmen had gone down over France in the one aircraft but an eleventh joined them, although his B-24 had returned to England. On a previous mission a waist gunner on Lt. Stone's 506th BS crew (S/Sgt. Strange) had watched a B-24 from another Group catch fire after the crew had vainly attempted to plug the flow of gas from ruptured tanks. The aircraft finally caught fire and several of the crew baled out, but with their parachutes also on fire. He remarked to the other gunner (Sgt. Foust) that if a similar situation occurred to their aircraft he would not hesitate to jump.

Now, a similar scenario erupted when TUFFY was hit and set on fire. Then 41-28767/ L + had its fuel transfer pump in the bomb-bay hit and the gunners were immediately liberally sprayed by the gas. Sgt. Foust was busy throwing out 'Chaff' bundles, and thought nothing of it when Strange handed over his chest-pack. A few seconds later, while releasing his flak vest, he looked up just in time to see his fellow-gunner dropping out of the rear hatch! Lt. Stone was informed of the fact (he thought that Strange had actually been wounded because he called back to ask how bad was the injury, but was then informed of the exact situation) and now offered the same choice to any of the other airmen still on board 42-95209/W, but said he was sticking with his bomber all the way home. This was enough incentive for his offer to be rejected. On the way back T/Sgt. Brown (Eng.) managed to stop the flow of fuel by inserting a crude 'plug' made from an ammunition box splinter torn off and fashioned in shape by Brown's teeth! The landing at Shipdham was made on the grass in order to prevent the likelihood of sparks that could then create a fire.

The ninth mission for Lt. Carter' 67th BS crew on 42-52616/C-Bar – GLORY BEE proved to be the last for his co-pilot Lt. Arterburn. Flak took out the instrument wires and a hydraulic line along with three fingers on the unfortunate officer's right hand. The subsequent landing was fraught with danger, as one engine was 'out', the brakes and the left aileron were inoperable and one main tire had been punctured. Despite these problems the landing came off in good order, and Lt. Arterburn was swiftly removed for hospitalisation.

Group participation in 8th USAAF operations on the 28th was confined to the 66th BS, which dispatched six crews to provide PFF services for other Groups. It was back to full strength next day when a Krupp aircraft factory in Magdeburg was briefed as the target. Thirty-six crews flew the mission for the Group with an additional four PFF crews heading other units. Madgeburg was a large industrial center and was accordingly well provided with flak defences. The gunners threw up a concerted barrage against the attackers that in the 44th BG's case damaged the majority of the thirty-five B-24s completing the bomb-run.

The need to fly tight formation for the purposes of defence concealed the reverse risk of mid-air collision; any deviation from the formation raised this dreadful spectre, as occurred on this day. It was the 506th BS that for the second consecutive mission was to be involved in the loss of crews in this manner. Lt. Landahl's 42-511821/K – CAPE COD SPECIAL flying Lead in its element was one of the aircraft struck by flak just after 'bombs away'. S/Sgt. Rinaldo (TG) had his turret's Plexiglas shattered and was thrown backwards into the fuselage

Ground crew pose with 'Myrtle The Fertile Turtle', a B-24 J-55-CO 42-99967/E. This bomber was later coded Q following transfer to the 67th and then H with the 506th!

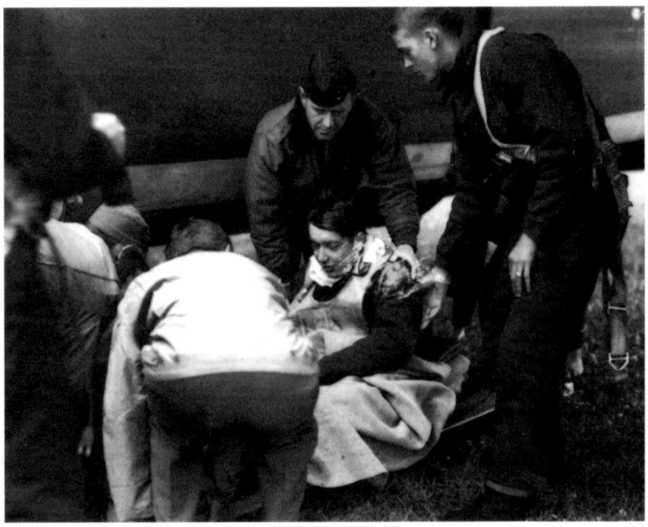

Captain Comer, flight surgeon gives first aid to right waist gunner S/Sgt. John H. Shelton from 1/Lt. Joy M. Smith's crew on return from the 21 June 1944 mission to Genshagen/Berlin.

by the shell's impact. He was barely back on his feet when a second impact again bowled him over, which he assumed was due to another flak strike.

Flying as right wingman in the same element was Lt. Westcott in 41-28829/Bar-H – MY EVER LOVIN' GAL. His B-24 was also being struck and after one burst S/Sgt. Lawrence (LW) was sent into the bomb-bay to check its condition; he found hydraulic fluid streaming out from the reservoir tank and reported the fact before returning to his position when an explosion occurred that literally threw him out into mid-air.

What Rinaldo and Lawrence had experienced was the collision between their B-24s, but which had run into the other was unclear from subsequent reports. The MACR for Landahl's bomber states that it slipped to the right and when attempting to pull out of formation its right wing struck the other B-24 behind the cockpit; it then went into a flat spin. Lt. Conzoner (B) said he saw Westcott's aircraft receive a strike that broke it up with the wreckage falling on his aircraft. Whatever the exact circumstances of the incident, two B-24s and nineteen airmen had been peremptorily 'written off'.

A total of nine who were alive at this point either baled out or was thrown out from the shattered remains. Lt. Conzoner remembered falling virtually alongside the nose section of his aircraft with assorted wreckage littering the sky. He was one of five survivors from his crew although six landed alive. The exception was Lt. Landahl who had received terrible lacerations to his abdomen as well as having both legs broken. Morphine was administered by Sgt. Lawrence and T/Sgt. DuBose from the Westcott crew, who had landed close to where the pilot lay. All their efforts proved to be in vain as Landahl slipped out of life shortly after.

A 67th BS aircraft flown by Lt. Henry came back with a wounded waist gunner, S/Sgt. Tillner. Flak strikes on 42-99967/ Q-Bar – MYRTLE THE FERTLE TURTLE left the gunner with a shell fragment in one leg. Lt. Jones (B) provided First Aid by applying sulfa powder, but did not add a tourniquet due to the blood-flow virtually ceasing thanks to the sub-zero temperature. Tillner also refused the offer of morphine and he endured a three-hour flight back. A following ambulance picked him up once the B-24 had taxied in, and after recovering from his injury he was transferred out to Italy where he completed his combat tour.

The pace of operations in this ultimately decisive month of June 1944 was almost non-stop. The Group combat crews had put in no less than twenty-four missions or an average of almost one per day. In addition the figure had put Shipdham

Lt. Harold Morrison and crew from the 66th BS.

well on the way to completing its second century of missions – a total that would be achieved in no more than one third of the time spend in completing the first century!

July 1944

July was to witness a more balanced division between strategic and tactical targets for the RAF and USAAF 'heavies', but it would be the middle of September before Gen. Eisenhower handed back un-fettered control of the bombers to ACM Harris and Gen. Spaatz. The start of the V-1 'Flying Bomb' offensive on June 13 had given added urgency to the task of at least blunting the robotic assault by bombing the numerous launching pads. (Known as 'ski-jumps' due to their ramp-like structures). The 44th BG was not involved on these 'No Ball' missions of 1-2 July, and it was not until the 4th that the 44th BG dispatched twenty-eight crews to bomb Beaumont-le-Roger airfield. This was part of the latest ground-support effort for the Allied armies, still fiercely locked in battle with the Wehrmacht within the Normandy bridgehead. On the way over Lt. Schaefer (68th BS) was forced to 'abort' in 42-100412/V – V FOR VICTORY. The initial problems caused by both the No.2 engine and propeller developed to a point where it would not have been safe to attempt a landing, and so the pilot called for a bale-out south of London. The bomber crashed in a field near Guildford, Surrey.

Only part of the 2nd BD that did not include the 44th BG was called upon for the 5 July missions, but Kiel (6th) demanded the services of the 14th CBW out of the three CBWs dispatched; the 66th BS flew PFF Lead for no less than four other Groups as well as its own Group. All aircraft returned safely but there was still one 'write-off'. This was 42-100637/F whose pilots had 'aborted' after losing No.1 engine. The bomber was on the landing approach when it faltered and crashed heavily just off the airfield. It was a miracle that the bomb-load did not display its potential volatility and blow aircraft and crew apart; in fact all crewmembers emerged with little or no injury!

A mix of oil and aircraft-production sources in Germany were selected next day with the 14th CBW going in to blast Bernburg in the face of moderate but accurate flak as well as the Luftwaffe. The latter form of resistance largely came from twin-engine Me 410s, and when the Group circled to land at Shipdham it was short three crews.

The losses had occurred as the Group was beginning its run from the I.P. The first attack came in from ahead and among the bombers hit was 42-110053/Y – ANY GUM CHUM flown by Lt. Steinke (68th BS). This B-24 was in the process of moving up front to take the place of the Lead bomber when the fighters struck. Returning personnel stated that the No.4 engine was shot out after which the B-24 developed a steep right-hand bank and was seen to crash. Lt. Mitchell (N) was on his twenty-ninth mission and feels sure that his escape from the spinning bomber was due to his being pushed out by Lt. Hybarger (B) after he had vainly tried to push open the nose wheel doors. The navigator had a broken leg and was paralysed below the waist. When he landed, he removed his Mae West and waved it to attract attention. Civilians then arrived, who placed him on a cart and took him to a barn; there he remained until later picked up by military medical personnel to begin a three-month spell in traction. He was told that his crew were alive, but in fact only S/Sgt. Malinwycz (ROG) had shared Mitchell's good luck.

The initial fighter attack took care of a second 68th BS crew flying in 42-99966/W – FULL HOUSE and on their 23rd mission. Lts. Weaver and Shambarger managed to correct the resultant descent out of and behind the formation after losing a good proportion of their engine power. Worse still was the inability to feather two of the propellers as the crippled bomber made for England. In the end, fire took hold of these engines as the aircraft was crossing the Dutch/German border close to Emmen. All ten airmen jumped or in the case of the seriously injured Sgt. Nalipa (LW) were assisted out; unfortunately, although he was conscious at the time, he did not act on the advice to pull the ripcord and was killed. Lt. Shambarger was apparently stabbed to death by a member of the Dutch Nazi Movement who had apprehended him. (This man was tried and sentenced to an 8 1/2 prison-term after the war). Lt. Weaver

'Feudin Wagon' was a B-24H-20-CF, 42-50339/ C of the 506th BS. Received on 4 May 1944, the Aircraft was finally 'written off' following a crash landing at Kingsnorth in Kent on return from Creil, in France on 27 June 1944.

'Full House', a B-24J-55-CO, 42-99966/W of the 68th BS was received on 21 January 1944 and survived until 7 July 1944 when it was MIA. Lt. Weaver (pilot) managed to evade capture and seven of his crew survived to become POWs.

had the luck to crawl into hiding and was later picked up by the Resistance who sheltered him for many months before he effected a return to Allied-liberated territory. The other seven crewmembers joined the long list of American 'Kriegies'.

The third loss also came from the 68th BS. Lt. Wilson's 42-100170/G – PATSY ANN II fell out of formation with a disabled No.1 engine and trailed behind as the turn for home was made. Fighters then closed in on the straggler, their gunfire starting a fire in the bomb-bay as well as knocking out the rudder controls. This latter item of damage probably caused the bomber to enter into a spin, whereupon those still on board at this stage also baled out. There was one fatality, S/Sgt. Yocco

(ROG) being the airman in question. (Lt. Wilson was a substitute for the crew's regular pilot Lt. Morrison who had finished up ahead of the others; they had arrived in late February and were another team well on their way to tour-completion).

The diary notes of Sgt. Uvanni (67th BS ROG) flying with Lt. Bieber on their first mission paint a starkly simple picture of the Bernberg run; "On the wall-map a red line stretched all the way to Bernberg. We were briefed to expect fighters as this is a fighter region, as well as flak. About five minutes before target time we were hit. We flew in the Lead element and were right up front. Approximately sixty fighters lined fifteen abreast came from one o'clock and slightly high. You could see orange shells coming through the air. None of our 67th BS planes was hit, but an entire Sqdn of twelve was knocked out on this first pass; some blew up and others went into dives and never came out. Several chutes came out ... the Germans were strafing some of these." (Uvanni's B-24 had over 200 holes in its airframe but none of the crew was even injured. This was a bad day for both the 14th CBW and the 2nd BD. Nine crews were lost by the CBW and twenty-eight by the Division; the worst affected unit was the 'hard luck' 492nd BG with twelve, and destined to lose one crew for each mission of its short existence).

It was a very small formation of ten that participated in next day's short run that was largely intended to strike tactical targets. Bad weather forced a 'recall' for most of the Groups, but several sought out Targets of Opportunity. The 44th BG had been heading for Esternay in France, but diverted eastward to bomb a railroad bridge on the Island of Zuid Beveland in southwest Holland.

Munich was located deep in southern Germany and meant a prolonged, tiring flight for the crews on the 11th. Twenty-two aircraft formed the basic Group contingent with eight more 66th BS aircraft functioning in their specialist role. The main formation was initially reduced by two when Lts. Bartlett and Herring (67th BS) 'aborted', and was then further reduced by one MIA aircraft; in addition one of the PFF contingent failed to return.

During the bomb-run on Munich (the Primary of Reim airfield was clouded-out and so a PFF run on the city was substituted) Lt. Bonnet lost the No.4 engine oil-pressure on 41-29544/T – FLAK ALLEY II. He switched off power, 'feathered' the propeller and proceeded with his bomb-run. Formation was held until well on the way back when a similar failure led to the same action being taken with No.2 engine.

Lt. James D. Moos, bombardier on Lt. Morrison's 66th BS. crew.

B-24J-125-CO, 42-110035Y 'Any Gum Chum' displays its nose art. This bomber was another loss on 7 July 1944.

Above: Lead aircraft of this 'elephant train' is 'Down De Hatch' of the 506th BS. A B-24H-20-FO 42-95016/Z, this aircraft joined the 506th BS on 1 May 1944. It would be RZI on 31 May 1945 and by the wars end the aircraft would acquire ninety-two bomb symbols under the cockpit window. She was one of just a few aircraft to gain such combat longevity.

Right: B-24J-75-CO, 42-100170G of the 68th BS failed to return on 7 July 1944. This aircraft was shot down seven kilometers south of Halberstadt in Germany. Lt. Wilson and all but one of his crew survived their bomber's demise.

Now on its own, the B-24 was picked up by P-38s. Just as the coast was reached No.3 engine went out, so the pilot called Colgate in accordance with 'distress' procedure while jettisoning all available equipment. Hopes of maintaining altitude quickly faded and the crew were ordered to their 'ditching' stations. The frailty of the B-24 airframe when subjected to the brutal pressures of 'ditching' was fully exposed. The fuselage broke apart in the middle as well as fracturing around the top turret area. The four crewmembers in the rear section were lost when it immediately sank beneath the waves, while T/Sgt. Kushinski (Eng.) was probably trapped or crushed by the top turret. The remaining four airmen were later rescued.

The 66th BS loss involved 41-28776/E+ whose pilot was Lt. Zweig and which was also bearing the Command Pilot, Major Conrad. Flak over Munich had inflicted damage to this B-24 that included serious fuel loss. Over Belgium on the way home Lt. Zweig indicated to the Deputy Lead aircraft of the 448th BG that he should take over, since he (Zweig) was critically short of fuel and therefore going to make a more direct route back. The aircraft was near Lille in Northern France when power began to fail and bale-out procedure was started. Sadly, only four out of the twelve airmen got out before the aircraft reportedly went into a spin and crashed. Lt. Zweig, Lt. Quail (N) and Major Conrad were soon in contact with the Resistance after being sheltered by the local population and ultimately returned to England; Lt. Mollen (radar op.) had broken a leg and ended up a POW.

Major Lehnhausen (68th BS CO) was Command Pilot when the Group went back to Munich twenty-four hours later. Bombing was again conducted by PFF method but this time around all participating crews returned, having delivered their bombs upon the city's marshalling-yard facilities. The next two missions (13th and 16th) also involved a double run to the same location, in this case Saarbruecken. On both occasions the 2nd BD was assigned to hit the city's marshalling-yard complex, which was an important potential 'feed-point' for reinforcements filtering through to Normandy. Bombing was again conducted by PFF method; no aircraft losses were suffered while battle damage was minimal.

A more direct form of tactical mission was flown on the 18th when the bombers effort was in support of Gen. Montgomery's drive against the city of Caen. In the case of the 44th BG all but the 506th BS struck positions at Troarns; the latter squadrons took on the 'last resort' target of marshalling-yards at Mezidon.

Three German-based targets occupied the 19th to the 21st. First up was Ruesselheim but cloud over the Primary saw the Group swinging back northwest towards Koblenz, whose marshalling-yards were pounded. Erfurt/North airfield was the selected target for the 14th CBW (20th). In contrast to several consecutive 'deep penetration' missions, today's target was bombed visually, but with the same pleasant lack of aircraft and personnel losses being experienced.

The third consecutive run was yet another 'deep penetration' run to Oberpfaffenhofen situated near Munich, and which possessed important armament production plants. The absence of the Luftwaffe over the past two weeks was broken today when a Force estimated at around thirty fighters make intermittent assaults from six o'clock. Flak was moderate but intense and contributed to the latest 'black day' for the Group.

Nose art of Lt. Allen's aircraft that went down on 21 July 1944. Bomber was 42-110034, a B-24J-125-CO named 'Southern Comfort II.' All but one of Lt. Allen's crew survived as POWs.

Lt. J. Anderson (68th BS) had managed a two-engine return from the Creil mission on 27 June, but would not come home this time round, although the fates were still kind to all but one of his crew. Flak had knocked out No.1 engine and bombs had been salvoed ahead of reaching the target; Lt. Hewlett (N) recalled that the bomb-doors were still closed when this action was taken! S/Sgt. Babin (Eng.) then informed the pilots that his estimate of fuel reserves was not sufficient to get back to England. The navigator was taken aback when Lt. Anderson asked for a heading to 'Sweden'. When he was tactfully reminded that he was a long way away from that country he corrected himself by yelling "No, no, I mean Switzerland!" Its neutral soil was invitingly at hand and the B-24 was headed in that direction. Lt. Hewlett had only his flak map with which to fly a course and when his calculations indicated they were there, the pilots could find no airfield on which to deposit their aircraft. Finally, all ten airmen baled out; a partially opened parachute was attached to the harness of S/Sgt. Hoffman (LW) when his dead body was discovered near St. Gallen. The bomber crashed at Silberplatte. (Lt. Hewlett felt a sense of guilt at contributing to Hoffman's fate, however unwittingly. He reasoned that had he possessed a proper map of Switzerland, he could have directed Lt. Anderson to an airfield, thereby preventing a bale-out

Ground crews take a welcome break for coffee from the Red Cross bus.

A second 68th BS crew were MIA in 42-95226/C – CHANNEL HOPPER, but shared their fellow squadron airmens' fate. Their B-24 was flak damaged after 'bombs away' and suffered the loss of the hydraulic system as well as having the bomb-bay doors open. The latter problem was of concern as the aircraft was headed towards Switzerland, because this could signal a hostile intent and therefore invite a defensive reaction from the Swiss gunners! However, the crew's dilemma lay in the fact that the central fuel tanks had ruptured and sprayed the interior – the doors had to remain open in order to let the fuel escape and thereby reduce the risk of an explosion As it so happened, the Swiss fighters picking up the bomber held their fire and the landing at Dubendorf was brought off at the expense of a collapsed nose wheel.

The two remaining losses came from the 506th BS, and although the crews were not as fortunate as the 68th BS duo in being interned, all but one of the personnel concerned survived as POWs. Lt. Allen's 42-110034/Bar-R – SOUTHERN COMFORT II was another victim of flak batteries around Munich that knocked out one engine and led to contact with the formation being lost. Further flak hits on the way towards a possible haven in Switzerland shot off part of a stabiliser as well as firing one wing, where-upon the crew jumped. S/Sgt. Kempowicz (ROG) had been present at Pearl Harbor on 7 December 1941 and had also reportedly been involved in a mid-air collision during his training-up period in the States. Today's incident was a case of 'third time unlucky' since his parachute did not open. (The fact that he was pushed out by his fellow crewmembers suggests he was injured or disoriented in some way).

Lt. Butler's 42-95142/Bar-K – CAPE COD SPECIAL #2 suffered a large hole in one wing and was steered towards Switzerland, but took further hits on the way that took out an engine and blew off part of one stabiliser. The pilots realised that they were not going to gain neutral airspace and baled out the crew, all ten of whom ended up as POWs.

Among the returning bombers in the Shipdham landing pattern was 42-95207/Bar-Q, also from the 506th BS. This aircraft had suffered damage to the left wing including the landing gear while the right tire was shot out. The pilots brought off a successful crash-landing in the circumstances, but the extent of the damage resulted in the B-24J being declared 'salvage' around one week later.

It had been seven weeks since the Allied Forces had stormed the Normandy beaches. Since then, the ground battle had proved to be a hard slog in the Bocage countryside. Narrow roads with high sides and enclosing hedges provided an excellent defensive background to the Germans' dogged resistance. Forward progress had been made albeit slowly and at considerable cost in men and their weaponry. However, the U.S. Armies on the right flank positioned in front of St. Lô were now in a position to launch a massive thrust that would take their armour and infantry eastwards. At the same time the British and Canadian Forces battling on the left flank were finally breaking through beyond the city of Caen to begin their advance that was ultimately intended to link up with the Americans.

B-24H-25-FO 42-95226/C 'Channel Hopper' from the 68th BS sits tail high after landing at Dubendorf, Switzerland on 21 July 1944. The aircraft was hit by flak near the target shortly after 'bombs away.'

The role of the USAAF bombers in what was code-named Operation COBRA was to destroy or disrupt the Wehrmacht defensive positions ahead of the ground advance. The weather once again intruded upon the planning by proving unsuitable on the 24th although about one third of the 1500 'heavies' dispatched did manage to drop their loads. The thirty-seven crews of the 44th BG were not among this number although they were granted mission 'credit'. Next day provided clear conditions with little or no danger of bombs falling short and among the 1st. Army soldiers. (Unfortunately, two incidents

Two 67th BS ground crew shelter from the wind: they are Cpl. Grady Fogelman and Horace Grisham.

did occur, causing the deaths of some 102 personnel including Gen. McNair; this added to a similar incident on the 24th when twenty-four fatalities were incurred). Thirty-six 44th BG crews went over to add their ordnance to the assault while leading the entire 2nd BD; the immediate result of the aerial assault was to leave the German defenders in no position to resist the breakthrough around and past St. Lô. The moderate attack altitude of 13,000ft. led to a number of bombers being struck by flak but all returned to Shipdham. One of the damaged aircraft was 42-99997 flown by Lt. Green (67th BS), but the Fortunes of War were destined to be cruelly unkind to the pilot and his crew just four days later.

Three frustrating days passed with each involving 'scrubbed' missions before the next mission was completed (29th). Bremen possessed a large oil-refinery at Oslebshausen that was allocated to the 2nd BD. In the course of flying the last forty-one missions, the hitherto embattled 67th BS had witnessed a complete change in fortune, in that no crew had been lost in action. That record was now broken in the most tragic manner possible, since it was self-inflicted.

The Group had formed up and were departing the coast over Cromer. Flying in the No.3 position in the 506th BS second element was Lt. Eberhardt in 42-95309/V-Bar. In the same position within the left Low element was Lt. Green (67th BS) in 42-109820/N-Bar – THE WASPS NEST. The formation made a left turn that saw Lt. Green's element slide under that of Lt. Eberhardt's element. At the same time Lt. Eberhardt's aircraft nosed downwards under the malign influence of prop wash, and a collision occurred. The No.2 propeller literally excised the entire tail on THE WASPS NEST, which threw the bomber into an uncontrollable dive. The other B-24 went into a flat spin and joined its hapless companion in smashing into the sea. All but one of the nineteen airmen was lost. Just three bodies were recovered by ASR boats called to the scene, with a fourth reclaimed from the sea at a later date. (S/Sgt. Favors, Lt. Eberhardt's engineer, had anticipated what was about to happen and had snapped on his chest-pack. He was still lucky to survive, especially as he had to fight against centrifugal forces as his aircraft spun down).

Bremen was attacked through solid cloud and proved to be the penultimate mission for July. The chemical-production facilities at Ludwigshafen absorbed the brunt of an assault by 447 B-24s on the 31st of which over thirty were provided by Shipdham.

Mission return. Tired crews taxi back to their hardstands after yet another mission to the Invasion area. The outboard right engine is 'feathered' on the lead B-24.

Chapter Ten

Breakout to Stalemate

The U.S. Armies' breakout at St. Lô in late July was the beginning of a two-month period of dramatic Allied advance through France, Belgium and southern Holland. At one stage in September the prospects of penetrating Germany's natural western barrier – the river Rhine – and gaining access to that nation's heartland, and by extension forcing a general capitulation by the year-end, appeared bright. (The tension between Russia and its current Allies that would lead to the Cold War was already in evidence. Consequently, within some Allied circles, a political as well as a military benefit was regarded as an important secondary gain arising from this scenario, in that the Soviet advance was likely to end considerably further east than actual events were to dictate).

The strategic Bomber Commands were still splitting their overall effort between tactical support and the hammering of Nazi industry during August. Airfields and bridges at Rouen and around Paris were the assigned targets to open the month for the 2nd BD. The 44th BG had only partial success when attempting to bomb a railroad bridge at Corbie through 9/10 clouds. The 67th BS element did unload its ordnance on an alternative bridge but the other two Sqdns. had no such luck. The 66th BS had none of its PFF aircraft assigned to this mission but next day the reverse situation occurred when it alone sent out three B-24s equipped with H2X or G-H for allocation to the 458th BG and 466th BG. The indifferent weather continued to hinder the bombing of 2nd BD targets on the first of two missions launched on the 3rd; part of the 44th BG managed to strike a Target of Opportunity however.

The 8th USAAF completed a 'double-header' for the second successive day, the first of which struck at German targets and the second at V-sites and Franco/Belgian coastal batteries. Kiel proved to be a major effort for the Group with thirty-nine crews taking part, with thirty-eight completing the run and results assessed as 'good to poor'. The second Group mission was, by comparison, small in terms of numbers with just four crews participating to form a composite Group with the 392nd BG and 492nd BG. The latter operation was of some significance for the Shipdham fliers and their ground support because it marked the 200th time the Group had been granted credit for a mission!

Brunswick had already been visited by both the 2nd BD and the 44th BG on several occasions and received its latest baptism of fire next day (5th). The Group ordnance was released with PFF assistance although the target was visible; the poor results achieved by the 67th BS were made up for by the other two squadrons. Then it was back to another prime – and highly respected, if not feared – target in the form of Hamburg and its oil refineries. Germany's second industrial city was packed with flak batteries whose gunners managed to damage a high proportion of the 310 B-24s getting through to their Primary targets as well as culling a number from our of the formations.

One of the MIA losses involved a 66th BS crew assigned to the Deputy Lead position within the 492nd BG. The Group was starting to withdraw after the bomb-run, having survived an intensive sequence of flak barrages, when Lt. McKenna flying 42-95561/I+ was forced out and down, supposedly to avoid a collision with another B-24 that was on its back and coming down from above. The bomber was levelled off and the pilots began to climb back up, but a tracking-pattern of flak shells caught up with its prey at this point. The No.3 engine disintegrated and parts of two cylinders burst through the side to land on the lap of Lt. LeRoux (Radar-Nav.). The Lt.'s hands were badly burnt in dislodging these large fragments but he was fortunate in the circumstances that he was not more seriously injured or killed. The bomb-bay was well alight and LeRoux's attempts to gain access to the fire-extinguisher on the bulkhead behind the co-pilot were thwarted by another crewmember who had 'frozen' at his post and was blocking the way. All normal escape routes from the cockpit appeared to be closed off, with LeRoux now unable to use his hands to clamber out by the roof hatch. Then he remembered the hole blasted in the fuselage by the engine cylinders and made for the gap. Fortune was on his side. He was wearing a backpack parachute and was able to squeeze out into mid-air – an action that would have been impossible to achieve with the standard chest-pack, given the narrow nature of the split. (Fortune favoured him even further because one foot snagged as he attempted to exit and it was only the force of the slipstream along with his determined wriggling that finally got him free!). His descent and swift capture was by comparison almost an anti-climax. Only Lt Tucker (Pilotage-Nav.) out of the six-officer complement joined LeRoux in surviving, whereas all but one of the six Enlisted Men – T/Sgt. Sheldon (Eng.) – baled out safely. (The fire in the bomb-bay must have subsided at some stage because Lt. Tucker baled out from this position).

Hamburg, Germany 6 August, 1944. The 44th BG are high above the major industrial city's dock area and on the bomb run. Lt. Bentcliff is at the controls of B-24J-1-FO 42-50626 'My Gal Sal.'

Preparations for the 200th mission celebrations were made over the next four days, but in the meantime the Group went out on three occasions. Two of the run were to northern and central France respectively, with tragedy striking on the latter date. First sortie was to Saleux close to Amiens where the 14th CBW at the head of the 2nd BD was itself led by the 44th BG. A cascade of M47 incendiaries went down on a fuel storage dump.

The second day's run into France was deeper, being to Romilly southeast of Paris, whose airfield at La Perthe was bombed with M47 incendiaries. The crew led by Lt. Komasinski was on its seventh mission and on the way to becoming a thoroughly seasoned combat team. Today was to be the end of the line for their operational career, however. Their B-24 (42-100415/Y -MY PEACH) was last reported with two engines 'out' and a third on fire. In fact the doomed bomber was destined to fly onward after the pilots had set the autopilot and ordered a bale-out. Not only did all ten airmen parachute safely, but also nine of them got into Resistance hands and were sheltered until American ground forces liberated the region!

T/Sgt. Schaeffer (Eng.) recalled how the No.2 propeller began to 'runaway' up to 4500 revs, a condition that no amount of counter-action with throttle, feathering button, or synchronisation switch could adjust. Schaeffer had gone into the bomb-bay to turn off the fuel selector valve, fuel booster pump and generator but with equal lack of success. Lt. Gippert (CP) ordered the feathering fuse be replaced but this bomber was configured for circuit breakers. The co-pilot pressed all four red buttons but this proved useless since the breaker did not pop. By now, engine oil pressure was zero, which rendered any feathering action null and void. (The sub-zero temperature had probably thickened the oil in the propeller spinner).

Schaeffer's bid to bale out following the order to jump nearly proved fatal. While manoeuvring round the outside of the bomb-bay catwalk his chest-pack's ripcord handle snagged on a bomb-shackle, spilling the canopy. A momentary thought about seeking out a spare chest-pack was quickly dispelled, and he took the chance of the canopy snagging or ripping as he crouched and rolled out into mid-air. His descent was interesting, the parachute swinging him almost through 180

Left to right: Lt. James P. McKenna Pilot and Lt. Paul Greno. This photo was taken during December 1943. Both men lost their lives on 6 August 1944 while flying the mission to Hamburg.

degrees at times with the attendant danger of canopy collapse. The harness straps were cutting into his crutch thanks to the force of the parachute deploying that had pushed him downwards and the thin air at the bale-out height left him weak.

Having got down safely and disposed of his harness he was shot at and missed, but managed to evade capture and get in contact with the local population some of whom who provided him with clothes, food and transport; others were (naturally) so afraid of what would be done to them by the Germans that they refused to do anything. His first move after being attended to was in a horse-drawn cart to a wood where he was temporarily concealed. Two men then turned up whistling a previously agreed tune as a recognition signal, and bearing a bottle of cider and a single cigarette. They left but reappeared at dusk, after which the trio began a lengthy cross-country hike that ended in a wood. Here a second pair of Frenchmen took charge for what turned out to be a continuation of the hike. It was midnight before the small group reached a house at Orlais L'Abbaye near Rheims where Schaeffer thankfully slumped onto a waiting bed.

Here he remained for the duration of his short time in enemy territory in the company of the Benier family. Although discouraged from going away from the house, he could enjoy fresh air and still escape observation in the high-walled garden. His activities were very restricted and a French playing-card pack was his sole, but very temporary, relief from boredom during the day. However, a regular companion during the evenings was a French secret agent 'Shorty' (Louis Guyomard) whom he assisted with his radio transmissions; on a more social level the two men pitched hay in the barn or looked after the hive of honeybees! On the 28th, the rumours of advancing American units reached fruition when Patton's Third Army arrived in Orlais L'Abbaye. The celebrations over the next day or so reached fever pitch with flowers, wine, homemade flags and numerous members of the F.F.I. sporting their armbands.

A second 506th BS crew had earlier 'aborted' the mission in 42-50328/D. This B-24H was originally named PREGNANT PEG. Following heavy damage off a late May mission to Poelitz, the aircraft had had its bomb-bay shored up with a telegraph pole prior to being transferred to 3rd SAD for repair. A reputed name-alteration to FLYING LOG was made in the light of this 'lash-up' adjustment, and the aircraft had returned to combat in early June. Lt. Jacobs brought his bomber back to Shipdham with one engine 'out'. After entering the airfield circuit the pilots inexplicably began a turn into the 'dead' engine. The inevitable result was that their aircraft fell into a spin and

A member of the 464th sub depot engineering section at work. The 464th were the specialists, who manufactured and repaired parts for the squadrons of the 44th.

A goodwill trip was made to the 8th USAAF bases by this RAF Avro Lancaster and crew. S for Sugar (R5868) served with Nos.83 and 467 (Australian) Sqdns. and she carries the PO codes for the latter unit. The bomber put in an astonishing 137 'Operations' (RAF term for missions) between late 1942 and April 1945. PO: S can still be seen today proudly displayed in the RAF Museum at Hendon, London.

the resultant impact and explosion of part of the bomb-load left no survivors.

It was probably the aftermath of this crash that Lt. McClane, a 68th BS navigator, commented upon later. He had come upon the crash site where members of a British bomb-disposal team were working. Found close to the main impact crater of the crash were the pilots, still secured in their seats. Their physical state was appalling, with arms and legs burnt to stumps and their entire frames charcoal black. The attempt of the team to pull one of the bodies out of the seat with a rope simply ended with the torso literally falling apart 'like an overdone roast' in the Lt.'s words. An un-burnt glove picked up by John was hastily dropped when he realised it was still occupied. Finally, as he walked around the crash-site, one of the team said, "Look what you are standing on, Guvernor" – it

Left: A 506th BS aircraft taxies past RAF Lancaster's parked in front of the Control Tower. The RAF crews couldn't make their own bases due to bad weather. Right: 'Lemon Drop' and 'Lili Marlene' share the same 68th BS hardstand.

was the top of a skull, cleanly cut off at the hair line. (This incident epitomised the typical, ghastly outcome ever liable to arise from the 'Clean Air War' that many a soldier or sailor imagined was the lot of his fellow-serviceman in the Air Force).

Sindelfingen just outside Stuttgart was due to be attacked on the 9th but adverse weather on the way over forced a turn-round and diversion to the Secondary target located in Saarbruecken. All crews returned but that led by Lt. Peterson (66th BS) was short one man. Courage has been aptly described as a human form of currency, with some individuals managing to remain permanently solvent and others running out or becoming bankrupt. The pressures arising from any form of combat were unpredictable, and probably contributed to what happened on board 41-28785/B+. Flak severed the main control cables during the bomb-run and, believing that the B-24 was out of control as it wallowed back and forth, Lt. Davies (CP) rang the bale-out bell and proceeded to bale out. (His descent landed him right in the middle of a flak battery!)

Meanwhile, a form of control had been re-established through engagement of the autopilot; in addition T/Sgt. Kelleher (Eng.) spliced together a severed stabiliser cable and the bomber was brought home. Lt. Davies was on his thirty-third mission, and acknowledged afterwards that he had responded to a gut reaction, having already witnessed bombers being hit and blowing up with no parachutes emerging.

Lt. Davies had missed the big celebration for the 200th mission by two days. Gen. Johnson was present during the entire day, during which volleyball and football games were organised and played between the senior and junior officers and the first sergeants and the privates. The beer flowed like a river but enough was available to last for the bulk of the festivities. Anyone who wore or even quoted rank was liable to be slung into the pond located near the Aero Club. This inevitably became a' sentence' that finally extended to all and sundry, regardless of whether they had transgressed or not. It included the general himself and even the female members of the base were not exempt from such primordial treatment! All in all, Democracy had had its way over normal strict Military conduct for this all-too-short interlude from the relentless pressure of combat flying.

The air war caught up with the Group less than twenty-four hours later when the two-day 'Stand-down' gave way to a briefing, in this instance to the airfield at Juvincourt. Death, which had taken a brief holiday, was again present on this mission and claimed three lives from among the 506th BS crew of Lt. McGuire, including the pilot. On the way home McGuire had called up to say he was low on fuel and was turning back. A subsequent message stated that one engine on 42-110024/ Bar-P – OLE COCK had failed and that the No.4 fuel tank was empty. The actual circumstances of the bomber's loss remained unclear at the time but of the seven survivors only two evaded capture; Lt. Crawford (N) and Sgt. Reiner (Gunner) were picked up and sheltered to be freed by advancing Allied soldiers and returned to duty by the month-end! (Lt. Turley (B) later stated that prior to take-off the Crew Chief had confirmed among other things that the fuel tanks had been topped. During Group assembly S/Sgt. Kramer (Eng.) reported a low reading on the

This photo shows a turret door embedded in the tail of a returning aircraft. The door was a part of a B-24 that exploded in the formation.

fuel gauges; the consensus of opinion between pilot and engineer went in favour of faulty gauge readings rather than inadequate fuel-content, as there was no reason to doubt the crew chief's statement. The Lt. also recalled the bomber being picked up by P-51s as a heading for an Allied airfield in Normandy was taken up. The descending glide being made to conserve fuel ended with the B-24 taking numerous strikes from ground fire as it skimmed the front-line zone, at which stage the call for a bale-out was made).

The niggling series of individual crew losses continued next day over France when road junctions between Le Havre and Roeun were picked out for assault. The absence of enemy fighters was almost equalised by the intense and accurate flak barrage through which the bombers had to track. Once again it was the 506th BS that suffered a loss, in this case 42-95150/ Bar-B – PASSION PIT. On board was the crew of Lt. Milliken, whose crew were sweating out what they believed to be their third-last mission (They had previously been informed that they were required to complete thirty-three missions under the revised rules; however, that figure had just been lowered to thirty-one in their absence today!).

The three road junctions to be attacked in tandem were in the Falaise area and the extended bomb-run gave the flak gunners ample time to zero-in on the bombers. Flak knocked out both inboard engines and set the B-24 on fire. The bomber's position as Deputy Group Lead made it difficult for the pilots to slip out of formation but this was done with all ten airmen baling out into captivity; their aircraft was seen to blow apart with the still-intact fuel tanks streaming huge tongues of flame as they dropped individually down.

In fact Lt. Milliken was only temporarily incarcerated. After baling out he did a free-fall and only opened his parachute when close to the ground. Having divested himself of harness and parachute, he started walking northwards, but was then captured. Soft cement in a corner of the building where he was held promised an escape route if dug out, but this effort was thwarted by his being moved out to a courtyard where he met up with his crew. His opportunity to escape came when the men were loaded onto a canvas-topped truck that set of after dark. The flap-cover over the rear entrance was loose, a fact that Milliken alerted the others to. However nobody else followed his unspoken suggestion that they follow him out. (Quite how the two guards accompanying the captives failed to notice his departure is almost unbelievable). For the next three days he resumed his northward march by night using the north star as a rough guide. The pangs of hunger he was suffering by the fourth day were assuaged when he came across an abandoned cow, which he relieved of some of its lactic content! Later that day he was shot at – not by Germans as he naturally thought, but by members of a Canadian Army unit deploying down from Caen. A matter of days later he was back in London.

'My Peach' a B-24J-100-CO 42-100415Y is seen lifting off from Shipdham. The B-24 was lost on 8 August 1944. No less than nine of Lt. Komaninski's crew not only got out of their doomed aircraft but also evaded capture!

Lt. Peretti's crew, of which Lt. John McClane was a member was granted official combat leave on the 10th and proceeded to the rest home (Stanbridge Earls) at Romsey down towards the south coast and located on top of a hill; this geographic feature was to play a key role in averting a disaster some two weeks later. Here was the chance to wear civilian clothes on a daily basis, no need to worry about disturbed sleeping patterns, organised sports, excellent food and the company of female staff with positive personalities who could and did discourse about all topics, other than War. These were the necessary ingredients to relax the bodies and minds of combat crewmembers over seven days before returning them to duty.

On their last evening, another 68th BS crew arrived. During the ensuing conversation between the two sets of officers, John and his fellow-officers made the promise of a 'return' to the Rest Home. Such a visit could only mean one thing, namely a fly-past. There was nothing out of order with this, but what was totally irresponsible in John's eyes was the subsequent manner of the fly-past. On the 25th, Lt. Peretti took off and headed southwest. John provided a pinpoint course that got the B-24 right on approach to Roke Manor. On the first of several runs, the propellers were thrown out of synchronisation to attract the residents' attention, a large crowd of which duly turned out in the front yard to wave and gesture. The final approach was over the nearby town nestling in a valley, whose tall church steeple proved a magnet for a low pass. The B-24 was now approaching at treetop level and up the hill slope towards Roke Manor. Flares were being fired from the top hatch as the pilots appeared to aim the huge bomber right at the building. John remembered his heart being in his mouth as the 'audience', anticipating a certain accident, dropped to the ground. At the last instant Peretti and Lt. Palmer pulled back on the control wheels and 'Lilli Marlene' seemed to mush into a semi-stall just above the roof before falling away into the provident airspace on the far slope of the hill, after which a safe airspeed was thankfully regained! There was a deep but momentary silence on board before bedlam broke out as the crew realised how near to a needless death its members had come. Several days later the other 68th BS crew returned from Roke Manor. On meeting their fellow-airmen, they gave full vent to their anger. They had had the living daylights scared out of them by (as John described it himself) 'a set of so-called intelligent and disciplined aviators'.

Security was of prime importance in denying the enemy any knowledge of one's intentions. One strict rule was never to divulge what the potential target was to anyone else before a mission briefing. However, this desired situation appeared to be regularly 'subverted' by, of all people, the Messhall KP Staff. Lt. Fisk, a 66th BS navigator, recalled being regularly informed of where the Group was bound for while having the pre-briefing meal served up. Sure enough, and without exception, when the cover was pulled off the target map, there was the named source for the mission! On one occasion, the meal was still in progress when a 'scrub' was announced; the Lt. inadvertently turned to Lt. Armstrong (CP) and blurted out "Well, I'm glad we are missing this trip to ——today!" It was his misfortune to be overheard by Major Berthong (66th BS Operations Officer). In his own words 'I found out quickly from the Major that 'this was not the Thing to Do'!!

The positive relationship between the combat and ground crews had its limitation, especially when it came to sharing the pleasures dispensed from the PX. Lt. Fisk recalled how the stock of 'goodies' in the small PX was replenished from time to time. However, any combat crew turning up at the Quonset hut after hearing about such deliveries was met by a "Closed for Inventory" notice on the door – which was usually removed just after the Group had taken off for a mission. On the rare occasion where Lt. Fisk managed to complete de-briefing and

Smoke billows up from the crash site of Lt. Jacobs aircraft on the Yaxham road, 8 August 1944. All the crew lost their lives in the resulting crash. The B-24 was 42-50328 of the 506th BS.

1/Lt. William Peterson's flak damaged B-24, seen after returning from the 9 August 1944 mission. The co-pilot was convinced the aircraft was going down so he rang the bail out bell and jumped. However, Peterson regained control and brought 41-28785 back to Shipdham and the co-pilot became a POW.

get to the hut before it closed he was greeted by a very depleted stock and range of items, which included Ping bars. This 'delicacy' was a chocolate glaze-covered marshmallow item whose taste in the Lt's opinion equated to leftover engine oil! Drastic action was called for and Bob took it in an unusual way. He bought up the stock on hand, forty-eight bars in all. He hauled them on board his B-24 for the next day's mission and threw them into the bomb-bay where they froze at altitude to become miniature missiles once the doors were opened for the bomb-run! (He also recalled a fellow-aviator saying this act could be construed as giving aid and comfort to the enemy. Bob's reaction was to suggest this airman could never have been reduced to attempting consumption of a Ping bar!)

Col. Gibson's period of tenure as Group commander came to an end on 14 August, when he was succeeded by Col. Eugene Snaveley. The new Commander had transferred from the 44th BG to the ill-fated 492nd BG, and had returned when that unit was disbanded. At squadron level, Major Felber, who had assumed charge of the 67th BS from Major Kolliner on 3 March 1944, gave way for the return of Major Bill Cameron. (Col. Gibson along with Col. Dent and Major Felber were due to return to the States with the Major receiving his orders on return from the mission of the 16th).

Captain. Raymond L. Craig (66th BS) brought R+ in a little too hot from the 9 August 1944 mission. Note the damage to the under belly near the waist gunners position. The bomber was R+ 42-50660 a B-24J-1-FO of the 66th BS.

The run of daily missions that began on the 12th did not end until the 17th. A French airfield at Lyon/Bron was struck as part of the prelude to Operation DRAGOON, the Allied Invasion of Southern France. This effort was followed by two runs into Germany, the first to an airfield at Wittmundhafen, one of five attacked by the 2nd BD. Then on the 16th, the complex of aircraft production plants around Magdeburg were hit by the Division, with the facility based at Koethen allocated to the 44th BG. Flak was the main deterrent over all three targets, and there were only two points of note. The first occurred on the 15th when another formation forced the Group to circle again for a second bomb-run. The second involved a failure of the sighting equipment on the 68th BS Lead ship that resulted in poor strike results compared to the remainder of the formation.

The stand-down announced on the 17th was generally welcomed as the respite, however brief, provided an opportunity to bring overall aircraft availability up to scratch. However, the normal frantic pace of work to achieve this position was to be easier paced, with one day's exception, thanks to the intervention of Mother Nature. Between now and the 23rd just one mission was flown to bomb the airfield at Nancy/Essay

These two photos shows the men of the 44th having fun during a "Stand Down" to celebrate the Group's 200th mission. The party was held on 11 August 1944.

(18th). One crew was forced to divert into Normandy due to damaged rudder controls, but twenty-two out of the other twenty-three crews returned to base. A second instance of being 'cut-up' by another formation and having to complete a second bomb-run was visited upon one squadron but this did not prevent an overall excellent strike being achieved.

Finally on the 24th, Langenhagen airfield that had been the subject of a 'scrubbed' briefing the day before was again put up on the board. The 6,000lb. bomb-loads were equally split between 500 GPs and M47 incendiaries and another excellent strike was achieved as the 14th CBW waded through barrage-pattern flak thrown up with its usual accuracy. Lt. Dittmer (68th BS) was flying in the rear Group echelon when strikes knocked out the No.4 engine and set fire to his B-24J (44-40098/B – LONE RANGER). This bomber had arrived in early 1944 and was the first natural metal finish aircraft assigned to the Group. Now its months of service were ended as its crew began to abandon the aircraft. Lt. Grueber (N) had the unnerving experience of watching the doomed B-24 make four complete circles around him as he floated down before expiring in a huge explosion very close to where the navigator also landed.

The main physical risk to downed Allied airmen over Germany generally came from the civilian population, whose sense of discipline was nothing like that of its military equivalent. Apart from this, was the human tendency to hand out summary punishment against those '*Terrorfliegers*' (Terror Fliers), as they had been branded in particular by Josef Goebbels, Nazi Minister for Propaganda. (Goebbels had made inflammatory remarks in this vein that virtually encouraged such 'vigilante' action by any German so influenced). Lt. Grueber was grabbed by a bunch of the local residents and was facing the distinct possibility of being lynched when German police arrived on the scene and stabilised matters before taking their captive to a nearby hospital. Both Lt. Dittmer and Sgt. Gasperetti (RW) were apparently not so fortunate when encountering civilian hostility, since they were lined up and shot before any official intervention could be made. The other waist-gunner S/Sgt. Braswell became the third crew fatality but the circumstances of his death were unclear.

The loss of LONE RANGER was the final such statistic for August but flak continued to inflict damage on aircraft as well as crewmembers. Over Langenhagen the 66th BS bomber flown by Lt. Henry (formerly head of a 67th BS crew before transfer-in) was having its bombsight lined up by Lt. Jones (B) when a flak fragment smashed through the Plexiglas, some of whose shattered remains temporarily blinded Jones. Almost at

2/Lt. Charles D. Peretti (Pilot) of the 68th BS poses with 'Lili Marlene' a B-24H-25-FO 42-95260/P. Peretti paid for the artwork to be painted, and Bob Kramer carried out the painting.

Below: A 68th BS aircraft makes a low pass down the main east/west runway at Shipdham.

once a second fragment knocked out the nose turret junction box and Jones's electrical system before slamming into and exploding an oxygen cylinder; this in turn set off ammunition stored in a box! In a final (unknown) act, the flak burst activated the release of the bombs; other bombardiers seeing this also released their bombs, which resulted in an under-shoot. Lt. Henry got both his charge and his crew back to England as did the pilots of three other extensively damaged aircraft. (The removal of bombers requiring large-scale repairs from the operations lists constituted a success for the enemy, even if it was only temporary in nature).

As the month approached its end the Allied Armies were enjoying continued swift success. The German 7th Army had been trapped in a 'pocket' centered upon the town of Falaise; most of its equipment had been destroyed although a sizeable proportion of the soldiers had escaped. Paris had been liberated and Patton's 3rd Army was thrusting ever deeper through central France. To the north, the British/Canadian Forces were enjoying similar success by sweeping up along the Channel coastal regions while ultimately heading for the Belgian Capital, Brussels.

The 8th USAAF for its part was keeping up activity on the issue of tactical support while still not neglecting its basic strategic brief. The 44th BG's contribution during the last week of the month was spread between these twin spheres of operations, with two of the three completed missions involving German targets. First up was the airfield at Schwerin (25th) followed by an attack on an oil refinery at Salzbergen next day. A planned run to Wesendorf with an aero-factory at Basdorf as the Secondary (27th) was the victim of weather; the entire strike-force was similarly affected, with less than 10% of the 1200 bombers dispatched picking out suitable Targets of Opportunity after the 'recall' signal was sent. Then on the 30th, a V-Site close to Abbeville was bombed; bombing was conducted with results unobserved, and was to prove the penultimate occasion on which the Group would be briefed for a target in France.

The tire of 'Down De Hatch' blew out while the bomber was landing from a mission.

September 1944

September's weather was to prove as unpredictable as the preceding month and led to a 'scrub' on the 1st and the 3rd; each time the target should have been at Foret-de-Haguenau north of Strasbourg. In fact the first week of the month resulted in just one completed mission on the 5th to Karlsruhe. Thirty-four crews were at the head of the 2nd BD and planted their bombs with good to poor effect on the city's marshalling-yards. Lt. Holmer (67th BS) was one of six pilots failing to return direct to Shipdham for a variety of technical reasons; in Holmer's case he was forced to divert into an airfield in France due to fuel shortage.

The second week opened with a happy reunion at Shipdham for twenty-two officers and enlisted men. All were survivors captured off the Ploesti mission. During August, Rumania had capitulated and the village in the central region where they were incarcerated was visited by trucks that transported them back to Bucharest. From there they were flown out by 15th USAAF aircraft and back to England. Eleven days later (19th) a farewell party organised by Major Cameron was laid on, at which Gen. Johnson and all four squadron COs were present.

Vultee A-35B Vengeance, 41-31367/A, from the 1st G & TT Flight based at Halesworth made a landing at Shipdham. Note the target tow attachment beneath the Star and Bar of the national insignia.

Karlsruhe was again the subject of assault by the 2nd BD on the 8th and this time round the Group ordnance was comprehensively good. This was also the second consecutive occasion that the Group led the entire division, with Capt. Konstand (68th BS) acting as Command Pilot. (This officer had survived the experience of flying with the now-disbanded 492nd BG, after it had lost an average of one crew per mission, but his luck was to run out right at the year-end).

Marshalling-yards continued to be the specific target-type for the division over the next two days, with the facilities at Mainz and Ulm struck; in addition the High Squadron going in as part of the Mainz mission diverted onto marshalling-yards at Worms after being forced off the original target by another formation. Both Primaries were bombed by the PFF method as was Worms. The weather continued to limit bombing by PFF assistance over the Hanomag factory at Misburg (11th), but this did not materially hinder the flak gunners, whose efforts damaged a number of B-24s. Lt. Hurst's 67th BS aircraft had the No.3 engine shot out, one main gear tire punctured, a large hole punched in one stabiliser and hundreds of holes all over the airframe. In addition Lt. Porter (B) collected a face-full of Plexiglas splinters. Misburg was again briefed twenty-four hours later but a nearby rail junction at Lehrte was chosen after the Primary was found to be blanketed by a solid smokescreen.

The airfield at Swabisch Hall was believed to be heavily involved with the Me 262 jet fighter, and was one of three Primaries struck by the 2nd BD on the 13th. Visibility was good enough for a visual sighting and release by all but four of the thirty-six crews, who were led by Major Cameron. The latter quartet of B-24s struck alternatives comprising Darmstadt's marshalling-yards and an un-identified location at Reichelshein. This was the Group's last mission for five days, and what they resumed on would have distinct similarity to the Ploesti run!

Aerial view of the 'Flak Home' at Roke Manor, which was regularly used by the Group crews when they were 'rested' from combat duties.

The crew of Lt. Mondloh (68th BS) had arrived at Shipdham on 8 July and were now flying their twenty-second mission. S/Sgt. Barton (LW) had noted in his own words; "As we approached the Ruhr Valley the Kaiser Wilhelm graduate school for 88s was holding its graduation exercises; the instructors were showing the 'new boys' how to pick off

Left: 2/Lt. Bure W. Palmer, co-pilot on the Peretti crew, checks the ready board. Right: Major. Robert Felber 67th BS CO (left) and Major Robert Lehnhausen (68th BS CO) watch a mission return while standing on the Tower.

bombers by firing just to the left side of the formation – at us! (Barton's B-24 was part of the Low left Squadron). When we picked up the flak we thought everybody was getting it, but when we called the Lead ship, they didn't know what we were talking about!" Strikes on the left wing led to the switching off and 'feathering' of No.2 engine and the puncturing of a fuel tank. The pilots decided to turn back and called for fighter cover. Two P-38s appeared and announced they were low on fuel but were calling in a P-51 in the vicinity. This fighter did turn up and escorted the bomber to Coulomniers south of Paris.

Once down, the damage was assessed, after which the crew spent a pleasant few hours in either the local town or Paris. Lack of dollars created no spending problems, because the escape kits contained 4000 Francs equalling $50 in value, which was totally used up. The next morning, having satisfied himself that the B-24 was still airworthy, Lt. Mondloh took off and got back to Shipdham. Then, in Sgt. Barton's words; "Next day we walked down to the Flight line and handed in our escape kits for new ones. A few days later we got a message to report to the finance office. It seems we were all short of 4000 Francs that we had spent in France. The USAAC wanted its money – no ifs, ands or buts. If we had been killed it would have been OK. The fact that we came back with a $250,000 plane almost intact cut no ice – we had to pay up!" Clearly, escape money was for emergency use, not self-indulgence.

The swift advance into Belgium and its borders with Holland during the first week of September had raised the intriguing possibility of a decisive if risky thrust up through the Dutch countryside as far as Arnhem whose bridges spanned the river Rhine. The proposal was put to Eisenhower and his staff by Gen. Montgomery. Should the Operation succeed then the Allied Armies would have the chance to sweep into Germany and surround and occupy the Ruehr in order to close off the enemy's chief source of industrial output, before spreading out across their hinterland. There was the even greater prospect of bringing the War to a close before the end of 1944. Whatever reservations were held by the SHAEF Command, of which there were several, the final decision to begin planning what was then code-named Operation MARKET-GARDEN was initiated around the 10th and all was to be ready no later than the 17th!

On Sunday the 17th three Airborne Divisions set off for Holland. The U.S. 82nd and 101st were to be dropped along the narrow road corrider stretching from south of Eindhoven up towards Arnhem. The British 1st Airborne would drop at Arnhem in order to hold the Rhine bridges. On the ground XXX Corps, of the British Army would launch its armour and supporting infantry units up the (hopefully) secured corridor.

The Group's yellow and black striped assembly ship 'Lemon Drop' was a 68th BS 'original' B-24D dating back to the Group's arrival in England during late 1942.

The paratroopers, particularly the contingent heading for Arnhem, could not have foreseen the disaster that was to unfold over the ensuing nine days of the operation. The initial drops in the clear weather conditions went off smoothly but the British soldiers were jumping straight into a clash with two Panzer Divisions. During this same day, the 44th BG crews were alerted for a practice mission – to be conducted at low level! The spectre of a second disastrous mission for those personnel who had participated in the 1 August sortie over Ploesti must have occupied their thoughts. As it so happened, the participating crews would face resistance but nothing on the scale of the Rumanian assault.

Paratroop units are very vulnerable to counter-attack should they not be swiftly relieved and/or backed up with further supplies. With this in mind the Allied authorities had prepared a comprehensive supply-drop for the 18th that in the case of the U.S. airborne troops was assigned to the 2nd BD. Over 250

Left: Col. John H. Gibson served as the 44th BG CO. between 29 March 1944 and 15 August 1944. He has previously flown with the 95th BG – a B-17 Group! Right: Col. Eugene H. Snaveley took over command of the 44th BG from Jack Gibson on 15 August 1944.

bombers from the 14th CBW and 20th CBW were laden with the necessary supplies and sent out in the late morning. The North Sea was traversed at around 1100ft. before a descent to the dropping-height of 400ft. was made on approach to Brest. Small-arms fire was encountered that damaged some aircraft and inflicted wounds upon several crewmembers. One or two crews experienced problems on releasing their loads and had to make renewed runs into the drop-zone. Seven aircraft were lost and although none came from the 44th BG, there were three incidents at Shipdham involving flat tires, a collapsed nose-wheel and a shot-up hydraulic system. No doubt there was great relief when it was determined that the mission would not be repeated!

Lt. John W. McClane, Jr. and Chaplin Harshaw.

'Jersey Jerk' of the 66th BS taxies past the Tower towards the west end of the main runway. The aircraft was a B-24J-60-CF, 44-10548/O+.

The remainder of the month would involve the Group in flying just six missions in that twelve-day spell. A run to Koblenz (21st) was 'scrubbed' as the first aircraft were lifting off. Next day, twenty of the twenty-four bombers got off to drop mixed explosive/incendiary loads upon marshalling-yards at Kassel. Two days of enforced operational inactivity followed thanks to the weather but an afternoon practice flight was flown on the 24th. The pre-occupation with marshalling-yards was a prominent operational feature up to the month-end, and was likely connected with the need to disrupt reinforcements for the defenders opposing the MARKET-GARDEN Forces. Koblenz on the 25th was followed next day to what was arguably the most extensive, if not infamous, marshalling-yard complex in Germany – Hamm. Two runs were made over the target area with the bombs being released under PFF direction.

The Hentschel tank-production plant at Kassel was a huge complex and came under assault on both the 27th and 28th. On both occasions the almost solid cloud-base merited the use of PFF equipment for bombing. Both missions passed off well for the Group although one crew had to divert into Belgium on the 28th after damage to three of their bomber's engines. Lt. Appelin's comment arising from the first Kassel mission was a telling one; "It was strange to see four bombers coming back out of a Group of thirty-two." He was referring to what was the aftermath of a 'Sturmgruppe' assault on the 445th BG that had despatched no less than twenty-five B-24s in a matter of minutes. (The Group had lost temporarily contact with the bomber-stream and were caught and decimated while in this fatally isolated position).

Left: Lt. Charles P. Norris and crew pose in front of K+ "WEARY" a 66th BS B-24H-25-FO 42-95189. This photo was taken shortly after Norris had brought 'Weary' in for this crash landing on return from Karlsruhe, Germany on 9 September 1944. Right: Lt. Norris and 'Weary.' The damage to the B-24 was such that it was declared 'Category E' and written-off Group records.

A second monthly sortie to Hamm on the 30th closed off the month's operations, but sadly also closed off the combat tour of a single 66th BS crew led by Lt. Ledford. Their B-24J (44-10531/ R+ – MY SAD ASS) originally belonged to the 68th BS but was then transferred into the 66th BS.

The flak barrage caught up with the aircraft in its exposed Low Squadron position after 'bombs away'. Strikes knocked out No.1 engine and adversely affected power on No.3 as well as setting it on fire; S/Sgt. Starr (TG) was believed to have been killed by one of these hits. The flames grew in intensity and quickly fired up the fuselage as well. The formation pulled away from the struggling bomber as it steadily descended. Finally, after it was confirmed that Starr was dead, the pilot ordered a bale-out to which the enlisted men responded, followed by the pilots. Lts. Tomblin (N) and Pascal (B) were attempting to free one of the nose wheel doors for their exit when the situation was brutally resolved – the aircraft blew up, throwing both airmen out into mid-air, from where they pulled their ripcords and floated safely down!

The Koblenz mission on the 25th coincided with the final tragic act of MARKET-GARDEN. The remnants of the British 1st Airborne were withdrawn that night across the swollen waters of the lower Rhine, having fought a gallant but hopeless battle against overwhelming forces. They had held the road bridge for four days, more than twice the expected time, but having been driven out of their positions had no option but to pull back into Arnhem. The attempt to reach the beleaguered aerial soldiers by road had stalled north of Nijmegen, but the loss of the vital Arnhem bridge spelled the death-knell of the entire operation. There was to be no swift and satisfactory conclusion to hostilities in 1944, and the Rhine barrier would not be crossed until the following March. Until then the Allied Armies would be locked in a sometimes fierce and protracted struggle with their desperately resisting adversaries.

These two Group 'hacks' are (left) 44-70285/B, a Noorduyn UC-64 Norseman and 42-7865/C, a Republic P-47D-1-RE Thunderbolt. The P-47 served as an unarmed formation monitor aircraft, having previously been declared 'War Weary' and passed over to the 44th BG. The P-47 was the thirteenth 1-RE variant to roll off the Republic production line.

The first of the many. "Lone Ranger" was the first NMF B-24 to join the 44th BG. She was assigned to the Group during April 1944 and was lost in combat on 24 August 1944.

Chapter Eleven

The Accent on Oil Targets

The priority-list of targets for the Strategic Bomber Commands had encompassed a number of industries when first set out at the Casablanca Conference in January 1943. During 1943 the 8th USAAF in particular sought to hammer specific product-lines, with ball bearings being brought to the fore. It was (erroneously) assumed that the destruction of this basic item would literally grind Nazi industry to a halt, or alternatively reduce production to a fatally low level of output. In fact, ample supplies were flowing in from Sweden and Switzerland, while the dispersal of the main industrial complex at Schweinfurt after the 'Black Thursday' mission of 14 October greatly reduced the continued vulnerability of that key production source.

Germany's dependence on oil was satisfied from oilfields in occupied Europe but also by the creation of synthetic oil production plants across the nation's landscape. None of these could be so easily concealed or indeed dispersed. The Nazi war machine would face ultimate ruin should these plants be taken out of commission. Gen. 'Tooey' Spaatz had led the way in the recommendation that the bombers turn their regular attention to this type of production, and the initial attacks had occurred in May 1944. Now, with the B-17s and B-24s back under his exclusive charge, he could grant even more concentration on oil targets. In addition RAF Bomber Command had also joined in this specific offensive although ACM Harris was never to totally divert his crews away from hammering the German cities before the War's conclusion.

Despite the priority accorded the Nazi oil industry, parallel assaults were also launched upon a range of other industrial categories. Communications continued to be another regular focus for attack, with marshalling-yards a particular choice. Hamm was selected for the 2nd BD on 2 October and was hammered by nearly 700 tons of ordnance. The Shipdham contingent of twenty-five aircraft was heading the entire Division but had to make two runs with bombing results being unseen. A vehicle production factory at Gaggenau (3rd) was nearly missed by the Group; a bombsight malfunction in the Lead aircraft caused the formation to drift to the right, but at least two Squadrons corrected their run and landed their bombs accurately. Another Group cutting across their path thwarted an alternative approach by the remaining Group elements to the secondary at Pforzheim. Finally, marshalling-yards located at Offenburg on the Franco/German border provided a suitable target of opportunity. Bombing results at Lippstadt airfield on the 5th ranged from good to poor but once again all crews returned safely.

So far, October was proceeding well in terms of either aircraft or crew casualties. This spell of fortune extended to the fourth monthly mission to Hamburg, where an armaments factory was struck. The flak coming up from this major city was intense but surprisingly inaccurate as far as the Group was concerned. What battle damage there was proved to be slight. Oil targets came the way of the 2nd BD for the first time in October on the 7th but the 44th BG was one of several units assigned to make a return to the Hentschel tank-production factory at Kassel. Over the past two months the 506th BS had borne the brunt of the Group's aircraft losses with four MIA and a fifth crashing after 'aborting' the mission. That unenviable state of affairs was to be further highlighted today with the loss of two Squadron crews. By this stage of the war flak had firmly taken over from fighters as the main deterrent to successful mission-completion.

Lt. Still's crew were on their first mission as a complete crew but the pilots had already flown one mission and had been shaken by an incident at take-off. Their aircraft was 44-40167/ Bar-Y –SIERRA BLANCA, which had barely scraped off the runway-end and demolished part of a fence in so doing. In addition the bomb-bay doors had stuck shut and the bombs were dropped through with the inevitable effect. On today's mission two engines had already failed and the aircraft was out of formation when a shell struck to set the bomb-bay ablaze. S/ Sgt. Lord (ROG) saw Lt. Welborn (CP) scramble up through the cockpit hatch but one of his hands had been burnt and the radio table that had previously been damaged had not been replaced thereby denying him a platform to reach the hatch. The dilemma was resolved in a most fortuitous manner when the bomber fell onto its back and Lord was propelled into the opening! Here his heating and intercom plugs temporarily snagged the edge but he quickly tore them loose and fell away to open his parachute. A large section of the bomber passed close by but he landed in reasonable order – close to a Signal Corps unit several of whose personnel secured his capture. Three enlisted men out of the remaining nine crewmembers failed to survive and a Major later told Sgt. Dahlin (LW) that three bodies had been discovered in the B-24's wreckage.

Lt. Salfen flying in 42-50789/Bar-A – LAKANOOKIE, led this crew's companion team in misfortune. This bomber had last been reported with both left-side engines stopped and trailing behind the Group. All but two of the crew ended up POWs; an unopened parachute caused one of the fatalities while the second airman apparently did not get out before the B-24 crashed.

The flak gunners were not quite finished with the 506th BS although in this third instance they inflicted just one serious crew casualty. Strikes in the bomb-bay and the Nos.1 and 2 engines on 42-50894/Bar-N also seriously injured Lt. J.W. Jones (P) on both legs as well as rendering Lt. Holcomb's (CP) left arm useless. Then No.4 engine caught fire but the strong slipstream extinguished the flames as the bomber dropped through several thousand feet. Adding to an already parlous situation was the compass, which was malfunctioning.

Jones was removed from his seat, and his place taken by S/Sgt. Kirkland (Eng.) who now assisted on the rudder pedals as well as handling the throttles, since Holcomb's arm injury precluded him from throttle manipulation. Control of the aircraft was difficult due to the power imbalance, but it was somehow kept roughly on course. Fuel was being lost, which raised the possibility of having to 'ditch', but this was not a good option

This B-24H -FO belonging to the 67th BS is photgraphed high over the target area.

for the pilot due to his injuries. Then Lt. Westenhiser (N) stated that a strip near Brussels (B-58) was available for an emergency landing. This was headed for and found in spite of the errant compass. The landing was risky due to the fact that the field was smothered in bomb craters, while a B-17 going in ahead of the 506th BS bomber crashed just short of the runway-end. Nevertheless, all went well and the aircraft was brought to an intact halt. Lt. Jones was rushed to a British Army hospital where his left leg was amputated. (The crew were flown back to Shipdham on a C-54 several days later).

The marshalling-yard theme continued to arise well into October, with this facility forming the Primary target on two occasions and the Secondary target for the remaining three missions flown up to the 17th. The yards at Koblenz were the alternate for a briefed airfield (9th). Three days later two sub-formations joined up with the 392nd BG and 491st BG as the 2nd BD headed for a clutch of airfields. However, it was Osnabrueck railroad rolling stock that bore the brunt of the bombing instead of Achmer airfield. Then, on the 14th the 44th BG was the sole 14th CBW unit dispatched within a reduced division effort comprising five Groups, when thirty-eight crews completed a PFF-assisted drop on Kaiserslautern marshalling-yards. (The Division dispatched a second much larger Force over Cologne that day).

B-24J-145-CO, 44-40071/P+ 'Sweat Box' of the 66th BS.

The city of Cologne was a massive conurbation packed with industrial and communications targets that were critical to the Nazi War effort. The 44th BG once again dispatched two sub-formations (A and B) with the latter leading the 14th CBW. Although apparently briefed to bomb a motor transport factory, the A Group was part of a large percentage of the Division that dropped on the Gereon marshalling-yards (Secondary), while the B Group took on a target of opportunity at Dormagen. S/Sgt. Allen (TG) made the following comment about this mission; "Took the familiar route in over Belgium, in and out." His words unconsciously confirmed just how the 8th USAAF's current domination of the skies over Europe meant that the bombers no longer had to conceal their approaches to and out from their targets, as had been the case just a few months previous.

A chemical works at Leverkusen in the northern sector of Cologne was the Primary two days later (17th) but 10/10 cloud forced a diversion to the Secondary; this was Nord marshalling-yard, one of a number located within the city's overall boundary. S/Sgt. Allen's B-24 did not suffer from the intense flak barrage, but his crew led by Lt. Struthers nearly 'bought the farm' during their landing at Shipdham. On final approach, progressive engine failure saw the aircraft scrape its nose and one wing through trees and touch down in a field before bouncing back up and over a boundary fence and onto the runway!

No less than four of Cologne's marshalling-yard complexes were on the 8th USAAF 'hit-list' (18th) but the same chemical works at Leverkusen was assigned to the 2nd BD. The Group Lead bomber flown by Lt. Bakalo was bearing the Command Pilot, Col. John Turnbull. (The Col. had come into the Group as its Operations Officer following the 492nd BG's disbandment, and had been a lacrosse-playing member of the U.S team at the 1936 Olympics in Berlin). This 67th BS crew were to be one of three not getting back to Shipdham, but their loss was to be the result of a self-inflicted act – mid-air collision.

The Group were on the way home and flying through persistent heavy cloudbanks featuring recurring electrical storms. Over Belgium a cloudbank stretching many thousands of feet above the bombers forced the pilots to penetrate 'blind' but to spread out in the process. Suddenly S/Sgt. Encimer (RW) felt a shudder run through the airframe of the Lead ship, 41-28944/Bar-D – FLYING GINNY. The bomber banked sharply left as the engines were throttled back and Col. Turnbull was heard to call out; "Center the needle! Center the needle!" Encimer was clipping on his chest-pack when FLYING GINNY flipped onto its back. The Sgt. suffered a broken arm with being

Lt. C.C. Spagnola's crew after returning from a mission. (left to right) Lt. Robert Lee Aston (navigator), ground crew, Sgt. Norman Sutherland (tailgunner) and Lt. K. Silverthorne. The aircraft is a B-24H-15-CF of the 67th BS.

tossed around, but still managed to scramble out of the wildly gyrating bomber along with the other waist-gunner, S/Sgt. Scott. These two were the sole survivors out of the twelve on board, and Scott required a blood transfusion due to the serious nature of his wounds. (Col. Turnbull was reported to have been found alive but expired two days after the incident).

The Lead ship's demise was later ascribed to a collision with Lt. Dayball's (68th BS) aircraft 42-50381/D, which plummeted to earth near Ghent and close by, all ten crewmembers being killed. S/Sgt. Encimer had observed another Group bomber behind and to the right that appeared to be creating steering problems for its pilots just as the formation entered the cloudbank, but whether or not it was Lt. Dayball's aircraft remained uncertain.

Lt. Ed. Lehnhausen was the brother of Major Bob Lehnhausen, a Group veteran and the 68th BS CO. He had joined his brother's squadron in August and was by this point

Nose art shot of 'Table for Ten', also known as "Wild Bill." The aircraft was B-24J-140-CO, 42-110185/C+ of the 66th BS.

Front and rear shots of 'Sweat Box' a B-24J-145-CO, 44-40071/P+ of the 66th BS. The incident was listed as 'crashed on take off' but in fact it involved a taxiing accident when the left main gear ran off the perimeter track and sank into the mud, causing the gear to buckle. The left wing was also badly damaged and the bomber was salvaged on 6 November 1944.

heading a reasonably experienced crew. His aircraft today was 42-50596/O, which became separated from the main formation after penetrating the cloudbank. The pilots appeared to have veered north of the return course because their B-24 was recorded as crossing over Walcheren Island on the north bank of the Schelde estuary. This was a heavily defended zone, whose flak gunners gave their lone target no chance of evasion. The shells impacted with the rear fuselage and blew the tail assembly clean off; all on board were either killed outright or trapped by the fierce centrifugal forces holding then down until the final impact.

Thirty more young Americans from Shipdham had failed to survive the constant rigours of combat flying, their names being added to the figure of approximately 26,000 airmen within the ETO who were destined never to savour the Fruits of Victory.

A fourth group bomber belonging to the 66th BS staggered back to a severe crash-landing inside Belgium. Lt. Norris (currently with the 68th BS but due to transfer to the 66th BS two days later) lost manifold pressure on No.1 engine of 4-51234/L+ and then experienced alternate power-surge and drop with No.4. Fuel was at a critical level as Belgium was being crossed, so the pilots turned about before letting-down. The B-24 iced-up during a prolonged descent that saw the aircraft breakout into the clear at only 2000ft. The first attempt to land at an airfield near Brussels failed and as the aircraft was circling for a second approach power began to falter. The bombs were still on board and these were salvoed with almost disastrous effect. All Plexiglas panels were blown out and the elevators rendered useless, while one engine caught fire. A flat stretch of ground was headed for with basic control of the bomber being maintained by an up and down movement of the nose through throttle manipulation. The wheels-down landing resulted in the nose wheel collapsing and the fuselage fracturing. Only minor injuries were reported in spite of this 'controlled crash', but the bomber was 'written-off' some weeks later.

Next day an armoured fighting vehicle (AFV) production plant at Gustavaburg was bombed using G-H by a reduced formation of nineteen accompanied by three PFF ships. This mission was the last flown for the following five days. A stand-down was declared on the 20th/21st and two consecutive briefings for Hamm and Gelsenkirchen (22nd/23rd) fell through as a result of bad weather. Finally, on the 24th the Group was not required for operations, but a practice flight was made. The 'scrubbed' Gelsenkirchen mission was resurrected and this time round completed on the 25th when a normal complement of twenty-nine crews backed up by six G-H or H2X B-24s dropped upon the cloud-obscured synthetic-oil plant. The same target-type at Bottrop was plastered twenty-four hours later when the Group headed the entire 2nd BD. The bombers waded through a flak barrage as intense and accurate as on the 25th; the Germans by now had realised the mortal threat to their oil industry and had packed each location with as many 88mm, 105mm and 128mm calibre weapons as could be spared from deployment elsewhere.

A 'scrubbed' mission to Frankfurt followed by two days 'stand down' occupied the month until the 30th when two refineries at Hamburg came the way of the 2nd BD; however, less than half of the 357 crews dispatched actually hit the assigned locations. The 44th BG was part of the Force going in on the site at Harburg. However, a combination of adverse weather and disruption caused by the preceding CBW resulted in the Group formation splitting up. All but eight struck the Secondary by PFF method while the others bombed Uetersen, a small town due west of Hamburg.

One B-24 from the 506th BS failed to return, which was carrying the experienced crew of Lt. Bentcliff. The MACR report indicated that just after 'bombs away' the bomber went into a very steep bank, recovered, and was last seen under apparent control on a southerly heading. Sgt. Fuller manning the top turret remembered the formation flying into a heavy weather front that enforced instrument flying action by the pilots. The Sgt.'s B-24 was leading the High right Squadron when another aircraft crossed over ahead; the wash-effect of its slipstream threw 44-10523/Bar-T onto its back and into a terminal spin. Only Fuller and two other enlisted men managed to fight their way out of the plunging machine before it bore the other eight airmen to their deaths. (Lt. Barefoot was the pilotage navigator and had been flying the mission in order to complete his combat tour. Sgt. Garza (LW) had been a member of Lt. Jewell's crew and had survived the risky forced-landing in Belgium on the 7th).

November 1944

The 8th USAAF's campaign against Nazi oil-production resources was well under way by the end of October, but to date the task had been primarily laid at the door of the 1st BD and 3rd BD. Now the 2nd BD's involvement was to intensify during November. The Shipdham experience was typical with six of the sixteen missions flown by 44th BG in the month involving synthetic-oil plants. The Bauer refinery at Gelsenkirchen was struck on the 1st, and next day similar punishment was handed out to the refinery at Castrop-Rauxel. On the 3rd, Gelsenkirchen was spared thanks to bad weather 'scrubbing' the mission, but over 200 B-24s plastered the plant located at Hannover/Misburg on the 4th. In all three instances, the 10/10 cloud-cover dictated the use of PFF-directed bombing.

In a switch reminiscent of the missions flown during the Battle of Normandy, the 8th USAAF attacked marshalling-yards ranging from southwards of Frankfurt towards the Black Forest. The intention was to hinder German reinforcements that could be directed against the U.S. Army's offensive in the Metz sector. The 44th BG records indicated an unspecified tactical target as the Primary but the bulk of the 2nd BD (including most of this Group) struck yards at Karlsruhe as its Secondary choice. The 506th BS flying Low left Squadron carried out a visual drop on Landau after becoming separated.

Crew Chief Pappy Hill (center) with his aircraft 'Lili Marlene.' Although the aircrew believed they owned the aircraft, in reality the crew chief was the boss, and a good pilot always listened to his crew chief.

'Southern Comfort III' of the 506th BS. This particular B-24J-5-FO, 42-50896, was the fourth aircraft to bear the name, and was received by the 44th BG sometime between July and 1 August 1944.

Oil was back on the mission 'menu' (6th) when Sterkrade on the western edge of 'Flak Valley" (The Ruhr) became the 2nd BD's latest victim. So far in November, the Group had suffered no aircraft casualties but the 'score' was opened on return to Shipdham. As it was landing the 66th BS aircraft 44-0071/P-Bar – SWEAT BOX suffered a folding of the left main gear after impact with a hole in the runway. The B-24 scraped along on the left wing before coming to a halt, but the scale of damage was enough for salvage action to be taken.

Marshalling-yards at Rheine just across the border from central Holland were put up for assault on the 8th but the small

Two shots of B-24H-25-FO, 42-95124 'Sand Bomb Special' of the 67th BS. The bomber blew a tire on take off. The name refers to the practice bombs in regular use by the USAAF.

44th BG Force of eleven crews experienced problems in picking out the Primary in the face of heavy cloud; visibility was even further compromised by thick contrails from preceding formations. In the end bombs were dropped on the railroad east of Enschede in Holland. The results were deemed to have fallen into the 'Gross Error' category and were more plainly described as 'pitiful' by a crewmember! There was no let-up in the operational pressure on the 9th when the second mission in support of the ground Offensive commenced on the 5th was sent out. This time round the 44th BG was involved in striking at reported gun positions around Metz, whose fire was harassing the 3rd Army's advance. The American soldiers, mindful of the ground-marker failures on 25 July at St. Lô that had contributed to 'friendly' bombing casualties, put up a barrage of fire to mark their presence.

This time round no such problems were experienced and the bomb-loads went down with the desired effect. (A 67th BS pilot had a brother with the Infantry who later told him how the German positions were so well hammered that the Americans had no problem in securing their gains at little or no cost).

The very indifferent weather patterns encountered during the autumn of 1944 autumn were reminiscent of the previous year. However, there were no longer the same inhibitions placed upon daylight operations compared to 1943. This was primarily thanks to the range of equipment that had commenced with H2X and had since expanded to the use of G-H and Micro-H, with which non-visual bombing of targets could be carried out. So it was that the Luftwaffe personnel serving at Hanua/Langendiebach near Frankfurt had no security from attack by the 2nd BD on the 10th. Over 400 tons of ordnance tumbled through the overcast and onto the airfield. Some flak at Koblenz did challenge the Group's inward progress, wounding several crewmembers including S/Sgt. Schofield (67th BS) in 42-50794/N-Bar. A shell fragment broke his jaw and went out through his cheek; Lt. Spencer immediately turned back for Shipdham, from where the gunner was rushed to hospital. Sgt. Kirk a 68th BS gunner also was seriously wounded.

Bombing under any condition could only be carried out if the bombers could safely get off and form up. Between the 12th and 15th the elements proved to be so restrictive that the 'heavies' were firmly pinned to the ground. The 8th USAAF only resumed full-scale operations on the 16th when enemy defensive positions west of Aachen were attacked prior to the U.S. Army advance in this area. Weather conditions at Shipdham were poor and the worsening situation permitted just eleven crews to get off before a total 'clampdown' set in. The

'Short Leg' was a B-24H from the 68th BS: the serial for this aircraft cannot be precisely established, as there are four possible individual serial numbers that could apply.

An 'in flight' shot of 'Sultry Sue' a B-24J-1-FO, 42-50539/U of the 67th BS. She was received by the 44th BG during July 1944 and was repaired at Woodbridge, Suffolk on 5 December 1944. She flew until the war's end and clocked up sixty-nine missions in the process, after which she flew back to the United States on 31 May 1945.

bomber flown by Lt. Kelly (68th BS) assumed the Lead for the 491st BG, which in turn headed the entire 8th USAAF. On board as Command Pilot was a full (unnamed) Colonel. Group assembly saw Lt. Lane (N) use up two full cases of red-red flares. Following 'bombs away' the Col. told the pilot to 'rack this thing around and let's get the Hell out of here' as the flak was pouring up. His reaction to the crew at this point singing 'Herr Hitler says we will never bomb this place' and then blowing a big raspberry was to say that he had never met a nuttier bunch! (However, he surely recognised that this act was by way of letting out some of the tension build-up that was an inevitable aspect of combat flying). All eleven crews were forced to divert to other airfields on return from what was regarded as a good bombing strike.

Weather was continuing to be the primary barrier to actual missions over the next four days. Just one attempt was made on the 20th but a 'recall' signal was issued after the Group had assembled. No such limitation applied next day when Harburg's oil refineries were struck. All thirty aircraft came back but the scene that greeted the ground crew for the 67th BS B-24 flown by Lt. Phillips was sickening in the extreme. Over the target an unexploded shell had penetrated the nose of 42-51552/M-Bar before passing on upwards. Lt. Burke (N) was right in its path and could have known nothing as the projectile literally tore his body apart and scattered it around. (Since World War II the film companies producing war films have generally portrayed death among military personnel as if their bodies remained intact. Gruesome incidents such as this once again highlighted the true situation and the extreme frailty of mankind when confronted by volatile explosive and heat-searing forces). In addition, S/Sgt. Kostocka (LW) was seriously injured by flak.

There was a break in missions caused by the weather for the third time in the month, but the first of the three days (22nd) involved a 'stand down'. Then on the 25th the 2nd BD plastered the marshalling-yards at Bingen, making the latest use of the Division's G-H equipment in order to deliver its assault. Bielefeld northeast of the Ruhr possessed a long railroad viaduct that had attracted previous and unsuccessful bombing runs. Today was to be no exception as the bomb-loads struck frustratingly close to, but not on, the narrow structure. (It would take the 22,000lb. aerodynamic bomb known as 'Grand Slam' to demolish the bridge's center-section when these were dropped by RAF Lancasters the following March).

Rail transportation featured in all three remaining November missions. Marshalling-yards at Offenburg (27th) and Neunkirchen (30th) were launched on either side of the 29th when a second key viaduct at Altenbecken was attacked using G-H. One of the Sqdns. over-shot the first-named target due to technical failure but the other crews confirmed a good visual strike. This was the only visual effort arising out of the trio of missions.

December 1944

The 44th BG had now been on combat status for just over two years, and the Christmas festivity looming up would be the third experienced far from home for many Group personnel, especially among the ground crew and other supporting organisations. The tantalising possibility that they would celebrate the fourth one on their own cherished soil was fully raised as the Nazi lust for conquest was being squeezed inexorably to death by the Allied armies. One last barrier in the form of the river Rhine lay between that desired goal and the Anglo/American involvement in its fulfillment.

Before December was out, the western Allies would find themselves on the back foot as Hitler made his final military gamble in the West. For weeks he had ordered the careful and secret build-up of a massive armoured and infantry force that would be launched against the thinly held Ardennes sector. The advance had the primary aim of driving northwest with the purpose of seizing the vital port of Antwerp and splitting the American and British forces. The Fuehrer's ultimate hopes arising from the perceived success of this counter-stroke was thought to be a negotiated settlement with his Western adversaries.

Left: Lt. Roy Owen of the 506th BS flew his first combat mission on 5 December 1944 as co-pilot with the Smith crew, when the target was Muenster, Germany. Right: Crew chief Sgt. Curtain with his arm inside one of the engine nacelles on 42-50896/K a B-24H-25-FO of the 67th BS.

Before the initial assault of what became known as the 'Battle of the Bulge' was launched on the 16th, the Strategic bombers continued to hammer at German resources, at least whenever the continuing poor weather conditions allowed. In the case of the 44th BG its crews put in eight missions prior to this date. The first went out on the 2nd and ended with the latest set of casualties inflicted upon the Group. It was back to Bingen and its marshalling-yards as the 8th USAAF hammered three such facilities in this quarter of Germany. The weather threw up a bank of cloud just ahead of the target and at a time when small numbers of enemy fighter were sighted. The formations were scattered as a result and when they emerged were short of several B-24s, including two from the Group.

The first of these was from the 68th BS and was 42-50805/T flown by Lt. Hobbs. He had pulled up to avoid possible collision and found his aircraft on its own when again out in the clear. S/Sgt. Montre (Eng.) remembered his B-24 coming under fighter attack whose strikes set the bomb-bay on fire. He grabbed his chest-pack and jumped down from his turret into the bomb -bay but had no further recollection of what happened until he was out in mid-air and had pulled his ripcord, having suffered severe burns. His parachute canopy had a large hole in its surface and he came down at a potentially lethal rate; however his rigging lines caught on the top of a tree to break his fall and save him from injury or death. He recalled the

German civilians being of assistance in getting him to a hospital. His condition was such that when he returned to America a few months later he had to have numerous skin grafts to both face and hands.

The second crew were actually Lead for the 392nd BG's Low left Squadron. This Group encountered the cloudbank just after passing the I.P. and was similarly scattered. Lt. Bayliss (506th BS) was also on his own in 42-50766/D-Bar and Bf 109s according to T/Sgt. Dosmann (ROG) duly attacked the isolated B-24. Fire erupted under the flight deck. T/Sgt. Moore (Eng.), realising the situation was irreversible, left his turret to open the cockpit roof hatch. He was then seen by Dosmann to drop down towards the bomb-bay but never emerged from the stricken bomber. Dosmann was very fortunate to survive, since he was thrown out through the top hatch when the pilots appeared to lose control and the bomber flipped onto its back. Lt. Louisa (CP) was equally fortunate to fight off the effects of centrifugal force and emerge via the same hatch. Lts. Brennan (B) and Jolovitz (N) later confirmed the source of the fire was under the flight deck; they knew this because they had no option but to exit through the nose-wheel doors as their route to the bomb-bay was blocked by the flames! Lt. Louisa evaded capture for ten days but was captured hiding alongside a river that he was seeking to cross. S/Sgt. Passantino in the nose turret was seen to snap on his chest-pack but he never made it out. He was one of the five crewmembers that failed to survive.

The Allied domination of the air was drastically reducing the casualty-rates among bomber crews caused by fighter attacks but could not do anything about flak or indeed about self-inflicted damage such as collisions or crashes on take-off or landing. The 'Grim Reaper's' tally was steadily diminishing but that spectre would continue to collect a blood debt until the conflict was long over.

The unfortunate start to December operations continued to some degree on the very next mission (4th) when marshalling-yards at Bebra south of Kassel were targeted. Problems with receiving precise G-H signals ended up with a PFF-assisted drop on a Target of Opportunity during the third bomb-run attempt. There was no enemy resistance offered but one crew was absent from among the numbers touching down at Shipdham. Reports indicated that the B-24 was seen going down in the target area with two engines 'out'. In fact the demise of 42-95124/P+ – SAND BOMB SPECIAL – was initially laid at the door of technical failure. Oil was seen streaming from both left-side engines. Asked to check the problem, Lt. Frazier (B) told his pilot to rely upon his instrument reading as he (Frazier) could not identify the liquid. Shortly after, both engines were switched off and their propellers were 'feathered'.

Out of formation and losing altitude, a course home was now taken up as all surplus gear was jettisoned, but calls for fighter cover were mistakenly transmitted on the ASR Channel. A single fighter did turn up, having probably spotted the distress flares being sent up, but he flew away after a short time. Lt. Rogers held course for what he believed would lead his bomber into France on 270 degrees. However, the B-24 seems to have wandered off to the southwest, since the bale-out (called for

This sequence of four photographs depicts the end of B-24J-5-DT, 42-51309/V from the 67th BS. Aircraft crashed on take off due to severe icing conditions on 18 December 1944. Lt. Collins and crew were on board.

This shot of 44th BG aircrew is a rare example as it was taken in Switzerland where the individuals concerned were all interned.

when fighters appeared) deposited the surviving crewmembers close to Freiburg in the Black Forest. At least two crewmembers were badly beaten-up, being Harkovich (LW) and Lt. Moir (CP). The Sgt. was kicked and punched all over by a group of civilians just after being apprehended by a rifle-bearing soldier; only the intervention of several other soldiers coming on the scene saved him from an even worse fate. Lt. McCracken (N) and Sgt. Spier who manned the nose turret were killed out of the ten on board.

Transportation targets monopolised operational activity up to the onset of the Battle of the Bulge, with marshalling-yards and key bridges attacked. A reduced Force of thirteen crews went out on the 5th for Muenster's yards. Next day it was back to Bielefeld railroad viaduct for the latest bid to bring it down. This time the Group's ordnance struck tantalisingly close to the bridge-span, as did the entire load released by the 14th CBW and 96th CBW bombers. The eleven crews taking part were integrated as the High Squadron within the 392nd BG. There then ensued a three-day enforced break from operations when weather either cancelled the planned missions (7th) or led to the day commencing with a 'stand-down' being announced.

Bingen's marshalling-yards received its latest course of treatment when all but two of the 2nd BD Groups were dispatched on the 10th but the 44th BG did not bomb. Failure of the G-H equipment forced the Group to circle for a second run. This time round the intention was to utilise the smoke markers dropped by the preceding formation as a guide. However, the circle was not yet complete when it was realised the smoke had drifted too far in order to provide any degree of accurate bomb-release. The run was duly abandoned and the Group headed home with bombs still on board. Lt. Kleiderer's 67th BS crew had continued bad fortune on this day. First, they lost one engine through a 'runaway' propeller while taxiing out. Changing over hastily to another B-24, they formed up and went over Bingen. On the way back their replacement aircraft had one engine go 'out' followed later by power-loss in a second. The bombs were dropped in the sea and full power was restored thanks to the engineer – who then suffered frostbite in one hand due to having to work with his gloves off. "Everything seems to have gone wrong today" was the terse summing-up of the day's events by S/Sgt. Chaffin (TG)!

Aircraft availability on the 11th was such that no less than forty-five were sent out in two sub-formations The Group figure mirrored the overall 8th USAAF bomber strength today, which at just under 1600 represented the pinnacle of operational achievement to date. Marshalling-yards at Hanau were assigned

The nearest aircraft is 44-10553/C a B-24J-65-CF of the 68th BS, which crash landed near Merville, France on the 28 December 1944. The OD aircraft is 42-110057Q a B-24J-130-CO. This aircraft crashlanded at Shipdham on 9 September 1944.

to the 2nd BD with bridges at Karlsruhe as the Secondary. It was the latter that the 44th BG dropped on with unobserved results. Lt. Thorne (506th BS) was flying his first mission that nearly became his last. On the return leg his B-24 entered into a cumulus-nimbus cloudbank. The lethal turbulence ever present within this weather feature threw the bomber over onto one wing and into a dive, whereupon the gyro instruments tumbled. Frantic pressure on the rudder pedals by both feet, plus the assistance of the co-pilot, finally enabled Thorne to bring the B-24 out into level flight at less than 500ft.!

Twenty-nine aircraft went out next day to Aschaffenburg, and for the first time in many missions the bomb-run was visual, which made the overall results all the more disappointing. The Lead Squadron suffered technical problems that led to a bombing 'gross error' caused by a premature release, while a lapse in promptly identifying the target forced the Low Squadron to link up with the High Squadron and so share in this failure However the High Squadron did sight and bomb very accurately, thereby salvaging something positive out of the day's mission. A senior staff promotion (and a very popular one at that) was announced today when Major Bill Cameron (67th BS CO) became a Lt. Col. His days as Squadron CO for the second and last time were numbered; three days following his promotion he was succeeded by Major Middleton (who had previously led the 506th BS) and he stepped up to Group HQ to assume the position of Group Deputy CO. Bill Cameron truly represented the spirit of the 'Flying Eightballs'. Both had experienced and survived very difficult times within their parallel operational lifetimes. The term 'Legend' often tends to be over-played but is still very pertinent when applied to the military career of this American airman and leader.

Hitler's Ardennes Offensive enjoyed the suitable murky weather conditions over its opening spell that effectively grounded the Allied air fleets. In truth, operations had already been severely restricted from the 13th onwards thanks to this malign factor. Four missions were launched by the 8th USAAF up to the 23rd but only the latter run saw the majority of the crew striking their primaries consisting of marshalling-yards and communications centers. The mission on the 16th resulted in less than half the 985 bomber striking either their Primary or Secondary targets, while the forces managing to assemble and bomb on the 16th and 19th were but a fraction of the available strength.

The 44th BG took part in the first two mentioned missions, but on both occasions the crews were recalled. The crews dispatched on the second occasion must have reacted strongly

The end of "Lili Marlene" of the 68th BS came on the morning of the 29 December 1944. These three photos were taken shortly after the crash of B-24H-25-FO 42-95260 P. All the crew killed in the ensuing crash.

to not receiving mission 'credit' since they were minutes away from the I.P. at Kyllburg, a railroad point close to the Ardennes sector, when the 'recall' signal was received! So it was that a full ten days were to elapse before the Group completed its latest mission, and then with just fifteen crews, of which four were attached to other Groups. The Germans' basic immunity from air attack in western Europe ended today. (The Ardennes Offensive was already in serious trouble due to a combination of fuel shortage for the German armoured units and the stubborn Allied resistance, in particular that shown by the 101st Airborne

An English farm house at the back of the 68th BS living Site with its aura of peace and tranquility affords a stark contrast with the implements of War just a short distance away.

at Bastogne, a town that possessed key road access for the enemy's westward advance).

The weather was still no better than indifferent but over 400 bombers still got off to batter communications points at widely-spread locations. Ahrweiler, close to Remagen on the Rhine (a location whose name was to feature prominently in the Allies crossing of that major water barrier in March 1945) was pounded by forty-eight B-24s. Elsewhere the 392nd BG, for whom Capt. Henry (66th BS) was flying Deputy Lead, experienced flak at the I.P., a location that was supposedly in Allied hands – and ran into continuous flak from thereon in! Lt. Jones (B) recalled that he did a G-H assisted run, but one bomb hung-up; fortunately the two bombs mounted above fell clear when released. Lt. Jones then had an interesting five minutes out on the bomb-bay catwalk with the doors open while he went about freeing the 'hung-up' weapon!

The figure of some 1600 bomber dispatched on the 11th was impressive enough, but it was eclipsed on Christmas Eve when just over 2000 B-17s and B-24s sallied forth in the clear, frosty conditions. A total of thirty-two locations were assaulted, of which all but seven were Primary-briefed targets; less than 150 crews were forced to bomb Secondaries. Everything that could fly went out, including several of the gaudily painted Assembly ships favoured by the 2nd BD, such was the desire to bring maximum relief to the hard-pressed troops in Luxembourg. The 44th BG contributed sixty-one crews, fifty-nine of whose ordnance fell on railroad bridges and tunnels at Ruwer, Pfazel, Wittlich and Eller. The 66th BS contributed two Lead aircraft for the 392nd BG and 491st BG with Lt. Pellow (67th BS) leading the former-named Group's High Squadron. Shortage of fuel was the reason used by Lt. Struthers (67th BS) to leave the Group on the way home, but his hope of reaching as far as Paris failed when Sgt. McDonald (Eng.) reported that the situation was critical according to the glass tubes recording fuel reserves. A French airstrip was sighted above which the pilots circled and made an approach, which was too high and forced an over-shoot. The second approach was eventful, since one engine cut out during the circuit, a second on final approach and a third after touching down! While refuelling was taking place, members of two stranded Bomb Groups along with several soldiers, asked the crew for a lift back. The personnel were disposed inside so that the B-24 was first sitting on its tail and put back on its nose before take-off was (successfully) attempted!

A total war such as World War II did not generally allow for 'human' gestures such as a Christmas truce, and the selected crews were alerted as usual on Christmas Day, with the 2nd BD and 3rd BD dispatched to strike railroad locations and communication centers. (Dense fog had closed down the bulk of the 1st BD bases the previous evening). However, the planned involvement of the 44th BG in proceedings was cancelled before take-off. This respite from the rigours of combat, however temporary, gave the personnel a chance to celebrate. Services at the Base chapels were well attended, as were the Christmas dinners laid on for the occasion. Many of the men went off into the surrounding district to visit British friends and acquaintances.

Right: Lead Pilot Captain Ernest C. Holmer seen on what was for him a non-mission day is watching the Group return from a mission.

Below: The 'Iron Corset', a 67th BS aircraft, ran up a tally of 120 plus missions during her combat tour, and returned to the Zone of the Interior in 31 May 1945. Aircraft was a B-24H-30-FO, 42-95318.

Left: from the left – Sgts. Norm Berg, Murray Kramer, Glen Barr and Harold Barnes. All four were a part of Lt. Rose's crew of the 68th BS. Right: 'Lemon Drop' sitting on her nest in the 68th BS area. This veteran B-24D had had more than her share of operational problems but, unlike her 'original' contemporaries, she had survived through the initial costly period of Group operations during 1942-1943.

The reaction of Lt. Fisk (66th BS) to his being a long way from home and not with his family round a candle-lit table on Christmas Eve was to manufacture his own candles. The inner boxes containing K-rations were wax-coated against moisture. The wax was scraped off and stored until sufficient was available to be rolled and kneaded into a rough candle-shape. The wicks were formed from GI shoelaces. Five of these items were placed around the Quonset hut and although each 'dweller' generally kept his thoughts to himself, Bob felt that the gesture, however basic was still appreciated. Later in the evening, somebody got the radio working and the carol singing broadcast by the Armed Forces Station brought a second reminder of the normality that all those present in this sparse, dimly-lit billet were risking life and limb to restore to the World

It was forty-eight hours before the call to arms recurred at Shipdham. In between, continuing poor conditions over central England on Boxing Day limited operations to the other two Bomb Divisions, and even then, the 2nd BD and 3rd BD dispatched just a fraction of their strength. The freezing fog still persisting on the 27th did not prevent all three Bomb Divisions sending out their bombers, including 182 B-24s. The latter went to three marshalling-yard locations, of which Homburg was allotted to the 14th CBW. A last-minute correction during the bomb-run put the formation on the correct heading but the Lead Bombardier was unable to synchronise properly in the time left before bomb-release. Accuracy was accordingly poor for most of the Group although the third Squadron did achieve good results.

Road and rail facilities at Kaiserslautern were pounded the next day by the 14th CBW, as the 8th USAAF maintained full pressure on communications in western Germany. Capt. Clements as in the Lead ship along with Col. Snavely the navigator operating the G-H set reported its failure. The Col. promptly issued the order for Clements to 'Turn over the Lead' to the Deputy Lead ship. Almost simultaneously came cries from up front that the so-far continuous undercast was breaking up to permit a visual bomb-run. Snavely then firmly muttered, "You guys had better be right!" as the crew maintained their lead status. The pilot's faith in the judgement of Lts. Bumbicka (B) and Boykin (N) proved justified – thought only just – as the cloud formation did clear almost at the last moment to permit a good strike. That evening in the Officer's Club the Col. was enthusiastically displaying the strike photo to all and sundry, but Capt. Clements always wondered what his reaction would have been had the cloud cover remained intact!

Only two bombers were MIA out of the 1158 given mission 'credit' on the 28th, but sadly one of this duo came from the 44th BG. In addition, one of the 68th BS crews that had 'aborted' the mission was lost over Shipdham. The single Group combat loss also involved the 68th BS. Capt. Konstand was piloting 44-10582/D and leading the 491st BG in his G-H equipped bomber. Flak was assessed at 'meagre to moderate' and was credited with bringing down this aircraft during the bomb-run. Two strikes right in the bomb-bay caused the B-24 to falter and drop down. Less than two minutes later it broke in two. S/Sgt. Davis (RW) remembered a box of flares on the flight deck being ignited by the first hit while the second threw him over in the waist. He donned his chest-pack and was on his way to assist S/Sgt. Stepanovic (TG) out of his turret when he suddenly found himself in mid-air; presumably he had fallen out at the point where the fuselage had separated. Only four others out of the twelve airmen on board survived the bomber's sudden

Just another day at Shipdham, as 42-110185 C+ taxies from the 66th BS hardstands past the Control tower for the start of yet another mission in 1944: the artwork is Table for Ten. The aircraft had been transferred into the 44th BG from the 491st BG.

The extreme winter conditions of 1944 can be seen here as B-24J-1-FO 42-50644 of the 506th BS is taxiing out for a mission during the critical 'Battle of the Bulge.' Ground crew direct the planes round the perimeter track.

disintegration and crash. (Capt. Konstand was a veteran flier who had originally served at North Pickenham before transfer to Shipdham, following the 492nd BG's dissolution).

Back at Shipdham the fire crews were already attending to the scattered remnants of the other 68th BS aircraft, LILI MARLENE (42-95260/P). This aircraft had been around since May and was being flown by Lt. Bledsoe. The No.2 engine that had occasioned the 'abort' action, was observed to be switched off as the landing approach was made. The pilots reportedly missed the runway and were forced to go around again. However, the turn was barely in progress when a second engine failed, whereupon the B-24 stalled and struck the ground. The chances of anybody among the ten airmen getting out alive were cruelly cancelled when part of the bomb-load went off. (The blast was so great that some personnel sitting at their workplaces or in the Mess Halls were lifted out of their seats). Compounding this day of tragedy for the 68th BS was the diversion by Lt. Van Dyke into an airfield near Brussels, where he crash-landed. The reason for the diversion was to gain urgent medical attention for his wounded navigator.

The year ran out its course with missions on all three remaining days, and with the emphasis for the 2nd BD still firmly focused on German communications. The communications center at Stadtkyll close to the Belgian border provided a disappointing result on the 29th. This was primarily due to a lack of intelligence information on the precise location to be attacked.

A rail bridge at Altenahr close to Ahrweiler provided a somewhat sounder prospect for good bombing next day although it was bombed 'blind' using G-H. There was all the more surprise, not to say consternation, expressed after the crews' return when those navigators operating on H2X asserted that Stadtkyll, and not the briefed Primary, had been struck. Examination of the radarscope prints confirmed this to be correct!

The 'Class of 44' bomber crews closed off 1944 with a combined hammering of enemy oil reserves by the 3rd BD and of communications by the other two divisions. Continued assault on marshalling-yards and rail bridges stretching along the Rhine between Bonn and Bingen involved the 2nd BD. A bridge spanning the river at Neuwied was to have been attacked by the 44th BG with G-H assistance. In fact the ordnance went down on a rail junction at Dorsel, some forty miles to the west, this error being attributed to failure of the electronic equipment. Flak damaged several aircraft including the 66th BS example flown by Lt. Ketchum, which was the first PFF aircraft flown by the Group after transfer from the 482nd BG in May. No.1 engine was fired and No.3 suffered a 'runaway' propeller on 41-28794/I+ – I'LL GET BY. The crew managed to divert into a Belgian airfield, where their aircraft was subsequently repaired and returned to Shipdham. (The bomber would survive to fly home in May 1945, but its crew for the 31 December mission would not be so fortunate). Lt. Henry (66th BS) had been the Lead for the 491st BG whose ordnance followed that of the 44th BG onto Dorsal.

Chapter Twelve

The Run-up to Victory

January 1945

Although the main crisis period arising out of the Ardennes Offensive was all but over, several weeks were to ensue before the Germans were finally driven back to their original starting positions. The fierce weather conditions for what was one of the worst European winters in many years dictated that all heavy clothing and support gear such as blankets deemed non-essential for 8th USAAF personnel was taken away for transfer to the hard-pressed GIs on the battlefield. This, in practice, affected the ground crews most of all and complaints were manifold if muffled; more careful consideration of the situation confirmed the higher priority for the men in the field who were literally stuck out in the open wastes of the continent. Indeed, it was not just equipment that was culled from the 8th USAAF but personnel also. Units were ordered to comb their ranks for airmen whose services could be dispensed with, but with little or no reduction in operational efficiency likely to occur.

Meanwhile, the air war proceeded at full pace with the 2nd BD still regularly assigned to harrying communications in behind the retreating German soldiers. Koblenz, a city located on the junction of the Rhine and Mosel rivers, was a key target. Rail bridges at Engers (392nd BG) and Lutzel (44th BG) just upstream from the city center were taken on but the results were very variable though generally good; the Group's Low Squadron was four miles short of the MPI thanks to accidental release by the lead ship, but the other two Squadrons dropped on the target. Next day the 44th BG was again assigned the bridge at Lutzel but solid cloud cover prevented any observation; Lt. Propper (66th BS) took the 392nd BG to the nearby rail bridge at Neuwied – the one that should have received the 14th CBW's ordnance on 30 December! The third consecutive monthly mission and the eighth in a row took the twenty-two crews to bomb marshalling-yards at Landau close to Karlsruhe with the help of G-H.

There was a double twenty-four hour break for all personnel between the 4th and 6th with a mission in between. Of the twenty-two crews dispatched to Oberstein, three 'aborted', one of which did so when the pilots discovered that the 491st BG whom they were briefed to act as Lead did not even take off! Four of those gaining mission 'credit' did so with other groups. An error by the Command Pilot in Lt. Henry's 66th BS lead ship found the Group trailing the 93rd BG instead of the 392nd BG, which threw the crews twenty miles off route. Requests for G-H to be used for the bomb-run were rejected in favour of a visual approach, after which the Lead ship's compass failed. Finally, with no prospect of searching out the primary, Lt. Jones (B) made a run on rail facilities at Neunkirchen with only 'fair' results recorded.

The Group was CBW Lead for the attack on Landau (7th) while two other crews led the 392nd BG and 491st BG; twenty-eight out of the thirty-three crews with the Shipdham contingent dropped on G-H. A communications center at Burg Reuland caught the brunt of twenty-one bomb-loads next day with G-H indications of a good concentration. This was the last mission flown for four days, apart from three crews of the 67th BS and 68th BS who were assigned to the Lead or Deputy Lead for the 392nd BG and 491st BG on the 10th. On the 13th the force of twenty-one crews (two more were flying Lead for the other two CBW Groups) was itself split in two, with each squadron flying the high position within the 392nd BG and 491st BG formations. The flak encountered was both meager and inaccurate and came up through the undercast as a G-H bomb-run was duly completed.

The oil campaign had so far mostly involved the two B-17 equipped Air Divisions – the new title introduced in 1 January 1945 – but this situation altered for the next few days at least, beginning on the 14th when the 2nd Air Division joined in. Three production or storage plants were struck including Hemmingstedt, located north of the mouth of the river Weser, which was assigned to the 14th CBW. The 44th BG was in the lead position, and for once the weather was clear. The bombardiers took full advantage of this and laid their loads around the MPI; the smoke from the destruction could be seen long after the bombers had turned for home.

Two days later, following a 'scrubbed' mission on the15th the crews flew deep into central Germany to the synthetic-oil plant at Ruhland. However, a combination of H2X malfunction in the Lead ship and low cloud intermingled with a smoke screen forced a diversion to the marshalling-yards in Dresden, approximately twenty miles due south. Bombing results were very poor; two Squadrons either under- or over-shot the target and the third was forced off its bomb-run by another unit! Several hours later, of the thirty-three bombers that had set out, a mere fifteen landed back at Shipdham. What fears that might have been expressed for another Group disaster were allayed when all but one of the missing crews was confirmed down in France or England. (Many or all of the crews who had diverted were among the fifty B-24s that landed at Orly airfield – in Paris!).

The one aircraft initially falling into the MIA bracket was the lead ship flown by Capt. Testa (68th BS) along with Col. Snavely as Command Pilot. Flak strikes over Ruhland had knocked out two engines on 42-50725/M, and a turn for home was made. The No.2 engine had caught fire with flames streaming back as far as the waist; the fire eventually went out but the engine still vibrated heavily. The inexorable loss of height suffered by the underpowered B-24 after two engines failed made it an easy target for flak gunners, who put one shell through the left wing that left the bomber with virtually no fuel. The crew abandoned their B-24 in the area where the German, Luxembourg and French national borders meet. Col. Snavely landed at Saarburg right on the Luxembourg/German border, while the others appear to have baled out over France, several of who received various injuries. The Group CO was in two minds about what to do with his '50-mission crusher' cap when preparing to bale out. He decided against its retention and left it behind. Some time later it was returned to him at Shipdham in an amazingly roundabout fashion.

A formation of 44th BG bombers flies through smoke markers released by a previous Group.This could spell disaster if the latter unit had not already bombed on the markers.

One of a party of GIs sifting through the B-24's wreckage had come upon the cap, which bore his name inside, and had taken it. Several days later this soldier was in Paris when his path coincided with the crew led by Lt. William Smith as they drank in a bar; the crew had diverted off the mission on the grounds of fuel shortage The GI was holding an officer's cap which when examined turned out to be that of Col. Snavely. The cap was bargained for and finally handed over on the pretext that the airmen wanted to forward it to Snavely's next of kin! (The cap had originally belonged to Lt. Dubowsky (68th BS). One day he was standing around when Col. Snavely entered the room, and enquired of Bob; "What head-size is your cap?" When discovering the measurement matched his own, he promptly took the item, stuck it on his head and left!).

The second total loss of a bomber occurred on return to England. Lt. Lindsay (68th BS) could not find a visible route to any airfield in the region and baled out his crew near Norwich, leaving 42-110095/G on autopilot and heading for a watery grave in the North Sea.

Nose art shot of B-24J-60-CF, 44-10542 G+ of the 66th BS, which was formerly with the 491st BG. This B-24 crash-landed on 28 January 1945 in Belgium.

"Corky" a B-24-H-20-DT, 42-51101H of the 68th BS was a veteran of sixty-five missions, but would be lost on her 66th mission. The aircraft took a direct flak hit in the bomb bay over the target area. Eight of 1/Lt. Corwine's crew were KIA, and S/Sgt. Kirkey was shot on the ground after landing.

A nice photo of the cleaned up nose art on B-14H-30-FO 42-50427/V of the 68th BS, which was originally named 'Puritanical Bitch.' Major Snavely was not happy about the name and made the ground crew re-paint name as 'Puritanical Witch.' The bomber was destroyed on 22 March 1945 while attempting to take off on what would have been its seventy-ninth mission.

Next day enough aircraft were dispatched to form one squadron within the 14th CBW and to bomb the oil refineries at Harburg. For those crews well advanced in their tour of duty the next ten days proved frustrating as the winter weather continued to restrict operations for the 2nd BD in particular with a single mission on the 21st to Heilbronn's marshalling-yards. Once again just eleven crews went out to form High Squadron within the 'B' Group of the 14th CBW. PFF guidance was compromised when the H2X equipment in the Lead ship went 'out' but the 44th BG contingent took up a course for a target of opportunity that resulted in a good visual strike on the same type of facilities located at Pforzheim. Lt. Franks (68th BS) first suffered a 'runaway' No.4 on 42-50725/M and later discovered he was running low on fuel. Problems with the electrical system and a gradual icing-up of the bomber led to a bale-out over French territory. One gunner was injured and hospitalised on the continent but the other members of the crew returned home on the 29th. Reputed fuel shortage forced several other crews to land at continental airfields for replenishment. In addition, missions were resumed on the 28th with a Group-strength force of twenty-eight aircraft that recorded strikes well past the MPI thanks to G-H equipment failure. Only twenty-five aircraft landed back at Shipdham, with the missing trio being 'written-off'. CORKY (42-51101/H) was a 68th BS bomber being flown by Lt. Corwine. A flak shell struck home in the bomb-bay during the bomb-run, and just three parachutes emerged before the aircraft blew up, but Lt. Corwine (P) and T/Sgt. Colosimo (ROG) were the sole survivors. The officer complement of CORKY's crew had shared Hut 17 with Lt. Ackerman's team. Lt. Graham (CP) recalled how he was first surprised when Lts. Lough (CP) and Scott (N) did not appear in the billet after de-briefing. Enquiries by Graham elicited scraps of information; "they went down … some chutes were seen … one, two, three?" The MIA airmen were not just hut-mates to the others, but had often laid on entertainment 'vignettes' in the form of song and dance routines. These were all the more whimsical in view of Lough's giant physique that towered above his companion's more average build – a true 'Mutt and Jeff' combination! Although each crew tended to keep itself to itself, the proximity of young, vulnerable men in the same living quarter led to some degree of social contact as in this instance. (Lt. Graham's final thought on their loss were very touching; "May God welcome them into his Kingdom, as they were welcomed into Hut 17").

"The Little Dutchman" is a Douglas A-20J Havoc with all guns removed, which is photographed at Shipdham. The medium attack bomber is thought to have been assigned to the 491st as a Group 'hack.' It had flown upwards of fifty missions as confirmed by the mission 'hash marks.'

Lt. Perrault's 506th BS crew were more fortunate when their bomber, 44-10542/G+ – TALLY HO II suffered progressive engine failure in Nos.1, 3 and 4, with the latter power plant catching fire. The airfield close to Brussels that they finally reached and over which they were orbiting under Ground Control was out of sight under the cloudbanks and the pilots were directed to break through the clouds and make a landing approach. It was just after getting into the clear that the third engine faltered. The attempted wheels-down landing in a snow-covered field ended with the nose and one main landing gear wheel collapsing and forcing a ground-loop action. The pilots had put up a good effort considering the crew was on its first mission, while an iced-up windshield had further hindered the landing effort! A second 68th BS aircraft was also declared 'Category E' when it was abandoned by Lt. Muldoon's crew while over Brussels/Melsbroek airfield; this was 42-52618/V+ – CHIEF WAPELLO.

A second 68th BS aircraft flown by Lt. Almonia was lost this day back at Shipdham while on a non-operational flight. The runway was covered in slush, which was cast up by a preceding B-24 onto the wings of 42-50349/F – FLAK MAGNET as it bored down the runway on a test-flight. The ice-accretion created as the spray solidified on the aircraft lifting surfaces quickly bit home as the aircraft was just off the airfield, and it fell out of the sky, to catch fire upon impact. Sgt. Scott (Eng.) was crushed when the top turret became unhinged, and although pulled free by the other crewmembers and hospitalised, passed away seven days later. What flak had failed to do to the veteran bomber of nine months operational standing had now accomplished by Mother Nature!

January ended with two missions launched in three days. The first (29th) was briefed for Altenbecken but the much-bombed marshalling-yards of Hamm (Secondary) caught their latest bout of punishment from two of the Group Squadrons. The Lead Squadron had experienced problems with its H2X equipment and looked for a target of opportunity that duly turned up in the form of Muenster's railroad facilities. The last day of the month involved a run to a steel works and blast furnace at Hallendorf, but it proved immediately for two reasons. The first affected the mission itself, which was recalled; the signal to return was not received until the bombers were bypassing the Dummersee. Then, weather over East Anglia forced the crews to divert northwards into RAF airfields in Yorkshire. (The anticipated grumbles at not gaining mission 'credit' were firmly quashed next day when the fliers returned to Shipdham, since such an award had already been granted in their absence!)

"Loco Moco" of the 66th BS in-bound to the target area.

February 1945

The loss of four aircraft on one day (28 January), though quite severe, was the last occasion that such a daily figure would occur at Shipdham before hostilities ceased. In addition the Group was reaching towards another mission milestone – the 300th – that would be recorded during February. The weather conditions were still poor and mission-launch was accordingly a matter of beating the elements. An added hazard was the sudden appearance of weather fronts that could endanger the safe launch and recovery of a mission – especially the latter condition when the aircraft were often critically short of fuel.

An example of this was witnessed by S/Sgt. Lundy (67th BS). The sound weather permitting take-off steadily deteriorated with high cloudbanks and snow flurries blurring vision as the day wore on. He was sheltering in the lee of the control tower as the snowfall increased to blizzard-level but with half the Group formation still aloft. One of the north/south runways had been forced into use thanks to a wind veering to the north. However, one B-24, whose pilots feared they were about to literally 'run dry', made an approach from the west onto the main runway. Suddenly, the control officer up on the tower roof was heard to yell out, run to the balcony railing and fire a red-red flare in an easterly direction. The Sgt. could see nothing as he strained his eyes against the murky vision surrounding the airfield. However, his ears almost immediately picked up the sound of four Pratt & Whitneys pushed to full power as the aircraft to which they belonged wended its upward but invisible path from right to left. It appeared that a second crew finding itself in a similar fuel predicament had almost simultaneously approached and settled down on the main runway and were therefore on a collision course. The control officer had noted the fact, and the flare had been discharged as a desperate warning for the pilots to clear the runway. Mercifully, there was still sufficient lateral distance between the two B-24s for the one that had been 'warned-off' to get airborne again!

It was not until the 3rd that the weather cleared sufficiently for thirty-three aircraft to take off for the oil refinery facilities at Magdeburg. However, the Secondary comprising the city's major marshalling-yards was hit after the Lead ship's bombsight failed. Another three-day period of inclement weather elapsed before the second monthly mission went out. Madgeburg was again visited when the Rothensee oil refinery was targeted. A similar situation to the 3rd ensued when the marshalling-yards were substituted for the Primary. (In fact, the Primary was to feature in all three of the Group's next missions!)

Maintaining flight on just two engines of a B-24 was an onerous duty, made more fraught when over enemy territory. This factor, combined with a radioed 'giveaway' of one's position, could end in the crew involved being added to the MIA list. Lt. Arnold Kleinschmidt (66th BS) recalled a mission conducted in early February to what was described as an airfield well north of Frankfurt. A violent snowstorm on the target approach, and the Squadron 'Mickey' operator's inability to pick it out, forced the Lead pilot to swing his formation towards Frankfurt, a major industrial city that was thoroughly ringed by flak batteries.

During the bomb-run a flak fragment penetrated the No.3 engine on Kleinschmidt's bomber and 'feathering' action had to be taken, and before the run was completed the No.2 engine had shed its propeller following another strike. By now, having been left behind and bereft of any anti-flak cover provided by the use of 'Carpet', the ailing B-24 was at the center of the gun barrage. Fortunately, the German gunners were not aware of the bomber's steady height loss so the vast bulk of their fire was reaching too high to have the desired affect.

Fighter cover was called for as the bomber's nose was pointed due west, and a single P-51 soon turned up to protect its charge as far as the bomb line in France. Almost immediately after this point was reached the P-51 pilot called up in the clear and said; "Sweetheart, I live next door – I believe you can make it now." This remark, light-hearted as it was, was to have an unfortunate and almost lethal consequence for the B-24 crew. The Germans always monitored the Allied airwaves, and in instances like this, could easily vector their fighters to intercept. Arnold called for his gunners to be alert and search for 'escorts' and sure enough, one turned up – in the form of a Bf 109! The fighter made just one pass that seemingly landed strikes behind the Nos.3 and 4 engines according to the navigator. By straining his neck, Arnold could see the black latex safety lining oozing out of the damaged area. His concern now was that the liner's proximity to the functioning and red-hot No.4 supercharger

Lt. Ryan's B-24 lies broken in a pond at the east end of the airfield. The pilots had tried to make a emergency landing at Shipdham on the morning of 8 January 1945 but were told to go round as their landing approach was too high. They attempted a second approach, but clipped some trees, tore the right hand wing tip off and skidded along the frozen ground before finally coming to rest in a duck pond. Lt. Ryan and crew were from the 466th BG at Attlebridge, and the aircraft was 'The Falcon', a B-24H-25-FO, 42-95248/S+ from the 785th BS.

could ignite and blowup the wing if not the entire bomber. A black blister the size of a five-gallon bucket had formed on the wing leading edge but this problem was currently less than the one caused by the pilot's evasive tactic of diving their aircraft. The speed was well above the 'red line' maximum level and the B-24 developed a high-speed stall when recovery into level flight was attempted. It took half of the former 17,000ft. altitude to effect recovery.

The IFF system was 'out' and the possibility of being fired upon by British AA batteries was real. Fortunately the necessary radio contact was made at the last moment, the crossing of the Channel safely made, and a heading taken up for Shipdam. Once on the ground, the cause of the potentially mortal damage to the wing was traced, not to a German cannon shell, but to part of the front turret. This segment had been blown off by a shell before gashing the wing leading edge and entering the gas tank – a true case of self-inflicted injury! (By the time the crew got to their barracks their personal belongings were already divided up, on the assumption – often tragically accurate – that the airmen in question were permanent absentees from the Group ranks).

It was a cold, hard fact that wartime aircraft were a threat to life and limb from the moment they were approached until each individual was again well distant from their presence. This fact applied equally to combat and ground crew, as an incident on 7 February was to confirm. The aircraft were being bombed-up for a planned mission to Osnabrueck (7th) when matters got drastically out of hand at a 506th BS hardstand containing 42-50509/Y – WANA. The main line and battery switches were tuned on, but the auxiliary power unit (APU) on the flight deck was out of fuel. The necessary replenishment from the service truck was made, but the mechanic involved returned the fuel container to the vehicle only after he had started the equipment.

A mixed formation of 44th BG bombers is being led by a 506th PFF ship. The photo was taken on the 13 January 1945 mission, and the Lead machine, which has the radome down, is a B-24JSH-10-FO, 42-51704/C flown by Lt. Ogden K. Hill (Lead crew 506th BS). The next bomber in trail is 42-51351/P: it was Lead element left wing, and was being flown by Lt. Ray Ciesielski (506th BS). The last B-24 is S/42-50763 flown by Captain. Ernest C. Holmer (67th Lead pilot): Holmer was flying as Deputy Lead for the mission. The target was the marshalling yards at Kaiserslautern in Germany.

A fire developed in this short interval and, despite the ground crew's efforts, it got out of control. Most of the ten 500lb. bombs nestling beneath the bomber and ready for loading were hastily rolled to one side of the hardstand but the balance had to be left in place as the flames became too fierce for the men. The fire-trucks summoned to the scene were just arriving when two bombs 'cooked off', indenting the concrete surface to a five-foot depth and scattering fragments of aircraft and bomb-casing hundreds of yards. There was just one fatality, but this airman's loss was particularly poignant. S/Sgt. Duckie (68th BS) had recently completed his tour of missions, and was currently serving as a guard while awaiting orders for homeward shipment. A piece of casing penetrated the shack in which he was sitting and killed him outright.

The coincidence of another three-day break in completed operations ended on the 9th with the third consecutive run to

Mosquito TA446 was on a local flight from Swannington. The crew was conducting a flight test for that night's mission, following engine repairs for combat damage received the previous day, when one of the engines burst into flame. The pilot made an emergency landing at Shipdham but the Mosquito broke its back and was scrapped.

Rothensee's oil refineries. (A mission to Bielefeld twenty-four hours before had been 'scrubbed' as Assembly was being made). Once again, a solid undercast over the Primary resulted in yet more ordnance being dropped upon Magdeburg's railroad system, even though this too was visually obscured.

The latest spell of adverse weather conditions grounded the Group for three days, while the crews were not called on for the 2nd Air Division mission sent out on the 11th. Then, weather conditions on St. Valentine's Day proved to be a stark contrast with excellent visibility permitting full mission launch – and a fourth attempt to demolish the Rothensee oil refinery system! The clear conditions over England were not matched by those at Magdeburg, which was again blanketed out by solid cloud. H2X bomb-runs were accordingly directed against the railroad system within the city boundaries. The 2nd Air Division was not yet finished with Rothensee, because it was the briefed target next day.

There was a change in bombing priorities, with the Primary also listed as the Secondary should cloud cover be present, and bombing have to be accomplished by H2X means. Sure enough, bombing was conducted with unobserved results. The flak, although moderate and fairly accurate, was arguably not the main danger to the 67th BS this day. The squadron's bomb-run saw the formation veer to the right, and directly under the path of another Group just as their bombs were being released! Thankfully, there were no casualties as the Shipdham fliers hastily manoeuvered out of the way, although at least one near-collision occurred in the process of evasion.

The final run to Madgeburg for the 44th BG was also the first of eleven missions it would fly by the month-end, although one (20th) was 'scrubbed' as the formations were over the French coast on their way to Nuernberg. The first completed run was on the 16th when marshalling-yards at Rheine were struck as the Secondary alternative to Salzbergen's oil refineries. Bad weather closed down Shipdham among numerous 8th USAAF bases and its crews diverted into airfields abroad before returning next day. It was the 21st before a full Group mission was next flown when the 'scrubbed' Nuernberg mission was resurrected. Over 1200 B-17s and B-24s hammered the railroad system in the Bavarian city through solid cloud.

Operation CLARION was initiated on the 22nd with the intention of landing a smashing blow against Germany's overall communications system. This included striking at road junctions deemed to be 'choke-points' regardless of the size of the surrounding built-up area. The town of Hohengandern just east of Kassel possessed a railroad station and junction and was

Above: Belgium civilians start to gather round 'Tally Ho II' a B-24J-60-CF 44-10542/G+ of the 66th BS, on 28 January 1945, after her unexpected arrival at Bonneff-Gerblou, twenty miles east of Brussels in Belgium.

Right: "Chief Wapello" a B-24H-15-FO 42-52618V+ of the 66th BS. Received by the 44th BG on 20th August 1944 from the 487th BG and assigned to the 506th BS, it was later assigned to the 66th BS and crashed at airfield B-58 Brussels-Melsbroek, Belgium, 28 January 1945.

laid on as the Primary; marshalling-yards further north at Goettingen constituted the Secondary. The twenty-nine crews that went out encountered a ground haze that obscured Hohengandern until the very last moment. The course for Goettingen was then taken up and a very good visual bombing was carried out at the inordinately low altitude of 8,000ft. So good was the result that it was later nominated as the best effort by a 2nd Air Division unit during February!

CLARION was completed next day with another mass effort by the Allied strategic bombers that in the 8th USAAF's case involved just over 1200 individual sorties. The 'A' Wing of the 14th CBW was led by the 44th BG with thirty crews out of fifty-seven participating against marshalling-yards at Weimer. Bombing was by H2X, no flak was encountered and the Luftwaffe also remained totally absent. However, compounding this pleasant set of statistics was the salient fact that the Group had now put in its 300th mission. Furthermore, the 67th BS crew led by Lt. Struthers had just completed its thirty-fifth and final mission. Their B-24 was another Shipdham veteran, on its 103rd mission, and all flown without a single 'aborted' example; this was 42-95318/J – OLD IRON CORSET, whose naturally proud ground crew was headed by M/Sgt. Nelson. (A further twenty-six missions would be put in by the bomber prior to her return home on 29 May. Her crew chief was an 'original' combat flier with the Group who had been grounded due to medical reasons).

Marshalling-yards as ever remained a regular priority for the 2nd Air Division with four of the five remaining monthly missions devoted to this target-type. The exception (24th) involved an oil refinery at Misburg, which was briefed for, and attacked by, a proportion of the Division's strength including the 44th BG. Today's strike on Misburg was conducted through 10/10 cloud. By now, the oil Campaign was virtually over and overall production levels reduced to less than a quarter of the May 1944 total when the campaign commenced.

Three of the railroad targets at Aschaffenburg (25th) Pankow (26th) and Siegen (28th) were struck, all of them with unobserved results. The fourth Primary at Halle (27th) was headed for but the H2X equipment provided too weak a signal; however the DR approach alternative to Halle was regarded as unsatisfactory and when Bitterfeld, which possessed a similar railroad facility, began to show up strongly on the H2X radar-scope, this was bombed instead.

There was an extra sense of trepidation when Pankow showed up on the briefing map – it was part of Berlin! 'Big B' still enjoyed a strong reputation as a tough target, even at this stage of World War II. As it so happened just three out of the entire force of 1100 bombers tracking over the cloud-covered metropolis were culled by the enemy defences. In the 44th BG's case, what flak was encountered proved to be meagre and well wide of the twenty-one-strong formation. Bombs were dropped through the several cloud layers that totally obscured visual sighting.

The Aschaffenburg mission had resulted in an aircraft loss although the crew were safe. Lt. Derrick's 42-51258/J+ had lost fuel due to a flak strike, and was running dangerously short by the time Belgium was reached. The emergency airfield they were close to could not be picked out, so the pilot elected to bale out the crew. Lt. Meyers (CP) landed so hard that he fractured his spine and spent months in hospital before recovery. The other eight airmen collected just one broken leg between them, the unlucky exception being T/Sgt. Brown (Eng.).

March 1945
Wacht am Rhein (Watch on the Rhine)

The daily mission-sequence begun on 21 February continued over the first five days of March, while the 'stand down' announced for the 6th provided little respite for the combat

Above: A tragic accident happened during the early hours of the 7th February 1945, while preparing 42-50509 "WANA" a B-24J-1-FO of the 68th BS for yet another mission. A fuel spillage caused a fire that cooked off part of the bomb load that consisted of 10x500lb. GP bombs. A 68th BS ground crewman checks out a blown bomb case.

Above right: This photo shows the total destruction of 'Wana.' The tragic irony of this accident was that just one man lost his life – he was a tour-expired airman waiting to be rotated back to the States! The largest recognizable parts of 42-50509 were the engines and propellers.

Right: The line shack out on the 67th hardstand area was over 300 yards from "Wana's" hardstand. Sgt. Frank Chowanski, found S/Sgt. Stanley H. Ducki in the line shack, which had been hit by a very large segment of a bomb casing. Sgt. Ducki, who had completed thirty-five combat missions, was sheltering from the cold. The dead airman bore no visible marks to indicate he had been struck by the bomb casing. The Fortunes of War had dealt Ducki one of the cruelest blows imaginable.

crews; many of their number had to fly practice missions that involved G-H equipment, instrument and camera bombing checks! The month began with an attack upon Ingolstadt's marshalling-yard complex. The mission generally proved to be routine in nature, but there was a brief moment of apprehension when a Me 262 jet-fighter made a lunge from six o'clock at the formation's Low Squadron and disappeared out ahead, fortunately without landing any strikes. However, there was one aircraft casualty that was due to fuel shortage. Lt. Crandall (67th BS) was flying in 42-95049/O –FEARLESS FOSDICK, a veteran B-24H enjoying many missions since arrival in May 1944. The crew took to their parachutes near Vermand, France and returned home several days later. (Sadly, the Crandall crew's lease on life had a bare twenty-three days to run at this stage). A second crew led by Lt. Maynard were also facing fuel shortage but managed to get down safely on a continental airfield.

Lt. Norman Nutt was forced to make a emergency landing on returning from the 17 February 1945 misson due to shortage fuel and damaged hydraulic system. B-24JSH-5-FO 42-51594/P+ would be repaired and put back into combat: it returned to the Zone of the Interior on 22 May 1945.

A B-24 of the 44th BG pulls contrails somewhere over Germany. These visual traces were both a giveaway of the USAAF formations to the enemy and a danger to the crews flying tight formation – in the latter case, the chances of a collision caused by flying through thick contrail patterns were ever high.

B-24J-1-FO 42-50643 Bar-K of the 506th BS is seen at Raydon Airfield in Suffolk after ferrying some ground personnel of the 353rd FG from the Continent.

A very familiar target appeared on the briefing map next day, when the Rothensee refinery was the focus for assault. The last attack had resulted in the refinery being bombed for the first time out of the five attempted strikes launched to date. Today's run did not add to the plant's destruction because a switch to the railroad system in Magdeburg was made. The 2nd Air Division's seventh appearance over Magdeburg since early February came on the 3rd, but this time round there was a degree of target visibility since the tall smoke-stacks could be seen peeking up through the ground haze. The moderate flak encountered did not interfere with a good concentration of ordnance around the MPI. On the other hand the escort cover, strong as it was, proved almost powerless in the face of the small group of Me 262s that descended upon the bomber formations. The German pilots took down four B-24s while literally leaving the P-51s standing still.

Aschaffenburg's tank production factory and Harburg's oil refinery were the next two day's briefed targets, but only the latter was attacked by H2X method. A heavy haze coupled with thick contrails spared the Primary on the 4th so the Division's units sought alternatives. This, for the 44th BG, evolved as marshalling-yards at Tuttlingen and Targets of Opportunity at Aach and Offenberg. The extended daily mission-run briefly ended after the Harburg mission, but fully fourteen missions were to be completed by the 23rd that included a 'double-header' on the 21st.

Rail targets dominated the bulk of missions for the Group up to the 14th. Two runs to the key viaduct at Bielefeld were sent out on the 7th and 10th with bombing conducted by G-H; the Shipdham contribution on the 7th was limited to just three crews assigned to other groups. It was almost inevitable that 'blind' bombing of such a narrow structure, even with the help of this precise electronic-aid, was unlikely to achieve a solid strike. The bridge still remained intact following the release of over eighty and 114 bomb-loads respectively. In between, the

2nd Air Division went to marshalling-yards at Betzdorf and Siegen, with the 44th BG dividing its effort between the two locations. The Siegen force, flying High Squadron within the 491st BG, experienced G-H problems and made an H2X run on what was believed to be Frankfurt, but turned out to be Limburg.

The second Bielefeld mission commenced a five-day operational sequence. The 11th saw a return to a target of grim historic significance at Shipdham; this was Kiel, where the Group had bled so badly on 14 May 1943. The contrast in fortunes could not have been greater this time round, because not one of the 352 Division bombers was lost after completion of an H2X bombing run that left its mark upon the city's U-boat construction yards. Marshalling-yards at Wetzlar (12th) and Gutersloh (14th) were struck with 'good' results. For once, there was clear visibility during the latter sortie, but the High Squadron ended up going over the target with the 20th CBW, while the low squadron's bomb-concentration unfortunately fell short and to the left. A German Army HQ at Zossen close to Berlin was assaulted on the 15th but the projected mission next day was 'scrubbed'.

One crew on the 12th took off with a full crew but were soon reduced by one member. Sgt. Logan on Capt. Macks's 506th BS crew had accidentally triggered off a smoke bomb while moving through the bomb-bay. Some of the weapon's acidic content sprayed the Sgt.'s face, so making it impossible for him to don his oxygen mask. He elected to bale-out, rather than force the aircraft to 'abort' on his behalf. A delayed drop from the aircraft's present 13,000ft. altitude was made to ensure his parachute did not carry him out over the coastline. He landed all right and within a few hours was receiving attention to his painful but not serious burns. (Logan was later awarded the DFC for his action)

The latest string of daily missions commencing on the 17th would extend to the 25th, during which time the last, vital land battle in western Europe would be launched. The bomber crews' minds were on more personal matters, with survival of their combat tour a priority item. Of course, the utter domination posed by the Allied fighters over the Luftwaffe meant that the chances of going down to an aerial adversary were virtually nil. The effectiveness of the flak defences was also diminishing, although not quite to the same degree, and the ground gunners would continue to cull bombers from the formations right up to the conclusion of the daylight Offensive.

Nose art of B-24M-5-FO 44-50597 J+ of the 66th BS, which was received by the 44th. BG prior to 10 March 1945: aircraft returned to the Zone of the Interior on 22 May 1945.

Muenster's key rail facilities came in for its latest hammering on the 17th when twenty-two Shipdham crews joined 145 other 2nd Air Division crews in a G-H assisted bombing. However, the High Squadron was forced to release on the smoke markers of preceding formations after its Lead ship had the G-H set fail. Berlin was set up for attack next day when the Rheinmetall-Borsig armaments plant was struck. However, the presence of heavy contrails from the IP onwards adversely affected the High Squadron's attempts to emulate the visual bombing result achieved by the other two Sqdns. Instead, its crews diverted to the city center on which the ordnance was dropped with H2X assistance. Flak damage was slight, although thirteen bombers elsewhere were downed from among the massive aerial Force.

A thick haze at the IP next day caused the Group to drop altitude in order to achieve a visual sighting of the aircraft-

Here a mixed group of NMF and OD B-24's taxi out for a mission. The aircraft wait their turn to start take off at the eastern end of the main runway.

assembly plant at Neuberg in Bavaria. The result was an excellent strike with the MPI smothered in hits. Five of the thirty-three bombers landed on the continent, while a sixth entered the MIA list. The Group had been homeward bound and not very far away from the Allied front-lines when Lt. Podojil (66th BS), whose B-24 was earlier observed to be bearing two 'feathered' propellers, called up to say he was confident of reaching friendly territory. That hope was cruelly denied when the crippled bomber was unfortunate enough to be intercepted and downed near Stuttgart by a pair of Bf 109s. Lt. Bail (N), along with both waist gunners and S/Sgt. Schmitz (TG), were the only ones to successfully bale out of 42-51907/B+. Schmitz had suffered a severe leg wound that necessitated its subsequent amputation, but gangrene had set in and he died. His companions were permitted to attend his funeral in Goeppingen. (Lt. Bail was on his second bale-out, the first being on 5 June 1944 out of the B-24 on which Col. Vance had been the Command Pilot. Today was also his twenty-fifth mission).

The operational momentum remained constant for the 8th USAAF, but the contribution of the 44th BG to the next mission (20th) proved surprisingly limited to eleven crews. An expanding smoke pall from the Hemmingstedt oil refinery forced the Lead Bombardier to use the 'off-set' method of bombing. Unfortunately, the offset rate was not properly computed and an 'overshoot' of the MPI ensued.

The perfect weather featured on the 21st – the first day of spring – was 'celebrated' by the dispatch of two missions. First, thirty-five crews headed out within the entire 2nd Air Division to attack the fighter airfield at Achmer. Later in the day just eleven crews formed up with the rest of the 14th CBW and headed for Muelheim airfield in the Ruhr. Bombing at Achmer ranged from very good to poor. The latter effort related to the Low Squadron after it had been forced out of its position in the order of bombing by the High Squadron. A total bombing failure over Muelheim was ascribed to the Lead bombardier being unaware that flak had severed the electrical circuits controlling his bombsight and the autopilot operation.

B-24H-25-FO, 42-95049 "Fearless Fosdick" of the 67th BS. was received by the Group between 27 April and 13 May 1944 and was finally abandoned on 1 March 1945. The crew bailed out, leaving their B-24 to come down at Vermand in France.

The 8th AF was enjoying a run of visual target sighting that continued over the next few days. Swabisch Hall's airfield (used by Me 262 jet fighters) was struck on the 22nd with excellent results. Marshalling-yards at Rheine were given similar treatment next day. One B-24 taking off on the 22nd got no further than an adjoining field. There was precious little runway length remaining even when the over-burdened bombers finally got airborne, and boundary fences were struck on occasions, sometimes with lethal effect. Today, 52-50427/V – PURITANICAL WITCH, did not even get airborne before running off onto the grass and through the boundary fence. It was a miracle that the 68th BS aircraft did not blow up although the nose section was twisted to one side, and Lt. Almonia's crew scrambled out and clear of the wreck.

Two different angle shots of 'Puritanical Witch' a B-24H-30-CF, 42-50427V of the 68th BS. The aircraft had failed to gain lift and ran headlong towards the bomb dump, and the resultant heavy landing twisted the nose off. The name "Puritanical Bitch" was changed by the Group CO Col. Snavely to 'Puritanical Witch.'

The removal of ball turrets from selected aircraft and the fitting of static line equipment around the apertures on the 23rd provided the first firm indication that something special was on the way for the 44th BG. In fact, the crews going out on the morrow would be indulging in their third bout of 'legalised' low flying along with elements from three CBWs of the 2nd Air Division. These would play a vital part in opening up western Germany to a land Invasion.

Operation VARSITY

For centuries the river Rhine had constituted a major barrier to an invasion of the Teutonic territories existing on the east bank. The expression 'Watch on the Rhine' was a very relevant way of describing how German security was dependent upon this major waterway's control.

By March 1945 the western Allies had their troops deployed along the greater length of the Rhine, and had even forged a crossing south of Cologne, when the U.S. 9th Division had managed to secure the Ludendorf rail bridge at Remagen on the 9th. However, the main campaign to pierce the German defences was not launched until the 24th in the region north of Cologne. Two Airborne Divisions (U.S. 17th and British 6th) were to provide over 20,000 troops with their support equipment jumping out of, or landing in, 3,000 transports or gliders respectively. A re-supply of the paratroopers was to be carried out shortly after the soldiers were down. This second logistic effort involved some 240 B-24s with a total of marginally under 600 tons due to be parachuted from the low-flying bombers.

The supplies were to be released both from the bomb-bays and the ball-turret apertures of the twenty-seven Group aircraft who were leading the 14th CBW. The height at which the drops were carried out brought the aircraft into direct confrontation with all types of ground-fire down to single rifles. Capt. Ursal Harvell (Photo Officer) was on board one of the B-24s, ready to shoot a film record of proceedings, and one of his sequences caught the first of two tragic incidents for the Group.

Lt. Chandler (506th BS) was flying 42-50896/Bar-R – SOUTHERN COMFORT III as the formation skimmed across the Rhine near Wesel and commenced the drop at around 200ft.

Light flak and small-arms fire was intense and strikes were soon registered on a number of bombers. Back in the waist of Chandler's B-24 Sgts. DeBlasio and Vance were dispensing their part of the 2 1/2 tons of supplies through the ball-turret opening. No sooner had they finished and the aircraft was banking for the homeward flight when it was hit and set on fire. Sgt. Clark, who had been attending to the bomb-bay

Three shots of the 68th BS, taken from the waist window of another Group bomber during the low-level support Mission to Wesel, Germany. The Group was dropping reinforcement supplies to the Allied parachute forces who had spear-headed Operation Varsity, the crossing of the Rhine on 24 March 1945.

release, shouted, "We've had it" and all three men assumed 'ditching' positions.

An observer in an adjoining bomber noticed that No.4 engine on the stricken bomber was exuding smoke as the machine sagged out of the air. The first contact was with the rudders and the belly, which momentarily bounced the B-24 back in the air. The second and final contact began with the right wingtip as the aircraft turned in that direction; this resulted in an incipient ground loop that ended in a complete 180 degree turn before it came to rest after splitting in two. Both DeBlasio and Vance miraculously survived after being partially thrown clear; the fact they were still wearing their flak-suits probably contributed to this positive outcome although both suffered broken limbs, cuts and bruises. None of the other seven men on board were so blessed and died when the truncated wreckage exploded several minutes later.

The two Sgts. painfully crawled over to and hid beneath a wagon. Each man attended to the other's wounds as best as possible, although Sgt. Vance's head wound left him incoherent at times. After an interval of time, a group of civilians came upon the airmen. One of them took possession of Sgt. DeBlasio's pistol, but not before he had managed to strip the mechanism. He was then asked to reassemble the weapon but played dumb, on the assumption (probably correct) that the German would have shot both captives!

The airmen were taken in charge by an officer, who was guarding a P-47 pilot, and all three Americans were held in a nearby wood until nightfall. Over the next few days, they were moved further back behind German lines, having either walked or ridden on a horse-drawn cart. They finally arrived at a hospital in Ahlen where their wounds were at least properly attended to, and where those still-mobile patients, including Sgt. Vance, were free to walk around. The Germans were short

'Kay Bar' was a B-24J-90-CO, 42-100314 G+ (66th BS) formerly of the 389th BG: the name was a play on her original individual letter (K-Bar). Aircraft was received by the 44th BG between 20 February and 22 March 1944. She was originally assigned to the 67th BS but later transferred to the 66th, when the code letter was changed from K̲ to V+, then to N+ and finally to G+. Lt. Leonard J. Crandell and his entire crew were KIA while flying this B-24 on the 24 March 1945 re-supply mission to Wesel in Germany.

of nearly everything including food – potato soup and lard-covered black bread was the regular diet!

On 1 April, the noise of tanks was heard, that turned out to be Shermans from a U.S. Army unit, so DeBlasio and Vance went out into the streets. The airmen's dirty and bloodstained appearance was such that they were recognised as fellow-Americans only when they began to speak to their liberators. They were initially transported to a U.S. Hospital in Munchen-Gladbach. Here they were separated, with Sgt. Vance being flown back to an English hospital before return to Shipdham. Sgt. DeBlasio was transferred to a Paris hospital and ultimate shipment to the States after VE-Day.

The second tragedy caught in the lens of Capt. Harvall's camera involved the B-24 flown by Lt. Crandell (67th BS).

'Southern Comfort', 42-50896/Bar-R, of the 506th BS leaves the English coast on 24 March, 1945. Only two of 2/Lt. Max E. Chandler's nine-man crew would still be alive by nightfall, being Sgts. DeBlasio and Vance, both of whom were badly injured.

A formation shot of the 66th BS; nearest aircraft with individual code of J+ is 'Loco Moco', a B-24M-5-FO, 44-50597. This B-24 would log twenty missions by the end of hostilities.

The squadron had enjoyed a lengthy run of loss-free missions that extended back to mid-October. The bomber in question on the Operation VARSITY mission was 42-100314/G+. It had been with the Group over thirteen months, and had transferred from the 67th BS to the 66th BS during September. The film sequence showed the aircraft suddenly rearing up before describing an arcing course into the ground and blowing up, killing all nine airmen.

A further personnel casualty occurred on 42-50535/Bar-O of the 506th BS. Sgt. Diaz (LW) was positioned between the ball turret aperture and the bomb-bay, hauling in the static-lines for the supply containers. How he managed to spill his chest-pack remained unclear, but the effect of the parachute streaming from its cover was to drag him inexorably out of the hole; the combination of high speed and minimal altitude guaranteed Sgt. Diaz's fate, and the discovery of his body was reported a few days later.

The 2nd Air Division suffered the loss of fourteen B-24s out of the total force involved in the supply mission. In contrast the day's second mission to bomb airfields saw no aircraft losses from among the force dispatched. The run to a fighter landing strip at Stormede passed off well for the twelve participating 44th BG crews whose aircraft formed a squadron within the 14th CBW Force. Flak damage was however incurred by nearly half the aircraft as the bombers were over-flying Koblenz on the way back. The breaching of the Rhine on this momentous day left the Nazis with no viable means of permanently delaying an Allied advance throughout Germany's western hinterland. The clock was now running inexorably down towards final Victory.

Chapter Thirteen

Victory

The success of Operation VARSITY was already con firmed within twenty-four hours, and the need for the B-24s to act in a subsequent supply-dropping role for the Allied paratroops was not necessary. Instead, the 2nd Air Division bombers went after oil-storage depots, with the 14th CBW assigned the one located at Hitzacker. High cloud-tops over the enemy coast gave way to good vision over the target area, which received over 300 tons of well-directed ordnance.

Operations over the next four days were either restricted or totally cancelled following a relapse in weather conditions. Normal service for the 2nd Air Division was resumed on the 30th when the focus was upon U-boat construction yards and port facilities. The yards and docks located at Wilhelmshaven were well hit using a mix of visual and H2X-assisted bombing in the face of variable cloud cover. March was closed off with a briefed run to Hoya near Bremen where an ammunition storage depot was located. Solid cloud cover forced a diversion to the Secondary further southeast at Brunswick. The vast bulk of the 2nd Air Division landed its ordnance on what the USSTAF Chiefs had long regarded as the Division's favored target-type – marshalling-yards!

The Group had completed twenty-five missions during this month. This was a figure almost equalling a full combat tour for any airmen fortunate enough to fly all twenty-five. It was also a figure whose realisation back in 1942-1943 would have taken up months rather than weeks to achieve, and was a measure of just how far the 8th USAAF had matured into a massive and well-coordinated combat Force since that pioneering period of operations.

The daylight Offensive had but twenty-five days to run as April was entered, but the numbers of suitable targets were already fast shrinking as Germany was being overrun. The occupation of the Ruhr that had been the principal anticipated prize arising from a successful Operation MARKET-GARDEN in September 1944 was now in hand. The U.S. Armies were advancing in leaps and bounds towards the east and southeast, while British/Canadian forces were sweeping up through Holland and northwest Germany.

The 8th USAAF did not commence operations until the 2nd when Denmark appeared on the briefing maps for the very first time. However, a build-up of bad weather resulted in a 'recall' being issued while the formations were traversing the North Sea. (An airfield at Tirstrup, one of a number targeted this day, had been assigned to the 44th BG; mission 'credit' was granted despite the cancellation). Concentration on targets in northern Germany took up the next two days although the 2nd Air Division was only called upon on the 4th when the 14th CBW went for Kaltenkirchen airfield north of Hamburg. Normal procedure when encountering weather conditions such as the undercast shrouding the target was to bomb either the Primary or a suitable alternative with G-H or H2X guidance. On this day, the issued orders were to bomb visually, or otherwise to bring the bombs back home.

No such limitation applied next day when the Division headed into southern Germany to attack a munitions depot at Bayreuth and marshalling-yards at Plauen. The blanked-out primary at Plauen meant that the bombing force, which included the 44th BG, used H2X to strike at the general traffic network in the town. Five out of the forty-three crews taking off failed to get back to Shipdham; four of this number later reported in from continental airfields, but not the 506th BS aircraft flown by Lt. Brown. It had last been seen trailing the formation on the way back. No.1 engine was 'feathered' and the pilots were maintaining a course for Allied-occupied territory.

Unfortunately, the eventual breakout through the clouds at 3000ft. was over the eastern edges of the Ruhr, and the bomber was quickly engaged by ground fire. A second engine was set on fire, the pilot wounded and S/Sgt. Nash (ROG) killed. The bale-out bell was finally rung and all eight men alive at this time jumped, leaving 44-40158/Bar-Q – TINKER BELLE to plunge into the ground. Sadly, the survival figure was later reduced to seven; Lt. Brown had suffered a head wound during the action and although he did bale out, he in fact died during or following his descent. Sgt. Sampley (WG) got hung up in a tree and while undoing his harness lost his balance. He ended up hanging from a branch with one foot wrapped in his parachute straps and twenty feet above the ground! He very carefully pulled himself back upright and clambered down to find himself almost immediately surrounded by soldiers brandishing rifles with bayonets attached! Sgt. Otto, manning the nose turret, did not hear the bale-out bell. By the time he became aware of his lonely status, he barely had sufficient time to get out and pull his ripcord. His parachute also got tangled in a tree from which he was cut down by a soldier.

Lt. Brown's B-24 had the unfortunate distinction of being the final Group casualty relating to combat operations. However, the fates had not yet finished with the Shipdham airmen, a number of whom would remain forever in their 'adopted' country.

Daily missions were the order of the day up to the 13th when a stand down was ordered. In that period the Group bombed marshalling-yards and airfields in particular. H2X was used over Halle (6th) but a visual run on the secondary next day proved disappointing since the ordnance landed short and to one side of Krummel's railroad center. In addition, there was a brief incursion by the Luftwaffe in the form of several Me 262s and Bf 109s. The attacks were uncoordinated although some pilots closed in to minimum distance and caused slight damage on several 66th BS aircraft. Better results were achieved over Leipheim airfield (9th) but the Low Squadron registered a 'Gross Error' when bombing Schweren airfield next day due to an operating accident by its Lead Bombardier. Finally, Neumarkt's marshalling-yards were well struck by most of the Group; the exception was the High Squadron, whose lead ship bombsight suffered a telescope motor failure, causing another 'short-bombing' result.

It was on the 14th that the Station observed 'Salute the Ground Man Week' when some 600 personnel paraded in front of Brig.Gen. Johnson, who presented ten Bronze Stars. He then delivered a short but inspiring talk on the vital nature of the men's part in the Offensive. He said it was not just the nine men in each bomber but the ninety ground men that got each aircraft into the air that should also receive credit for mission success. Finally, he recalled the day of his CMH award; "I received this highest honor, but do not consider it a personal one. The citation reads ... 'for the destruction of a highly important target'... I considerate it to be an award to the Group Commander for the work done by every member of this Group in destroying the target." The ovation the General received as he left the podium was not only loud but was truly heart-felt by all present. Col. Snavely who would hand over command of the 44th BG to Col. Vernon Smith next day closed off the ceremony with a short speech of thanks.

On the 21 January 1945 mission to Heilbronn marshalling-yards in Germany, 1/Lt. Habedank and crew were flying Group Lead in 44-48858 a B-24J-20-FO. On the bomb run the H2X failed, so Captain Holmer took over Lead, and visually bombed the marshalling yards at Pforzheim, Germany.

Cpl. Burford of the 506th BS stands near 'Iron Corset' of the 67th BS.

Ground crew check out an oil leak on the prop boss, as the combat crew due to fly the aircraft under scrutiny watch and wonder if they will be flying today's mission.

Early morning briefing for the crews: the target today is Tirstrup in Denmark, another long haul mission. In fact the mission was subsequently aborted.

This same day, the crews were initially puzzled when briefed for a target on France's Biscay coastline. The German garrison at Royan right on the mouth of the river Gironde was still holding out and pinning down Allied units. Thirty-six aircraft dropped their ordnance right on the MPI. The mission was repeated next day, but this time around the ordnance consisted of fighter drop-tanks filled with napalm except for three B-24s into which M-47 incendiaries were loaded. Fighter escort was dispensed with on both occasions, given the absence of any Luftwaffe units anywhere in the region. Flak proved to be both light and inaccurate and no damage or personnel injuries were sustained on either mission.

Although the Group had avoided losses on both Royan missions, heavy casualties were apparently sustained by French civilians. Lt. Arnold Kleinschmidt (66th BS) recalled his feeling of possible disaster when he heard that the ordnance consisted of P-47 drop-tanks, which had no directional fins and were not basically compatible to being hung in the B-24 bomb-racks. Gen. Johnson at the briefing had said, "If the ordnance does not go on the target area there are many French civilians within the same area, and killing a few could get a flight commander shot at dawn!" The pre-mission practice dropping of the tanks that was made in order to establish reliable data to feed to the bomb-sights did not leave Lt. Kleinschmidt with a good feeling about the likely accuracy of the subsequent strikes.

The briefed absence of heavy flak at Royan did not prove accurate, while the presence of a warship in the estuary added to the flak barrier. Then, as the 44th BG lined up for the IP a B-17 formation was seen some 3,000ft. above several B-24 formations and clearly ready to bomb. The ordnance fell through the B-24 ranks and although Arnold recollected what he described as 'one hell of a fireworks display' no bomber casualties were actually incurred. The poor ballistic properties of the tanks with widespread scattering was the likely the reason for 'friendly' casualties being incurred at Royan.

On return to Shipdam Arnold took a Jeep to the photo lab to check out the squadron strike photographs. These happily displayed a near-perfect record of hits on the actual target area. His sense of satisfaction took a severe knock on attending the de-briefing with the other Lead pilots; Gen. Johnson was present and on seeing Arnold ordered him to 'hit a brace', before delivering a tirade that would have made a sailor blush. It was only when the Gen. had finished that the reason for his state of mind emerged. He asked Arnold, "How in the Hell am I going to explain away your killing 256 French civilians?" When he was informed of the strike photo confirming the 66th BS accurate delivery of its ordnance, he asked; "Aren't you Lt….?" The officer in question was next to Arnold, who was very upset at not even receiving a subsequent apology for being wrongly 'cussed out'!

The 15th witnessed a structural change when the 405th Air Service Group was created from the HQ and base services squadron, the 655th Air Material Squadron and 831st Air Engineering Squadron. The personnel were re-assigned from the now disbanded 50th Complement Squadron, 464th Sub Depot and associated sub-units (Quartermaster Co., Ordnance Co., Finance Section, MP Co., Fire-fighting Platoon and Medical Dispensary).

The continuing swift advance by the ground forces was making the choice of targets for the 'Heavies' ever more limited. In the case of the 44th BG the crews were destined to respond to just four more CQ calls in the early hours. The first came on

'Glory Bee' a B-24H-15-FO, 42-52616/R+ tucks her gear away on the 12 April 1945 mission to Tirstrup, in Germany. In the event, the mission was recalled. This B-24 amassed no less than 101 missions by the end of the war.

A 506th crew chief gives a thumbs-up to the pilot of the aircraft. The B-24 would not see combat this day as the mission was aborted due to bad weather.

the 16th when marshalling-yards at Landshut north of Munich were targeted. A B-17 Group cutting across their path during target approach forced two Squadrons to 'abort' their visual bomb-runs and then jettison; the Low Squadron at least succeeded in making a solid strike. Two days later thirty aircraft headed out for the same region to bomb more marshalling-yards at Passau, and this time around all the ordnance went down to provide an accurate strike. On return, the 67th BS held softball game between officers and enlisted men (the latter won 5-2!), followed by a beer party in the evening that 'demolished' eight barrels of beer. Events were rounded off by an impromptu jam session and later a song-fest

The 44th BG's penultimate mission in World War II involved a rail junction at Schwandorf-Irlaching due east of Nuernberg that had been briefed but 'scrubbed' the previous day (19th). There was no opposition at all experienced by either the 2nd Air Division or the 44th BG as the Group's thirty aircraft led the 14th CBW over the target.

The 8th USAAF was dispatched on the 21st but only a relatively small proportion of its strength was involved, and the 44th BG was among the units not called upon. Indifferent weather caused the Primary targets to be abandoned, with 'last resort' alternatives including Ingolstadt's town center attacked by H2X. Then, four days late came the 'Mighty Eighth's' final strike in World War II, that only involved the 1st and 2nd Air Divisions. The latter Division's spread of targets was centered on Salzburg, right on the Austro/German border. Hallein just south of the city was an Austrian town whose marshalling-yards were assigned to the 44th BG. Just across the border from the target was Berchtesgaden, location for Hitler's infamous 'Eagles Nest' dwelling; flak batteries based there and at Salzberg provided a moderate and accurate barrage that only caused slight damage. As the weary fliers tracked back to England this day, they had no way of knowing that the daylight Offensive had finally run its course and the blood-letting was over.

The Aftermath

The ground war was to last just under two weeks more before the total surrender of all the German forces was confirmed at Rheims and in Berlin. During this time the B-17s of the 3rd AD participated in operation Manna/Chowhound, the dropping of supplies to the civilian population in the still-occupied section of Holland. Activities within the other two Divisions were more of a passive nature but did involve flights over western Germany

This 67th BS B-24 lifts off from the main runway for a local practice flight after the mission to Tirstrup on 12 April 1945 had been cancelled.

and the former Nazi-occupied countries. These were made with a view to demonstrating to the ground personnel what had been achieved during the Combined Bombing Offensive, as well as being a 'thank you' for their un-stinted effort in bringing about this stunning achievement.

The flights commenced at the beginning of May and were prefaced by a written 'itinerary' of the intended route and the places of note to be viewed, including targets struck by the Group. In the case of the 44th BG, the 3rd May saw forty B-24s loaded up with personnel, after which the aircraft took off and formed up into a loose formation. The entire flight was made at 1,000ft. and entered Europe at Ostend before crossing over Brussels; here was an important marshalling-yard complex. The southeasterly course headed into Germany until it reached Ludwigshafen. This city possessed a number of I.G. Farben chemical-production plants that had received four strikes. Then it was on to Aschaffenburg to the northeast where another marshalling-yard system had been twice bombed, as had the road and rail systems in nearby Frankfurt. A direct heading west took the aircraft over Mainz, Wiesbaden and the small town at Bingen on the bend of the Rhine and possessing yet another marshalling-yard that had received a triple hammering. North to Koblenz situated on the confluence of the Rhine and Mosel, and subject to four strikes against its multitude of industries as well as the key bridges spanning the twin waterways. Further north along the Rhine was Cologne, a truly massive conurbation packed full of key targets with marshalling yards high on the priority list and 'visited' the same number of times as Koblenz. Finally, the aircraft skirted the western fringe of the Ruhr or 'Flak Valley' as it was feelingly and accurately named by the 8th USAAF fliers before the turn to the left back over and out of northern Belgium and home to Shipdham.

In fact, the itinerary was sometimes varied. One ground crew individual recalled grabbing the nose turret for his vantage point. His recollections were quite revealing about the state of the Continent at this time; the Ardennes countryside churned-up wholesale by tank-tracks ... the German family on their bicycles who instinctively dived for cover as the bellowing herd of bombers flashed overhead at minimum altitude (a reaction the airmen could sympathise with as he remembered the first time a B-24 practice formation for Ploesti had done the same to him!) ... the huge German POW camp on the Rhine, with the same defensive reaction being taken by many of the occupants ... (this time round, the airman's reaction was one of quiet satisfaction at what was a small measure of revenge for the stresses and suffering these soldiers and their kind had placed upon the Free World) ... The stark contrast between the utterly ruined towns and the lush greenery of the surrounding countryside.

14 April 1945, and 506th BS B-24s drop Napalm on Fort-De-Royan, France, where the target was a German garrison holding out. This was the first use of Napalm, the volatile liquid being put in fighter drop tanks and fused.

Party time in the 67th BS area on 18 April 1945. A good time was had by all!

Particularly revealing was the virtually intact cathedral at Cologne, still standing amidst a sea of ruined structures that included the Anhalter rail station right alongside. The scale of destruction at all of the major sites was one that shocked the aerial onlookers, and made some wonder if Germany could ever be brought back to a normal economic and social state. The flooded regions of Holland, and the smiling Dutch faces as the formation crossed Amsterdam were final points of note. (The landing back at Shipdham with this eyewitness still sitting in his forward vantage point was eventful; the attempted three-point landing proved to be made marginally too high, causing the B-24 to hop and skip several times before finally settling down on the runway!)

This is the wreckage of Capt. Donald Edkins aircraft after a crash landing during a practice ATC flight on 11 May 1945. Problems with carrying out a propeller 'feathering' test had led to this drastic situation.

A nice photo of the heart of Station 115 at Shipdham airfield. "Pathway" was the Radio call sign for the Tower.

Thousands of USAAF POWs, including a sizeable number of 44th BG personnel, had survived months or years of alternate despair and hope as the events of World War II drew to their steady, but sometimes stuttering, conclusion. Military reverses such as operation MARKET-GARDEN and the Battle of the Bulge had cast their gloom into the minds of the 'Kriegies' before the ultimate joy of release came during April and May 1945. The experience of captivity for the average Shipdam airman could probably be summed up by that of Sgt. Archie Thomas, the sole survivor from Lt. Mayes crew 67th BS on 8 April 1944.

Following capture and interrogation at Dulag Luft, he had faced a five-day trip in a boxcar to Stalag 17B, Krems. The guards shared the interior with their POWs. And Thomas recalled how one of the Germans would sit at his bench and make hand movements similar to that on a piano – he was apparently a musician whose post-war desire was to be a concert pianist! There being no toilet facilities other than a single bucket inside the box-cars, the train was stopped at intervals to permit the POWs to relieve themselves. This act was conducted alongside the track regardless of any civilian presence – false modesty was clearly not a Germanic trait!

Arrival at a marshalling yard near the camp was followed by a march of several miles to the POWs new 'home'. Final release and assignment to a barrack block was only made after the men had been officially photographed. The newcomers would be an element of some 4000 USAAF personnel, who in turn were to be joined by a further 14,000 Allied POWs during the camp's existence.

The new arrivals were eagerly quizzed by the current 'Kriegies' as to events in the free world. However, the camp possessed a number of radios, from which daily reports were

A mixed formation of B-24Hs and Js taken on the 20 April 1945; the target was the railroad junction at Irlaching, Germany and all aircraft returned.

24 April 1945, and aircraft of the 506th BS are photographed high above Holkham Hall on the North Norfolk coast line, near the small seaside village of Wells next to the Sea. The camouflaged bomber is 'Down De Hatch', the NMF machine in the center is 'the Big Headed Kid' while the other NMF aircraft is 'Clean Sweep.'

formulated and read out to each barracks. As Thomas acidly commented, "we soon found out that we were less informed concerning the war effort that they were!"

Barrack 31A was home for Thomas for the vast bulk of the twelve months and twenty-eight days of his incarceration. It was one of four blocks previously occupied by Russian POWs that had been hastily cleared out for he and his group of POWs, and made available a few days after their arrival. Being on his own in terms of his crew could have led to a sense of isolation but friendships were soon struck up, including one with a Sgt. Robert V Black that endures to this very day.

The daily routine commenced with the guards entering the barracks yelling "Raus mit Ihnen, Appell, Appell!" This 'request' to get out onto the square for roll-call was responded to with the men lining up in columns of five for counting. Sometimes the personnel would deliberately shift around in order to hinder the count; this was sometimes done for a serious purpose following an attempt at escape. The basically monotonous diet provided by the Germans was supplemented by weekly deliveries of Red Cross parcels, although the interval between these welcome arrivals began to stretch during the final chaotic months of 1945.

Keeping warm was a constant problem. The daily single bucket of coal proved barely adequate to heat the barracks, and men slept in their clothing. The bunks were in triple layers and the 'mattresses' were burlap bags containing a none-too-generous quantity of wood shavings – good for the posture but making comfortable sleeping something of an acquired art!

On 8 April 1945, Krems was evacuated and the POWs began a 'forced march' destined to last more than two weeks and extend over 200 miles. This was a tough enough experience for fully fit and well-fed individuals, never mind men whose energy levels had been sapped by prolonged captivity. In addition, poor weather conditions involving a mix of rain and snow were still prevalent despite the onset of spring. On several occasions the men were forced to sleep out in the open, which further reduced their stamina. The presence of several blanket-covered bodies close to a huge camp near Linz was commented on by Thomas; he was told by a guard that the camp held 100,000 prisoners whose life expectancy was measured in days or weeks (This was probably the infamous SS concentration camp at Mauthausen). The beautiful scenery was of no consolation to the men, and their arrival at Braunau where they were officially 'camped out' was of no physical benefit, since they still had to exist out in the open. By now dysentery was striking home with a real prospect of a fatal outcome for many of those so affected, should proper accommodation not be immediately on hand.

Right: Lt. James Wright reads the paper with the headline that everybody was happy to see "Germany Quits" James was a bombardier in the 68th BS on Lt. Erickson's crew

Below: A very loose flight of 67th BS bombers over-fly Station 115 Shipdham – flying without being shot at by flak and no fighters trying to shoot you down!

It must have been a tremendous relief to all concerned when, on 5 May, contact was made with advance units of the American army. Next day, the German guards were relieved of their arms and the POWs moved into proper buildings within Braunau. The men's immediate ordeal was over, although medical problems created during the forced march would cast up their malign influence in the years ahead. (Thomas still has difficulties with his stomach and bowels, and suffers from spinal arthritis). Over the ensuing two weeks, Sgt. Thomas was flown out of the area in a C-47 to Camp Lucky Strike in France. From here he boarded a Liberty Ship 'Martin Luther' that transported him via Liverpool to Boston. Several months later his military career was ended when he was discharged at Ellington Field outside Houston, TX.

Archie Thomas's experience, at least while in Stalag 17B, was arguably no different from that of his fellow-POWs. However, all those who were captured went through an existence that was far worse and protracted than that meted out to their civilian criminal contemporaries. A normal prisoner knows the terms of his sentence, whereas the 'Kriegies' all received an open-ended sentence, with no firm release date, but rather one that was dependent upon the completion of hostilities whenever that might be. Not for them a comfortable cell, with guaranteed catering and even proper social facilities. Worse still, was the ever-constant threat of wholesale annihilation by Hitler's SS fanatics, should the Fuehrer so ordain this action as his Thousand-year Reich crumbled into dust.

Maj. Lehnhausen (68th BS CO, seen third from the right back row) and crew and passengers had this photograph taken prior to going on a "Trolley" mission.

Towards the middle of May, the 8th USAAF began preparations for its transfer back to the States and test-flying of the aircraft was made with a view to ensuring their overall readiness for the lengthy overseas haul. One of the drills involved 'feathering' practice, and this aspect of flight control was being indulged in on 11 May by Capt. Edkins and Lt. Whittle (506th BS). While flying at 5,000 feet, both outboard engines on 44-50698/Bar-C were 'feathered' one after the other. Lt. Whittle had a vague recollection that a pretence was then made of 'feathering' one of the functioning engines by momentarily depressing the feathering button but with no intention of completing the action.

It was at this point that things went drastically awry. The third engine's propeller 'feathered' and no amount of

VE Day Scottish style. The photograph is taken outside the American Red Cross building in Edinburgh.

Lt. Norman Nutt taxies "Glory Bee" to the main runway at Valley, Wales. This would be the last take off from the UK; next stop Meeks Field Iceland and then Bradley Field USA.

manipulation of any of the three buttons could induce a return to normal propeller configuration and therefore to a restoration of power. The B-24 was headed for an airfield several miles off to the right as it began to drop inexorably downwards. Despite there being no time to inform the crew of what was happening, those in the rear fuselage sensed the critical situation they were in and took up crash positions. The one functioning engine was on the right wing and the aircraft was manoeuvered into line with a runway. However, height was being lost so fast that a normal landing became ever more problematical; this was especially so in view of a bank of trees over which the pilots had to steer their charge. Lt. Whittle's last conscious recollection at this point was of attempting to pull back on the yoke in order to 'skip' over the trees. When he came to again the B-24 was down on the ground, with both wings sheered off between the inboard and outboard engines. Edkins had suffered serious head injuries that left him on the critical list for some time. Lt. Edward Smith (N) was equally affected; in his case he had been bodily thrown through the cockpit windshield and had broken his back. The three enlisted men in the rear were badly shaken but otherwise intact.

An investigation later determined that the crash could be ascribed to an inherent problem in B-24 design. All four 'feathering' mechanisms were run off a single master fuse. The fuse was not capable of handling a wholesale 'feathering' operation as indulged in by the pilots, and had 'blown'.

Death coming at any stage of a combat tour was a tragic enough occurrence. It was arguably worse still to complete a

RAF men wave good-bye to this 67th BS crew and aircraft as they depart for home from Valley in Wales.

"Bye Yank, its been good to Know you." The men of the 44th leave the village of Shipdham. The villagers are waving good bye for what they thought would be the last time, but the veterans of the 44th BG were destined to keep coming back to visit their old haunts year after year.

combat tour and then be killed. (An individual instance of this was S/Sgt. Duckie, a tour-expired 68th BS gunner killed while on guard duty on 7 February 1945) But arguably the worst fate of all was to survive the war and then be killed.

Lt. Jack Ketchum's crew had come through their run of missions and were preparing to fly to the States. The crew had picked up a B-24 at Warton and had reached the first staging airfield at Prestwick, Scotland, from where they then took off for Meeks Field, Iceland on 13 June. On board were the nine crewmembers and six passengers, five of who were also personnel from combat units. The initial route over Scotland took the bomber up over the western reaches of the Grampian Mountains to a point roughly level with the top of the Isle of Skye, where it would start across the Atlantic waters for Iceland.

Less than an hour after take-off 42-95095 was a shattered, fire-blackened wreck left strewn across high ground near Gairloch. A reconstruction of the incident suggested that the pilots, who had been flying on instruments due to the very heavy cloud formations over Scotland, had sought a visual confirmation of their position. Their decision to do so was to prove fatal because the B-24 was adjudged to have clipped the top of Slioch, a mountain standing 3,217ft. high on the eastern end of Loch Maree and almost due north of Prestwick. It then appeared to have veered off to the left and across the Loch before finally impacting with the ground several miles on from the first ground contact. The bright dreams of returning safely to their homeland had been cruelly expunged in an instant and fifteen Americans had just paid the final grim instalment on the 44th BG's blood debt in returning Freedom and Justice to an embattled Europe, most of whose peoples had been so long under the heel of an obdurate and harsh Invader.

42-95095 "Sleepy Time Gal" was a former 93rd BG aircraft. Lt. Jack B. Ketchum's crew and passengers were all killed in a tragic accident while flying this aircraft back to the ZOI. The 44th aircraft that they should originally have flown back was not on hand, having been involved in an accident at Shipdham.

The Group aircraft had been deploying to the States during the latter part of May, and the Ketchum crew must have been among the last to depart. Each aircraft had taken a proportion of the ground echelon on board; the 68th BS for example had loaded 346 personnel into its nineteen B-24s. The ground echelon personnel, in the meantime, were preparing for their own departure by sea. Arrival at Southampton around the 19th witnessed the men's 'reunion' with the same vessel that had brought them over to Britain, the 'Queen Mary'. Next day, the mighty liner up-anchored and steamed down the Southampton Water and out into the English Channel. The five-day voyage was naturally a much more relaxed affair compared to 1942 although arrangements for accommodation and feeding were arguably little improved. But who really cared – everybody was heading home!

Following arrival in New York the men were granted thirty days R & R after which some of them reported to Sioux Falls Field, SD. During July the Group was selected for recreation as a B-29 outfit, and moved to Great Bend Field, Kansas to

A line up of aircraft that had completed the first leg of the protracted journey home. This photograph also shows B-17's of the 96th and 100th BGs parked on the plank steel runway at Meeks Field, Iceland.

A consolidated OA-10 Catalina that was based at Meeks field Iceland is seen being refueled.

commence training. Twelve months would then elapse before aircraft and personnel were transferred-out to another unit and the 44th BG was officially inactivated on 12 July 1946. The War was finally over for the Shipdham-based Group, but this initial five-year period of activation was to be repeated. During 1951 reactivation took place as a B-29 Group within SAC, with subsequent conversion on to B-47 Stratojets and then Minutemen missiles in 1963.

Reflections

For at least two decades after it had ended, World War II remained largely a memory in the minds of the surviving participants as they established themselves in their chosen professions or trades as well as bringing up families. As time went by, the harsher aspects of the war began to slip into the background and an innate sense of former shared experiences, allied with a desire to reunite with one another, led to the foundation of numerous Group Associations as well as 'umbrella' organisations in the form of the 2nd Air Division Association and the 8th USAAF Historical Society.

The 44th BG Heritage Memorial Group was, and still is, a prominent structure that fosters the spirit of comradeship. There have been as many as 3000 names listed as Group members and the quarterly Newsletter is one of the finest and most comprehensive documents brought out by any similar 8th USAAF veterans organisation.

Shipdham airfield has partially slipped back into the English landscape from which it was arbitrarily constructed in response to the dictates of military needs. Part of one subsidiary runway is used by a private aviation concern. Many of the flight line buildings such as the hangars are intact and in use by several companies. The control tower still exists although it is bereft of windows and is just a hollow shell, albeit with intact floors and internal walls. Numerous structures within the scattered sites are on hand, some of which are used for storage or other purposes. There is enough of the base left for its former occupants to gaze at and reminisce whenever they return, and they do return, sometimes in groups but as often or not as single visitors.

What is in their minds and hearts is perhaps summed up by the statement of J.T. Elias, a former gunner who wandered around the airfield during a 1955 visit, when the ravages of Time and Nature were already taking their toll: "Seams and cracks in the concrete, sprouting weeds … derelict shells of wartime buildings … Out on the main runway stood an abandoned farm machine … Up in the control tower broken glass covered the floor, an open door creaked eerily in the breeze … Faces flitted through my mind, faces of men – boys really, who had become men before their time. Where were all those wonderful kids? … kids who didn't speak of patriotism, love of country, fear of death, but who went out, did the best they could – clumsily at times, perfectly sometimes, but always the best they could …"

The Annual Memorial Day ceremony at Madingley Military Cemetery just west of Cambridge, England, continues to be an occasion that is well attended by the members of

B-24JSH-5-FO 42-51508G+ sits at Meeks Field, Iceland. The aircraft had formerly served with the 453rd BG.

'Sultry Sue' at Meeks Field after completing the first part of the flight home.

Part of the Kleinschmidt crew at Bradley Field, after the second leg of the trip to the Zone of the Interior (USA).

'Friends of the Eighth'. This is a British organisation dedicated to perpetuating the history and achievements of the 8th USAAF. The cemetery still holds the mortal remains of 3,812 out of the 10,000 American Service personnel buried there during World War II. A further 5,216 names are inscribed on the 'Wall of the Missing'. At the base of the tall flagpole is recorded the telling phrase from John McCrae's World War I poem 'In Flanders Field'. It states; "TO YOU FROM FALLING HANDS WE THROW THE TORCH – BE YOURS TO HOLD IT HIGH."

Our members are conscious of the tremendous debt owed to the men and women who truly 'gave us our today' in sacrificing their lives. They would expect no less of our generation than that we would do our level best to ensure the fruits of victory arising out of VE-Day and VJ-Day were not wantonly cast away. And so they rest forever in Britain's soil, surrounded by our simple respect and – yes – love. The following few lines act as an apt valediction for them all:

Here under the wide, starry sky
Dig my grave and let me lie
Glad did I live and gladly die
And I laid me down with a will;
This be the verse that you grave for me
'Here he lies where he longed to be
Home is the sailor, home from the sea-
And the hunter, home from the hill'

Appendices

Appendix 1
44th Bombardment Group (Heavy) Missions

Mission Number	Mission Date	City	Country	Target
1	07 November 1942	Diversionary Mission	Germany	Diversion
2	09 November 1942	St. Nazaire	France	
3	14 November 1942	Diversionary Mission	France	Diversion
4	17 November 1942	Cherbourg	France	Airdrome
5	18 November 1942	Diversionary Mission	France	Diversion
6	06 December 1942	Abbeville	France	Airdrome
7	12 December 1942	Abbeville	France	Airdrome
8	20 December 1942	Romilly Sur Seine	France	Airdrome
9	03 January 1943	St. Nazaire	France	
10	27 January 1943	Lemmer	Holland	Target of Opportunity
11	04 February 1943	Hamm	Germany	Mission Recalled
12	15 February 1943	Dunkirk	France	German Radar Ship
13	16 February 1943	St. Nazaire	France	Airfield
14	26 February 1943	Wilhelmshaven	Germany	Port & Docks
15	27 February 1943	Brest	Germany	Porrt & U-boat Pens
16	04 March 1943	Diversionary Mission	Germany	Diversion
17	06 March 1943	Brest	France	Dock Facilities
18	08 March 1943	Rouen	France	Marshalling Yards
19	12 March 1943	Diversionary Mission	France	Diversion
20	13 March 1943	Diversionary Mission	France	Diversion
21	18 March 1943	Vegesack	Germany	Airfield
22	22 March 1943	Wilhelmshaven	Germany	Docks & U-boat Pens
23	28 March 1943	Rouen	France	Mission Recalled
24	31 March 1943	Rotterdam	Holland	No Bombs Dropped
25	04 April 1943	Diversionary Mission	France	Diversion
26	05 April 1943	Antwerp	Belgium	Truck Parts Plant
27	16 April 1943	Brest	France	Dock Area
28	01 May 1943	Diversionary Mission	France	Diversion
29	04 May 1943	Diversionary Mission	Holland	Diversion
30	14 May 1943	Kiel	Germany	Krupp Submarine Works
31	17 May 1943	Bordeaux	France	Docks & U-boat Pens
32	29 May 1943	La Pallice	France	Docks & Harbor Installations
33	02 July 1943	Lecce	Italy	Airdrome
34	05 July 1943	Messina	Sicily	Marshalling Yards
35	06 July 1943	Gerebina	Sicily	Air Drome
36	08 July 1943	Catania	Sicily	Communications
37	10 July 1943	Catania	Sicily	Marshalling Yards
38	12 July 1943	Reggio Di Calabria	Italy	Marshalling Yards
39	13 July 1943	Crotone	Sicily	Air Drome
40	15 July 1943	Foggia	Italy	Air Drome
41	17 July 1943	Naples	Italy	Marshalling Yards
42	19 July 1943	Rome	Italy	Littorio Marshalling Yards
43	01 August 1943	Ploesti	Romania	Oil Facilities
44	13 August 1943	Wiener-Neustadt	Austria	Aircraft Factory
45	16 August 1943	Foggia	Italy	North Airfield
46	19 August 1943	Foggia	Italy	Marshalling Yards
47	21 August 1943	Canciello	Italy	Railroad Facilities
48	07 September 1943	Leeuwarden	Holland	Air Drome
49	09 September 1943	Abbeville/Drucat	France	Air Drome
50	15 September 1943	Chatres	France	Air Drome
51	21 September 1943	Leghorn	Italy	Tactical
52	24 September 1943	Pisa	Italy	Marshalling Yards
53	25 September 1943	Lucca	Italy	Air Drome
54	26 September 1943	Diversionary Mission	France	Diversion
55	27 September 1943	Diversionary Mission	France	Diversion
56	01 October 1943	Wiener-Neustadt	Austria	Aircraft Factory
57	04 October 1943	Helgoland	France	Diversion
58	09 October 1943	Gdynia	Germany	Ship Yards
59	10 October 1943	Diversionary Mission	France	Diversion
60	18 October 1943	Diversionary Mission	France	Diversion
61	20 October 1943	Diversionary Mission	France	Diversion
62	03 November 1943	Wilhelmshaven	Germany	Ship Yards
63	05 November 1943	Munster	Germany	Railroad Junction
64	13 November 1943	Bremen	Germany	Port and Storage Facilities
65	16 November 1943	Rjukan	Norway	Hydro-Nitrate Plant

Mission Number	Mission Date	City	Country	Target
66	18 November 1943	Kjeller	Norway	Airfield
67	26 November 1943	Bremen/Leer	Germany	Industrial Areas
68	30 November 1943	Solingen	Germany	Manufacturing
69	01 December 1943	Solingen	Germany	Aero Casting Works
70	05 December 1943	Cognac/Chateaubernard	France	Airfield
71	11 December 1943	Emden	Germany	Boat & Rail Traffic
72	13 December 1943	Kiel	Germany	Ship & Submarine Building
73	16 Der-ember 1943	Bremen	Germany	
74	20 December 1943	Bremen	Germany	
75	22 December 1943	Munster	Germany	Railway &Waterway
76	24 December 1943	Pas De Calais Area	France	Construction
77	30 December 1943	Ludwigshaven	Germany	Chemical Works
78	31 December 1943	St- Jean D'Angely	France	Airdrome
79	04 January 1944	Kiel	Germany	Docks & Rails
80	05 January 1944	Kiel	Germany	Docks & Harbor Facilities
81	07 January 1944	Ludwigshaven	Germany	Recalled
82	11 January 1944	Meppen	Germany	Factory & Rails
83	14 January 1944	Ecalles Sur Buchy	France	Military Installations
84	21 January 1944	Ecalles Sur Buchy	France	Military Installations
85	29 January 1944	Frankfurt	Germany	
86	30 January 1944	Braunsweig	Germany	Target of Opportunity
87	02 February 1944	Watten	France	Military Installations
88	05 February 1944	Tours	France	Airdrome
89	06 February 1944	Siracourt	France	Military Installations
90	08 February 1944	Watten	France	Military Installations
91	11 February 1944	Siracourt	France	Military Installations
92	12 February 1944	Siracourt	France	Military Installations
93	13 February 1944	Ray-Sur-Authie	France	Military Installations
94	20 February 1944	Helmstadt/Oscherteben	Germany	Target of Opportunity
95	21 February 1944	Handorf	Germany	Airdrome
96	22 February 1944	Gotha	Germany	Recalled
97	24 February 1944	Gotha	Germany	Aircraft Assembly Plant
98	25 February 1944	Furth	Germany	Bomber Components & Military Installations
99	02 March 1944	Frankfurt	Germany	Piston Ring Factory
100	03 March 1944	Oranienburg	Germany	Recalled
101	05 March 1944	Cognac/Bergerac	France	Airdromes
102	06 March 1944	Berlin	Germany	Templehof Airdrome
103	08 March 1944	Berlin (Erkner)	Germany	Ball Bearing Factory
104	09 March 1944	Brandenburg	Germany	Airframe Factory
105	12 March 1944	Siracourt	France	Military Installations
106	15 March 1944	Brunswick	Germany	Bomber Components
107	16 March 1944	Fredrichshaven	Germany	
108	18 March 1944	Fredrichshaven	Germany	Aircraft Components
109	21 March 1944	Watten	France	Military Installations
110	22 March 1944	Berlin	Germany	Target of Opportunity
111	23 March 1944	Achmer	Germany	Airfield
112	24 March 1944	St. Dizier/Robinson	France	Airdrome
113	26 March 1944	Tillencourt	France	Military V-1 Sites
114	27 March 1944	Mont De Marson	France	Airdrome
115	01 April 1944	Schaffhausen	Germany	Switzerland River Front
116	06 April 1944	Watten	France	V-1 Sites
117	08 April 1944	Langenhagen	Germany	Airdrome
118	09 April 1944	Tutrow	Germany	Airdrome
119	11 April 1944	Burngerg	Germany	Aircraft Assembly Plant
120	12 April 1944	Zwickau	Germany	Recalled
121	13 April 1944	Lechfeld	Germany	Twin-Engine Fighter Plant
122	18 April 1944	Cuxhaven/Rathenow	Germany	Target of Opportunity
123	19 April 1944	Gutersloh	Germany	Airfield
124	20 April 1944	Pas DeCalais (Marquise)	France	Recalled
125	22 April 1944	Hamm	Germany	Marshalling Yards
126	26 April 1944	Gutersloh	Germany	Recalled
127	27 April 1944	Moyenneville	France	
128	27 April 1944	Chalone-Sur-Marne	France	Marshalling Yards
129	29 April 1944	Berlin	Germany	
130	01 May 1944	Liege	Belgium	Marshalling Yards
131	03 May 1944	Wizernes	France	V-1 Sites
132	04 May 1944	Brunswick	Germany	Recalled
133	07 May 1944	Osnabruck	Germany	
134	08 May 1944	Brunswick	Germany	
135	09 May 1944	St. Trond/Brustem	Belgium	Airfield
136	11 May 1944	Orleons/Bricy	France	Airdrome & Belfort Marshalling Yards
137	12 May 1944	Zeitz	Germany	Synthetic Oil Plant
138	13 May 1944	Tutow	Germany	Airfield & Air Park

Mission Number	Mission Date	City	Country	Target
139	15 May 1944	Siracourt	France	Constructional Work
140	19 May 1944	Brunswick	Germany	Marshalling Yards
141	21 May 1944	Siracourt	France	V-1 Sites
142	23 May 1944	Avord	France	Airfield
143	24 May 1944	Melun	France	Airfield
144	25 May 1944	Belfort	France	Marshalling Yards
145	27 May 1944	Saarbrucken	Germany	Marshalling Yards
146	27 May 1944	Fecamp	France	V-1 Sites
147	28 May 1944	Zeitz	Germany	Oil Plants
148	29 May 1944	Politz	Germany	Oil Plants
149	30 May 1944	Rotenburg	Germany	Airfield
150	31 May 1944	Brussels	Belgium	No Bombs Dropped
151	02 June 1944	Berck-Sur-Mer	France	Defended Locality
152	03 June 1944	St. Albins	France	Defended Locality
153	03 June 1944	Berck Area	France	Field Battery
154	05 June 1944	Boulogne Area	France	Coastal Defenses
155	06 June 1944	Colleville/St. Laurent	France	D-Day Invasion
156	06 June 1944	Ferets-De-Cerisy	France	Invasion Targets
157	06 June 1944	Caen (Vire)	France	Invasion Targets
158	07 June 1944	Lisieux	France	Rail Choke Points
159	08 June 1944	Angers	France	Marshalling Yards & Locomotives
160	10 June 1944	Orleans/Bricy	France	Airfield
161	11 June 1944	Montfort	France	Airfield
162	12 June 1944	Illiers L'Eveque	France	Airfield
163	14 June 1944	Chateaudun	France	Airfield
164	15 June 1944	Tours	France	Bridge
165	17 June 1944	Melun	Germany	Airfield
166	18 June 1944	Bremerhaven/Wesemunde	Germany	Target ofOpportunity
167	19 June 1944	Authreaux	France	V-1 Sites
168	20 June 1944	Politz	Germany	Oil Refineries
169	20 June 1944	Pas-De-Calais Area	France	No Bombs Dropped
170	21 June 1944	Berlin	Germany	Target of Opportunity
171	22 June 1944	Nucourt	France	Military Installations
172	22 June 1944	St. Cyr	France	Airfield
173	23 June 1944	Laon/Athies	France	Airfield
174	24 June 1944	Toussus Le Noble	France	Airfield
175	25 June 1944	Doullens	France	Powerhouse
176	26 June 1944	Bretigny	France	
177	27 June 1944	Criel	France	Rail Tunnel and Marshalling Yards
178	28 June 1944	Saarbrucken	Germany	
179	29 June 1944	Magdeburg	Germany	Krupp Aircraft Factory
180	04 July 1944	Beaumont Le Roger	France	Airfield
181	06 July 1944	Kiel	Germany	Submarine Pens and Docks
182	07 July 1944	Bernburg	Germany	Aircraft Factory
183	08 July 1944	Zuid Beveland	France	Railroad Bridge
184	11 July 1944	Munich	Germany	
185	12 July 1944	Munich	Germany	Marshalling Yards
186	13 July 1944	Saarbrucken	Germany	Rail and Communications
187	16 July 1944	Saarbrucken	Germany	Rail and Communications
188	18 July 1944	Troarns (Caen Area)	France	Troop Support
189	19 July 1944	Koblenz	Germany	Marshalling Yards
190	20 July 1944	Erfurt	Germany	North Airfield
191	21 July 1944	Oberpfaffenhofen	Germany	Armaments
192	24 July 1944	St. Lô	France	Support American Troops
193	25 July 1944	St. Lô	France	Support American Troops
194	29 July 1944	Oslebshausen	Germany	Ship Building Buildings
195	31 July 1944	Ludwigshaven	Germany	Chemical & Dye Works
196	01 August 1944	Aimes	France	Railway Junction
197	02 August 1944	Wadiscourt	France	Three Targets (Villers L'Hopital & Belloy)
198	03 August 1944	Mery-Sur-Oise	France	Recalled
199	04 August 1944	Kiel	Germany	Port Facilities
200	04 August 1944	Villers L'Hopital	France	V-1 Sites
201	05 August 1944	Brunswick	Germany	Aircraft Factory
202	06 August 1944	Hamburg	Germany	Oil Refinery
203	07 August 1944	Saleaux	France	Fuel Storage Dump
204	08 August 1944	La Perth	France	Airfield at Romilly
205	09 August 1944	Saarbrucken	Germany	Marshalling Yards
206	12 August 1944	Juvincourt	France	Airdrome
207	13 August 1944	Le Harve/Rouen	France	Road Junction (Lisieux)
208	14 August 1944	Lyon/Bron	France	Airfield
209	15 August 1944	Wittmundhafen	Germany	Ardorf Airfield
210	16 August 1944	Kothen	Germany	Aircraft Factory
211	18 August 1944	Nancy/Essey	France	Airfield

Mission Number	Mission Date	City	Country	Target
212	24 August 1944	Langenhagen	Germany	Airfield
213	25 August 1944	Schwern	Germany	Assembly plant for Fw 190s
214	26 August 1944	Salzbergen	Germany	Oil Refinery
215	27 August 1944	Basdorf	Germany	Aero Engine Factory
216	30 August 1944	Haute-Maisnil	France	Military Installations
217	05 September 1944	Karlsruhe	Germany	Marshalling Yards
218	08 September 1944	Karlsruhe	Germany	Marshalling Yards
219	09 September 1944	Mainz & Worms	Germany	Marshalling Yards
220	10 September 1944	Ulm	Germany	Marshalling Yards
221	11 September 1944	Misburg	Germany	Hanomag Works
222	12 September 1944	Leharte	Germany	Rail Junction
223	13 September 1944	Schwabish/Hall	Germany	Airfield
224	18 September 1944	Best	Holland	Low-Level Supplies, Troops
225	22 September 1944	Kassel	Germany	Marshalling Yards
226	25 September 1944	Koblenz	Germany	Marshalling Yards
227	26 September 1944	Hamm	Germany	Marshalling Yards
228	27 September 1944	Kassel	Germany	Tank Factory
229	28 September 1944	Kassel	Germany	Motor Works
230	30 September 1944	Hamm	Germany	Marshalling Yards
231	02 October 1944	Hamm	Germany	Marshalling Yards
232	03 October 1944	Offenburg	Germany	Marshalling Yards
233	05 October 1944	Lippstadt	Germany	Airfield
234	06 October 1944	Hamburg	Germany	Air Armament Factory
235	07 October 1944	Kassel	Germany	Tank Factory
236	09 October 1944	Koblenz	Germany	Marshalling Yards
237	12 October 1944	Osnabruck	Germany	Marshalling Yards
238	14 October 1944	Kaiserlautern	Germany	Marshalling Yards
239	15 October 1944	Cologne/Geron	Germany	Marshalling Yards
240	17 October 1944	Cologne	Germany	Nord Marshalling Yards
241	18 October 1944	Leverkusen	Germany	Chemical Works
242	19 October 1944	Gustavsburg	Germany	Diesel Works
243	25 October 1944	Gelsenkirchen	Germany	Synthetic Oil
244	26 October 1944	Bottrop	Germany	Synthetic Oil
245	30 October 1944	Hamburg/Ueterson	Germany	Oil Refinery
246	01 November 1944	Gelsenkirchen	Germany	Bauer Oil Refinery
247	02 November 1944	Dortmund	Germany	Castrop-Rauxel Oil Refinery
248	04 November 1944	Gelsenkirchen	Germany	Nordston Refinery
249	05 November 1944	Karlsruhe	Germany	Marshalling Yards
250	06 November 1944	Sterkrade	Germany	Oil Refinery
251	08 November 1944	Enschede	Germany	Railroad
252	09 November 1944	Metz	France	Gun Positions
253	10 November 1944	Hanau	Germany	Lanzendiebach Airfield
254	11 November 1944	Bottrop	Germany	Synthetic Oil Plant
255	16 November 1944	Eschweiler	France	Troop Support
256	21 November 1944	Harburg	Germany	Crude Oil Refinery
257	25 November 1944	Bingen	Germany	Marshalling Yards
258	26 November 1944	Bielefeld	Germany	Railroad Viaduct
259	27 November 1944	Offenburg	Germany	Marshalling Yards
260	29 November 1944	Altenbeken	Germany	Railway Viaduct
261	30 November 1944	Neunkirchen	Germany	Marshalling Yards
262	02 December 1944	Bingen	Germany	Marshalling Yards
263	04 December 1944	Wetzlar/Koschausen/Bebra	Germany	Target of Opportunity
264	05 December 1944	Munster	Germany	Marshalling Yards
265	06 December 1944	Bielefeld	Germany	Marshalling Yards
266	10 December 1944	Bingen	Germany	Marshalling Yards
267	11 December 1944	Karlsruhe	Germany	Railroad Bridge
268	12 December 1944	Aschaffenburg	Germany	Marshalling Yards
269	23 December 1944	Arhweiler	Belgium	Road Choke Point
270	24 December 1944	Ruwer	Germany	Bridges & Tunnels
271	27 December 1944	Homburg	Germany	Marshalling Yards & Choke Point
272	28 December 1944	Kaiserlauten	Germany	Railroad & Road Junction
273	29 December 1944	Stadtkyll	Germany	Communications
274	30 December 1944	Altenahr	Germany	Rail & Road Junctions
275	31 December 1944	Dorsel	Germany	Railroad Junction
276	01 January 1945	Koblenz	Germany	Koblenz-Lutzel Railroad Bridge
277	02 January 1945	Koblenz	Germany	Koblenz-Lutzel Railroad Bridge
278	03 January 1945	Landau	Germany	Ordnance Supplies
279	05 January 1945	Neunkirchen	Germany	Marshalling Yards
280	07 January 1945	Landau	Germany	Rail & Road Junction
281	08 January 1945	Burghreuland	Germany	Rail & Road Junction
282	10 January 1945	Dasburg	Germany	
283	13 January 1945	Kaiserslautern	Germany	Marshalling Yards
284	14 January 1945	Hemmingstedt	Germany	Oil Refinery

Mission Number	*Mission Date*	*City*	*Country*	*Target*
285	16 January 1945	Dresden	Germany	Marshalling Yards
286	17 January 1945	Harburg	Germany	Oil Refinery
287	21 January 1945	Pforzheim	Germany	Marshalling Yards
288	28 January 1945	Dortmund	Germany	Coking Plant
289	29 January 1945	Hamm	Germany	Marshalling Yards
290	31 January 1945	Hallendorf	Germany	Recalled
291	03 February 1945	Madgeburg	Germany	Marshalling Yards
292	06 February 1945	Madgeburg	Germany	Marshalling Yards
293	09 February 1945	Madgeburg	Germany	Marshalling Yards
294	14 February 1945	Madgeburg	Germany	Marshalling Yards
295	15 February 1945	Magdeburg	Germany	Rothensee Oil Refinery
296	16 February 1945	Rheine	Germany	Marshalling Yards
297	19 February 1945	Siegen	Germany	Marshalling Yards
298	21 February 1945	Nurnberg	Germany	Marshalling Yards
299	22 February 1945	Gottingen	Germany	Marshalling Yards
300	23 February 1945	Weimar	Germany	Rail Center
301	24 February 1945	Misburg	Germany	Oil Refinery
302	25 February 1945	Aschaffenburg	Germany	Marshalling Yards
303	26 February 1945	Berlin	Germany	Pankow Marshalling Yard
304	27 February 1945	Bitterfeld	Germany	Marshalling Yards
305	28 February 1945	Siegen	Germany	Marshalling Yards
306	01 March 1945	Ingolstadt	Germany	Marshalling Yards
307	02 March 1945	Magdeburg	Germany	Marshalling Yards
308	03 March 1945	Magdeburg	Germany	Rothansee Oil Refinery
309	04 March 1945	Tuttlingen	Germany	Three Targets Tuttlingen, T/O at
310	05 March 1945	Harburg	Germany	Oil Refinery
311	07 March 1945	Bielefeld	Germany	Railway Viaduct
312	08 March 1945	Betzdorf & Frankfurt	Germany	Marshalling Yards
313	10 March 1945	Bielfeld	Germany	Railway Viaduct
314	11 March 1945	Kiel	Germany	Sub Pens & Shipbuilding
315	12 March 1945	Wetzlar	Germany	Marshalling Yards
316	14 March 1945	Gutersloh	Germany	Marshalling Yards
317	15 March 1945	Zossen	Germany	Military Headquarters
318	17 March 1945	Munster	Germany	Marshalling Yards
319	18 March 1945	Berlin	Germany	Rheinmetal Borsig Armament
320	19 March 1945	Neuburg	Germany	Jet Aircraft Factory
321	20 March 1945	Hemmingstadt	Germany	Oil Refinery
322	21 March 1945	Achmer	Germany	Airfield
323	21 March 1945	Essen	Germany	Airfield
324	22 March 1945	Schwabisch Hall	Germany	Airfield
325	23 March 1945	Rheine	Germany	Marshalling Yards
326	24 March 1945	Wesel	Germany	Low-Level Supply on Rhine River
327	24 March 1945	Stormede	Germany	Landing Strip
328	25 March 1945	Hitzacker	Germany	Oil Storage
329	30 March 1945	Wilhelmshaven	Germany	Dock Area
330	31 March 1945	Brunswick	Germany	Marshalling Yards
331	04 April 1945	Kaltenkirchen	Germany	Airfield
332	05 April 1945	Plauen	Germany	Transportation
333	06 April 1945	Halle	Germany	Marshalling Yards
334	07 April 1945	Neumunster	Germany	Railway Center
335	08 April 1945	Bayreuth	Germany	Ordnance Supplies
336	09 April 1945	Leipheim	Germany	Airfield
337	10 April 1945	Parchim	Germany	Airfield
338	11 April 1945	Neumarket	Germany	Marshalling Yards
339	14 April 1945	Fort-De-Royan	France	German Troops
340	15 April 1945	Fort-De-Royan	France	German Troops
341	16 April 1945	Landshut	Germany	Marshalling Yards
342	18 April 1945	Passau	Germany	Marshalling Yards
343	20 April 1945	Irlaching	Germany	Railroad Junction
344	25 April 1945	Hallein	Austria	Marshalling Yards

Appendix 2
44th Bombardment Group (Heavy) Chronological Index of B-24s Lost, Crashed or Salvaged

06-12-1942	41-23786	B	68	
03-01-1943	41-23771	E or I	66	
03-01-1943	41-23806	Z	68	BAT OUTA HELL
03-01-1943	41-23808	P	67	TEXAN
27-01-1943	41-23690	O or O	68	
27-01-1943	41-23776	W	68	SPIRIT OF '76
15-02-1943	41-23783	M	67	GALLOPIN' GHOST
				BETTY-ANNE
15-02-1943	41-23794	Q	67	RAILWAY EXPRESS/BOARDWALK EXPRESS
15-02-1943	41-23800	Y	68	THE CAPTAIN AND THE KIDS
16-02-1943	40-2354	C	66	SNAFU
16-02-1943	41-23818	R	67	MISS MARCIA ANN
20-02-1943	41-23703	A	66	SCRAPPY'S PAPPY
26-02-1943	41-23777	H	66	MAISEY
26-02-1943	41-23804	J	66	SAD SACK
	41-23784	T	67	MISS DIANNE
08-03-1943	41-23988	E	67	EMMA LOU/ DOUBLE PLAYMATE
22-03-1943	41-24191	X	506	CACTUS
22-03-1943	41-23832	N	67	MAGGIE
14-05-1943	41-24014	P	66	SCRAPPY
14-05-1943	42-40126	T	67	ANNIE OAKLEY "CRACK SHOT"
14-05-1943	41-24278	Q	67	MISS DELORES
14-05-1943	41-24295	J	506	WICKED WITCH
14-05-1943	41-23807	U	67	LITTLE BEAVER
14-05-1943	41-23819	A	68	RUGGED BUGGY
17-05-1943	42-40130	H	66	AVENGER II
02-07-1943	42-40094	E	68	MISS VIRGINIA
02-07-1943	42-40745	A	68	SEED-O-SATAN
17-07-1943	42-63763	F	67	LADY FIFINELLA
01-08-1943	41-24015	R	66	WING DINGER
01-08-1943	41-24153	L	66	SAD SACK II
01-08-1943	42-40182	A	66	FORKY II
01-08-1943	42-40267	N	67	HORSE FLY
01-08-1943	42-40371	Q	67	G I GAL
01-08-1943	42-40375	G	66	SCRAPPY II
01-08-1943	42-63761	D	67	L'IL ABNER
01-08-1943	42-40777	N	66	FLOSSIE FLIRT
01-08-1943	42-40780	H	67	AVAILABLE JONES
01-08-1943	42-40995	W	68	MARGUERITE
16-08-1943	42-41021	T	67	BLACK SHEEP
16-08-1943	41-24229	P	67	BUZZIN BEAR/SEEDS OF SATAN
16-08-1943	42-40373	Z	68	NATCHEZ BELLE
16-08-1943	42-40606	X	506	TIMB-A-A-AH!
16-08-1943	41-23778	F	66	LADY LUCK/JENNY
16-08-1943	42-40778	T	506	SOUTHERN COMFORT
16-08-1943	41-23817	L	67	SUZY Q
01-10-1943	42-41017	L	67	
01-10-1943	41-23811	K	66	FASCINATING WITCH
01-10-1943	41-23816	X	68	BLACK JACK
01-10-1943	42-72853	Q	67	COUNT BRUGA/COUNT GRUCA
01-10-1943	42-72857	X	506	
01-10-1943	42-72877	A	66	
01-10-1943	41-23918	O	67	BELA
01-10-1943	41-23936	J	66	QUEEN ANNE
04-10-1943	42-40989	B	506	HOLIDAY MESS
11-10-1943	42-40764	M	66	HELEN B HAPPY
11-11-1943	42-7647	R	506	SABRINA
13-11-1943	41-29168	F	66	
13-11-1943	42-7650	J	67	OLE MISS BAD PENNY
13-11-1943	42-40973	D	66	BATTLE AXE
18-11-1943	41-29139	E	67	
18-11-1943	41-29161	H	67	
18-11-1943	41-29164	I	67	
18-11-1943	42-7545	D	67	TOUCH OF VENUS

18-11-1943	42-7603	L	67	RAGGEDY ANN
18-11-1943	42-63971	W	68	HELEN HYWATER
26-11-1943	41-24234	N	66	MR 5 BY 5
01-12-1943	42-7544	C	67	SEED OF SATAN
11-12-1943	41-24232	M	67	CALABAN
16-12-1943	41-23788	S	66	AVENGER
20-12-1943	42-7630	P	506	
21-12-1943	42-72878	A	67	MISS EMMY LOU II
22-12-1943	42-7533	E	66	HOLIDAY MESS II
22-12-1943	42-7638	A	66	LILI MARLENE/BIG BANNER
30-12-1943	42-7548	I	66	BULL OF THE WOODS
03-01-1944	42-7536	M	66	THE BANSHEE
04-01-1944	42-7476	H	66	NICE 'N NAUGHTY
13-01-1944	42-7551	Y	68	THE JINX
14-01-1944	41-23779	G	67	4-Q-2
21-01-1944	42-7501	P	68	BING'S BIG BOX
21-01-1944	42-7514	O	68	VALIANT LADY
21-01-1944	42-7635	Q	68	RAM IT - DAMN IT!
21-01-1944	41-23813	V	68	VICTORY SHIP/REBEL
21-01-1944	42-72813	L	66	QUEEN MARLENE
21-01-1944	42-99970	M	67	LIB-ERTY BELLE
29-01-1944	41-29157	J	66	
29-01-1944	42-7547	X	506	SKY QUEEN
02-02-1944	41-24282	Y	506	RUTH-LESS
05-02-1944	42-100181	Z	68	STAR VALLEY
09-02-1944	41-29236	F	66	HELL'S KITTEN
20-02-1944	42-64166	A	66	BIG FAT BUTTERFLY
20-02-1944	42-100285	J	66	
20-02-1944	42-100373	Y	68	
22-02-1944	42-100402	M	67	
22-02-1944	42-72865	F	67	F FOR FREDDIE
24-02-1944	41-29148	B	66	
24-02-1944	41-24225	T	68	FLAK ALLEY
25-02-1944	41-29231	J	67	THE IMPATIENT VIRGIN
02-03-1944	42-100295	V	68	
05-03-1944	42-63965	Q	506	
07-03-1944	42-7582	F	66	ICE COLD KATY
09-03-1944	42-99980	H	66	BANSHEE IV
12-03-1944	42-7507	X	68	HEAVEN CAN WAIT
15-03-1944	42-52332	K	QK 68	MY ASS'AM DRAGON
16-03-1944	42-7549	K	NB 67	THE SHARK
18-03-1944	42-100073	H	NB 67	SACK ARTISTS
18-03-1944	42-100112	Q	WQ 68	PAPER DOLL
				LADY DOT
18-03-1944	41-29172	T	GJ 506	LUCKY STRIKE
18-03-1944	42-52305	P	GJ 506	
18-03-1944	42-100400	Y	GJ 506	(*One of these two was named*
18-03-1944	41-29431	Q	GJ 506	SHOO SHOO BABY)
18-03-1944	42-7618	C	QK 66	SCOURGE OF THE SKIES
18-03-1944	42-109800	T	WQ 68	
23-03-1944	41-29538	X	WQ 68	NAUGHTY NEL
27-03-1944	42-100107	R	GJ 506	
27-03-1944	41-29554	J	NB 67	TEXAS ROSE
27-03-1944	42-109836	B	QK 66	
08-04-1944	42-110020	Z	WQ 68	
08-04-1944	42-110023	T	GJ 506	RUBBER CHECK
08-04-1944	42-110083	X	NB 67	
08-04-1944	41-29153	Z	GJ 506	GREENWICH
08-04-1944	42-100423	A	GJ 506	OH! MY SUFFERIN' HEAD
08-04-1944	42-73506	X	GJ 506	
08-04-1944	42-7767	C	NB 67	SHACK RABBIT
				STAR SPANGLED HELL
08-04-1944	42-109822	O	WQ 68	TOWNSEND'S TERRIBLE TEN
08-04-1944	42-109827	Q	GJ 506	
08-04-1944	42-99987	S	WQ 68	PIZZ AND MOAN
				TOOTIE BELLE
08-04-1944	42-99996	I	QK 66	
09-04-1944	42-72858	U	WQ 68	PISTOL PACKIN' MAMA
11-04-1944	42-7522	S	GJ 506	SOUTHERN COMFORT
13-04-1944	42-100330	L	NB 67	
13-04-1944	42-99986	D	NB 67	D-BARFLY
21-04-1944	41-29418	U	WQ 68	TURNIP TERMITE

27-04-1944	42-110067	O	NB 67	
27-04-1944	41-29467	X	NB 67	
29-04-1944	42-100279	I	NB 67	TUFFY
29-04-1944	41-29471	X	WQ 68	
29-04-1944	41-29513	Z	GJ 506	
08-05-1944	41-28795	D+	QK 66	
09-05-1944	42-100110	P	WQ 68	NORTHERN LASS
11-05-1944	42-94999	-B	GJ 506	
12-05-1944	42-110042	J	NB 67	
25-05-1944	42-94962	I	NB 67	
28-05-1944	42-110045	K	GJ 506	THE BANANA BARGE
29-05-1944	42-73500	F	WQ 68	
29-05-1944	42- 63962	W	GJ 506	PRINCESS
05-06-1944	42-7509	V	GJ 506	GALLAVANTIN' GAL OLD CROW
05-06-1944	41-28690	B+	QK 66	MISSOURI BELLE MISSOURI SUE
20-06-1944	42-94892	U	WQ 68	BATTLIN' BABY
21-06-1944	42-100411	E	NB 67	
27-06-1944	42-110082	O	WQ 68	WENDY W
27-06-1944	42-50339	C	GJ 506	FEUDIN WAGON
27-06-1944	41-29496	Q	GJ 506	RAM IT - DAMN IT!
29-06-1944	42-51181	K	GJ 506	CAPE COD SPECIAL
29-06-1944	41-28767	L+	QK 66	
29-06-1944	41-28829	H	QK 66	MY EVERLOVIN' GAL
04-07-1944	42-100412	V	WQ 68	V FOR VICTORY
06-07-1944	42-100367	F	NB 67	
07-07-1944	42-110035	Y	WQ 68	ANY GUM CHUM
07-07-1944	42-100170	G	WQ 66	PATSY ANN II
07-07-1944	42-99966	W	WQ 68	FULL HOUSE
11-07-1944	41-29544	T	WQ 68	FLAK ALLEY II
11-07-1944	41-28776	E+	QK 66	
15-07-1944	42-110088	T	GJ 506	
21-07-1944	42-110034	R	GJ 506	SOUTHERN COMFORT II
21-07-1944	42-110049	A	WQ 68	
21-07-1944	42-95142	K	GJ 506	CAPE COD SPECIAL #2
21-07-1944	42-95207	Q	GJ 506	
21-07-1944	42-95226	C	WQ 68	CHANNEL HOPPER
29-07-1944	42-95309	E	GJ 506	
29-07-1944	42-109820	N	67 NB	WASP NEST, THE
06-08-1944	42-95561	I+	QK 66	
08-08-1944	42-50328	D	GJ 506	PREGNANT PEG FLYING LOG
08-08-1944	42-100415	Y	GJ 506	MY PEACH
12-08-1944	42-110024	P	GJ 506	OLE COCK
13-08-1944	42-95150	B	GJ 506	PASSION PIT
23-08-1944	42-50733	E	GJ 506	
24-08-1944	44-40098	B	WQ 68	LONE RANGER
30-08-1944	42-50626	H	GJ 506	MY GAL SAL
05-09-1944	42-95189	K+	QK 66	WEARY .....
09-09-1944	42-110057	Q	WQ 68	
13-09-1944	41-28785	B+	QK 66	
13-09-1944	42-94952	A	GJ 506	SHACK RAT
30-09-1944	44-10531	R+	QK 66	MY SAD ASS
07-10-1944	44-40167	Y	GJ 506	SIERRA BLANCA
07-10-1944	42-50789	A	GJ 506	LAKANOOKIE
18-10-1944	42-51234	L+	QK 66	
18-10-1944	42-50381	K	WQ 68	
18-10-1944	42-50596	O	WQ 68	
18-10-1944	41-28944	D	NB 67	FLYIN' GINNY
30-10-1944	44-10523	T	GJ 506	
05-11-1944	44-40071	P+	QK 66	SWEAT BOX
30-11-1944	44-40437	H	GJ 506	HAIRLESS JOE
02-12-1944	42-50766	D	GJ 506	
02-12-1944	42-50805	T	WQ 68	
04-12-1944	42-95124	Z	NB 67	SAND BOMB SPECIAL
18-12-1944	42-51309	V	NB 67	
24-12-1944	42-50894	N	GJ 506	
28-12-1944	42-95260	P	WQ 68	LILI MARLENE
28-12-1944	44-10553	L	WQ 68	
28-12-1944	44-10582	D	WQ 68	
16-01-1945	42-110095	G	WQ 66	LUCKY STRIKE HELLSADROPPIN'

16-01-1945	42-52293	G	NB 67	JUDY'S BUGGY
16-01-1945	42-50660	A	WQ 68	
16-01-1945	42-50711	X	WQ 68	
21-01-1945	42-50725	M	WQ 68	
28-01-1945	42-51101	H	WQ 68	CORKY
28-01-1945	42-50349	F	WQ 68	FLAK MAGNET
28-01-1945	44-10542	G+	QK 66	TALLY HO II
28-01-1945	42-52618	V+	QK 66	CHIEF WAPELLO
07-02-1945	42-50509	Y	WQ 68	WANA
16-02-1945	42-94895	R	NB 67	
23-02-1945	42-51552	J	GJ 506	
25-02-1945	42-110031	H	NB 67	PHYLLIS
25-02-1945	42-51258	J+	QK 66	
01-03-1945	42-95049	O	NB 67	FEARLESS FOSDICK
01-03-1945	44-49525	E	GJ 506	
19-03-1945	42-51907	B+	QK 66	
22-03-1945	42-50427	V	WQ 68	PURITANICAL BITCH/PURITANICAL WITCH
24-03-1945	42-100314	G+	QK 66	
24-03-1945	42-50896	R	GJ 506	SOUTHERN COMFORT III
05-04-1945	44-40158	Q	GJ 506	TINKER BELLE
08-05-1945	42-110185	S+	QK 66	WILD BILL
11-05-1945	44-50698	C	GJ 506	
29-05-1945	41-29475	M	NB 67	
29-05-1945	42-94975	M	GJ 506	
29-05-1945	42-99997	P	NB 67	
31-05-1945	42-100177	L	GJ 506	
01-06-1945	41-23699	N	68	LEMON DROP

Appendix 3
44th Bombardment Group (Heavy)
B-24s in Ascending Order of the Last Three Figures of the Serial Number

(followed by incomplete details such as name or date of loss of B-24s not yet identified by serial number)

B-24H-20 FO 42-95001 — Z — 68 (WQ) — T S TESSIE >108<
OD — BECK'S BAD BOYS
Name was T S TESSIE but the Beckingham crew called it BECK'S BAD BOYS.
Received between 8 & 26 Apr 44.
Flew truckin' operation with 458th BG retaining 44th BG markings on 18 Sep 44.
Landed at airstrip B-51 (Lille/Vendeville, France) on return from 16 Jan 45 mission to Ruhland (but Dresden bombed) because of fog blanket over England.
RZI 28 or 30 May 45.

B-24D-15 CO 41-24009 — W — 68 — MARGARET ANN >9<
OD
Received 20 Apr 43.
Transferred to MTO on 13 or 15 Oct 43 and assigned to 98th BG.

B-24D-125 CO 42-41013 — D — 506 — TROUBLE >12<
OD — R — 506 — TEXAN II
First trace: 13 Aug 43.
Letter changed from D to R between 21 Aug and 6 Sep 43.
Name was TROUBLE (see photo on page 325 of "Liberator America's Global Bomber" and also, possibly, TEXAN II.
Transferred to 389th BG between 1 & 18 Oct 43.

B-24D-15 CO 41-24014 — P — 66 — SCRAPPY >4<
OD
Received 15 Apr 43? (it appears on 28 Mar formation plan as a 66th BS spare and has a sortie credit with 68th BS on 31 Mar 43 [Pilot: Jansen]).
Shot down 14 May 43 in the North Sea off Sheringham by a flight of Spitfires piloted by Poles after being abandoned on return to Shipdham. (Kiel)

B-24D-15 CO 41-24015 — R — 66 — WING DINGER >11<
OD
Received before 17 May 43.
Lost 1 Aug 43 - crashed and exploded after leaving the target area. (Ploesti, Rumania)

B-24H-20 FO 42-95016 — -Z — 506 (GJ) — DOWN 'DE HATCH >92<
OD — Z — 506 (GJ)
Was picked up on 2 Apr 44 from Hamilton Field, California, by a 453rd BG replacement crew who left the aircraft at BAD 2, Warton, Lancashire.
Received by 44th BG on 1 May 44.
RZI 31 May 45 (photographed at Willow Run with 90 mission marks).

B-24D-125 CO 42-41017 — L — 67 — >5<
OD
Lost 1 Oct 43 - set on fire by flak and fighters after releasing bombs. (Wiener Neustadt, Austria)

B-24J-125 CO 42-110020 — Z — 68 (WQ) — >1<
OD
Received 26 Mar 44.
Lost 8 Apr 44 - shot down by flak. (Langenhagen)

B-24D-125 CO 42-41021 — T — 67 — BLACK SHEEP >1<
OD
May have been named BLACK SHEEP.
Lost 16 Aug 43 - crashed on return on the beach at Cape Stilo, Calabria, Italy - see also 41-23817. (Foggia, Italy)

B-24H-20 FO 42-95021 — T — 67 (NB) — LIMPIN' OLE SADIE >96<
OD — T — 68 (WQ) — SAN ANTONIO ROSE
Name changed from LIMPIN' OLE SADIE to SAN ANTONIO ROSE.
Received before 3 May 44.
Transferred from 67th BS to 68th BS on 20 Feb 45.
Repaired at Woodbridge, Suffolk, 20 Jul - 10 Aug 44 - #4 engine, spar work, fuel cell change and heavy battle damage on 19 Jul 44 mission to Koblenz.
Hit by flak in port outer engine and bomb bay and landed at B-80, Volkel, Netherlands, after 5 of the crew bailed out on 3 Mar 45 mission to Magdeburg - returned to Shipdham before 10 Mar 45.
RZI 28 or 31 May 45.

B-24J-125 CO 42-110023 — T — 506 (GJ) — RUBBER CHECK >2<
OD
Received between 18 Mar & 1 Apr 44.
Lost 8 Apr 44 - shot down by fighters. (Langenhagen)

B-24J-125 CO 42-110024	P	506 (GJ)	OLE COCK >46<
OD	-P		
P		506 (GJ)	

Position of bar changed from below the letter to before the letter on 27 Apr 44 and to above the letter on 21 May 44.
Received between 18 & 26 Mar 44.
Lost 12 Aug 44 - left formation, losing altitude, low on gas with #3 engine out and #4 tank empty, crashed at Pont-l'Evêque, France. (Juvincourt, France)

B-24J-125 CO 42-110030	S	506 (GJ)	>90<
OD	_S	506(GJ)	
	S	506 (GJ)	
	U+	66 (QK)	

Bar added before the letter on 27 Apr 44 and moved above the letter on 21May 44. Transferred from 506th BS to 66th BS on 31 Dec 44.
Received between 11 & 18 Apr 44.
Repaired at Woodbridge, Suffolk, 10 - 14 Feb 45 - hydraulic system and bomb bay doors - damaged on 9 Feb 45 mission to Magdeburg.
Completed 90 missions.
RZI 31 May 45.

B-24J-125 CO 42-110031	H	67 (NB)	PHYLLIS >86<
OD			

Received between 18 & 27 Mar 44.
Crash-landed 25 Feb 45 at A-50 (Orléans/Bricy, France) - attempted an emergency landing with the G box out, compass inoperative and low on fuel. The nose turret gunner, Sgt Grau, was recovered, seriously injured, from an open field 1/2 mile short of A-69 (Laon/Athis, France). (Aschaffenburg) Salvaged battle damaged 25 - 28 Feb 45 by 5 SAD.

B-24J-125 CO 42-110034	R	506 (GJ)	SOUTHERN COMFORT II >39<
OD -R 506 (GJ)	R	506 (GJ)	

Bar below the letter moved before the letter on 27 Apr 44 and above the letter on 21 May 44.
Received between 27 Mar & 17 Apr 44.
May have crash landed 27 Jun 44 at Manston, Kent, on return from mission to Creil, France, but must have been repaired.
Lost 21 Jul 44 - shot down by flak. (Oberpfaffenhofen)

B-24J-125 CO 42-110035	Y	68 (WQ)	ANY GUM CHUM >24<
OD			

Received 27 Mar 44.
Lost 7 Jul 44 - hit by enemy aircraft and shot down between the initial point and the target. (Bernburg)

B-24J-130 CO 42-110042	J	67 (NB)	>17<
OD			

Received between 27 & 31 Mar 44.
Lost 12 May 44 - went down on the way out after being hit by four fighters. (Zeitz)

B-24J-130 CO 42-110045	K	66 (QK)	THE BANANA BARGE >26<
OD	-K	506 (GJ)	
	K	506 (GJ)	

Transferred from 66th BS to 506th BS on 27 Apr 44. Bar changed from before to above the letter on 21 May 44.
Received between 15 & 22 Mar 44.
Lost 28 May 44 - hit in #2 engine by flak in the vicinity of Dümmer Lake, the aircraft turned back and went down after the crew bailed out. (Zeitz)

B-24H-25 FO 42-95049	O	67 (NB)	FEARLESS FOSDICK >98<
NMF			

Name was followed by the words "WRIT BY HAND".
Received between 27 Apr & 13 May 44.
Landed at A-47 (Paris/Orly, France) on return from 16 Jan 45 mission to Ruhland (but Dresden bombed) because of fog blanket over England.
Repaired at Lissett, Yorkshire, 3 - 8 Feb 45 - #1 engine damaged on 31 Jan 45 mission to Hallendorf re-called after the formation reached the Dümmer Lake area.
Abandoned 1 Mar 45, low on gas on return and unable to locate a field for landing, the crew bailed out and the airplane went down at Vermand, France. (Ingolstadt) Salvaged 30 Mar 45 on the Continent by 5 SAD.

B-24J-130 CO 42-110049	P	66 (QK)	>33<
OD	A	68 (WQ)	

Transferred from 66th BS to 68th BS on 27 Apr 44.
Received before 8 Apr 44.
Lost 21 Jul 44 - crashed and was destroyed at Silberplatte Santis, Nesslau, St Gallen canton, SWITZERLAND. (Oberpfaffenhofen)

B-24J-130 CO 42-110057	Q	68 (WQ)	>48<
OD			

Received between 18 & 31 Mar 44.
Crashed 9 Sep 44 at Shipdham. (Mainz) Salvaged 9 Sep 44 - cracked aux spar, pulled laminated skin.

B-24J-130 CO 42-110067	B	66 (QK)	>4<
OD	O	67 (NB)	

Transferred from 66th BS to 67th BS on 27 Apr 44.
Received between 27 Mar & 1 Apr 44.
Crashed 27 Apr 44 at Shipdham. (Creil, France) Salvaged 27 & 28 Apr 44 - stations 1 - 6 washed out, left gear pulled out.

B-24D-30 CO 42-40068 N 506 LYNN BARI <4>
OD
Original aircraft received 4 Mar 43.
It is said to have crashed 29 Mar 43 on take-off from a modification centre in Northern Ireland (Langford Lodge or Greencastle?) but this seems unlikely. It appears on the formation plans for 22 & 23 Mar and 5 Apr 43 (pilot: Anderson on all three) and has a sortie credit for 31 Mar 43 (pilot: O'Brien [68th BS]). Was succeeded by 42-40172 -N 506th LYNN BARI II - first trace on 14 May 43 crew interrogation form.

B-24D-30 CO 42-40071 C 66 SATAN'S HELL CATS >17< OD MARGARET ANN II
Name was SATAN'S HELL CATS on Jansen's loading list to Africa in May 43. On Ploesti mission list it becomes MARGARET ANN II.
Received before 17 May 43.
Flew on 1 Aug 43 Ploesti mission.
Left in Tunis - transferred to MTO 16 or 19 Oct 43.

B-24J-145 CO 44-40071 D+ 66 (QK) SWEAT BOX >20<
NMF P+ 66 (QK)
ex 492nd BG.
Received by 44th BG between 18 & 27 Aug 44.
Crash landed 5 Nov 44 at Shipdham - landing gear hit a hole in the runway on return. (Karlsruhe). Salvaged 5 & 6 Nov 44 - left gear went out and left wing badly damaged.

B-24J-65 CO 42-100073 H 67 (NB) SACK ARTISTS >12<
OD
Received before 13 Jan 44.
Lost 18 Mar 44 - crashed at Fehraltdorf, Zurich canton, SWITZERLAND. (Friedrichshafen)

B-24J-130 CO 42-110082 O 68 (WQ) WENDY >21<
OD
Received between 8 & 19 Apr 44.
Crash-landed 27 Jun 44 at Manston, Kent, on return. (Creil) Salvaged 27 - 29 Jun 44 - nose wheel retracted.

B-24J-130 CO 42-110083 X 67 (NB) >1<
OD
Received before 8 Apr 44.
Lost 8 Apr 44 - hit by enemy aircraft before the target, went down in a tight spin on fire and exploded when it hit the ground in the vicinity of the target. (Langenhagen)

B-24H-25 FO 42-95087 A 67 (NB) Backward Katie/Shy little Lady >120<
NMF K 67 (NB)
Letter changed from A to K on 12 Oct 44.
Received between 18 Apr & 7 May 44.
Completed 120 missions. Name was given by the spagnola crew no photo to confirm name.
RZI 31 May 45.

B-24J-130 CO 42-110088 T 506 (GJ) >19<
OD -T 506 (GJ)
T 506 (GJ)
Bar changed from below to before the letter on 27 Apr 44 and again changed from before to above the letter on 21 May 44.
Received between 8 & 19 Apr 44.
Crashed and burned at Shipdham. Salvaged 15 Jul 44.

B-24D-30 CO 42-40094 E 68 MISS VIRGINIA >5<
OD
Received 27 Apr 43.
Lost 2 Jul 43 - ditched in the Mediterranean, short of fuel, flak having damaged the gas tanks. (Lecce, Italy)

B-24J-135 CO 42-110095 S+ 66 (QK) LUCKY STRIKE >25<
OD D 68 (WQ) HELLSADROPPIN'
G 68 (WQ)
GH lead aircraft until at least 16 Nov 44. After that its call letter was changed to G and it flew missions as a wing aircraft from 4 Dec 44.
ex 93rd BG. Received by 44th BG before 2 Aug 44.
Will Lundy gives the name as HELLSADROPPIN'.
Lost 16 Jan 45 - on return found Shipdham fogged-in solid as well as other fields in the area so the crew bailed out 6 or 7 miles from Norwich after setting the automatic pilot. Presumably, the aircraft went down in the North Sea. (Ruhland but could not be located so Dresden was bombed)

B-24J-145 CO 44-40098 B 68 (WQ) LONE RANGER >37<
NMF
Received before 22 Apr 44 (first NMF B-24 assigned to 44th BG).
Lost 24 Aug 44 - shot down by flak. (Langenhagen).

B-24J-70 CO 42-100100 K 68 DOUBLE TROUBLE >1<
OD
Letter believed to be K.
Received 10 Dec 44.
Transferred to 392nd BG after 31 Dec 43.

B-24H-20 DT 42-51101 E 68 (WQ) CORKY >66<
NMF H 68 (WQ)
Letter changed from E to H on 12 Oct 44.
Received before 10 Jun 44.
Repaired at Woodbridge, Suffolk, 26 Oct - 14 Nov 44 - #4 engine, electrical work, tab cables, horizontal stabilizer and hydraulic system damaged on 25Oct 44 mission to Gelsenkirchen.
Lost 28 Jan 45 - received a direct hit in the bomb bay over the target. (Dortmund)

B-24HSH-20 DT 42-51103 C+ 66 (QK) >0<
NMF
Received between 31 Jul & 13 Sep 44.
Transferred to 392nd BG.

B-24J-70 CO 42-100107 R 506 (GJ) >19<
OD
Received 29 Jan 44.
Crash-landed 27 Mar 44 at Tangmere, Sussex. (Mont-de-Marsan, France) Salvaged 28 & 29 Mar 44 - right landing gear collapsed.

B-24H-25 DT 42-51108 68 (WQ) ARROWHEAD >0<
NMF
ex 453rd BG after 10 Apr 45.
Flew no combat missions with 44th BG.
RZI 28 or 31 May 45.

B-24J-70 CO 42-100110 P 68 (WQ) NORTHERN LASS >30<
OD
Received 27 Jan 44.
Crash-landed 9 May 44 at Swannington or Attlebridge due to heavy battle damage caused by the premature explosion of bombs beneath the aircraft while near the target. (St-Trond-Brustem, Belgium) Salvaged 9 & 10 May 44 at Attlebridge.

B-24D-20 CO 41-24112 Y 68 CAPTAIN & HIS KIDS RIDE AGAIN >2<
OD
Received 9 May 43? (it appears on 28 Mar & 16 Apr 43 formation plans).
Transferred to 389th BG after 29 May 43.
Re-named by Jack Benny after transfer to 389th BG.

B-24J-70 CO 42-100112 Q 68 (WQ) PAPER DOLL >17<
OD LADY DOT
Name was PAPER DOLL or LADY DOT.
Received 31 Jan 44.
Lost 18 Mar 44 - crashed at Dietschwil, St Gallen canton, SWITZERLAND. (Friedrichshafen)

B-24HSH-1 CF 41-29120 >1<
OD
ex 445th BG.
May have been assigned to 44th BG but flew no missions with that Group prior to conversion by BAD 1 to B-24HSH PFF (H2S) and assignment to 482nd BG - call letter A - on 20 Dec 43. (Have 1 confirmed mission on September 18,1944. Lt Horricks crew)

B-24H-25 FO 42-95124 P+ 66 (QK) SAND BOMB SPECIAL >12<
NMF D+ 66 (QK)
D 67 (NB)
Z 67 (NB)
P+ 66 (QK)
GH aircraft?
Letter changed from P+ to D+ on 18 Oct 44, transferred from 66th BS to 67th BS on 2 Nov 44, letter changed from D to Z on 29 Nov 44 and reverted to 66th BS as P+ on 4 Dec 44.
ex 93rd BG.
Received by 44th BG between 25 Jul & 5 Oct 44 - probably before 10 Sep 44.
Landed on one wheel on 29 Nov 44.
Lost 4 Dec 44 - lost #1 & #2 engines and crew bailed out near Freiburg. (Wetzlar)

B-24D-30 CO 42-40126 T 67 ANNIE OAKLEY "CRACK SHOT" >4<
OD
Received before 5 Apr 43.
Lost 14 May 43 - crashed and burned. (Kiel)

B-24HSH-25 DT 42-51126 D+ 66 (QK) UMBRIAGO >2<
NMF
Received before 31 Jul 44.
Transferred to 392nd BG between 5 & 8 Aug 44.

B-24D-30 CO 42-40130 H 66 AVENGER II >4<
OD
Received before 4 Apr 43.
Landed 17 May 43 at Alama de Aragon fighter base, north west of Saragossa, SPAIN, after developing engine trouble before the target and was interned. (Bordeaux, France)

B-24H-1 CF 41-29139 E 67 >3<
OD
Received before 12 Nov 43.
Lost 18 Nov 43 - went down in the North Sea. (Oslo-Kjeller, Norway)

B-24H-25 FO 42-95142 K 506 (GJ) CAPE COD SPECIAL #2 >10<
NMF
Received 1 Jul 44.
Lost 21 Jul 44 - shot down by enemy fighters south-west of Munich, headed for Switzerland, having already a large flak hole in the wing. (Oberpfaffenhofen)

B-24H-1 CF 41-29148 B 66 >26<
OD
Received between 1 Oct & 13 Nov 43.
Lost 24 Feb 44 - crashed at Dippach, near Fulda. (Gotha)

B-24HSH-25 DT 42-51149 E+ 66 (QK) BLOOD AND GUTS >0<
NMF
Received between 11 & 20 Jul 44.
Transferred to 389th BG between 20 Jul & 10 Aug 44 and then to 453rd BG between 12 & 24 Aug 44.

B-24HSH-25 DT 42-51150 N+ 66 (QK) I WALK ALONE >0<
NMF
Received before 6 Aug 44.
Transferred to 392nd BG before 9 Aug 44.

B-24H-25 FO 42-95150 -B 506 (GJ) PASSION PIT >47<
NMF B 506 (GJ)
Received between 11 & 19 May 44.
Lost 13 Aug 44 - exploded and fell in pieces after flak knocked out #1and #2 engines and set fire to the aircraft on the bomb run. (Road junctions between Le Havre and Rouen, France)

B-24D-20 CO 41-24153 L 66 SAD SACK II >8<
OD
Lost 1 Aug 43 - badly shot up, crashed in a cornfield and burned after leaving the target. (Ploesti, Rumania)

B-24H-1 CF 41-29153 Z 506 (GJ) GREENWICH >42<
OD
Bar added below letter Z in Nov 43.
Received between 1 & 9 Oct 43.
Lost 8 Apr 44 - started to go down, hit by flak and by fighters in the vicinity of the target. (Langenhagen)

154 67 (NB)
It was on the strength of 67th BS on 21 May 45 when the pilot was Lt Lee - see page 200 of "The History of the 67 Bombardment Squadron". According to Webb Todd on page 400 of "History of the 68th Bomb Squadron", it flew its last mission on 13 Mar 45. According to Roger Freeman in "Mighty Eighth War Diary", weather restricted operations on that date and Webb Todd states on page 260 of the History that there was only practice flying on that date. Although 42-52154 was at Thorpe Abbotts undergoing repair to #1 engine from 11 - 17 Mar 45 and Webb Todd's information would seem to eliminate it from possibles, I suspect it was this ex 453rd BG plane named MALE CALL. Other possibilities are: 41-29154, 42-100154, 42-64154, 42-110154 (original 491st BG plane named JOHNNY COME LATELY, recorded with that Group until Nov 44 and salvaged war weary on 29 May 45), 44-51154 and 44-42154.

B-24H-1 CF 41-29156 R 68 (WQ) V-PACKET >63<
OD R 68 (WQ)
Bar below letter R deleted in Nov 43.
Received before 18 Oct 43.
Classed war weary 9 Aug 44 after 56 missions - last on 5 Aug 44?
To USA from ATC Valley terminal 21 Mar 45.

B-24H-1 CF 41-29157 J 66 >14<
OD
Received between 1 Oct & 16 Nov 43.
Lost 29 Jan 44 - trying to reach Switzerland, it was shot down and crashed between Illfurth and Zillisheim, near Mulhouse, France. (Frankfurt)

B-24J-150 CO 44-40158 Q 506 (GJ) TINKER BELLE >53<
NMF
ex 492nd BG.
Received by 44th BG on 13 Aug 44.
Landed at B-53 (5 SAD, Merville, France) with #1 engine out on 14 Jan 45 mission to Hemmingstedt when there was adverse weather in England. Returned to Shipdham on 2 Mar 45.
Lost 5 Apr 45 - shot down by flak and crashed near Wipperfürth. (Plauen)

B-24H-1 CF 41-29161 H 67 >16<
OD
Received 9 Oct 43 and flown on that date by crew from 392nd BG, 579th BS.
Crash-landed 18 Nov 43 at Shipdham on one wheel with severe battle damage. (Oslo-Kjeller, Norway) Salvaged 19 Nov 43.

B-24J-140 CO 42-110161 M+ 66 (QK) JAIL BAIT >36<
OD
ex 491st BG.
Received by 44th BG on 22 Aug 44.
Landed at A-47 (Paris/Orly) on return from 16 Jan 45 mission to Ruhland (but Dresden bombed) because of fog blanket over England.
RZI 31 May 45.

B-24HSH-1 CF 41-29163
OD
It is thought to have been assigned to 44th BG but to have flown no missions with that Group prior to conversion by BAD 1 to B-24HSH PFF (H2S) and assignment to 482nd BG - call letter B - on 15 Dec 43.
Flew as lead aircraft with 44th BG on 30 Jan 44 mission.
Later assigned to 392nd BG, then to 492nd BG - 2nd Organisation and finally transferred to MTO on 30 Jan 45.

B-24H-1 CF 41-29164 I 67 >7<
OD I 67
Bar added below letter I in Nov 43.
Received before 3 Nov 43.
Lost 18 Nov 43 - went down in the North Sea. (Oslo-Kjeller, Norway)

B-24J-5 CF 42-64166 A 66 BIG FAT BUTTERFLY >7<
OD
Received between 22 Dec 43 & 20 Jan 44.
It would not surprise me if the true identity of this ship were B-24H-1 CF 41-29166 because, otherwise, it is the only aircraft from Block J-5 CF to have been traced in the 8th AF.
Lost 20 Feb 44 over Belgium. (Helmstedt)

B-24J-150 CO 44-40167 Y 506 (GJ) SIERRA BLANCA >15<
NMF
ex 492nd BG.
Received by 44th BG on 13 Aug 44.
Lost 7 Oct 44 - hit by flak and set on fire. (Kassel)

B-24H-1 CF 41-29168 F 66 >2<
OD
Received between 9 Oct & 12 Nov 43.
Belly-landed 13 Nov 43 at Frogshall, Northrepps. (Bremen) Salvaged 13 & 14 Nov 43 - fuselage damaged to station 6.

B-24J-75 CO 42-100170 A 66 PATSY ANN II >46<

OD G 66 (QK)
G 68 (WQ)
Letter changed from A to G in 66th BS on 25 Feb 44. Transferred from 66th BS to 68th BS on 27 Apr 44.
Received between 20 & 24 Feb 44.
Lost 7 Jul 44 - shot down 7 km south east of Halberstadt. (Bernburg)

B-24H-1 CF 41-29172 T 506 (GJ) LUCKY STRIKE >45<
OD
Received before 13 Nov 43.
Lost 18 Mar 44 - crashed near the coast in France or in the English Channel. (Friedrichshafen)

B-24D-35 CO 42-40172 N 506 LYNN BARI II >5<
OD
Received before 14 May 43.
Flew on 1 Aug 43 Ploesti mission.
Left at Gibraltar in need of extensive repairs - transferred to MTO 31 Aug 43, recorded on 12 May 44 to go to BAD 1 for modification and later assigned to 801st BG(P).

B-24H-1 CF 41-29174 U 67 AMBLIN' OKIE >1<
OD
Received before 13 Nov 43.
Transferred to 392nd BG between 16 Nov 43 & 28 Jan 44.

B-24J-75 CO 42-100177 L 66 (QK) >65<
OD -L 506 (GJ)
L 506 (GJ)
No name visible on the starboard side but this had a picture of a goofy type wearing a flying helmet and GI fatigues holding a magnifying glass in his left hand and a bomb between the thumb and forefinger of his right hand.
Received between 21 Jan & 13 Feb 44.
Transferred from 66th BS to 506th BS between 26 Apr & 3 May 44.
No trace with 44th BG after 10 Sep 44.
Flew truckin' operation with 458th BG on 18 Sep 44 with 44th BG markings.
War weary when salvaged 31 May 45 by BADA, Greencastle, Northern Ireland.

B-24H-25 DT 42-51181 K 506 (GJ) CAPE COD SPECIAL >9<
NMF
Received between 28 May & 3 Jun 44.
Lost 29 Jun 44 - collided with 41-28829 after being hit by flak following bombs away, went into a flat spin and exploded. (Magdeburg)

B-24J-75 CO 42-100181 Z 68 STAR VALLEY >1<
OD
Received 28 Jan 44.
Lost 5 Feb 44 - went down with the FW 190 which had shot off the plane's wing. (Tours, France)

B-24D-35 CO 42-40182 A 66 FORKY II >16<
OD
Received before 4 Apr 43.
Lost 1 Aug 43 - crashed into a corn field on leaving the target and exploded. (Ploesti, Rumania)

B-24J-140 CO 42-110185 C+ 66 (QK) WILD BILL >23<
OD S+ 66 (QK)
Had a picture on the nose, drawn in white paint, of a 10-men crew standing at a bar with a diminutive barman behind the bar.
ex 491st BG.
Received by 44th BG between 13 Sep & 2 Oct 44.
Landed at A-84 (Chièvres, Belgium) for refuelling on return from the 25 Feb 45 mission to Aschaffenburg and returned to Shipdham 26 Feb 45.
Landed at A-94 (Conflans, France) on 1 Mar 45 mission to Ingolstadt - lost oil pressure in #3 engine, engine being changed, internal failure.
It was salvaged at 1 SAD, Troston (Honington) – date unknown - see photo on page 203 of American Bomber Aircraft Vol.1 "Consolidated B-24 Liberator" by John M & Donna Campbell.

B-24H-25 FO 42-95189 J 67 (NB) >40< WEARY xxx (the remainder is illegible)
NMF K+ 66 (QK)
Received between 9 and 24 May 44.
Crash-landed 5 Sep 44 in a ploughed field near Shipdham on return when the aircraft ran out of gas and four engines cut out. (Karlsruhe) Salvaged 5 & 6 Sep 44 - main bulkheads torn out stations 3 to 4.

B-24MEA-20 CO 44-42189 68 (WQ) (EAGLE)
ex 482nd BG. NMF
Date received by 44th BG unknown.
RZI 28 or 31 May 45.

B-24D-20 CO 41-24191 X 506 CACTUS >1<
OD
Original aircraft received 4 Mar 43.
Lost 22 Mar 43 - went down off the Netherlands coast. (Wilhelmshaven)

B-24H-25 FO 42-95193 I 67 (NB) THREE KISSES FOR LUCK >83<
NMF Y 68 (WQ)
I 67 (NB)
Transferred from 67th BS to 68th BS on 14 Feb 45 and back to 67th BS on 10 Mar 45.
Received 6 Jun 44.
Landed at A-47 (Paris/Orly, France) on return from 16 Jan 45 mission to Ruhland (but Dresden bombed) because of fog blanket over England.
Landed at A-70 (Laon/Couvron, France) low on fuel on 1 Mar 45 mission to Ingolstadt. Returned to Shipdham on 2 Mar 45.
RZI 27 May 45.

B-24D-20 CO 41-24201 O 506 BALDY AND HIS BROOD >53<
OD O 506
Original aircraft received 4 Mar 43.
Bar above O deleted and bar below O added in Nov 43.
Flew on 1 Aug 43 Ploesti mission.
Assigned to 801st BG(P) on 28 Feb 44 after conversion by BAD 1 between 14 & 28 Feb 44.

B-24H-25 FO 42-95207 Q 506 (GJ) >8<
NMF
Received between 27 Jun & 6 Jul 44.
Crash-landed 21 Jul 44 at Shipdham according to 3 SAD salvage report but Will Lundy gives the location as Warningford (probably Wormingford, near Colchester, Essex, - Station AF 159, a 9th Air Force fighter base). Will
also gives the pilot's name as Lt. Atkins but according to the formation plans for this mission, the airplane was flown by Lt. Bentcliff. Right tyre blown out, left main landing gear and wing damaged. (Oberpfaffenhofen)
Salvaged 27 - 29 Jul 44.

B-24H-5 CF 41-29208 D 66 (QK) SHOO SHOO BABY >20<
OD
ex 448th BG.
Received by 44th BG between 23 & 30 Dec 43.
Had a modified nose - Bell power boost unit from a B-26 incorporated.
Repaired at Manston, Kent, 9 Feb - 13 Mar 44 - change 4 engines.
Recorded on 14 Apr 44 that top turret and ball turret had been removed and lights for pre-dawn forming installed. Aircraft lightened by removal of arms and armour.
To USA 7 Mar 45 from ATC Valley terminal.

B-24H-25 FO 42-95209 W 506 (GJ) SILVER HAIRED DADDY >105<
NMF
Received before 27 May 44.
RZI 30 May 45.

B-24D-20 CO 41-24211 U 68 WING AND A PRAYER >9<
OD
Received 22 May 43.
Flew on 1 Aug 43 Ploesti mission.
Force landed 13 Aug 43 on return, out of fuel, on a small landing strip in Sicily. (Wiener Neustadt, Austria)
Transferred to MTO 28 Aug 43.

B-24H-30 DT 42-51224 W 68 (WQ) >78<
NMF
Received between 7 & 16 Jul 44.
Landed at A-83 (Denain/Prouvy, France) low on gas on return from 16 Jan 45 mission to Ruhland (but Dresden bombed) because of fog blanket over England - overshot the runway and stuck in mud. Returned to Shipdham on 3 Mar 45.
RZI 31 May 45.

B-24D-25 CO 41-24225 T 68 FLAK ALLEY >47<
OD T 68
Received 26 Mar 43.
Bar below T deleted in Nov 43.
Flew on 1 Aug 43 Ploesti mission.
Lost 24 Feb 44 on its 42nd mission - crashed on a small village south of the target. (Gotha)

B-24H-25 FO 42-95226 C 68 (WQ) CHANNEL HOPPER >32<
NMF
Received before 21 May 44.
Lost 21 Jul 44 - hit by flak immediately after bombing the target, with its hydraulic system knocked out, crash landed near Dübendorf, Zürich canton, SWITZERLAND, overshooting the runway. (Oberpfaffenhofen)

B-24D-25 CO 41-24229 P 67 BUZZIN BEAR >12<
OD SEEDS OF SATAN
Name changed from SEEDS OF SATAN (see also SEED-O-SATAN - 42-40745 and SEED OF SATAN - 42-7544) to BUZZIN BEAR.
Received before 29 May 43.
Flew on 1 Aug 43 Ploesti mission.
Lost 16 Aug 43 - broke in two shortly after leaving the target. (Foggia, Italy)

B-24H-5 CF 41-29231 J 67 THE IMPATIENT VIRGIN >15<
OD
ex 448th BG.
Received by 44th BG between 7 & 30 Dec 43.
Belly-landed 25 Feb 44 at Lympne, Kent, on return. (Fürth) Salvaged 26 & 27 Feb 44.

B-24D-25 CO 41-24232 M 67 CALABAN >20<
OD M
Received 2 Mar 43.
Bar below M added in Nov 43.
Flew on 1 Aug 43 Ploesti mission - landed at Malta on return.
Lost 11 Dec 43 - crashed near Wybelsum after bombs from a B-24 flying above broke off the right wing at #4 engine and the tail assembly. (Emden)

234 68 (WQ)
Shown on 16 Jul 44 formation plan without a call letter (Pilot: Lt Clair W Hill Jr) but no other trace of it has been found. Unless it was borrowed for this mission, it was not 42-51234 because that was assigned to 492nd BG
as a repacement aircraft on 13 Jul 44 and flew 14 missions with that Group - see page 92 of "The Fortunes of War". The formation plan for 16 Jul 44 is handwritten and the "4" looks as if it may have been changed to "1" but the only 231 assigned to 44th BG was 41-29231, salvaged in Feb 44, so it could not have been that one. It is just possible that it was 42-51231 which was assigned to 466th BG and with which it flew its first mission on 5 Oct 44 - see "The Attlebridge Diaries".

B-24D-25 CO 41-24234 U 506 MR 5 BY 5 >19<
OD E 66
N 66
Original aircraft received 4 Mar 43.
Transferred from 506th BS to 66th BS in Sep 43 and letter changed in Nov 43 from E to N with a bar above.
Repaired at Shipdham 11 Sep - 15 Oct 43 - nose gear collapsed.
Lost 26 Nov 43 - crashed into the sea after losing the tail section in a mid-air collision with 42-7501. (Bremen)

B-24J -1 DT 42-51234 L+ 66 (QK) >17<
NMF
ex 492nd BG.
Received by 44th BG between 15 Aug & 1 Sep 44.
Crash-landed at Veltem or Heultje, near Westerlo, about 25 miles north east of Brussels - ran into mechanical trouble and left the formation, heading for Brussels. Due to poor visibility, missed the field and, running short of fuel, salvoed its bombs. The blast blew out the windows in the plane and damaged the elevator. The pilot tried to land in a grassy meadow but the landing gear collapsed and split the plane, rendering it a complete washout. (Leverkusen) Salvaged on the Continent, battle damaged, by 8 ASC (salvage recorded on 14 Nov 44, an administrative date, not the date on which the aircraft was actually salvaged).

B-24D-25 CO 41-24235 C 506 EARTHQUAKE McGOON >16<
OD P 67
Original aircraft received 4 Mar 43.
Transferred from 506th BS to 67th BS in Sep 43.

Flew on 1 Aug 43 Ploesti mission.
Crash landed 1 Oct 43 on the beach at Salerno, Italy. (Wiener Neustadt, Austria)
Transferred to MTO 15 Oct 43 and condemned 30 Nov 43.

B-24H-5 CF 41-29236 F 66 HELL'S KITTEN >12<
OD
ex 448th BG.
Received by 44th BG on 29 or 30 Dec 43.
Crashed on take-off or crash landed 9 Feb 44 at Shipdham. (Mission to Gotha re-called shortly after take-off). Salvaged 10 Feb 44 - left landing gear pulled out and left wing damaged.

247
The North Pickenham control tower log lists the arrival of a new 491st BG replacement aircraft, 247, from Shipdham on 7 Mar 45.
No record of missions with 44th BG - may never have been assigned to 44th BG
Possible complete serials:
B-24H-5 CF 41-29247
B-24H-10 FO 42-52247
B-24J-85 CO 42-100247
B-24L-20 FO 44-50247 (this is probably the aircraft)
B-24J-1 DT 42-51258 J+ 66 (QK) >45<
NMF
ex 492nd BG.
Received by 44th BG between 6 Aug & 8 Sep 44.
Landed at B-67 (Ursel, Belgium) on 1 Jan 45 for refuelling.
Landed at Bentwaters, Suffolk, on return from 16 Jan 45 mission to Ruhland (but Dresden bombed) when Shipdham was closed by fog.
Landed at airfield A-83 (Denain-Prouvy, France) on 21 Feb 45 mission to Nürnberg - #4 engine changed. Returned to Shipdham on 23 Feb 45.
Crashed 25 Feb 45 on the Continent - hit, probably by flak, the plane lost fuel and had to be abandoned very close to an auxiliary landing field at Charleroi, Belgium. (Aschaffenburg) Salvaged 9 Mar 45 on the Continent by 5 SAD.

B-24H-25 FO 42-95260 P 68 (WQ) LILI MARLENE >47<
NMF
See also 42-7638 with the same name.
Received between 9 & 24 May 44.
Crashed and burned 28 Dec 44 at Shipdham - had to turn back with #2 engine out, missed the runway, began a right turn and stalled. A bomb exploded demolishing the airplane. (Kaiserlautern) Salvaged 28 & 29 Dec 44.

B-24D-45 CO 42-40267 N 67 HORSE FLY >9<
OD
Received before 17 May 43.
Lost 1 Aug 43 - seriously damaged, it landed in TURKEY and was interned. (Ploesti, Rumania)

B-24J-155 CO 44-40276 Q+ 66 (QK) SCOTTY MAC >42<
NMF R 68 (WQ)
Transferred from 66th BS to 68th BS on 8 Jan 45.
ex 493rd BG.
Received by 44th BG between 11 & 25 Sep 44.
Landed at an airfield in Belgium or France on return from 16 Jan 45 mission to Ruhland (but Dresden bombed) because of fog blanket over England.
Landed at A-82 (Verdun-sur-Meuse, France) on 25 Feb 45 mission to Aschaffenburg, having lost #1 engine. Returned to Shipdham 16 Mar 45.
RZI 31 May 45.

B-24D-25 CO 41-24278 Q 67 MISS DELORES >1<
OD
Lost 14 May 43 - hit by flak over the target and crashed in the sea near Danish territorial waters south of the Island of Æro. (Kiel)

B-24J-85 CO 42-100279 I 67 (NB) >24<
OD
Received before 13 Feb 44.
Lost 29 Apr 44 - damaged by flak, it was attacked by FW 190s and with only 50 galls of fuel left when about 40 miles east of the Zuyder Zee, the aircraft was pointed in the direction of Germany and the rest of the crew bailed out. (Berlin)

B-24J-155 CO 44-40279 K+ 66 (QK) HENRY >47<
NMF
ex 490th BG, probably originally 493rd BG.
Received by 44th BG between 5 & 21 Sep 44.
Landed at A-47 (Paris/Orly, France) on return from 16 Jan 45 mission to Ruhland (but Dresden bombed) because of fog blanket over England.
Repaired at Woodbridge, Suffolk, 29 Jan - 14 Feb 45 - extensive damage to hydraulic system on 28 Jan 45 mission to Dortmund.
RZI 22 May 45.

B-24D-25 CO 41-24282 Y 506 RUTH-LESS >33<
OD
Original aircraft received 4 Mar 43.
Flew on 1 Aug 43 Ploesti mission.
Crashed and burned 2 Feb 44 on return at Butt's Lane, Willingdon, near Eastbourne, East Sussex. (Watten V-1 site, France) Salvaged 4 & 5 Feb 44.

B-24MEA-25 CO 44-42282 67 (NB) EIGHT BALL (Eagle)
NMF

May have been named EIGHT BALL.
ex 482nd BG.
Date received by 44th BG unknown.
RZI 31 May 45.

B-24D-25 CO 41-24283 Z 506 OLD CROW >25<
OD GALVINATIN GAL
Name was OLD CROW (nose art represents a label from a liquor bottle, Old Crow) but also said to have been named GALVINATIN GAL (see 42-7509 GALLAVANTIN GAL).
Original aircraft (received 4 Mar 43?).
Flew on 1 Aug 43 Ploesti mision.
Transferred to MTO 18 Oct 43, having landed at Palermo, Sicily, on return from 1 Oct 43 mission to Wiener Neustadt, Austria, when the left main wing spar was cracked, hit by a 20mm shell. It was apparently left at Tunis and scrapped.

B-24MEA-25 CO 44-42283 (Eagle)
NMF
ex 482nd BG.
Received by 44th BG on or after 30 Apr 45.
RZI 31 May 45.

B-24J-85 CO 42-100285 J 66 >3<
OD
Received beween 29 Jan & 11 Feb 44.
Crash-landed 20 Feb 44 at Holbrook, Suffolk, after running out of fuel on return. (Helmstedt) Salvaged 22 - 24 Feb 44 - tyre blew.

B-24H-10 FO 42-52293 G 67 (NB) JUDY'S BUGGY >38<
OD
ex 458th BG - received by 44th BG between 14 Jan & 20 Feb 44.
Repaired at Beccles, Suffolk, 9 Apr - 22 May 44 - #3 & 4 engines, surface changes and fuselage damage to station 8 - after force landing at Ellough, Suffolk, on return from 8 Apr 44 mission to Langenhagen.
Repaired at Heston, Middlesex, 31 May - 12 Jul 44 - nose gear collapse, #1 engine.
Recorded on 14 Jul 44 that a request had been made for war weary status.
Flew truckin' operation with 458th BG on 18 Sep 44 bearing 44th BG markings.
Crashed 16 Jan 45 at A-47 (Paris/Orly, France) after the crew bailed out - flak hit #3 engine. #2 propeller governor out. (Dresden) Salvaged 4 Feb 45 on the Continent.

B-24D-25 CO 41-24295 J 506 WICKED WITCH >3<
OD
Original aircraft received 4 Mar 43.
Lost 14 May 43 - #2 engine was damaged by flak before the target, bombs were salvoed and the aircraft was finished off by fighters over the Baltic. (Kiel)

B-24J-85 CO 42-100295 V 68 >5<
OD
Received between 21 Jan & 20 Feb 44.
Crash-landed at Thorpe Abbotts on four dead engines due to failure of the fuel transfer system. (Frankfurt) Salvaged 2 - 5 Mar 44 - left main landing gear and wing damaged.

B-24H-15 FO 42-52305 P 506 (GJ) >17<
OD
Possibly ex 458th BG.
Received by 44th BG between 29 Jan & 8 Feb 44.
Lost 18 Mar 44 - went down over Austria - crashed near Wintersulgen. (Friedrichshafen)

B-24J-5 DT 42-51309 V 67 (NB) >21<
NMF
Received before 2 Oct 44.
Crashed 18 Dec 44 at Shipdham on take-off probably due to the severe icing condition in the freezing fog. (Mission to Kyllburg re-called) Salvaged 18 & 19 Dec 44 - left main gear collapsed.

B-24H-30 FO 42-95309 E 506 (GJ) >23<
NMF
Received before 27 May 44.
Lost 29 Jul 44 - went down in the North Sea 6 miles off Cromer after sliding under the centre section of the formation just after leaving the English coast when its #2 propeller chewed off the tail of 42-109820 which also went down. (Bremen)

B-24J-90 CO 42-100314 K 67 (NB) Kay Bar >57<
OD V+ 66 (QK)
N+ 66 (QK)
G+ 66 (QK)
ex 389th BG.
Received between 20 Feb & 22 Mar 44.
Transferred from 67th BS to 66th BS on 10 Sep 44. Letter changed from V+ to N+ on 7 Oct 44 and from N+ to G+ on 22 Mar 45.
Lost 24 Mar 45 with a 67th Sqn crew - after the supplies were dropped the aircraft having been hit by flak suddenly went into a steep climb with #1 engine smoking. It then stalled, nosed directly into the ground and exploded. (Wesel assault area supply drop)

B-24H-30 FO 42-95318 B 67 (NB) OLD IRON CORSET >130<
NMF J 67 (NB)

Letter changed from B to J on 12 Oct 44.
Landed at A-42 (Paris/Villacoublay, France) on return from 16 Jan 45 mission to Ruhland (but Dresden bombed) because of fog blanket over England.
Completed 129 missions.
RZI 31 May 45 - left Shipdham on 29 May 45.

B-24LHO-5 FO 44-49322 D 506 (GJ) >30<
NMF
Received before 8 Jan 45.
RZI 20 or 22 May 45.

B-24LHO-5 FO 44-49323 C 67 (NB) >15<
NMF
Received before 28 Jan 45.
RZI 22 May 45.

B-24MEA-25 CO 44-42324 (Eagle)
NMF
ex 482nd BG.
Date received by 44th BG unknown.
RZI 20 or 31 May 45.

B-24H-20 CF 42-50328 -D 506 (GJ) PREGNANT PEG >14<
OD FLYING LOG
D 506 (GJ)
Name may have been changed from PREGNANT PEG to FLYING LOG.
Received 8 May 44.
Flown from Shipdham to 3 SAD, Watton, on 29 May 44 on return from a mission to Politz for repair with a telegraph pole to brace the catwalk - repaired 29 May - 9 Jun 44 - left wing and surfaces.
Crashed and burned 8 Aug 44 at Yaxham - aborted because of mechanical reasons, returned to Shipdham and while flying the traffic pattern the aircraft suddenly spun in and crashed with a full load of bombs aboard. (Romilly, France).
Salvaged 8 & 9 Aug 44.

B-24H-30 FO 42-95329 S 67 (NB) FIFINELLA >112<
NMF H+ 66 (QK)
See also 42-63763.
Transferred from 67th BS to 66th BS on 5 Sep 44.
Received before 24 May 44.
Landed at Fulbeck, Lincolnshire, on return from 16 Jan 45 mission to Ruhland (but Dresden bombed) when Shipdham was closed by fog.
RZI 30 May 45.

B-24J-90 CO 42-100330 L 67 (NB) >22<
OD
Received before 31 Jan 44.
In the picture on page 20 of "Strangers in a Strange Land" and on page 22 of "Liberator Album - Vol 2", there is a picture of a blonde in a bathing suit in a flying or diving posture on the starboard side of the nose but no name is visible.
Repaired at Manston, Kent, 25 Mar - 9 Apr 44 - #4 engine.
Lost 13 Apr 44 - landed at Dübendorf, Zürich canton, SWITZERLAND. (Lechfeld)

B-24H-15 FO 42-52332 K 66 (QK) MY ASS'AM DRAGON>11<
OD
ex 458th BG.
Received by 44th BG between 29 Jan & 13 Feb 44.
Lost 15 Mar 44 - crashed at Nieuwleusen, Netherlands. (Brunswick)

B-24H-20 CF 42-50339 -C 506 (GJ) FEUDIN WAGON >23<
OD _ C 506 (GJ)
Received 4 May 44.
Belly-landed 27 Jun 44 at Kingsnorth, Kent, on return. (Creil, France). Salvaged 27 - 29 Jun 44.

B-24H-20 CF 42-50349 X 68 (WQ) FLAK MAGNET >60<
OD F 68 (WQ)
Received between 29 Apr & 4 May 44.
Flew truckin' operation with 458th BG on 18 Sep 44 retaining 44th BG markings.
Crashed and burned 28 Jan 45 at Whinburgh, 2 miles east of Shipdham, just after take-off due to icing-up from spray thrown up by the preceding aircraft taking-off. (Dortmund). Salvaged 28 & 29 Jan 45.

B-24J-5 DT 42-51351 P 506 (GJ) CLEAN SWEEP >78<
NMF dragon nose
Received between 9 & 24 Aug 44.
Repaired after crash landing at Old Buckenham on return from 24 Aug 44 mission to Langenhagen - two engines out, supercharger on #3 engine and hydraulic system.
Landed at A-47 (Paris/Orly, France) on return from 16 Jan 45 mission to Ruhland (but Dresden bombed) because of fog blanket over England.
RZI 29 May 45.

B-24D CO 40-2354 C 66 SNAFU >2<
OD
Received 20 Sep 42.
Sent to Bovingdon, Hertfordshire, in Sep 42 for evaluation of armament modifications made at Wright Field
Lost 16 Feb 43 - collided with 41-23818, caught fire, exploded and fell through a formation of B-17s into the English Channel off Selsey, Sussex. (St-Nazaire, France)

B-24LHO-5 FO 44-49356 D+ 66 (QK) >12<
NMF
Received before 28 Jan 45.
RZI 22 May 45.

B-24J-95 CO 42-100367 F 67 (NB) >36<
OD
Received between 21 Feb & 3 Mar 44.
No name visible on crash photos received from Will Lundy of both sides of nose.
Fitted with large B-24M type navigator's windows.
Crash-landed 6 Jul 44 in a field at the end of the runway at Shipdham when coming back in with a full load of bombs after the mission was aborted due to loss of # 1 engine. (Kiel). Salvaged 6 & 7 Jul 44 - lost hydraulic fluid and sheared landing gear.

B-24D-53 CO 42-40370 V 506 HEAVEN CAN WAIT II >12<
OD PETE THE POM INSPECTOR
See also 42-7507 named HEAVEN CAN WAIT.
Re-named PETE THE POM INSPECTOR after transfer to 467th BG.
Flew on 1 Aug 43 Ploesti mission but turned back to Cyprus.
It is said to have been abandoned on 28 Oct 43 at Devasair, Cyprus, but this may have been Deversoir, where the Suez Canal enters the Bitter Lake, Egypt, and the RAF had base MEAF 10 in what was the Canal Zone.
Was returned to ETO, assigned to 389th BG in Nov 43 and later to 467th BG to become the latter Group's 1st assembly ship - salvaged at Rackheath 27 Oct 44 (Note the proximity of dates in different years).

B-24D-53 CO 42-40371 Q 67 GI GAL >9<
OD
Lost 1 Aug 43 - severely damaged, it was abandoned 80 miles from the target. (Ploesti, Rumania)

B-24D -53 CO 42-40373 Z 68 NATCHEZ BELLE >11<
OD
Received 20 Jun 43.
Flew on 1 Aug 43 Ploesti mission.
Lost 16 Aug 43 - attacked by FW 190s and set on fire. (Foggia, Italy)

B-24J-95 CO 42-100373 Y 68 >1<
OD
Received between 11 Jan & 9 Feb 44.
Lost 20 Feb 44 with a 506th Sqn crew - due to mechanical problems it became a straggler and was shot down by fighters over Belgium. (Helmstedt)

B-24D-53 CO 42-40375 G 66 SCRAPPY II >11<
OD
Lost 1 Aug 43 - crash landed after leaving the target area and exploded. (Ploesti, Rumania)

B-24H-25 CF 42-50381 D 68 (WQ) >56<
NMF K 68 (WQ)
Letter changed from D to K on 15 Oct 44.
Received before 21 May 44.
Repaired at Manston, Kent, 27 Jun - 26 Jul 44 - extensive battle damage and #2 engine damaged on 27 Jun 44 mission to Creil, France.
Lost 18 Oct 44 - collided in mid-air with 41-28944 during an electrical storm over Belgium and crashed near Dienze, south west of Ghent, Belgium. (Leverkusen)

B-24LHO-5 FO 44-49387 D 68 (WQ) >15<
NMF
Received between 28 Dec 44 & 17 Jan 45.
RZI 22 or 27 May 45.

B-24J-100 CO 42-100400 Y 506 (GJ) SHOO SHOO BABY >11<
OD
Either this aircraft or 41-29431 was named SHOO SHOO BABY.
Received between 2 & 21 Feb 44.
Lost 18 Mar 44 - nose wheel collapsed on landing at Dübendorf, Zürich canton, SWITZERLAND. (Friedrichshafen)

B-24J-100 CO 42-100402 M 67 (NB) >3<
OD
Received between 20 Jan & 20 Feb 44.
Lost 22 Feb 44 over the Netherlands or over the North Sea. (Mission to Gotha recalled when 100 miles inland - targets of opportunity sought but strong winds caused the formation to drift over the Netherlands where some aircraft bombed Enschede, Arnhem, Nijmegen and Deventer unintentionally)

B-24J-100 CO 42-100411 E 67 (NB) >31<
OD
Received before 3 Mar 44.
Lost 21 Jun 44 with a 506th BS crew. (Genshagen)

B-24J-100 CO 42-100412	V	68 (WQ)	V FOR VICTORY >39<
OD			

Received between 2 & 18 Mar 44.
Crashed 4 Jul 44 at Shalford, near Guildford, Surrey, in an open field - the aircraft developed propeller trouble and was forced to turn back to England where the crew bailed out. (Beaumont-le-Roger, France) Salvaged 7 Jul 44.

B-24J-100 CO 42-100415	Y	506 (GJ)	MY PEACH >38<
OD	-Y	506 (GJ)	
	Y	506 (GJ)	

Received between 18 Mar & 1 Apr 44.
Lost 8 Aug 44 - with engines out or on fire shortly after the target, the aircraft continued in flight, burning, after the crew bailed out 60 miles east of Paris. (Romilly-sur-Seine, France) Salvaged battle damaged by 8 ASC (recorded on 14 Nov 44, an administrative date, not the date on which the aircraft was actually salvaged)

B-24H-15 CF 41-29418	U	68 (WQ)	TURNIP TERMITE >3<
OD			

See also 42-7624 with the same name.
ex 486th BG.
Received by 44th BG between 9 & 17 Apr 44.
Crashed and burned 21 Apr 44 at Taverham Mill Lake, 5 miles north west of Norwich and 1 mile north east of Ringland Hills, due to severe icing conditions - the aircraft stalled, spun and fell apart. (Mission to Zwickau re-called) Salvaged 21 - 23 Apr 44.

B-24J-100 CO 42-100423	A	506	>9<
OD	A	506 (GJ)	

Received before 21 Feb 44.
Repaired at Manston, Kent, 26 Feb - 18 Mar 44 - #3 and #4 engines and structural damage on 25 Feb 44 mission to Fürth.
Lost 8 Apr 44 - the aircraft caught fire after a FW 190 collided with the port engines. (Langenhagen)

B-24LHO-5 FO 44-49425	C	68 (WQ)	>13<
NMF			

Received before 28 Jan 45.
RZI 22 May 45.

B-24H-30 CF 42-50427	V	68 (WQ)	PURITANICAL BITCH >78<
NMF			PURITANICAL WITCH

Name changed from PURITANICAL BITCH to PURITANICAL WITCH on the order of Col Snavely when a WAAF was assigned to the base.
Received 26 Jun 44.
Crashed 22 Mar 45 at Shipdham on take-off - the pilot could not make the plane airborne. (Schwabisch Hall) Salvaged 22 Mar 45 - nose section completely twisted off.

B-24J-100 CO 42-100429	O	506 (GJ)	CONSOLIDATED MESS >69<
OD	-O	506 (GJ)	
	O	506 (GJ)	
	G	506 (GJ)	
	R	506 (GJ)	

The bar was placed before the letter on 27 Apr 44 and above the letter on 21 May 44. The letter was changed to G with a bar above on 16 Nov 44 and changed again after 24 Mar 45 to R with a bar above.
Received 18 Feb 44.
Flew truckin' operation with 458th BG bearing 44th BG markings on 18 Sep 44.
Landed at A-47 (Paris/Orly, France) on return from 16 Jan 45 mission to Ruhland (but Dresden bombed) because of a fog blanket over England.
Repaired at Carnaby (Bridlington), Yorkshire, 2 - 28 Feb 45 - station 5 through station 7.3 damaged on re-called mission to Hallendorf.
RZI 31 May 45.

B-24H-15 CF 41-29431	Q	506 (GJ)	SHOO SHOO BABY >1<
OD			

Either this aircraft or 42-100400 was named SHOO SHOO BABY. (No name visible in the photo on page 14 of "Strangers in a Strange Land" but it shows a girl painted on the starboard side of the nose.)
Received between 3 & 17 Mar 44.
Lost 18 Mar 44 - landed at Dübendorf, Zürich canton, SWITZERLAND. (Friedrichshafen)

B-24J-160 CO 44-40437	H	506 (GJ)	HAIRLESS JOE >8<
NMF			

ex 493rd BG.
Received by 44th BG before 17 Oct 44.
Force landed 30 Nov 44 on the Continent. (Neunkirchen) Salvaged battle damaged 28 Dec 44.

B-24H-15 CF 41-29467	X	67 (NB)	>3<
OD	X	67 (NB)	

Received between 8 & 22 Apr 44.
Lost 27 Apr 44 - received a direct hit by flak in #3 & #4 engines, right wing fell off, the aircraft tipped on its left wing, started down in a tight spiral, became enveloped in flames and exploded. (Moyenneville, France)

B-24H-15 CF 41-29471	X	68 (WQ)	>11<
OD			

Received 26 Mar 44.
Lost 29 Apr 44 - hit by enemy fighters and exploded. (Berlin)

B-24H-15 CF 41-29475	M	67 (NB)	>45<
OD			

Received between 21 Feb & 26 Mar 44.
Repaired at Friston, Sussex, 6 - 26 Jun 44 - # 1 engine, # 2 generator.
Repaired at Woodchurch, Kent, 27 Jun - 26 Jul 44 - # 4 engine, hydraulic lines, radio and electrical work - damage caused by flak on 27 Jun 44 mission to Creil, France.
No trace with 44th BG after 13 Sep 44.
Flew truckin' operation with 458th BG on 18 Sep 44 bearing 44th BG markings.
War weary when salvaged 29 May 45 by BAD 3.

B-24H-1 FO 42-7476	H	66	NICE 'N NAUGHTY >10<
OD			

Received before 3 Nov 43.
Crash-landed 4 Jan 44 at Shipdham on return. (Kiel) Salvaged 4 Jan 44 - both landing gears collapsed.

B-24J-401 CF 42-50480	B+	66 (QK)	BIG TIME OPERATOR >69<
NMF	T+	66 (Q)	

Letter changed from B+ to T+ on 14 Oct 44.
Received before 21 Sep 44.
Landed at A-47 (Paris/Orly, France) on return from 16 Jan 45 mission to Ruhland (but Dresden bombed) because of fog blanket over England.
Landed at Brussels (probably B-58, Brussels-Melsbroek), Belgium, for re-fuelling on 26 Feb 45 mission to Berlin. Returned to Shipdham on the same day.
RZI 27 May 45.

B-24H-15 CF 41-29496	Q	506 (GJ)	RAM IT Dammit >21<
OD	-Q	506 (GJ)	
	Q	506 (GJ)	

See also 42-7635 with the same name.
ex 486th BG.
Received by 44th BG between 8 & 17 Apr 44.
Lost 27 Jun 44 - hit by flak just before bombs away - went down at Creil, France. (Creil, France)

B-24J-50 CO 42-73500	F	68 (WQ)	>23<
OD			

Received before 8 Apr 44.
Lost 29 May 44 - landed at Söve, near Göteborg, SWEDEN.
Brought back to England 29 May 45.

B-24M-5 FO 44-50500	S	506 (GJ)	
NMF			

Received before 30 Mar 45.
RZI 27 May 45.

B-24H-1 FO 42-7501	P	68	BING'S BIG BOX >17<
OD	P	68	

Bar below letter P deleted in Nov 43.
ex 392nd BG but flew no missions with that Group.
Received by 44th BG 8 Oct 43.
Lost 21 Jan 44 - went down at Toupray, France. (Escalles, France)

B-24J-60 CF 44-10503	E	67 (NB)	MISS MARION >27<
NMF	X	67 (NB)	

Letter changed from E to X on 29 Jan 45.
Received before 25 Nov 44.
Landed at Brussels (probably B-58, Brussels-Melsbroek), Belgium, to re-fuel on 25 Feb 45 mission to Aschaffenburg. Returned to Shipdham on 26 Feb 45.
Landed at A-89 (Le Culot, Belgium) on 27 Feb 45 mission to Halle (but Bitterfeld bombed) - #2 turbo, left mag on #2 and #4 engine out and short of fuel.
Returned to Shipdham on 16 Mar 45.
RZI 30 or 31 May 45.

B-24J-60 CF 44-10504	J	68 (WQ)	LADY GERALDINE >53<
NMF			

Received between 13 Sep & 6 Oct 44.
Landed at Faldingworth, Lincolnshire, on return from 16 Jan 45 mission to Ruhland (but Dresden bombed) when Shipdham was closed by fog.
RZI 31 May 45.

B-24J-50 CO 42-73506	X	506 (GJ)	Black Jack >19<
OD			

Received between 29 Jan & 9 Feb 44.
Lost 8 Apr 44 - hit by flak, it caught fire over Brunswick. (Langenhagen)

B-24H-1 FO 42-7507	X	68	HEAVEN CAN WAIT >36<
OD			

See also 42-40370 with the same name.
ex 392nd BG but flew no missions with that Group.
Received by 44th BG between 1 & 18 Oct 43.
Crash-landed 12 Mar 44 on return and caught fire at Friston, near Beachy Head, Sussex. (Siracourt, France) Salvaged 16 - 20 Mar 44.

B-24JSH-5 FO 42-51508 G+ 66 (QK) >0<
NMF
ex 453rd BG.
Received by 44th BG after 9 Apr 44.
Flew no combat missions with 44th BG.
RZI 31 May 45.

B-24H-1 FO 42-7509 V -V V 506 (GJ) GALLAVANTIN' GAL >30< OLD CROW
OD
It had an OLD CROW painted on one side but with the name GALLAVANTIN' (or GALLIVANTIN') GAL on the other. Part of the original OLD CROW (41-24283) crew flew on this plane so it appears they retained the original 392nd BG name and had OLD CROW added.
Letter remained V throughout but had a bar below until Apr 44 when the bar preceded the letter and in May 44 it was placed above.
ex 392nd BG but flew no missions with that Group.
Received by 44th BG between 8 Oct & 3 Nov 43.
Aborted on 13 Nov 43.
It was war weary when salvaged 5 - 15 Jun 44 at BAD 2, Warton, Lancashire, landing gear collapsed and wing damaged.
Nose art photo confirms this as a FO a/c.

B-24J-1 FO 42-50509 Y 68 (WQ) WANA >51<
NMF
Received between 7 & 16 Jul 44.
Caught fire in the early hours of 7 Feb 45 when fuel spilled and ignited while the auxiliary power unit was being filled. Of the ten 500 lb general purpose bombs beneath the aircraft in preparation for loading, seven were removed but two of them detonated, destroying the aircraft. Salvaged 7 Feb 45.

B-24M-5 FO 44-50512 H 68 (WQ) >20<
NMF
Received before 10 Mar 45.
RZI 28 or 31 May 45.

B-24H-15 CF 41-29513 Z 506 (GJ) >3<
OD
Received between 8 & 22 Apr 44.
Lost 29 Apr 44 - ditched on return. (Berlin)

B-24H-1 FO 42-7514 O 68 VALIANT LADY >19<
OD
Flown from USA on orders dated 24 Sep 43.
Received by 44th BG before 13 Nov 43.
Lost 21 Jan 44 - shot down by Me 109s. (Escalles, France)

B-24H-1 FO 42-7520 C 67 >1<
OD
Letter may not have had a bar below.
Recorded on only one mission with 44th BG which may have been scrubbed - 4 Dec 43?
Transferred to 445th BG.

B-24H-1 FO 42-7521 B 67 POOP DECK PAPPY >3<
OD
ex 392nd BG but flew no missions with that Group.
Received by 44th BG before 9 Oct 43.
Repaired at Shipdham 26 Nov 43 - 21 Jan 44 - extensive damage to fuselage stations 5 & 6 on crash landing on return from 26 Nov 43 mission to Bremen.
Nose turret changed at some stage from Emerson A-15 to Consolidated MPC A-6B.
Transferred to 448th BG - probably on completion of repairs (last mission with 44th BG was 26 Nov 43).

B-24H-1 FO 42-7522 S 506 (GJ) SOUTHERN COMFORT >42<
OD
See also 42-40778 with the same name.
ex 392nd BG but flew no missions with that Group.
Received by 44th BG before 9 Oct 43.
Lost 11 Apr 44 - right bomb bay door failed to open, fragmentation bomb hit closed door setting the ship on fire and causing it to break in two at mid-section. (Bernburg)

B-24J-60 CF 44-10523 T 506 (GJ) >12<
NMF
Received before 1 Sep 44.
Lost 30 Oct 44 - probably due to flak - went down after bombs away. (Hamburg or Uetersen)

B-24J-60 CF 44-10524 L 506 (GJ) >70<
NMF
Received between 10 & 26 Sep 44.
Landed at B-51(Lille/Vendeville, France) for refuelling on 21 Feb 45 mission to Nürnberg. Returned to Shipdham on the same day.
RZI 22 or 31 May 45.

B-24LHO-5 FO 44-49525 E 506 (GJ) >7<
NMF
Received before 29 Jan 45.

Landed at A-80 (Mourmelon-le-Grand, France) or A-89 (Le Culot, Belgium) on the 23 Feb 45 mission to Weimar - #2 engine and low on gas. Returned to Shipdham on 24 Feb 45.
Crash-landed 1 Mar 45 at A-84 (Chièvres, Belgium) low on fuel and the nose wheel collapsed on landing. (Ingolstadt) Salvaged 10 or 13 Mar 45 on the Continent by 5 SAD.

B-24JSH-1 FO 42-95531 Unk 66 (QK) >53<
NMF J 67 (NB)
B 67 (NB)
Transferred from 66th BS to 67th BS on 11 Sep 44 and letter changed from J to B on 12 Oct 44.
Received 4 Aug 44.
RZI 22 May 45.

B-24J-60 CF 44-10531 G 68 (WQ) MY SAD ASS >17<
NMF R+ 66 (QK)
Transferred from 68th BS to 66th BS on 8 Sep 44.
Received between 7 Jul & 5 Aug 44.
Lost 30 Sep 44 - hit by flak after bombs away, caught fire and went down. (Hamm)

B-24H-1 FO 42-7533 E 66 HOLIDAY MESS II >14<
OD
ex 392nd BG but flew no missions with that Group.
Received by 44th BG between 25 Sep & 9 Oct 43.
Lost 22 Dec 43 - shot down by accurate barrage-type flak and crashed at Den Ham, Netherlands. (Münster)

B-24H-1 FO 42-7535 U 506 PEEP SIGHT >19<
OD
ex 392nd BG but flew no missions with that Group.
Received by 44th BG between 1 & 9 Oct 43.
Repaired at Shipdham 6 Nov - 6 Dec 43 - flak damage on 5 Nov 43 mission to Münster.
Repaired at Hawkinge, Kent, 13 Feb - 26 Mar 44 - flak damage on 13 Feb 44 mission to Petit Bois Tillencourt (sic - possibly Thiescourt or Millencourt, France?)
Last mission with 44th BG.
Transferred to 3 SAD for use as a transport after removal all turrets.

B-24J-1 FO 42-50535 C 506 (GJ) JOPLIN JALOPY >66<
NMF O 506 (GJ)
Letter changed from C to O on 9 Oct 44.
Received 24 Jul 44.
RZI 31 May 45.

B-24H-1 FO 42-7536 M 66 THE BANSHEE >11<
OD M 66
Bar below the letter deleted in Nov 43.
ex 392nd BG but flew no missions with that Group.
Received by 44th BG between 1 & 9 Oct 43.
Repaired at Rackheath 18 - 29 Dec 43 - #3 engine and battle damage on 16 Dec 43 mission to Bremen.
Salvaged 3 & 4 Jan 44 at Deopham Green - landing gear torn off and nose crushed.

B-24M-5 FO 44-50536 X 68 (WQ) ONE WEAKNESS >9<
NMF
Received before 30 Mar 45.
RZI 22 May 45.

B-24H-15 CF 41-29538 X 68 (WQ) NAUGHTY NEL >0<
OD
Received between 12 & 23 Mar 44.
Crashed 23 Mar 44 at Shipdham on take-off. (Osnabrück) Salvaged 24 & 25 Mar 44 - left gear collapsed and wing damaged.

B-24J-1 FO 42-50539 U 67 (NB) SULTRY SUE >69<
NMF
ex 34th BG.
Received by 44th BG before 25 Jul 44.
Repaired at Woodbridge, Suffolk, 5 Dec 44 - hydraulic system, propeller governer - damaged on 4 Dec 44 mission to Soest (but Wetzlar or Kolschausen bombed).
RZI 31 May 45.

B-24H-1 FO 42-7541 506 SWEATIN' IT OUT
OD
Possibly assigned to 44th BG (but no record of any missions) before assignment to 445th BG.

B-24J-60 CF 44-10542 E+ 66 (QK) TALLY HO II >42<
NMF G+ 66 (QK)
Letter changed from E+ to G+ on 15 Oct 44.
ex 491st BG.
Received by 44th BG on 22 Aug 44.
Crash landed 28 Jan 45 at Bonneff-Gernblou (sic), about 20 miles east of Brussels, Belgium - damaged by flak just at bombs away, headed for an emergency field and, losing remaining engines when landing gear was partly
down, the plane crashed in about 2 ft of snow and caught fire. (Dortmund) Salvaged 13 Mar 45 by 5 SAD.

B-24H-15 CF 41-29544 T 68 (WQ) FLAK ALLEY II >40<
OD
Received between 18 & 26 Mar 44.
Lost 11 Jul 44 - ditched 15 miles off Beachy Head, Sussex, after being seriously damaged by flak. (Munich)

B-24H-1 FO 42-7544 C 67 SEED OF SATAN >7<
OD
See also SEEDS OF SATAN (41-24229) and SEED-O-SATAN (42-40745).
ex 392nd BG but flew no missions with that Group.
Received by 44th BG before 10 Oct 43.
Lost 1 Dec 43 - abandoned over Belgium short of fuel on return, it went down in the English Channel. (Solingen)

B-24H-1 FO 42-7545 D 67 TOUCH OF VENUS >5<
OD
ex 392nd BG but flew no missions with that Group.
Received by 44th BG before 3 Nov 43.
Lost 18 Nov 43 - went down in the North Sea on return. (Oslo-Kjeller, Norway)

B-24H-1 FO 42-7547 X 506 SKY QUEEN >12<
OD
ex 392nd BG but flew no missions with that Group although it was abortive on that Group's 4 Oct 43 diversion mission.
Received by 44th BG between 4 Oct & 3 Nov 43.
Repaired at Thorpe Abbotts 22 - 28 Dec 43 - #3 engine, minor skin damage.
Lost 29 Jan 44 - damaged by flak and shot down by fighters - crashed near the Rhône-Rhine canal, outside Illfurth in the direction of Zillisheim, France. (Frankfurt)

B-24H-1 FO 42-7548 I 66 BULL OF THE WOODS >13<
OD I 66
Bar under letter I deleted in Nov 43.
ex 392nd BG but flew no missions with that Group.
Received by 44th BG before 18 Oct 43.
Lost 30 Dec 43 - shot down by enemy fighters and crashed at Pont-Saint-Mard, (44th Bomb Group Roll of Honor gives the crash site as Chavigny), north of Soissons, France. (Ludwigshafen)

B-24J-60 CF 44-10548 O+ 66 (QK) JERSEY JERK >60<
NMF
No nose art but the name JERSEY JERK was painted in small letters under the pilot's side window.
Received before 26 Sep 44.
Landed at A-47 (Paris/Orly, France) on return from 16 Jan 45 mission to Ruhland (but Dresden bombed) because of fog blanket over England.
Repaired at Woodbridge, Suffolk, 27 Feb - 5 Mar 45 - #3 engine damaged on 26 Feb 45 mission to Berlin.
RZI 31 May 45.

B-24H-1 FO 42-7549 K 67 THE SHARK >39<
OD
ex 392nd BG but flew no missions with that Group.
Received by 44th BG before 9 Oct 43.
Crash-landed 16 Mar 44 on return at Woodchurch, near Kingsnorth, Kent. (Friedrichshafen) Salvaged 19 - 21 Mar 44 - both landing gears collapsed.

B-24H-1 FO 42-7551 Y 68 THE JINX >10<
OD
ex 392nd BG but flew no missions with that Group.
Received by 44th BG 7 Oct 43.
Repaired at Attlebridge 14 Nov - 18 Dec 43 after crash landing at Garveston, near Shipdham, with extensive battle damage on return from 13 Nov 43 mission to Bremen.
Crashed and burned 13 Jan 44 at Letton Hall, Cranworth, on return from a training flight - apparently it made an overshoot and then whilst turning back towards the airfield it lost height and crashed into a fir spinney 2 miles away from the runway. Salvaged 13 & 14 Jan 44.

B-24H-1 FO 42-7552 K 66 LIL COOKIE >38<
OD A 67 (NB)
Transferred from 66th BS to 67th BS in Dec 43.
ex 392nd BG but flew no missions with that Group.
Received by 44th BG between 1 & 9 Oct 43.
Repaired at Goodnestone Park, Kent, 31 Dec 43 - 26 Jan 44 as a result of damage on 30 Dec 43 mission to Ludwigshafen - temporary runway built.
Assigned to 489th BG after 18 Apr 44 to become that Group's assembly ship.

B-24J-5 FO 42-51552 M 67 (NB) >33<
NMF J 506 (GJ)
Transferred from 67th BS to 506th BS between 25 Nov & 10 Dec 44.
Received between 13 & 25 Sep 44.
Damaged by an 88mm shell that hit and killed the navigator as he was leaning over his table on the 21 Nov 44 mission to Harburg - the plane was repaired.
Landed at B-51(Lille/Vendeville, France) on return from 16 Jan 45 mission to Ruhland (but Dresden bombed) because of fog blanket over England.
Crash-landed 23 Feb 45 at A-64 (St-Dizier, France) - hydraulics shot out and #2 engine out. (Weimar) Salvaged 4 Mar 45 by 5 SAD.

B-24J-65 CF 44-10553 C 68 (WQ) >44<
NMF L 68 (WQ)
Letter changed from C to L on 12 Oct 44.
Received between 21 Jul & 3 Aug 44.
Crash-landed 28 Dec 44 near 5 SAD base, Merville, France. (Kaiserlautern) Recorded by 5 SAD as missing on operations on 28 Dec 44.

B-24H-15 CF 41-29554 J 67 (NB) TEXAS ROSE >1<
OD
Received between 25 Feb & 27 Mar 44.
Lost 27 Mar 44 - crashed near San Sebastian, SPAIN, after the crew had bailed out. (Mont-de-Marsan, France)

B-24LHO-10 FO 44-49556 D 67 (NB) >14<
NMF
Received before 9 Feb 45.
RZI 22 May 45.

B-24JSH-1 FO 42-95561 I+ 66 (QK) >4<
NMF
Received before 31 Jul 44.
Lost 6 Aug 44 while flying as deputy lead with 492nd BG - received a direct hit by flak over the target. (Hamburg)

B-24M-5 FO 44-50578 Q 67 (NB) MYRTLE THE FERTILE TURTLE >15<
NMF
ex 491st BG.
Received by 44th BG on 7 Mar 45.
RZI 22 May 45.

B-24H-1 FO 42-7582 F 66 ICE COLD KATY >2<
OD
ex 389th BG.
Received by 44th BG between 9 & 20 Feb 44.
Crashed and burned 7 Mar 44 at Shipdham after being hit by a P-47 on a practice flight. Salvaged 8 Mar 44.

B-24J-65 CF 44-10582 R 68 (WQ) >14<
NMF D 68 (WQ)
Letter changed from R to D on 25 Nov 44.
Received between 5 Aug & 25 Sep 44.
Lost 28 Dec 44 leading 491st BG - hit by flak in the bomb bay, caught fire, dropped bombs, broke in two at the waist and went down. (Kaiserlautern)

B-24M-5 FO 44-50588 M 68 (WQ) >15<
NMF
Received before 14 Mar 45.
Landed at B-80 (Volkel, Netherlands) to re-fuel on 15 Mar 45 mission to Zossen. Returned to Shipdham on 16 Mar 45.
RZI 22 or 27 May 45.

B-24JSH-5 FO 42-51594 E+ 66 (QK) >48<
NMF P+ 66 (QK)
Letter changed from E+ to P+ on 6 Feb 45.
Received between 12 & 17 Oct 44.
Repaired at Shipdham 15 Feb 45 by 464th Sub Depot after landing with a collapsed gear on return from the 15 Feb 45 mission to Magdeburg.
RZI 22 May 45.

B-24J-1 FO 42-50596 O 68 (WQ) >30<
NMF
Received 2 Jul 44.
Lost 18 Oct 44 - received a direct hit, lost complete tail section and crashed near Buttinge, Walcheren, Netherlands. (Leverkusen)

B-24M-5 FO 44-50597 J+ 66 (QK) LOCO MOCO >20<
NMF
Received before 10 Mar 45.
RZI 22 May 45.

B-24H-1 FO 42-7603 L 67 RAGGEDY ANN >2<
OD
Received between 1 & 6 Oct 43.
Lost 18 Nov 43 - went down in the North Sea on return. (Oslo-Kjeller, Norway)

B-24D-75 CO 42-40606 X 506 TIMB-A-A-AH! >13<
OD
Received 14 Mar 43.
Flew on 1 Aug 43 Ploesti mission.
Lost 16 Aug 43 - shot down by enemy fighters about 10 minutes after the target. (Foggia, Italy)

B-24H-15 FO 42-52616 C 67 (NB) GLORY BEE >101<
OD Q+ 66 (QK)
R+ 66 (QK)
Received between 8 & 19 Apr 44.
Transferred from 67th BS to 66th BS on 10 Sep 44 - letter changed from Q+ to R+ on 30 Oct 44.
Repaired at Woodbridge, Suffolk, 22 - 27 Jul 44 - #1 fuel cell.
Completed 98 missions.
RZI 31 May 45.

B-24H-1 FO 42-7618 N 66 SCOURGE OF THE SKIES >28<
OD C 66 (QK)
Letter changed from N to C in Nov 43.
ex 93rd BG.
Received by 44th BG before 9 Oct 43.
Lost 18 Mar 44 - landed at Dübendorf, Zürich canton, SWITZERLAND. (Friedrichshafen)

B-24H-15 FO 42-52618 B 506 (GJ) CHIEF WAPELLO >17<
OD V+ 66 (QK)
ex 487th BG
Received by 44th BG on 20 Aug 44.
Landed at A-47 (Paris/Orly, France) on return from 16 Jan 45 mission to Ruhland (but Dresden bombed) because of a fog blanket over England.
Crashed 28 Jan 45 at B-58 (Brussels-Melsbroek, Belgium) - lost # 3 engine and the crew bailed out. (Dortmund) Recorded by 5 SAD as missing on operations on 28 Jan 45.

B-24JSH-1 FO 42-95619 L+ 66 (QK) BI-U-BABY >4<
NMF
Received before 5 Aug 44 on which date it led the 491st BG.
Transferred to 491st BG on 18 Aug 44.

B-24JSH-1 FO 42-95622 J+ 66 (QK) TUNG HOI II >4<
NMF
Received before 21 Jul 44.
Transferred to 491st BG on 18 Aug 44.

B-24H-1 FO 42-7624 Z 68 TURNIP TERMITE >1<
OD
See also 41-29418 with the same name.
Received 2 Nov 43.
Transferred to 392nd BG after 16 Nov 43.

B-24J-1 FO 42-50626 H 506 (GJ) MY GAL SAL >17<
NMF
Received 1 Jul 44.
Nose wheel collapsed 30 Aug 44 on landing at Shipdham. Salvaged 30 Aug 44.

H-1 FO 42-7630 P 506 >10<
OD
Received before 13 Nov 43.
Lost 20 Dec 43 - due to flak and enemy fighters. (Bremen)

B-24H-1 FO 42-7635 Q 68 (RAM IT - DAMN IT!)* >18<
OD
See also 41-29496 with the same name.
Received 7 Nov 43.
Lost 21 Jan 44. (Escalles, France)

B-24H-1 FO 42-7638 A 66 LILI MARLENE >8<
OD BIG BANNER
Name was LILI MARLENE (see also 42-95260 with the same name) and/or BIG BANNER.
Received between 1 & 18 Oct 43.
Repaired at Rackheath 19 Nov - 17 Dec 43 - battle damage on 18 Nov 43 mission to Oslo-Kjeller, Norway.
Lost 22 Dec 43 - damaged by accurate barrage-type flak and ditched in the Zuidelijk-Flevoland (Zuyder Zee), Netherlands. (Münster)

B-24H-1 FO 42-7642 N 506 (GJ) M'DARLING >54<
OD -N 506 (GJ)
N 506 (GJ)
X 506 (GJ)
Letter N until Apr 44 when bar preceded N then bar above N in May 44 until letter changed to X in Dec 44.
Received before 13 Nov 43.
It went to Sub-Depot 8 Jul 44 for repair of battle damage on 7 Jul 44 mission to Bernburg when flown by 68th BS crew after many previous missions.
Flew truckin' operation with 458th BG on 18 Sep 44 bearing 44th BG markings.
Monitor on 28 Dec 44 mission.
War weary when RZI 31 May 45.

B-24J-1 FO 42-50643 K 506 (GJ) >23<
NMF
Received by 44th BG before 2 Oct 44.
Landed at A-47 (Paris/Orly, France) on return from 16 Jan 45 mission to Ruhland (but Dresden bombed) because of fog blanket over England.
RZI 22 May 45.

B-24H-15 FO 42-52643 S 68 (WQ) JOSE CARIOCA >101<
OD
ex 486th BG
Received by 44th BG between 8 & 17 Apr 44.
Repaired at Manston, Kent, 15 - 28 May 44 - battle damage.
Landed at B-60 (Grimberghen, near Brussels, Belgium) for refuelling on 25 Feb 45. Returned to Shipdham on 26 Feb 45.
RZI 31 May 45.

B-24HSH-1 FO 42-7644 >0<
OD
Thought to have been assigned to 44th BG but to have flown no missions with that Group prior to conversion by BAD 1 to B-24SH PFF (H2S) and assignment to 482nd BG - call letter D - on 20 Dec 43.
Flew as one of the two deputy lead aircraft on 44th BG 11 Jan 44 mission (formation plan erroneously shows 'last three' as 664) and as lead aircraft with 93rd BG on 29 Jan 44 mission when it retained its 'A' in a circle 44th
BG marking.

B-24JSH-1 FO 42-50644 I+ 66 (QK) >42<
NMF H 506 (GJ)
A 506 (GJ)
Transferred fro 66th BS to 506th BS on 31 Aug 44 and letter changed from H to A on 12 Oct 44.
Received between 6 & 31 Aug 44.
RZI 22 May 45.

B-24H-1 FO 42-7647 B 506 SABRINA >5<
OD R 506
Letter changed from B with a bar above to R in Nov 43.from USA on orders dated 24 Sep 43.
Received by 44th BG between 4 & 18 Oct 43.
Crash-landed 11 Nov 43 at Shipdham in a clump of trees. Salvaged 11-13 Nov 43.

B-24H-1 FO 42-7650 J 67 OLE MISS >1<
OD BAD PENNY
Received before 6 Nov 43.
Named OLE MISS and/or BAD PENNY.
Lost 13 Nov 43 – crash-landed at Schoterzijl, south of Lemmer and west of Blokzijl, Netherlands. (Bremen)

B-24JSH- 1 FO 42-50660 R+ 66 (QK) >29<
NMF G 68 (WQ)
A 68 (WQ)
Transferred from 66th Sqn to 68th Sqn on 26 Aug 44 and letter changed from G to A on 15 Oct 44.
Received before 9 Aug 44.
Lost 16 Jan 45 - lost two engines (#4 engine had a blown cylinder and oil pressure dropped off in #2 engine) due to accurate flak near the target, dropped from the formation and losing altitude, salvoed bombs near Bernburg
and went down, abandoned by the crew, over the Alsace-Lorraine area of France. (Ruhland - but Dresden bombed) Salvaged 20 Mar 45 on the Continent by 5 SAD.

B-24JSH-1 FO 42-50668 E+ 66 (QK) >0<
NMF
Received between 31 Jul & 18 Aug 44.
Transferred to 491st BG on 18 Aug 44.

B-24HSH-1 FO 42-7672 PEACE OFFERING >0<
OD
Name may have been PEACE OFFERING.
Thought to have been assigned to 44th BG but to have flown no missions with that Group prior to conversion by BAD 1 to B-24HSH PFF (H2S) and assignment to 482nd BG - call letter F - on 29 Dec 43.
Flew as one of two deputy lead aircraft on 44th BG 11 Jan 44 mission.

B-24JSH-1 FO 42-50672 F+ 66 (QK) >33<
NMF A+ 66 (QK)
Letter changed from F+ to A+ on 1 Oct 44.
Received before 27 Aug 44.
RZI 27 May 45.

B-24M-10 FO 44-50681 >0<
NMF
Date received unknown.
RZI 22 May 45.

B-24M-10 FO 44-50682 G 506 (GJ) >19<
NMF
Received between 1 & 10 Mar 45.
RZI 22 May 45.

B-24D-1 CO 41-23690 O 68 (3m) >4<
OD O
Original aircraft received 20 Sep 42.
Lost 27 Jan 43 a FW 190 crashed into it causing it to go down in the Wadden See, Netherlands. (Wilhelmshaven was the target but bombs were released over Lemmer, near the Zuider Zee, Netherlands)

B-24HSH-10 DT 41-28690 B+ 66 (QK) MISSOURI BELLE >14<
OD MISSOURI SUE
Name was MISSOURI BELLE or MISSOURI SUE.
ex 389th BG, originally 482nd BG.
Received by 44th BG before 29 May 44.
Lost 5 Jun 44 - ditched off Broadstairs, Kent, after leading 489th BG on a mission to Boulogne-sur-Mer, France. Salvaged 5-6 Jun 44.

B-24M-10 FO 44-50690 R 67 (NB) >1<
NMF
Received between 16 Feb & 14 Mar 45.
RZI 27 May 45.

B-24M-10 FO 44-50691 F 506 (GJ) >6<
NMF
Received before 14 Apr 45.
RZI 22 May 45.

B-24MSH-10 FO 44-50698 C 506 (GJ) >0<
NMF
Received after 3 Feb 45.
Crash-landed 11 May 45 one mile south of Watton - was returning from Southern England, fulfilling Air Transport Command requirements, including feathering propellers - all four engines were probably cut out. Salvaged
11 May 45
D-1 CO 41-23699 P 68 LEMON DROP >47<
OD N 68
Original aircraft received 20 Sep 42.
Letter changed to N between Oct & Nov 43.
Flew on 1 Aug 43 Ploesti mission.
Became the Group's assembly ship after 8 Feb 44.
Repaired at Bradwell Bay, Essex, 1 - 25 Jan 44 - #1 engine, left aileron. left outer wing panel.
Repaired at Speke (Liverpool), 18 Aug - 6 Sep 44 - left outer wing panel tip, belly stations 7.6 - 7.9.
Failed POM inspection and ordered to salvage yard 1 Jun 45.

B-24D-1 CO 41-23703 A 66 SCRAPPY'S PAPPY >5<
OD
Original aircraft received 20 Sep 42.
Crashed and caught fire 20 Feb 43 at Clermont Hall, near Watton, while performing practice flying - salvaged 20 Feb 43.

B-24JSH-10 FO 42-51704 O 506 (GJ) >30<
NMF C 506 (GJ)
A 68 (WQ)
Letter changed from O to C on 19 Oct 44 and transferred from 506th BS to 68th BS on 6 Feb 45.
Received between 13 & 25 Sep 44.
RZI 22 May 45.

B-24J-1 FO 42-50711 X 68 (WQ) >30<
NMF
Received between 13 & 26 Sep 44.
Repaired at Woodbridge, Suffolk, 26 & 27 Oct 44 - hydraulic system damaged on 25 Oct 44 mission to Gelsenkirchen.
Force landed 16 Jan 45 at Y-34 (Metz-Frescaty, France) with #2 engine hit by flak and low on fuel on return. (Ruhland - but Dresden bombed). Salvaged 4 Feb 45 on the Continent.

B-24H-10 DT 41-28712 M 66 (QK) TUFFY >35<
OD D 67 (NB)
X 67 (NB)
L+ 66 (QK)
Q+ 66 (QK)
Received before 13 Feb 44.
Transferred from 66th BS to 67th BS between 18 & 22 April 44, letter changed from D to X between 13 Sept & 9 Nov 44, transferred back to 66th BS between 16 Nov & 11 Dec 44 and letter changed from L+ to Q+ in Feb 45.
Recorded on 14 Jul 44 that a request for war weary status had been made.
Flew truckin' operation with 458th BG on 18th Sep 44 bearing 44th BG markings.
RZI 31 May 45.

B-24H-5 FO 42-7717 Z 68 THE EXTERMINATOR >10<
OD
ex 389th BG, originally 448th BG.
Received by 44th BG between 5 & 21 Feb 44.
Transferred to BAD 3 after 27 Mar 44 and to USA on 25 Apr 45.

B-24J-1 FO 42-50725 A 68 (WQ) >60<
NMF M 68 (WQ)
Letter changed from A to M on 15 Oct 44.
Received 16 Jul 44.
Lost 21 Jan 45 - #4 engine ran away and could not be feathered, ran very low on fuel with #1 and #2 engines running dry, electrical system out, aircraft started icing up so the crew were ordered to bail out. The aircraft is said to have gone down at Taconville (sic), probably Tanconville, France. (Pforzheim)

B-24D-90 CO 42-40731 N 68 EAGER EVE >16<
OD HAG MAG, THE MOTH BALL QUEEN
Name on the aircraft in photo on page 159 of the "History of 68th Bomb Squadron" is clearly EAGER EVE as listed on page 436 of the same book but the caption under the photo gives the name as EAGER BEAVER. The name was apparently later changed to HAG MAG, THE MOTH BALL QUEEN.
Received 15 Jun 43.
Flew on 1 Aug 43 Ploesti mission.
Crashed 6 Oct 43 at Marrakech, Morocco, after hitting a wall on take-off when returning to England from MTO - transferred to MTO 9 Oct 43.

B-24J-1 FO 42-50733 E 506 (GJ) >9<
NMF
Received between 29 Jul & 4 Aug 44.
Salvaged 23 Aug 44 at Shipdham - left front auxiliary spar cracked.

B-24J-1 FO 42-50741 P 67 (NB) >63<
NMF
Received between 11 & 21 Sep 44.
Landed at A-47(Paris/Orly, France) on return from 16 Jan 45 mission to Ruhland (but Dresden bombed) because of fog blanket over England.
Landed at A-82 (Verdun-sur-Meuse, France) with #3 engine out and short of fuel on 25 Feb 45 mission to Aschaffenburg. Returned to Shipdham on 26 Feb 45.
RZI 30 May 45.

B-24D-95 CO 42-40745 A 68 SEED-O-SATAN >1<
OD
See also SEEDS OF SATAN (41-24229) and SEED OF SATAN (42-7544).
Received 14 Jun 43.
Lost 2 Jul 43 - shot down by a Me 109 near the target area on the way in. (Lecce, Italy). Salvaged 28 Aug 43.

B-24MSH-10 FO 44-50748 J 506 (GJ) THE BIG HEADED KID >14<
NMF
Received between 22 Feb & 21 Mar 45.
RZI 27 May 45.

B-24M-10 FO 44-50751 T 67 (NB) >24<
NMF
Received between 9 Feb & 10 Mar 45.
RZI 22 May 45.

B-24M-10 FO 44-50755 Y 68 (WQ) >21<
NMF
Received between 4 & 10 Mar 45.
RZI 22 May 45.

B-24H-5 FO 42-7758 I 67 DOWN AN GO >1<
OD
ex 448th BG - received between 18 Nov & 2 Dec 43.
Returned to 448th BG between 13 & 21 Dec 43.

B-24J-5 FO 42-50761 A+ 66 (QK) KING PIN >75<
NMF F+ 66 (QK)
Letter changed from A+ to F+ on 12 Oct 44.
Received before 25 Sep 44.
Landed at Bungay after aborting on 16 Jan 45 mission to Ruhland.
RZI 27 May 45.

B-24D-1 CF 42-63761 D 67 L'IL ABNER >12<
OD
Received before 17 May 43.
Lost 1 Aug 43 - on fire 40 miles from the target, it belly-landed near Visnia Dombovitsa. (Ploesti, Rumania)

B-24J-5 FO 42-50763 S 67 (NB) Cow town Katy >65<
NMF
Received between 27 Aug & 27 Sep 44.
Landed at B-48 (Amiens/Glisy, France) low on gas and with the Gee box out on the 1 Mar 45 mission to Ingolstadt. Returned to Shipdham on 2 Mar 45.
RZI 22 May 45.

B-24D-1 CF 42-63763 F 67 LADY FIFINELLA >7<
OD
See also 42-95329.
Lost 17 Jul 43 - damaged by flak and shot down by enemy fighters over the target. (Naples, Italy)

B-24D-95 CO 42-40764 M 66 HELEN B HAPPY >13<
OD
Flew on 1 Aug 43 Ploesti mission.
It was forced to make an emergency landing at Palermo, Sicily, on 1 Oct 43 where damage on the same day's mission to Wiener Neustadt, Austria, was repaired.
Crashed 11 Oct 43 shortly after take-off from Oudna, Tunisia, for Marrakech, Morocco, on the first leg of the return trip to England. (Had been transferred to MTO on 9 Oct 43).

B-24JSO-5 FO 42-50766 D 506 (GJ) >12<
NMF
Received before 19 Oct 44.
Lost 2 Dec 44 - went down after being set on fire by enemy fighters while leading the 392nd BG's low left squadron. (Bingen)

B-24HSH-15 DT 41-28767 L+ 66 (QK) >2<
OD
ex 389th BG.
Received by 44th BG between 26 Apr & 29 May 44.
Crash-landed 29 Jun 44 at Covehithe flying deputy lead with 392nd BG. (Magdeburg) Salvaged 30 Jun & 1 Jul 44 - left wing torn off and fuselage broken.

B-24H-5 FO 42-7767 C 67 (NB) SHACK RABBIT >19<
OD STAR SPANGLED HELL
Name was SHACK RABBIT (A 44th BG veteran has sent Will Lundy a nose shot showing 12 rabbits and one swastika). Also said to have been named STAR SPANGLED HELL.
ex 448th BG.
Received by 44th BG between 4 Dec 43 & 4 Jan 44.
Repaired at Biggin Hill, Kent, 16 - 29 Jan 44 - #2 engine, minor sheet metal work.
Lost 8 Apr 44 - hit by enemy fighters, it exploded and crashed in the suburbs of Hannover. (Langenhagen)

B-24D-5 CO 41-23769 B 66 PRINCESS CHARLOTTE (34)
OD SURE SHOT
Names attributed to it are PRINCESS CHARLOTTE (Will Lundy has a photo of the airplane airborne showing on the starboard - pilot's - side the name PRINCESS printed with CHARLOTTE or CHARLETTE apparently added afterwards by hand) and SURE SHOT (on the port - co-pilot's - side)
Original aircraft received 20 Sep 42.
Damaged 1 Oct 43 and landed at Salerno, Italy. (Wiener Neustadt, Austria)
Transferred to MTO 15 Oct 43.

B-24M-10 FO 44-50769 V 68 (WQ) >6<
NMF
Received between 22 & 30 Mar 45.
RZI 22 or 27 May 45.

B-24HSH-15 DT 41-28770 H+ 66 (QK) >22<
OD A 67 (NB)
Transferred from 66th Sqn to 67th Sqn on 15 Oct 44.
Received between 26 Apr & 6 Jun 44.
Deputy lead PFF with 489th BG on 13 Jul 44 - see page 97 of "A History of The 489th Bomb Group".
Later assigned, after 1 november 44 to 492nd BG - 2nd Organisation.

B-24D-5 CO 41-23771 E 66 >3<
OD or I
Original aircraft received 20 Sep 42.
Crash landed 3 Jan 43 short of fuel on return near New House Farm, Ambleston, 2 miles south of Puncheston, Pembrokeshire, Wales. (St-Nazaire, France)

B-24HSH-15 DT 41-28772 C+ 66 (QK) EL CAPITAN >14<
OD
Received by 44th BG between 22 Apr & 3 Jun 44.
Made a precautionary landing on 18 Mar 44 at Connel, Strathclyde, Scotland, en route from Iceland to Prestwick, Scotland, and ran off the end of the runway but was repaired and flown to Prestwick.
Transferred to 491st BG on 18 Aug 44 and later to 392nd BG.

B-24D-5 CO 41-23774 S 67 HITLER'S NIGHTMARE >6<
OD S 68
Letter may have been S in 67th BS.
No name visible on any photos seen.
Transferred from 67th BS to 68th BS before 27 Feb 43.
Original aircraft received 20 Sep 42.
Transferred to 93rd BG after 18 Mar 43.

B-24D-5 CO 41-23776 W 68 SPIRIT OF '76 >9<
OD
42-52776 (487th BG, 2 BAD & MTO) may also have been named SPIRIT OF '76.
Original aircraft received 20 Sep 42.
Lost 27 Jan 43 - exploded after being attacked by FW 190s. Rear fuselage and tail units fell into the harbour at Terschelling and the rest was scattered over the Noordsvaarder shallows and Terschelling beach, West Friesian Islands, Netherlands. (Wilhelmshaven was the target but bombs were released over Lemmer, near the Zuider Zee, Netherlands)

B-24HSH-15 DT 41-28776 E+ 66 (QK) >6<
OD
Probably ex 389th BG.
Received by 44th BG between 20 Apr & 6 Jun 44.
Lost 11 Jul 44 leading 448th BG - crashed and exploded near Lille, France. (Munich) MACR 7511.

B-24D-5 CO 41-23777 H 66 MAISEY >7<
OD
Original aircraft received 20 Sep 43.
Lost 26 Feb 43 - caught fire and exploded after being attacked by fighters from the time it reached Texel Island until almost Oldenburg. (Wilhelmshaven)

B-24D-95 CO 42-40777 N 66 FLOSSIE FLIRT >8<
OD
Lost 1 Aug 43 - landed in Turkey after being badly shot up on leaving the target. (Ploesti, Rumania)

B-24D-5 CO 41-23778 F 66 LADY LUCK >26<
OD JENNY
Name changed from JENNY to LADY LUCK.
Original aircraft received 20 Sep 42.
Flew on 1 Aug 43 Ploesti mission.
Lost 16 Aug 43 - exploded after being attacked by fighters and went down over Ruoti. (Foggia, Italy)

B-24D-95 CO 42-40778 T 506 SOUTHERN COMFORT >5<
OD
See also 42-7522 with the same name.
Received 14 Mar 43.
Flew on 1 Aug 43 Ploesti mission.
Lost 16 Aug 43 - exploded and crashed about 15 minutes after bombing the target under continued attack by enemy fighters. (Foggia, Italy)

B-24D-5 CO 41-23779 G 66 4-Q-2 >42<
OD G 67
G 67
Transferred from 66th BS to 67th BS after 27 May 43.
Bar added below letter G in Nov 43.
Original aircraft received 20 Sep 42.
Flew on 1 Aug 43 Ploesti mission - landed at Malta on return.
Lost 14 Jan 44 - attacked by fighters near Duclair, about 15 km west of Rouen, it caught fire, exploded and crashed near Bolbec, France. (Estouteville Ecalles, near Buchy, France)

B-24D-95 CO 42-40780 H 67 AVAILABLE JONES >11<
OD
Lost 1 Aug 43 - ditched on return 30 miles south of Corfu having been damaged by flak, a balloon cable and fighters. (Ploesti, Rumania)

B-24D-5 CO 41-23783 M 67 GALLOPIN' GHOST >4<
OD BETTY-ANNE
Name was GALLOPIN' GHOST but the name BETTY-ANNE was also carried under the pilot's window (his daughter).
Original aircraft received 20 Sep 42.
Lost 15 Feb 43 - was hit by flak immediately after releasing bombs and went down after the right wing came off. (Dunkirk, France)

B-24HSH-15 DT 41-28783 M+ 66 (QK) >18<
OD
Received by 44th BG between 18 Apr & 6 Jun 44.
Transferred to 491st BG on 18 Aug 44.

B-24D-5 CO 41-23784 T 67 MISS DIANNE >10<
OD
Original aircraft received 20 Sep 42.
Lost 8 Mar 43 - went down in flames after being hit by flak and attacked by FW 190s mistaken for P-47 escort. (Rouen, France)

B-24HSH-15 DT 41-28785 B+ 66 (QK) >14<
OD
ex 389th BG, originally 482nd BG.
Received 6 Jun 44.
Hit by flak on the bomb run on 9 Aug 44 flying with another Group on a mission to Saarbrücken, the co-pilot bailed out but the pilot brought the aircraft back and it was repaired.
Lost 13 Sep 44 possibly while on loan to 458th BG. Salvaged by 8 ASC (recorded on 14 Nov 44, an administrative date, not the date on which the aircraft was actually salvaged)

B-24D-5 CO 41-23786 B 68 >4<
OD
Original aircraft received 20 Sep 42.
Lost 6 Dec 42 - was attacked by FW 190s and burst into flames when it went down in the English Channel. (Abbeville-Drucat, France)

B-24D-5 CO 41-23787 B 506 >10<
OD
Transferred to MTO 28 Aug 43 after being left damaged at Benina Main, Libya, but was lost on 21 Sep 43 while flying with 389th BG on its mission to Leghorn, Italy, or Bastia, Corsica.

B-24D-5 CO 41-23788 D 66 AVENGER >37<
OD S 68
Transferred from 66th BS to 68th BS between 10 & 21 Sep 43.
Original aircraft received 20 Sep 42.
Flew on 1 Aug 43 Ploesti mission.
Belly-landed, exploded and burned 16 Dec 43 in a minefield on the beach in the mouth of the river Humber, off Skeffling, East Riding, Yorkshire. (Bremen)
Salvaged 29 & 30 Dec 43.

B-24HSH-15 DT 41-28788 F+ 66 (QK) FEATHER MERCHANT >13<
OD
Named FEATHER MERCHANT when assigned to 44th BG in the summer 1944. Transferred to 392nd BG.
ex 93rd BG - between 8 Jan & 12 May 44.
Transferred to 392nd BG between 7 & 26 Oct 44.

B-24JSH-5 FO 42-50789 A 506 (GJ) LAKANOOKIE >11<
NMF
Received between 8 & 21 Sep 44.
Lost 7 Oct 44 - crashed and burned after being hit by flak in the tail section and wing, taking out #1 and #2 engines. (Kassel)

B-24D-5 CO 41-23794 Q 67 RAILWAY EXPRESS/BOARDWALK FLYER >4<
OD
Original aircraft received 20 Sep 42.
Lost 15 Feb 43 - damaged by flak and attacked by FW 190s, it went down and exploded as it hit the water about half way across the English Channel. (Dunkirk, France)

B-24HSH-15 DT 41-28794 G+ 66 (QK) I'LL GET BY >32<
OD I+ 66 (QK)
Letter changed from G+ to I+ on 24 Dec 44.
ex 389th BG, previously 482nd BG.
Received by 44th BG on 7 May 44 when it was the first PFF aircraft flown by 44th BG and was probably still bearing its original 389th BG call letter Q.
Flew with 458th BG on 28 Jun 44 mission to Saarbrücken and was damaged but repaired because it flew again with 458th BG on 7 Jul 44 mission to Lutzkendorf.
Hit by flak on 31 Dec 44 mission to Neuwied railroad bridge (Dorsal railroad junction was in fact bombed) and landed in Belgium but was repaired.
RZI 30 May 45.

B-24HSH-15 DT 41-28795 D+ 66 (QK) >0<
OD
Letter may have been D+.
ex 389th BG.
Received by 44th BG on 5 May 44.
Crashed and burned 8 May 44 at Halvergate after being attacked by a lone German intruder at 23,000 ft while on a PFF practice flight making a simulated run on Great Yarmouth. Salvaged 8 & 9 May 44.

B-24J-5 FO 42-50795 D 67 (NB) >60<
NMF N 67 (NB)
Letter changed from D to N on 14 Oct 44.
Received between 13 & 26 Sep 44.
Landed at A-47 (Paris/Orly, France) on return from 16 Jan 45 mission to Ruhland (but Dresden bombed) because of fog blanket over England.
Landed at A-73 (Roye/Amy, France) because of low batteries on 21 Jan 45 mission to Heilbronn (but Pforzheim bombed). Returned to Shipdham on 22 Jan 45.
Landed at A-82 (Verdun-sur-Meuse, France) on 25 Feb 45 mission to Aschaffenburg, having lost #3 engine. Returned to Shipdham before 25 Mar 45.
RZI 31 May 45.

B-24D-5 CO 41-23800 Y 68 THE CAPTAIN AND THE KIDS >9<
OD
Original aircraft received 20 Sep 42.
Crash-landed 15 Feb 43 without flaps or landing gear, 10 - 15 yards from the water's edge on Sandwich Flats, about 1 mile south of Ramsgate, Kent. (Dunkirk, France)

B-24HSH-15 DT 41-28800 A+ 66 (QK) >28<
OD E 506 (GJ)
Transferred from 66th BS to 506th BS on 8 Sep 44.
Received between 22 Apr & 12 May 44.
Lead PFF with 44th BG on 12 Jul 44 and with 489th BG on 13 Jul 44 - see page 97 of "A History of The 489th Bomb Group"
Assigned to 492nd BG - 2nd Organisation as a B-24HSH NITE after 16 Nov 44.

B-24J-105 CO 42-109800 T 68 (WQ) >10<
OD
Received between 24 Feb & 2 Mar 44.
Lost 18 Mar 44 - landed at Dübendorf, Zürich canton, SWITZERLAND. (Friedrichshafen)

B-24D-5 CO 41- 23804 J 66 SAD SACK >7<
OD
Original aircraft received 20 Sep 42.
Lost 26 Feb 43 - the crew bailed out over Oldenburg with the Swedish coast in sight. (Wilhelmshaven)

B-24J-5 FO 42-50805 T 68 (WQ) >39<
NMF
Received 4 Jul 44.
Repaired at Woodbridge, Suffolk, 7 - 9 Aug 44 - hydraulic system damaged on 7 Aug 44 mission to Saleux, near Amiens, France.
Lost 2 Dec 44 - went down after being attacked by enemy fighters and set on fire. (Bingen)

B-24J -105 CO 42-109805 J 66 (QK) GIPSY QUEEN >55<
OD J 68 (WQ)
Transferred from 66th BS to 68th BS on 27 Apr 44.
See also 42-109896 with the same name.
Received between 20 Feb & 2 Mar 44.
Flew truckin' operation with 458th BG on 18 Sep 44 bearing 44th BG markings.
No trace with 44th BG after 13 Sep 44 but RZI 30 May 45.

B-24D-5 CO 41-23806 Z 68 BAT OUTA HELL >3<
OD
Original aircraft received 20 Sep 42.
Crash-landed 3 Jan 43 out of fuel 3 miles east of Talbenny, south west of Haverfordwest, Pembrokeshire, Wales. (St-Nazaire, France)

B-24JSH-5 FO 42-50806 E 68 (WQ) LOUISIANA BELLE >57<
NMF
Received between 6 & 18 Oct 44.
Landed at A-71 (Clastres, France) low on fuel, on 1 Mar 45 mission to Ingolstadt. Returned to Shipdham on 2 Mar 45.
RZI 26 or 31 May 45.

B-24D-5 CO 41-23807 U 67 LITTLE BEAVER >19<
OD
Original aircraft received 20 Sep 42.
Lost 14 May 43 - hit by flak after leaving the target and caught fire. (Kiel)

B-24D-5 CO 41-23808 P 67 TEXAN >5<
OD
Original aircraft received 20 Sep 42.
Crash landed 3 Jan 43 short of fuel in a field on the approach to Aberporth (Blaenannerch) airfield, Cardiganshire, Wales. (St-Nazaire, France)

B-24D-5 CO 41-23811 K 66 FASCINATING WITCH >33<
OD
According to the pilot who flew the aircraft on its last mission, it had no name.
Original aircraft received 20 Sep 42.
Flew on 1 Aug 43 Ploesti mission - landed at Malta on return.
Lost 1 Oct 43 - set on fire in an attack by Me 109s after bombs away. (Wiener Neustadt, Austria)

B-24D-5 CO 41-23813 V 68 VICTORY SHIP >49<
OD REBEL
Name was VICTORY SHIP and/or REBEL.
Original aircraft received 20 Sep 42.
Flew on 1 Aug 43 Ploesti mission.
Lost 21 Jan 44 - 3 engines knocked out by Me 109s and FW190s - went down near Auffay, France. (Escalles, France)

B-24D-155 CO 42-72813 L 66 QUEEN MARLENE >14<
OD L 66
Bar deleted from under letter in Nov 43.
Lost 21 Jan 44 - shot down by FW 190s after bombs away. (Escalles, France)

B-24H-20 FO 42-94816 TIGER'S REVENGE >0<
OD
Ex 489th BG No evidence of any missions flown with the 44th.
This a/c and two oters showed up at Shipdham at the same time. 816 flew its first mission with the 492nd BG (carpetbaggers) 20/21 Feb 45. MIA over Norway on the night of the 20/21 April 45.

B-24D-5 CO 41-23816 X 68 BLACK JACK >34<
OD
Original aircraft received 20 Sep 42.
Lost 1 Oct 43 - received a direct hit by flak over the target. (Wiener Neustadt, Austria)

B-24D-5 CO 41-23817 L 67 SUZY Q >29<
OD
Original aircraft received 20 Sep 42.
Is recorded at BAD 3, Langford Lodge, Northern Ireland, and reputed in Lockheed Overseas Corporation records to have left for the USA! (LOC operated BAD 3 on behalf of 8th AFSC)
Flew on 1 Aug 43 Ploesti mission.
Lost 16 Aug 43 - crashed and burned on an Italian beach believed to be at Cape Stilo - see also 42-41021. (Foggia, Italy)

B-24D-5 CO 41-23818 R 67 MISS MARCIA ANN >8<
OD
Original aircraft received 20 Sep 42.
Lost 16 Feb 43 - collided with 40-2354, caught fire, exploded and fell through a formation of B-17s into the English Channel off Selsey, Sussex. (St-Nazaire, France)

B-24D-5 CO 41-23819 A 68 RUGGED BUGGY >14<
OD
Original aircraft received 20 Sep 42.
Lost 14 May 43 - was hit by flak over the Friesian Islands but continued to the target and went down near the Danish-German border when attacked by Me109s and FW 190s. (Kiel)

B-24J-105 CO 42-109820 G 66 OH! MY SUFFERIN HEAD >45<
OD A 66 (QK)
N 67 (NB)
Transferred from 66th BS to 67th BS on 27 Apr 44.
Received between 13 & 24 Feb 44.
Repaired at Manston, Kent, 26 Feb - 3 Mar 44 - battle damage on 25 Feb 44 mission to Fürth.
Repaired at Nuthampstead, Hertfordshire, 10 - 22 Jun 44 - #1 engine could not be feathered on 8 Jun 44 mission to Angers, France. The aircraft was transferred to 3 SAD for an engine change.
Lost 29 Jul 44 - went down in the North Sea 6 miles north east of Cromer - tail was chewed off by #2 propeller of 42-95309 which slid under the centre section of the formation just after leaving the English coast causing the aircraft to go into a dive. (Bremen)

B-24JHO-20 FO 44-48821 A 67 (NB) >7<
NMF
Received before 24 Dec 44.
RZI 31 May 45.

B-24J-105 CO 42-109822 O 68 (WQ) TOWNSEND'S TERRIBLE TEN >15<
OD
Received 26 Feb 44.
Lost 8 Apr 44 - shot down by fighters. (Langenhagen)

B-24JHO-10 FO 42-51823 C+ 66 (QK) >24<
NMF
Received between 12 Oct & 16 Nov 44.
RZI 22 May 45.

B-24J-105 CO 42-109827 Q 506 (GJ) >6<
OD
Received between 18 & 24 Mar 44.
Lost 8 Apr 44 - shot down by fighters. (Langenhagen)

B-24H-15 DT 41-28829 H 66 (QK) MY EVERLOVIN' GAL >28<
OD -H 506 (GJ)
H 506 (GJ)
Transferred from 66th BS to 506th BS on 27 Apr 44 and bar changed from before to above the letter on 21 May 44.
Received by 44th BG before 27 Mar 44.
Repaired at Wendling 9 Apr 44 by 465th Sub-Depot.
Lost 29 Jun 44 - was hit in the bomb bay area after bombs away and struck by the right wing of 42-51181 near the top turret before catching fire and exploding. (Magdeburg)

B-24D-7 CO 41-23832 N 67 MAGGIE >16<
OD
Original aircraft received 20 Sep 42.
Is recorded at BAD 3, Langford Lodge, Northern Ireland.
Lost 22 Mar 43 - damaged by flak, it lost altitude and went down in the vicinity of Alte Mellum Island. (Wilhelmshaven)

B-24D-160 CO 42-72833 U 506 TORNEY >7<
OD
Received between 13 Aug & 6 Sep 43.
Transferred to 389th BG between 1 & 9 Oct 43.

B-24J-105 CO 42-109836 B 66 (QK) >5<
OD
Received between 24 Feb & 5 Mar 44.
Lost 27 Mar 44 - ditched 1 mile from the French coast, headed for Spain. (Mont-de-Marsan, France)

B-24H-20 FO 42-94846 L 67 (NB) MI AKIN ASS >127<
OD
Received between 12 & 19 Apr 44.
According to Stephen Adams, it had the front view of the donkey painted on the right hand side.
Landed at A-47 (Paris/Orly, France) on return from 16 Jan 45 mission to Ruhland (but Dresden bombed) because of fog blanket over England.
Completed 127 missions.
RZI 22 May 45.

B-24H-20 FO 42-94842 ? ? FORDS FOLLY >0<
OD
Photograph confirms this aircraft to be ex 489th BG,did not fly any missions with 44th. Transferred to 453rd BG, later rzi 389th BG 21 May 45.

B-24D-160 CO 42-72853 Q 67 COUNT BRUGA >5<
OD COUNT GRUCA
Received 1 Sep 43.
Named COUNT BRUGA or COUNT GRUCA.
Lost 1 Oct 43 - attacked by fighters. (Wiener Neustadt, Austria)

B-24D-160 CO 42-72857 X 506 >5<
OD
Received between 16 Aug & 6 Sep 43.
Lost 1 Oct 43 - attacked by fighters. (Wiener Neustadt, Austria)

B-24D-160 CO 42-72858 U 68 (WQ) PISTOL PACKIN' MAMA >35<
OD
Received before 3 Oct 43.
Lost 9 Apr 44 - landed at Bulltofta (Malmö), SWEDEN. (Tutow)
Left in Sweden in May 45.

B-24JSH-20 FO 44-48858 B 506 (GJ) >14<
NMF
Received before 24 Dec 44.

Landed at A-47 (Paris/Orly, France) on return from 16 Jan 45 mission to Ruhland (but Dresden bombed) because of fog blanket over England.
Landed at A-68 (Juvincourt, France) on 21 Jan 45 mission to Heilbronn (but Pforzheim bombed) - complete electrical failure. Returned to Shipdham on 22 Jan 45.
RZI 22 May 45.

B-24D-160 CO 42-72860 N 67 MISS EMMY LOU >7<
OD
Received 1 Sep 43.
Crash-landed 1 Oct 43 on return from mission to Wiener Neustadt, Austria.
Transferred to MTO 9 Oct 43 and salvaged 30 Nov 43 (Photo taken on 21 Oct 43 shows collapsed nose wheel and damaged nose).

B-24D-165 CO 42-72865 F 67 F FOR FREDDIE >30<
OD
Received before 3 Oct 43.
Lost 22 Feb 44 - heavy damage by FW 190s. (Mission to Gotha recalled when 100 miles inland - targets of opportunity sought but strong winds caused the formation to drift over the Netherlands where some aircraft bombed Enschedd, Arnhem, Nijmegen and Deventer unintentionally)

B-24D-165 CO 42-72870 G 66 >21<
OD G 66
Bar below letter deleted in Nov 43.
Received before 3 Oct 43.
Recorded 16 Feb 44 to re-deploy for Carpetbagger modifications.
Assigned to 801st BG(P) after 13 Feb 44.

B-24D-165 CO 42-72873 E 67 RAGGEDY ANN II >29<
OD B 67 (NB)
Letter changed from E with bar above to B in Mar 44.
Received before 4 Oct 43.
Repaired at Shipdham 5 Oct - 10 Nov 43 - extensive battle damage on 4 Oct 43 diversion mission off Heligoland to asist B-17 attack on Frankfurt.
Crash-landed 5 Feb 44 at West Malling, Kent, where it was repaired 6 Feb - 9 Mar 44 - #2 engine, fuel cell change and battle damage. The aircraft was forced to land with two wounded officers. The aircraft was flown back to
Shipdham on 20 Mar 44.
Recorded 12 May 44 to go to BAD 1 for modification.
Assigned to 801st BG(P) after 7 May 44.

B-24D-165 CO 42-72877 A 66 >4<
OD
Received before 9 Sep 43.
Lost 1 Oct 43 - attacked by fighters, crashed and burned. (Wiener Neustadt, Austria)

B-24D-165 CO 42-72878 A 67 MISS EMMY LOU II >9<
OD
Received before 3 Oct 43.
Crashed and burned on 21 Dec 43 at Richards Farm, West Bradenham, near Shipdham. Salvaged 23 & 24 Dec 43.

B-24H-20 FO 42-94883 Y 506 (GJ) HIT PARADE >47<
OD
ex 489th BG, previously 34th BG, originally 486th BG.
Received by 44th BG between 7 & 15 Oct 44.
Landed at A-75 (Cambrai/Epinoy, France) on 21 Jan 45 mission to Pforzheim and returned to Shipdham 22 Jan 45. (It is thought that Lt Kyes and his crew flew this aircraft in place of 42-50535 O (bar above) JOPLIN JALOPY which,
according to the formation plan, they were scheduled to fly).
Repaired at Carnaby (Bridlington), Yorkshire, 4 - 8 Feb 45 - #1 engine.
RZI '45 via Valley.

884
The North Pickenham control tower log lists the arrival of a new 491st BG replacement aircraft, 884, from Shipdham on 7 Mar 45.
Transferred by 491st BG to 44th BG on 20 Mar 45.
No record of missions with 44th BG.
Possible complete serials:
B-24J-110 CO 42-109884
B-24J-5 FO 42-50884
B-24J-20 FO 44-48884
B-24M-15 FO 44-50884 (RZI 20 May 45 by BAD 2, Warton, Lancashire)

B-24H-20 FO 42-94892 U 68 (WQ) BATTLIN' BABY >19<
OD
Received between 20 Apr & 3 May 44.
Lost 20 Jun 44 - landed at Bulltofta (Malmö), SWEDEN, - received a flak hit which knocked out control of supercharger waste gates on the bomb run, started to descend and fall behind but continued on the bomb run alone.
After bombs away, tried to open up the waste gates with the spare amplifier but with no luck. Also had flak damage to fuel cells. (Politz)
Brought back to England on 19 Jun 45.

B-24J-5 FO 42-50894 N 506 (GJ) >27<
NMF
Received between 8 & 25 Sep 44.
Force landed 24 Dec 44 on the Continent. (Ruwer, Pfazel, Wittlich or Eller) Salvaged 20 Jan 45 on the Continent by 5 SAD.

895
The North Pickenham control tower log lists the arrival of a new 491st BG replacement aircraft, 895, from Shipdham on 7 Mar 45.
No record of missions with 44th BG - may never have been assigned to 44th BG
Possible complete serials:
B-24J-115 CO 42-109895
B-24H-15 DT 41-28895
B-24J -5 FO 42-50895
B-24J-15 FO 42-51895
B-24J-20 FO 44-48895
B-24L-15 FO 44-49895 (probably this one)
B-24M-15 FO 44-50895

B-24H-20 FO 42-94895 R 67 (NB) >67<
OD
Received before 27 Apr 44.
Crash landed 16 Feb 45 at A-72 (Peronne, France) battle damaged - tyre blew out and nose strut broken. (Rheine)
Salvaged 13 Mar 45 on the Continent by 5 SAD.

B-24J-5 FO 42-50896 R 506 (GJ) SOUTHERN COMFORT III >63<
NMF
Received between 22 Jul & 1 Aug 44.
Landed at A-47(Paris/Orly, France) on return from 16 Jan 45 mission to Ruhland (but Dresden bombed) because of fog blanket over England - #4 starter would not engage and two amplifiers were out. Returned to Shipdham on 14 Feb 45.
Lost 24 Mar 45 - at 300 ft #4 engine began to smoke and the plane hit the ground with its belly and the bottom part of the rudders, came up again for about 1 1/2 minutes, then the right wing dipped, struck the ground and pinwheeled into the ground before starting to burn. (Wesel assault area supply drop)

B-24J-115 CO 42-109896 H 67 (NB) GYPSY QUEEN >0<
OD
See also 42-109805 with the same name.
ex 453rd BG after 11 Apr 45, originally 392nd BG.
Flew no missions with 44th BG.
RZI 31 May 45.

B-24JSH-15 FO 42-51907 B+ 66 (QK) >20<
NMF
Received before 24 Dec 44.
Landed at A-47 (Paris/Orly, France) on return from 16 Jan 45 mission to Ruhland (but Dresden bombed) because of fog blanket over England.
Landed at B-58 (Brussels-Melsbroek, Belgium) on 21 Feb 45 mission to Nürnberg - #4 engine knocked out by flak. Returned to Shipdham before 10 Mar 45.
Lost 19 Mar 45 - shot down by two Me 109s near Stuttgart. (Neuburg)

B-24D-10 CO 41-23918 O 67 BELA >19<
OD
Received before 1 May 43.
Lost 1 Oct 43. (Wiener Neustadt, Austria)

B-24D-13 CO 41-23933 W 506 SWEET ADELINE II >1<
OD
Original aircraft (received 4 Mar 43?)
Transferred to 389th BG after 29 May 43.

B-24D-13 CO 41-23936 J 66 QUEEN ANNE >19<
OD
Received before 16 Apr 43.
Flew on 1 Aug 43 Ploesti mission.
Crash-landed 1 Oct 43 about 4 miles from Foggia, Italy. (Wiener Neustadt, Austria)

B-24H-20 FO 42-94941 PIN UP GIRL
OD
Ex 489th BG, no evidence of 941 ever flying missions with the 44th, but was photographed at Shipdham with two other 489th a/c. Was lost with the 705BS, 446th BG 5 April 45.

B-24H-20 DT 41-28944 D 67 (NB) FLYIN' GINNY >5<
NMF
Call letter changed from N to D on 14 Oct 44 (N was its call letter in 93rd BG, 329th BS).
ex 93rd BG (may also have been assigned to 489th BG).
Received by 44th BG between 11 Sep & 4 Oct 44.
GH aircraft.
Was fitted with a B-24M type navigator's window and the anti-glare panel extended to the nose turret as on a B-24H CF.
Lost 18 Oct 44 - collided in mid-air with 42-50381 during an electrical storm over Belgium and crashed 1 km from Petegem, near Deinze, south-west of Ghent, Belgium. (Leverkusen)

B-24H-20 FO 42-94952 -A 506 (GJ) SHACK RAT >57<
OD A 506 (GJ)
Received between 8 & 26 Apr 44.
Lost 13 Sep 44 (probably while on loan to 458th BG for truckin' operations). Salvaged by 8 ASC on the Continent (salvage recorded on 14 Nov 44, an administrative date, not the date on which the aircraft was actually salvaged)

B-24D-15 CF 42-63959 F 66 SOUTHERN QUEEN IV >3<
OD
Appears 26 Sep (diversion) and 3 & 9 Oct 44 combat mission formation sheets.
Transferred to 389th BG and later assigned to 801st BG (P).

B-24D-15 CF 42-63962 W 506 PRINCESS >51<
OD W 506 (GJ) PRINC-ASS
-W 506 (GJ)
W 506 (GJ)
Letter remained W throughout assignment to 44th BG, 506th BS, but originally without bar, bar below added in Nov 43, replaced by bar in front in Apr 44 and finally by the bar above in May 44.
Name originally PRINCE, then PRINC-ASS and finally PRINCESS.
Lost 29 May 44 - landed at Bulltofta (Malmö), SWEDEN, short of fuel after attack by fighters. (Politz)
Left in Sweden in Jun 45 or RZI?

B-24H-20 FO 42-94962 I 67 (NB) >7<
OD
Accepted from Ford Motor Co. on 21 Feb 44, assigned to 2nd AF in Topeka, Kansas, on 19 Mar 44, picked up by a 453rd BG replacement crew (Pilot: Rudy Kremer) on 1 Apr 44 and left Morrison Field, Florida, on 4 Apr 44. Arrived
Valley, Anglesey, Wales, on 17 Apr 44 via Puerto Rico; Trinidad; Belem & Natal, Brazil; Dakar, Senegal; Marrakech, Morocco, and St Mawgan, Cornwall, and was taken to BAD 2, Warton, Lancashire, on 18 Apr 44 where the aircraft and crew were separated.
Received by 44th BG between 29 Apr & 4 May 44.
Lost 25 May 44 - shot down by flak having left the formation with #2 engine feathered and #3 engine smoking, headed for Switzerland but crashed in the Champagne area of France. (Belfort, France)

B-24JSH-15 FO 42-51965 B 68 (WQ) >25<
NMF
Received before 15 Oct 44.
Landed at A-74 (Cambrai-Niergnies, France) with #3 engine out on 16 Jan 45 mission to Ruhland (but Dresden bombed). Returned to Shipdham on 9 Feb 45.
Landed at A-64 (St-Dizier, France) low on fuel, on the 1 Mar 45 mission to Ingolstadt. Returned to Shipdham on 2 Mar 45.
RZI 27 May 45.

B-24D-15 CF 42-63965 A 506 >22<
OD Q 506
Q 506
Letter changed from A with a bar above to Q in Oct 43 and a bar below was added in Nov 43.
Crashed 5 Mar 44 at Shipdham on take-off - swerved off the runway at the lower end of the field. (Cognac or Bergerac, France)

B-24J-55 CO 42-99966 W 68 (WQ) FULL HOUSE >45<
OD
Received 21 Jan 44.
Lost 7 Jul 44 - crashed near Valthe, near Odoorn, Netherlands. (Bernburg)

B-24J-55 CO 42-99967 E 66 (QK) MYRTLE THE FERTILE TURTLE >70<
OD Q 67 (NB)
H 506 (GJ)
Transferred from 66th BS to 67th BS in Apr 44 and then to 506th BS in Feb 45.
Received between 22 Dec 43 & 30 Jan 44.
Repaired at Ford, Sussex, 20 Mar - 9 Apr 44 - #1 engine and supercharger, #2 propeller.
RZI 31 May 45.

B-24J-55 CO 42-99970 M 67 LIB-ERTY BELLE >2<
OD
Received between 11 Dec 43 & 14 Jan 44.
Belly-landed 21 Jan 44 at Brambling Down, Wingham, Kent, on return. (Escalles, France) Salvaged 22 & 23 Jan 44.

B-24D-15 CF 42-63971 E 68 HELEN HYWATER >7<
OD W 68
Letter changed from E with a bar above to W in Nov 43.
Received 5 Oct 43.
Lost 18 Nov 43 - landed at Trollhåtten, SWEDEN, and was set on fire by the crew. (Oslo-Kjeller, Norway)
Parts were sold in 1945.

B-24D-120 CO 42-40973 Z 66 BATTLE AXE >12<
OD D 66
Letter changed from Z to D in Sep 43.
Flew with 98th BG on loan from 44th BG on 1 Aug 43 Ploesti mission.
Lost 13 Nov 43 - went down in the North Sea - probably ditched but some of the crew bailed out over the Netherlands and their bodies were recovered from the Ijsselmeer. (Bremen)

B-24H-20 FO 42-94975 -M 506 (GJ) >53<
OD M 506 (GJ)
Received before 4 May 44.
No trace with 44th BG after 25 Sep 44.
War weary when salvaged 29 May 45 by BAD 3, Langford Lodge, Northern Ireland.

B-24J-55 CO 42-99980 H 66 BANSHEE IV >11<
OD E Z DUZIT
Received between 4 & 13 Jan 44.
According to Will Lundy, this aircraft was named BANSHEE IV and E Z DUZIT.
Crash-landed 9 Mar 44 at Shipdham on return, having been hit by flak just as bombs were released. (Brandenburg) Salvaged 9 - 21 Mar 44 - extensive damage to nose back to station 4.

B-24J-60 CO 42-99986 D 67 (NB) D-BARFLY >27<
OD
Received between 18 Nov 43 & 13 Jan 44.
Crash-landed 13 Apr 44 at Shipdham - salvaged 14 Apr 44 - left landing gear and wing damaged.

B-24J-60 CO 42-99987 S 68 (WQ) PIZZ AND MOAN >18<
OD TOOTIE BELLE
Name was PIZZ AND MOAN or TOOTIE BELLE.
Received 15 Jan 44.
Lost 8 Apr 44 - shot down by fighters close to the target. (Langenhagen)

B-24D-15 CO 41-23988 E 67 EMMA LOU >6<
OD DOUBLE PLAYMATE
Received before 23 Jan 43.
Per Will Lundy, according to Leo Frazier, this was Lt Blaine's plane and was named both EMMA LOU and DOUBLE PLAYMATE.
Lost 8 Mar 43 - shot down by FW 190s between St-Valéry-en-Caux and Rouen on the way to the target and went down at Maromme or Sierville, France. (Rouen, France)

B-24D-120 CO 42-40989 B 506 HOLIDAY MESS >1<
OD
Lost 4 Oct 43 - a shot-up Me 109 crashed into it and both planes exploded over the North Sea. (Diversion mission off Heligoland to assist a B-17 attack on Frankfurt)

B-24D-120 CO 42-40995 C 68 MARGUERITE >2<
OD W 68
There is considerable doubt about this aircraft.
Was it ever assigned to 44th BG?
Was its letter C or W with a bar above the letter)?
Was it lost 1 Aug 43 - shot down while leaving the target area or belly-landed near the initial point - on the mission to Ploesti or was it salvaged on 31 Jan 44 by 8 AFHQ?

B-24J-60 CO 42-99996 I 66 (QK) >8<
OD
Received between 30 Dec 43 & 31 Jan 44.
Repaired at Shoreham, Sussex, 21 Feb - 20 Mar 44 - #3 & #4 engines, empennage change - damage on 25 Feb 44 mission to Fürth (repair date taken from 3 SAD Field Engineering records is suspect).
Lost 8 Apr 44 - went down in the vicinity of Salzwedel. (Langenhagen)

B-24J-60 CO 42-99997 C 66 (QK) Available Jones #2 >56<
OD P 67 (NB)
ex 389th BG.
Received between 18 & 22 Mar 44.
Changed from 66th BS to 67th BS on 27 Apr 44.
No trace with 44th BG after 11 Sep 44.
Flew on truckin' operation with 458th BG on 18 Sep 44 but retained 44th BG markings.
War weary when salvaged 29 May 45.

B-24H-20 FO 42-94999 -B 506 (GJ) >2<
OD
Received 8 May 44.
Lost 11 May 44 - shot down by Me 109s over Patay, 20 km north west of Orléans, France. (Mulhouse, France, but target obscured by clouds so Orléans-Bricy, France, was selected as a target of opportunity)

B-24D B 506
OD
On 29 May 43 formation plan.
Was one of the following:
B-24D-95 CO 42-40781 (Assigned to 93rd BG, 329th BS as U, named HELL'S ANGELS and lost 1 Aug 43 at Ploesti)
B-24D-1 CO 42-63781 (Assigned to 479th ASG, 8 AFSC and converted to CB-24D, assigned to 801st BG(P), 406th BS, and salvaged 4 Jul 44 due to nose wheel collapse after landing battle damaged)

B-24 BEVERLY JEAN
Pilot: Capt. McDonnell.

B-24 BOARDWALK FLYER
OD
Crew Chief: Sgt Bagley

B-24J 68 (WQ) DEAN
NMF
Stephen Adams has a photo taken in Belgium. This may be the aircraft in the photo on page 249 of the History of the 68th BS by Webb Todd.

B-24H? OD Not 42-99980.	66	E Z DUZIT
B-24H DT		FLAK DODGING FANNY
B-24 See page 436 of the "History of 68th Bomb Squadron"		GUS GREMLIN
B-24	67	THE HORNET'S NEST
B-24J CO OD 302 on nose.		HOT STUFF
B-24 See page 436 of the "History of 68th Bomb Squadron"		JEN
B-24H FO OD Photo in "Liberators over Europe" by Ursel P Harvell.		KING HIGH
B-24H		LADY LIGHTNING
B-24 See page 437 of the "History of 68th Bomb Squadron".		MARY ANN
B-24 See page 437 of the "History of 68th Bomb Squadron".		MARY ANN II
B-24 See page 438 of the "History of 68th Bomb Squadron".		MISS IT
B-24 See page 438 of the "History of 68th Bomb Squadron".		PATSY ANN
B-24H FO See page 439 of the "History of 68th Bomb Squadron". I have photo of nose art, 8 Ball visable.		SHORT LEG
B-24 See page 439 of the "History of 68th Bomb Squadron".		TEN GUN DOTTIE
B-24 See page 439 of the "History of 68th Bomb Squadron.		UN-HAPPY
B-24 In 1944, E D Rozman or Martin mentioned this as their plane.		VALIANT VIRGIN

Appendix 4
44th Bombardment Group (Heavy) Roll of Honor 1942-1945

Cemetary Location	*Wall of Missing*	*Interred*	*Total*
AR = Ardennes	23	79	102
BR = Brittany	0	1	1
CA = Cambridge	116	47	163
EP = Epinal	0	7	7
FL = Florence	13	1	14
HC = Henri Chapelle	1	2	3
LO = Lorraine	0	27	27
LX= Luxembourg	0	2	2
NE = Netherlands	46	29	75
NO = Normandy	3	26	29
NA = North Africa	13	1	14
RH = Rhone	4	1	5
SR = Sicily-Rome	4	9	13
Total	**223**	**232**	**445**

Total of 44th BG men KIA: 860
Total of 44th men NUA: 223

Rank	*ASN*	*Name*	*Sqdn.*	*Pilot*	*Dat of Loss*	*Cemetary Location*
2 Lt	0-798720	Ackerman, Edward J.	506	Bolin	02 Feb 1944	Interred in USA
Sgt	34735355	Adams, Carl E.	68	Lehnhausen	18 Oct 1944	Interred in USA
Capt	0-23946	Adams, Howard F.	66	Adams	26 Feb 1943	AR B33-5
SSgt	14120178	Adams, Richard W.	67	Roach	14 May 1943	Interred in USA
SSgt	32323720	Adams, Victor J.	68	Mathisen	21 Jan 1944	Interred in USA
Sgt	34251163	Aguirre, Adolph P.	67	Bateman	16 Aug 1943	NA Wall of Missing
Sgt	31121510	Aho, Augustus	506	Maynor	20 Dec 1943	NE Wall of Missing
2 Lt	0-759546	Airoldi, John A.	506	Eberhardt	29 Jul 1944	CA Wall of Missing
1 Lt	0-800804	Albert, Frank L.	506	Albert	18 Mar 1944	LO K37-22
SSgt	13087450	Albine, Robert L.	66	Decker	20 Feb 1944	Interred in USA
SSgt	37430255	Allen, Norbert G.	67	O'Neill	11 Dec 1943	Interred in USA
1 Lt	0-676714	Almlie, Harlan C.	66	Almlie	13 Nov 1943	NE Wall of Missing
2 Lt	0-2045026	Altemus, William B.	68	Altemus	08 Apr 1944	Interred in USA
SSgt	15016119	Andello, David F.	506	Albert	18 Mar 1944	LO K48-18
1 Lt	0-885575	Anderson, Everett P.	66	Scrivner	01 Aug 1943	Interred in USA
Maj	0-411678	Anderson, William N.	506	Cookus	21 Jan 1944	Interred in USA
Cpl	?	Andrews, Stanley C.	66	Frawley	18 May 1942	Interred in USA
SSgt	16028759	Andris, Eugene E.	506	Johnson	04 Oct 1943	NE Wall of Missing
SSgt	15087738	Appeldorn, Thomas J.	66	Trolese	26 Nov 1943	AR A23-3
SSgt	32540668	Arcamone, Frank	66	Maynard	29 Jan 1944	EP B5-70
2 Lt	0-738953	Archambault, William S.	67	Bronstein	01 Oct 1943	Interred in USA
Sgt	17035780	Arnold, Ernest F.	68	Bledsoe	28 Dec 1944	CA F2-82
SSgt	16171652	Artym, Frank Jr.	506	Westcott	29 Jun 1944	Interred in USA
TSgt	14042027	Aswell, Harold L.	66	Billings	16 Feb 1943	CA Wall of Missing
Sgt	35579833	Atchley, Monroe A.	2033	Firefight	04 Jun 1944	Interred in USA
1 Lt	0-789432	Augenstene, Jacob A. Jr.	67	Price	08 Mar 1943	AR C25-9
2 Lt	0-734779	Ayers, John T.	66	Gentry	01 Aug 1943	Interred in USA
1 Lt	0-699752	Bakalo, Michael	67	Bakalo	18 Oct 1944	Interred in USA
2 Lt	0-734296	Baker, WaHace P.	67	Hager	16 Aug 1943	SR G15-54
SSgt	15070162	Balca, Michael J.	66	Decker	20 Feb 1944	Interred in USA
TSgt	34283420	Bales, James H.	506	Bolin	02 Feb 1944	Interred in USA
2 Lt	0-681300	Ballangrud, Norris S.	68	Mathisen	21 Jan 1944	Interred in USA
SSgt	39175097	Balsley, Lucius M.	66	Miller	18 Mar 1943	CA D6-69
SSgt	12012298	Banning, Charles E.	68	Bonnet	07 Jul 1944	CA Wall of Missing
SSgt	34163105	Barber, Thomas G. Jr.	66	Folsom	07 Mar 1944	Interred in USA
1 Lt	0-1995910	Barefoot, Chester L.	506	Bentclitf	30 Oct 1944	AR 13-35-9
2 Lt	0-730337	Barnett, Edward	66	Winger	01 Aug 1943	FL Wall of Missing
Sgt	42069644	Barth, David	68	Bledsoe	28 Dec 1944	Interred in USA
1 Lt	0-726980	Bartmess, Thomas E.	67	Phillips	14 Nlav 1943	Interred in USA

Rank	ASN	Name	Sqdn.	Pilot	Dat of Loss	Cemetary Location
1 Lt	0-680595	Bartol, Stockton R.	506	Mccaslin	08 Api- 1944	CA C-2-15
1 Lt	0-796281	Bateman, Walter R.	67	Bateman	16 Aug 1943	NA Wall of Missing
SSgt	36832427	Battenburg, Walter R	67	Crandell	24 Mar 1945	Interred in USA
2 Lt	0-685420	Baum, Paul F.	66	Harlemail	27 Mar 1944	RH C-9-18
TSgt	39020115	Bauman, Francis A.	68	Whitaker	01 Oct 1943	LO C-19-71
TSgt	18193549	Baxter, Orus Jr.	66	Zweig	11 Jul 1944	Interred in USA
1 Lt	0-768414	Bayless, Herbert L	506	Bayless	02 Dec 1944	Interred in USA
2 Lt	0-756831	Bean, Loran M. Jr.	67	Scarborough	16 Mar 1944	CA D-6-29
SSgt	38345296	Beggs, William A.	506	Bayless	02 Dec 1944	AR C-34-5
Sgt	32736648	Behnke, George C	506	Eberhardt	29 Jul 1944	CA Wall of Missing
2 Lt	0-699505	Beirne, Milton R.	506	Eberhardt	29 Jul 1944	CA Wall of Missing
Sgt	11106940	Bell, Robert J.	506	Jacobs	08 Aug 1944	Interred in USA
1 Lt	0-675984	Bellard, Harold W.	68	Altemus	08 Apr 1944	Interred in USA
SSgt	33300775	Belsky, George	506	Bonnet	11 Jul 1944	CA Wall of Missing
1 Lt	0-815806	Bentcliff, Clifford J.	506	Bentcliff	30 OctI944	Interred in USA
Cpl	19074373	Berg, Albert H.	66	McCoy	20 Feb 1943	Interred in USA
TSgt	18104589	Berkstresser, George B.	67	Bronstein	01 Oct 1943	FL Wall of Missing
SSgt	39234569	Bernstein, David G.	68	Garrett	02 Jul 1943	NA Wall of Missing
SSgt	38194491	Besse, Wilson P.	68	Jones	16 Dec 1943	CA E-0-43
SSgt	20227109	Bessen, Theodore	66	Folsoin	07 Mar 1944	Interred in USA
SSgt	16077154	Bethke, Elmer J.	66	Decker	20 Feb 1944	Interred in USA
SSgt	11113894	Bettley, Conrad R. Jr.	66	Dayball	18 Oct t944	Interred in USA
SSgt	18045226	Beverly, Paul E.	68	Du Bard	06 Dec 1942	AR Wall of Missing
1 Lt	0-411918	Billings, Fred M. Jr.	66	Billinas	16 Feb 1943	CA Wall of Missing
1 Lt	0-676728	Billings, James R.	66	Heskett	30 Dec 1943	EP A-20-41
Cpl	11032802	Binienda, Walter	66	McCoy	20 Feb 1943	Interred in USA.
TSgt	14080954	Birge, Edward E.	66	Miller	22 Dec 1943	Interred in USA
Sgt	16063878	Bitmer, Harry H.	67	Carpenter	01 Oct 1943	Interred in USA
1 Lt	0-423910	Blaine, Robert W.	67	Blaine	08 Mar 1943	AR Wall of Missing
SSgt	11055810	Blake, Foster A.	506	Money	11 Apr 1944	Interred in USA
2 Lt	0-718848	Bledsoe, Jesse W.	68	Bledsoe	28 Dec 1944	CA D-2-43
SSgt	33204357	Blitz, Aulis L.	66	Heskett	30 Dec 1943	EP B-22-53
SSgt	12067159	Bloomfield, Philip J.	68	Sullivan	27 Jan 1943	NE A-3-26
SSgt	33213653	Boggess, Boyd Jr.	67	O'Neill	11 Dec 1943	Interied in U.SA.
1 Lt	0-735031	Bohnisch, Carl A.	68	Bohnisch	05 Feb 1944	Interred in USA
1 Lt	0-424895	Bolin, James O.	506	Bolin	021 Feb 1944	CA F-3-83
SSgt	35397686	Bolster, Harry T.	67	Bronstein	01 Oct 1943	FL Wall of Missing
SSgt	15125248	Bonham, Robert W.	506	Whitlock	16 Aug 1943	Interred in USA
Sgt	39917713	Borgstrom, Rolori D.	506	Jacobs	08 Aug 1944	Interred in USA
Sgt	20135511	Boutin, Albert L. Jr.	67	Oliphant	15 Feb 1943	CA Wall of Missing
SSgt	11013585	Bowie, Donald R.	66	Adams	26 Feb !943	AR B-33-6
1 Lt	0-717169	Bradshaw, Eugene T.	67	Bakalo	18 Oct 1944	Interred in USA
SSgt	37232782	Brady, Lloyd J.	506	Albert	18 Mar 1944	Interred in USA
SSgt	14105559	Braswell, Homer H.	68	Dittmer	24 Aug 1944	Interred in USA
SSgt	33408973	Breakey, Karl D.	506	Jacobs	0 8 Aug 1944	CA E-4 53
SSgt	39092835	Breniser, Norman A.	67	Blaine	08 Mar 1943	Interred in USA
1 Lt	0-727081	Brenner, Joseph L.	506	Fouts	22 Mai 1943	NE Wall of Missing
SSgt	39826187	Brewer, Scott E.	66	Adams	26 Feb 1943	AR B-33-7C
1 Lt	0-523516	Bronstein, George	67	Bionstein	01 Oct 1943	FL Wall of Missing
Sgt	34623016	Broome, Garland R.	07	Green	29 Jul 1944	CA Wall of Missing
2 Lt	0-831104	Brown, Georae F.Jr.	506	Brown	05 Apr 1945	Interred in USA
SSgt	1531-7559	Brown, Harry H. Jr.	68	Hobbs	0' Dec 1944	Interred in USA
SSgt	34316177	Brown, James M, Jr.	67	Crandell	24 Mai 1945	Interred in USA
2 Lt	0-727307	Brown, John C.	66	Mccov	20 Feb 1943	CA D-1-14
1 Lt	0-727161	Brown, Richard C.	67	Warne	22 Mar 1943	NE Wall of Missing
SSgt	18063845	Brown, Walter L.	67	Carpenter	01 Aug 1943	SR Wall of Missing
2 Lt	0-547126	Bruce, James C. Jr,	66	Zweig	I I Jul 1944	Interred in USA
Sat	14159347	Bruce, W. B.	66	Richardson	08 Apr 1944	Interred in USA
2 Lt	0-727309	Bryant. Charles W.	6 7	Oliphant	15 Feb 1943	CA Wall of Missing
SSgt	10601101	Bryl, Edward B.	67	Carpenter	01 Oct 1943	LO E-14-222
1 Lt	0-669980	Buckholts, John J.	68	Jones	16 Dec 1943	Interred in USA
Sgt	1311-4177	Buckley, Francis X.	506	Salfen	07 Oct 1944	Interred in USA
2 Lt	0-739538	Buechsenstem, John L.	66	Etheridge	24 Feb 1944	LO B-20-9
Sgt	39621427	Buhl, Vernon	506	Still	07 Oct 1944	NE 1721-18
Pvt	32756508	Bunalski, Ted R.	2033	Fire Fighting	04 June 1944	Interred in USA
2 Lt	0-697098	Burge, Harold L.	66	Zweig	11 July 1944	Interred in USA
Sgt	14091412	Burk, William J.	67	Mayes	08 Api 1944	Interred in USA
2 Lt	0-886703	Burke, Robert A.	67	Phillips	21 No, 1944	Interred in USA
TSgt	13044534	Burns, Harry B.	67	Oliphant	15 Feb 1943	CA Wall of Missing
2 Lt	0-661588	Burroughs, Sidney M.	67	Dobson	IS Nov 1943	CA Wall of Missing
SSgt	13044499	Butler, Richard J.	68	Bonrwt	11 July 1944	CA Wall of Missing
Sgt	37704580	Byers, Clifford L	67	Green	29 July 1944	CA Wall ofMissing
Capt	0-25011	Byrne, Austin P. (492nd BG)	66	McKenna	06 Aug 1944	Interred in USA
2 Lt	0-727313	Caldwell, Paul D.	67	Cullen	15 Feb 1943	Interred in USA

Rank	ASN	Name	Sqdn.	Pilot	Dat of Loss	Cemetary Location
TSgt	32316551	Caflahan, Cornelius J.	66	Zweig	11 Jul 1944	Interred in USA
SSgt	07010352	Calvin, William A.	68	Ground Crew	24 Aug 1943	CA D5-69
2 Lt	0-727170	Canfield, Dale K.	66	Hilliard	03 Jan 1943	CA D2-27
2 Lt	0-734422	Campbell, Donald G.	67	Stamos	04 Oct 1943	CA Wall of Missing
TSgt	32533914	Capizzi, Thomas F.	68	Sobotka	21 Jan 1944	Interred in USA
1 Lt	0-427211	Cargile, Nolan B.	68	Cargile	27 Jan 1943	NE Wall of Missing
TSgt	37464353	Cargill, Lawrence E.	66	Musgrave	08 May 1944	Interred in USA
SSgt	14037452	Carlton, Clyde W.	68	Houston	01 Aug 1943	AR C6-29
1 Lt	0-671279	Castellotti, Paul E.	506	Albert	18 Mar 1944	Interred in USA
Sgt	20366318	Cate, Richard E.	67	Brown	14 May 1943	NE Wall of Missing
1 Lt	0-703026	Celentano, Louis S.	506	Bentcliff	30 Oct 1944	AR D11-34
SSgt	13145502	Chalan, Andy	67	Goodwin	14 Jan 1944	NO B21-6
2 Lt	0-2059456	Chandler, Max E.	506	Chandler	24 Mar 1945	Interred in USA
TSgt	32142986	Chapman, Robert D.	67	Bateman	16 Aug 1943	NA Wall of Missing
1 Lt	0-740744	Charleson, Norman	67	Dobson	18 Nov 1943	CA Wall of Missing
MSgt	06890102	Charletta, Henry	66	Billings	16 Feb 1943	CA Wall of Missing
1 Lt	0-1051904	Chase, Dudley S.	66	Podojil	19 Mar 1945	LO A-19-16
TSgt	39333461	Cheek, Hillburn L.	66	Ketchum	13 Jun 1945	CA ?
TSgt	19087860	Childers, James C.	66	Miller	22 Dec 1943	Interred in USA
F/O	T-190738	Chorzelski, Michel	66	Gentry	01 Aug 1943	Interred in USA
SSgt	37281658	Christensen, George E.	506	Swanson	14 May 1943	AR D8-57
SSgt	14094288	Christian, Charles M.	68	Steinke	07 Jul 1944	Interred in USA
TSgt	14266875	Christian, James W. Jr.	66	Oakley	22 Dec 1943	Interred in USA
SSgt	16108271	Churchill, Douglas E.	68	Townsend	08 Apr 1944	Interred in USA
SSgt	34288192	Cianciolo, Michael A.	67	Bateman	16 Aug 1943	NA Wall of Missing
Sgt	32491716	Cieply, Eugene B. Jr.	68	Starring	21 Jan 1944	NO B11-34
1 Lt	0-676748	Clarey, Howard A. Jr.	67	Clarey	27 Apr 1944	Interred in USA
SSgt	11033143	Clark, Frederick W.	68	Sullivan	27 Jan 1943	NE B1-8
2 Lt	0-675337	Clark, Raymond C.	67	Goodwin	14 Jan 1944	Interred in USA
Sgt	12100209	Clark, Thomas W.	506	Chandler	24 Mar 1945	Interred in USA
SSgt	35229520	Clark, William N. Jr.	66	Podojil	19 Mar 1945	Interred in USA
TSgt	15015217	Clemons, Archie D.	68	Townsend	08 Apr 1944	NE Wall of Missing
TSgt	15115001	Click, George	67	Bronstein	01 Oct 1943	LO K48-12
Pvt	31088145	Closson, William E.	68	Ground Crew	24 Aug 1943	CA D4-69
1 Lt	0-735857	Cobane, William E.	66	Harleman	27 Mar 1944	RH Wall of Missing
2 Lt	0-691634	Cole, Edward A.	68	Hovens	21 Apr 1944	Interred in USA
1 Lt	0-741099	Cole, Woodrow W.	67	Cookus	21 Jan 1944	CA D1-35
TSgt	13051982	Coll, William F.	66	Scrivner	01 Aug 1943	Interred in USA
1 Lt	0-393514	Collins, Richard K.	66	Oakley	22 Dec 1943	Interred in USA
SSgt	35371803	Confer, Charlie H.	67	Henderson	01 Oct 1943	Interred in USA
2 Lt	0-662333	Cook, Harold C.	67	Long	16 Feb 1943	CA Wall of Missing
TSgt	35307128	Cooney, Woodrow J.	68	Peterson	02 Jul 1943	Interred in USA
TSgt	38148230	Cooper, Harold E.	67	Henderson	01 Oct 1943	Interred in USA
2 Lt	0-829129	Cooper, Warren H.	68	Hobbs	02 Dec 1944	Interred in USA
Sgt	12100258	Cordes, Thomas H.	506	Chandler	24 Mar 1945	NE K7-15
Sgt	32466223	Corsilli, Gene	67	Fish	22 Feb 1944	CA Wall of Missing
TSgt	20649538	Cottington, Oma E.	67	Long	16 Feb 1943	CA Wall of Missing
Sgt	38494335	Couvillion, Wilbert L.	68	Dayball	18 Oct 1944	Interred in USA
Sgt	31240322	Cowan, Henry Jr.	68	Hobbs	02 Dec 1944	Interred in USA
Sgt	?	Crabtree, Mansfield	66	Frawley	18 May 1942	Interred in USA
Major	0-23925	Cramer, Thomas R.	68	Peterson	02 Jul 1943	Interred in USA
1 Lt	0-720197	Crandell, Leonard J.	67	Crandell	24 Mar 1945	NE H-16-26
SSgt	13046804	Crane, Paul M.	68	Cargile	27 Jan 1943	NE Wall of Missing
1 Lt	0-785168	Crane, Walter W.	66	Podojil	19 Mar 1945	LO A-19-28
2 Lt	0-727320	Crawford, George A.	68	Du Bard	06 Dec 1942	CA Wall of Missing
SSgt	34267452	Crawford, Michael S.	67	Mitchell	18 Nov 1943	CA Wall of Missing
SSgt	16041926	Crigger, William C.	67	Long	16 Feb 1943	CA Wall of Missing
SSgt	34430758	Crocker, John L. Jr.	66	Decker	20 Feb 1944	Interred in USA
2 Lt	0-2058627	Croll, William B.	67	Crandell	24 Mar 1945	Interred in USA
Sgt	13040353	Crook, Thomas W. Jr.	68	Sullivan	27 Jan 1943	NE Wall of Missing
1 Lt	0-741141	Crowl, Wayne D.	68	Howington	21 Jan 1944	Interred in USA
TSgt	36318179	Crump, John W.	68	Cramer	15 Feb 1943	CA Wall of Missing
2 Lt	0-670981	Curelli, Rocco A.	66	Curelli	16 Aug 1943	SR J5-63
TSgt	33361905	Curry, Francis X.	67	Hager	16 Aug 1943	SR 114-55
1 Lt	0-748585	Curtis, Herman M.	68	Howington	21 Jan 1944	Interred in USA
SSgt	38197204	D'Amico, Anthony	68	Whitaker	01 Oct 1943	LO A22-20
Sgt	32669213	Daniels, Carl E.	506	McGuire	12 Aug 1944	Interred in USA
2 Lt	0-2072657	Dantzler, Robert T.	506	Chandler	24 Mar 1945	Interred in USA
F/O	T-122578	Davidowitz, Edward	67	Vance	12 May 1944	Interred in USA
Sgt	34248774	Davis, Byron C.	68	Lehnhausen	18 Oct 1944	NE M5-3
TSgt	36343869	Davis, Donald A.	66	Almlie	13 Nov 1943	Interred in USA
2 Lt	0-691878	Davis, Milton H.	66	Richardson	08 Apr 1944	AR C2-13
SSgt	35151144	Davis, Raymond E.	66	Ketchum	13 Jun 1945	Interred in USA
2 Lt	0-723022	Davis, Richard H.	68	Dayball	18 Oct 1944	Interred in USA

Rank	ASN	Name	Sqdn.	Pilot	Dat of Loss	Cemetary Location
1 Lt	0-701907	Dayball, Julian H.	68	Dayball	18 Oct 1944	Interred in USA
SSgt	36175723	Deal, Manford S.	68	O'Brien	27 Jan 1943	CA C0-50
2 Lt	0-443161	Deavenport, Thomas G.	68	Erwin	03 Jan 1943	Interred in USA
1 Lt	0-2044424	Decker, Donald R.	66	Decker	20 Feb 1944	Interred in USA
SSgt	13124616	Dewald, George M.	506	Bolin	02 Feb 1944	Interred in USA
Sgt	34530358	Diaz, Anibal C.	506	Pyle	24 Mar 1945	Interred in USA
Sgt	31033519	Dick, Charles S.	68	Du Bard	06 Dec 1942	AR Wall of Missing
TSgt	32453614	Dickinson, John L.	68	Mathisen	21 Jan 1944	AR Wall of Missing
TSgt	18160347	Dillahunty, Jack C.	67	Houle	18 Nov 1943	CA Wall of Missing
2 Lt	0-818843	Dittmer, Arthur H.	68	Dittmer	24 Aug 1944	NE E-14-14
SSgt	16055011	Dobbins, Maurice H.	506	Fouts	22 Mar 1943	NE Wall of Missing
1 Lt	0-668216	Dobson, Edward M.	67	Dobson	18 Nov 1943	CA Wall of Missing
SSgt	13039292	Doherty, Robert L.	506	Salfen	07 Oct 1944	AR B-43-48
2 Lt	0-825804	Dolan, Charles Jr.	68	Lelmhausen	18 Oct 1944	NE B-3-32
SSgt	12039389	Doria, Frank N.	67	Blaine	08 Mar 1943	Interred in USA
SSgt	34261978	Douthit, William E.	67	Oliphant	15 Feb 1943	CA Wall of Missing
SSgt	12193464	Downey, John J. 111	506	Bentcliff	30 Oct 1944	AR B37-14
1 Lt	0-410225	Du Bard, James D. Jr.	68	Du Bard	06 Dec 1942	AR Wall of Missing
SSgt	?	Ducki, Stanley H.	68	Collins	07 Feb 1945	Interred in USA
2 Lt	0-684699	Dudrich, John	506	Johnston	04 Oct 1943	CA Wall of Missing
MSgt	6376260	Duke, Benjamin F.	68	Sullivan	27 Jan 1943	Interred in USA
SSgt	32313726	Dunajecz, Hugo Jr.	506	Whitlock	16 Aug 1943	SR E8-40
SSgt	33281841	Duncan, Joseph B.	506	Swanson	14 May 1943	Interred in USA
SSgt	12126659	Dunn, Edward K.	68	Steinke	07 Jul 1944	Interred in USA
2Lt	0-670043	Dunn, Robert F.	66	Hobson	01 Oct 1943	LO A- 16-50
SSgt	16021949	Durand, Frederick W.	67	Carpenter	01 Aug 1943	SR Wall of Missing
2 Lt	0-681359	Eberhardt, Bernard J. Jr.	506	Eberhardt	29 Jul 1944	CA Wall of Missing
1 Lt	0-729151	Ede, Hubert J.	68	Bohnisch	05 Feb 1944	Interred in USA
SSgt	31281654	Edgerton, Eugene C.	68	Bohnisch	05 Feb 1944	NO A- 16-5
2 Lt	0-734660	Edmonds, David	67	Scarborough	16 Mar 1944	CA D3-75
SSgt	18218286	Edmonson, Roger W.	68	Hovens	21 Apr 1944	Interred in USA
SSgt	32455476	Einarsen, Emil (314th Trp Car Gp)	66	Ketchum	13 Jun 1945	CA?
SSgt	31157299	Ela, DeForest L.	66	Curelli	16 Aug 1943	Interred in USA
TSgt	38132105	Elkin, Alton M.	66	Decker	20 Feb 1944	Interred in USA
Sgt	31378866	Elliott, Eugene L.	506	Chandler	24 Mar 1945	NE K7-14
SSgt	34038466	Ellis, John B. Jr. (314th Trp C Gp)	66	Ketchum	13 June 1945	CA?
2 Lt	0-676452	Ellis, John T.	67	Bateman	16 Aug 1943	NA Wall of Missing
TSgt	6245362	Emery, Albert W.	67	Cullen	15 Feb 1943	AR Wall of Missing
2 Lt	0-742572	Erickson, Charles R.	67	Bronstein	01 Oct 1943	Interred in USA
1 Lt	0-437436	Erwin, Roy B. Jr.	68	Erwin	03 Jan 1943	Interred in USA
2 Lt	0-?	Everhart, James H.	66	Frawley	18 May 1942	Interred in USA
SSgt	14055946	Falls, Charles E.	67	Warne	22 Mar 1943	Interred in USA
2 Lt	0-798775	Farm, Irwin	67	Johnson	18 Nov 1943	CA Wall of Missing
1 Lt	0-755660	Farrell, John A.	506	Scudday	27 Jun 1944	EP B31-8
Sgt	34927059	Faulkner, James L.	68	Hobbs	02 Dec 1944	Interred in USA
Sgt	32297428	Faust, David F.	67	Dobson	18 Nov 1943	CA Wall of Missing
TSgt	39466210	Feeney, Larry L.	67	Crandell	24 Mar 1945	NE H-17-27
Sgt	35162685	Feichter, Herschel H.	67	Dobson	18 Nov 1943	CA Wall of Missing
Sgt	42068546	Fidares, Nicholas J.	68	Bledsoe	28 Dec 1944	CA D-6-23
TSgt	33522224	Fields, Edwin D.	68	Konstand	28 Dec 1944	LO E-35-36
2 Lt	0-733298	Finder, Sheldon	506	Austin	16 Aug 1943	SR J-11-62
SSgt	33574486	Fink, Ivan W.	68	Dayball	18 Oct 1944	Interred in USA
2 Lt	0-803799	Fish, George E.	67	Fish	22 Feb 1944	CA Wall of Missing
1 Lt	0-713157	Fiskum, Lowell A.	506	Bentcliff	30 Oct 1944	Interred in USA
2 Lt	0-681534	Flaugh, Harold E.	67	Evans	22 Feb 1944	HC Wall of Missing
SSgt	12035273	Fleshman, Lewis J.	67	Price	08 Mar 1943	AR C33-18
1 Lt	0-727327	Flynn, Robert K.	68	Cramer	15 Feb 1943	Interred in USA
1 Lt	0-745068	Folsom, Glenn R.	66	Folsom	07 Mar 1944	Interred in USA
2 Lt	0-676584	Forest, Richard P.	67	Goodwin	14 Jan 1944	Interred in USA
2 Lt	0-695641	Forrest, George W.	67	Clarey	27 Apr 1944	Interred in USA
2 Lt	0-727979	Forrest, Robert E.	67	Price	08 Mar 1943	NO A8-16
1 Lt	0-437434	Fouts, Virgil R.	506	Fouts	22 Mar 1943	CA Wall of Missing
1 Lt	0-717050	Fowls, Ralph A.	67	Bakalo	18 Oct 1944	Interred in USA
SSgt	31309090	Francis, Robert J. (162nd Reinf)	66	Ketchum	13 Jun 1945	CA?
SSgt	12036607	Frangos, Theodore W.	68	Bledsoe	28 Dec 1944	CA Wall of Missing
1 Lt	0-789463	Franklin, Charles B.	67	Oliphant	15 Feb 1943	CA Wall of Missing
2 Lt	0-707579	Franson, Quinten A.	67	Tomer	25 May 1944	Interred in USA
2 Lt	0-?	Frawley, Herbert W.	66	Frawley	18 May 1942	Interred in USA
2 Lt	0-727328	Frazee, Winthrop T.	67	Long	16 Feb 1943	CA Wall of Missing
2 Lt	0-734663	Fredricks, Adrian E.	506	Johnston	04 Oct 1943	CA Wall of Missing
SSgt	39092033	Frye, Richard E.	67	Oliphant	15 Feb 1943	CA Wall of Missing
SSgt	35495933	Funkhouser, Eugene H.	506	Johnston	04 Oct 1943	CA Wall of Missing
SSgt	18194853	Fuxa, Ernest C.	68	Lehnhausen	18 Oct 1944	NE B-12-12
SSgt	12143699	Gaffney, William J.	68	Altemus	08 Apr 1944	NE Wall of Missing

Rank	ASN	Name	Sqdn.	Pilot	Dat of Loss	Cemetary Location
Sgt	31071580	Gallagher, Joseph W.	67	Dobson	18 Nov 1943	CA Wall of Missing
TSgt	18085234	Gandy, Guy E.	67	Warne	22 Mar 1943	NE Wall of Missing
Sgt	31388309	Garrett, James J.	68	Bledsoe	28 Dec 1944	Interred in USA
SSgt	35431909	Garrett, Kenneth 0.	66	Bridges	01 Oct 1943	AR C-30-16
Sgt	39294443	Garrett, Wayne D.	506	Eberhardt	29 Jul 1944	CA Wall of Missing
Sgt	38541707	Garza, Raul	506	Bentcliff	30 Oct 1944	AR D-11-36
Sgt	39043892	Gasperetti, Raymond	68	Dirtmer	24 Aug 1944	NE C-10-8
2 Lt	0-672946	Gatens, Frederick B.	66	Decker	20 Feb 1944	Interred in USA
2 Lt	0-663253	Gates, Jack A.	66	Trolese	26 Nov 1943	Interred in USA
Sgt	11054081	Gaziukeviczus, Albert	67	Brown	18 Nov 1943	CA C-0-41
1 Lt	0-704835	Gempel, Charles L.	506	Bentcliff	30 Oct 1944	AR D-13-40
Capt	0-727983	Gentry, Rowland M.	66	Gentry	01 Aug 1943	Interred in USA
TSgt	39389081	Gentry, William H.	67	Mitchell	18 Nov 1943	CA Wall of Missing
SSgt	33038923	Geriok, Michael	68	Cargile	27 Jan 1943	NE Wall of Missing
SSgt	39047565	Germolus, Irwin E.	67	Crandell	24 Mar 1945	Interred in USA
SSgt	19055445	Gibby, Gola G.	67	Smith	16 Aug 1943	Interred in USA
1 Lt	0-805903	Giffin, John S.	68	Bohnisch	05 Feb 1944	NO A-16-30
SSgt	34339959	Gilbert, Joseph D.	67	Dobson	18 Nov 1943	CA Wall of Missing
SSgt	15102189	Gilbert, Robert N.	68	Altemus	08 Apr 1944	NE L-5-13
SSgt	36275004	Gilles, Eldon J.	66	Ketchum	13 Jun 1945	CA E-0-56
SSgt	18110321	Gilligan, Eugene G.	66	Folsom	07 Mar 1944	CA C-4-5
1 Lt	0-885283	Girard, Louis V.	68	Houston	01 Aug 1943	FL Wall of Missing
SSgt	37197914	Glasscock, Kenneth J.	67	Johnson	18 Nov 1943	CA Wall of Missing
Sgt	13049367	Gleason, Robert J.	68	Bell	24 Feb 1944	Interred in USA
2 Lt	0-702411	Gleichenhaus, Seymour	506	Eberhardt	29 Jul 1944	CA Wall of Missing
SSgt	36196961	Glemboski, Stanley W.	506	Swanson	14 May 1943	NE Wall of Missing
SSgt	34265714	Goddard, Cecil D.	67	Oliphant	15 Feb 1943	CA Wall of Missing
1 Lt	0-671345	Goldman, Arthur	66	Talbott	15 Mar 1944	Interred in USA
SSgt	14048874	Goldman, Carl S.	66	Billings	16 Feb 1943	CA Wall of Missing
1 Lt	0-711390	Goo, William L.Y.	66	McKenna	06 Aug 1944	NE Wall of Missing
SSgt	38235476	Goode, Armel M.	67	Houle	18 Nov 1943	CA Wall of Missing
SSgt	33442228	Gooden, Ray C.	66	Spelts	21 Jan 1944	Interred in USA
TSgt	11042195	Goodfellow, George E.	67	Houle	18 Nov 1943	CA Wall of Missing
TSgt	11011586	Goodman, Earl E.	66	Gentry	01 Aug 1943	Interred in USA
1 Lt	0-794123	Goodnow, Edward W.	66	Spelts	21 Jan 1944	AR C-14-49
2 Lt	0-675337	Goodwin, Henry C. Jr.	67	Goodwin	14 Jan 1945	Interred in USA
SSgt	13066720	Goolsby, Ray K.	66	Richardson	08 Apr 1944	Interred in USA
SSgt	13089150	Gordon, Rhodes C.	68	Jones	16 Dec 1943	Interred in USA
SSgt	14069419	Gosline, Roy E.	67	Price	08 Mar 1943	Interred in USA
Sgt	12055796	Gotts, Howard F.	66	Winger	01 Aug 1943	FL Wall of Missing
SSgt	20641515	Grabowski, Barney J.	67	Phillips	14 May 1943	Interred in USA
Sgt	19005806	Gradwohl, Jacob	66	Winger	01 Aug 1943	Interred in USA
TSgt	37428100	Graff, Andrew C.	506	Money	11 Apr 1944	AR B36-54
TSgt	39381894	Graham, Sidney W.	67	Roach	14 May 1943	Interred in USA
2 Lt	0-727334	Grant, Reginald D.	68	O'Brien	27 Jan 1943	Interred in USA
SSgt	16048131	Greattinger, Gordon J.	67	Griffin	17 Jul 1943	Interred in USA
SSgt	35462147	Green, Donald	506	Johnston	04 Oct 1943	CA Wall of Missing
2 Lt	0-700447	Green, William F.	67	Green	29 Jul 1944	CA Wall of Missing
1 Lt	0-817662	Greno, Paul J.	66	McKenna	06 Aug 1944	NE Wall of Missing
SSgt	37120507	Grett, Gerald L.	67	Smith	16 Aug 1943	Interred in USA
Capt	0-727211	Griffin, Curtis S.	67	Griffin	17 Jul 1943	SR Wall of Missing
2 Lt	0-828160	Griffith, Warren W.	68	Bledsoe	28 Dec 1944	Interred in USA
1 Lt	0-885961	Grimes, George G.	67	O'Neill	11 Dec 1943	NE Wall of Missing
TSgt	36241507	Grinde, John H.	66	Curelli	16 Aug 1943	Interred in USA
SSgt	16034619	Gritsonis, Nickolas C.	67	Warne	22 Mar 1943	AR C4-23
SSgt	33566080	Grogg, Emil L.	506	Jacobs	08 Aug 1944	Interred in USA
SSgt	39167088	Gross, Gale H.	506	Eberhardt	29 Jul 1944	CA F-1-71
2 Lt	0-727336	Gross, Morton P.	67	Price	08 Mar 1943	NO B17-43
SSgt	32501788	Grushkevich, Aron	67	Houle	18 Nov 1943	CA Wall of Missing
Sgt	14195404	Gunter, Noah	68	Lehnhausen	18 Oct 1944	Interred in USA
Sgt	18081540	Haaf, Howard S.	506	With 389th BG	27 Aug 1943	NO Wall of Missing
2 Lt	0-531342	Hacker, William E.	66	Almlie	13 Nov 1943	NE Wall of Missing
Sgt	39393257	Hagmann, Paul A.	67	O'Neill	11 Dec 1943	AR B44-55
SSgt	18157469	Hall, Clifton C.	68	Peterson	02 Jul 1943	Interred in USA
SSgt	14044753	Hall, Franklin P.	66	Spelts	21 Jan 1944	AR Wall of Missing
SSgt	11114148	Hall, Kenneth E.	68	Bohnisch	05 Feb 1944	Interred in USA
TSgt	35323302	Hall, Kenneth H.	66	Spelts	21 Jan 1944	NO A9-17
SSgt	12046305	Hallisey, John H. (93rd BG)	66	Ketchum	13 Jun 1945	Interred in USA
Sgt	07000408	Hammond, Charles P.	67	Wame	22 Mar 1943	AR C-16-10
Sgt	14161472	Hammontree, James A.	68	Bell	24 Feb 1944	Interred in USA
Sgt	32254108	Hancock, Earl W.	66	Ground Crew	19 Apr 1943	CA F5-48
2 Lt	0-727337	Hannan, William J.	66	Adams	26 Feb 1943	AR B33-8
2 Lt	0-671429	Hansen, James E.	67	Mitchell	18 Nov 1943	CA Wall of Missing
SSgt	32509732	Hantober, Manuel	67	Thom	03 Feb 1944	Interred in USA

Rank	ASN	Name	Sqdn.	Pilot	Dat of Loss	Cemetary Location
2 Lt	0-746482	Hardwick, Robert E.	67	Mitchell	18 Nov 1943	CA Wall of Missing
1 Lt	0-799767	Harleman, Richard E.	66	Harleman	27 Mar 1944	CA Wall of Missing
2 Lt	0-556125	Hannon, Howard K.	506	Jacobs	08 Aug 1944	Interred in USA
SSgt	12153113	Hastings, Alexander W. (314th TCG)	66	Ketchum	13 Jun 1945	Interred in USA
Sgt	39120898	Hawkes, Hazen E.	66	Folsom	07 Mar 1944	Interred in USA
SSgt	35610332	Haynam, Richard D.	68	Lehnhausen	18 Oct 1944	LX 17-10
Sgt	34572318	Haynes, Wiley W. Jr.	68	Bell	24 Feb 1944	AR B21-9
SSgt	17058569	Heller, Clayton E.	68	Shannon	16 Aug 1943	Interred in USA
Sgt	39013517	Helphrey, Aaron L.	67	Dobson	18 Nov 1943	CA Wall of Missing
1 Lt	0-665686	Henderson, Charlie P. Jr.	67	Henderson	01 Oct 1943	Interred in USA
2 Lt	0-817211	Henderson, Gordon W.	506	Howe	21 Jun 1944	NE Wall of Missing
Sgt	?	Hepler, Lewis J.	66	Frawley	18 May 1942	Interred in USA
2 Lt	0-817213	Herman, Bernard L.	67	Bakalo	18 Oct 1944	Interred in USA
2 Lt	0-670542	Hersh, George P.	68	Shannon	16 Aug 1943	Interred in USA
TSgt	15095162	Hess, William H.	67	Mitchell	18 Nov 1943	CA Wall of Missing
SSgt	18076405	Hester, Milton Jr.	67	Mitchell	18 Nov 1943	CA Wall of Missing
Sgt	35809558	Hibbs, Leo R.	506	Still	07 Oct 1944	NE F-17-16
Sgt	14094125	Higgins, Hartwell J.	68	Hovens	21 Apr 1944	Interred in USA
SSgt	11088586	Hill, Herbert S. Jr.	506	Money	11 Apr 1944	Interred in USA
Sgt	34117846	Hilley, James A.	67	Cullen	15 Feb 1943	AR C31-4
1 Lt	0-692312	Hine, Thomas L.	506	Westcott	29 Jun 1944	AR D2-52
2 Lt	0-752855	Hinkle, Glenn E.	67	Clarey	27 Apr 1944	Interred in USA
TSgt	17129255	Hites, Harold B.	66	Spelts	21 Jan 1944	Interred in USA
SSgt	34117537	Hobbs, Herbert J. Jr.	67	Roach	14 May 1943	Interred in USA
2Lt	0-828430	Hobbs, John C.	68	Hobbs	02 Dec 1944	Interred in USA
SSgt	13173525	Hoffman, Leo J. Jr.	68	Anderson	21 Jul 1944	Interred in USA
SSgt	19176656	Hoffman, Walter G. Jr.	68	Hovey	13 Jan 1944	CA C5-79
TSgt	37009698	Hogan, Harry C.	68	Diehl	17 May 1943	CA Wall of Missing
TSgt	13110122	Holabaugh, John W.	67	Bakalo	18 Oct 1944	Interred in USA
TSgt	37299913	Holland, Earl M.	67	Johnson	18 Nov 1943	CA Wall of Missing
1 Lt	0-789472	Hook, Robert D.	66	McCoy	20 Feb 1943	CA D5-14
SSgt	15339517	Houchens, George B. Jr.	68	Hovens	21 Apr 1944	Interred in USA
1 Lt	0-526201	Houle, Joseph L.	67	Houle	18 Nov 1943	CA Wall of Missing
Capt	0-727991	Houston, Rowland B.	68	Houston	01 Aug 1943	Interred in USA
2 Lt	0-676805	Hovey, Glenn C.	68	Hovey	13 Jan 1944	Interred in USA
1 Lt	0-727992	Howell, Malcolm C.	68	Howell	14 May 1943	AR B37-28
1 Lt	0-800356	Howington, Hartwell R.	68	Howington	21 Jan 1944	Interred in USA
SSgt	19144166	Howley, Robert M.	67	Scarborough	16 Mar 1944	Interred in USA
1 Lt	0-864127	Howser, Earl P.	68	Corwine	28 Jan 1945	Interred in USA
Sgt	37120505	Hubbard, Gaylord F.	67	Phillips	14 May 1943	Interred in USA
SSgt	32468888	Hughes, John R.	66	Curelli	16 Aug 1943	SR J13-57
2 Lt	0-783265	Hummer, William M.	67	Crandell	24 Mar 1945	NE C15-4
SSgt	35288918	Hurst, Clifford C. Jr.	66	Hart	13 Nov 1943	Interred in USA
1 Lt	0-436139	Hutchinson, Amos	66	Billings	16 Feb 1943	Interred in USA
1 Lt	0-666673	Hybarger, Tom P.	68	Steinke	07 Jul 1944	Interred in USA
Sgt	17015167	Idlet, Philip D.	506	Johnston	04 Oct 1943	NE Wall of Missing
SSgt	18025712	Iorgov, George W.	66	Almlie	13 Nov 1943	NE B1-3
SSgt	37071188	Irwin, John F.	67	Carpenter	01 Oct 1943	Interred in USA
2 Lt	0-700615	Jacobs, Myron G.	506	Jacobs	08 Aug 1944	Interred in USA
2 Lt	0-683457	Jarrett, Daniel D.	67	Johnson	18 Nov 1943	CA Wall of Missing
2 Lt	0-681994	Jeffs, Robert H.	67	Fish	22 Feb 1944	CA Wall of Missing
Sgt	38104143	Jefson, Harold E.	66	Billings	16 Feb 1943	CA Wall of Missing
SSgt	38267506	Jessen, Max M.	66	Zweig	11 Jul 1944	NO J-17-35
TSgt	17023590	Jester, Donald E.	67	Price	08 Mar 1943	AR C-36-14
SSgt	39236097	John, Glenn G.	506	Larson	13 Feb 1944	Interred in USA
1 Lt	0-799569	Johnson, Earl T.	67	Johnson	18 Nov 1943	CA Wall of Missing
F/O	T-1010	Johnson, Farmer A. Jr.	67	Houle	18 Nov 1943	CA Wall of Missing
1 Lt	0-681431	Johnson, Guy W.	506	Johnson	08 Apr 1944	AR A-36-2
1 Lt	0-749695	Johnson, Melvin J.	66	Harleman	27 Mar 1944	RH Wall of Missing
SSgt	18021146	Johnston, David W. Jr.	66	McCoy	20 Feb 1943	CA D-7-44
2 Lt	0-675349	Johnston, Frederick V.	506	Johnston	04 Oct 1943	CA Wall of Missing
2 Lt	0-738559	Johnston, William P.	506	Rawson	20 Feb 1944	NE H-12-9
SSgt	34258309	Jones, Linwood F.	66	Adams	26 Feb 1943	Interred in USA
TSgt	37049716	Jones, Norman H.	67	Warne	22 Mar 1943	Interred in USA
1 Lt	0-674587	Jones, Parke H. Jr.	68	Jones	16 Dec 1943	CA B7-3
SSgt	36726983	Jones, Philip G.	68	Steinke	07 Jul 1944	Interred in USA
Sgt	39680958	Jones, Shirley A.	506	Jacobs	08 Aug 1944	Interred in USA
2 Lt	0-679073	Jorgensen, Roy G.	66	Decker	20 Feb 1944	Interred in USA
2 Lt	0-727999	Kaitala, Henry B.	68	Du Bard	06 Dec 1942	AR Wall of Missing
SSgt	16051552	Kallal, Lawrence B.	66	Hobson	01 Oct 1943	LO E9-8
1 Lt	0-683831	Kasten, Richard J.	68	Howington	21 Jan 1944	NO Wall of Missing
SSgt	16144626	Katz, Ervin	67	Tomer	25 May 1944	Interred in USA
1 Lt	0-727349	Keilman, Paul H.	68	Cargile	27 Jan 1943	NE Wall of Missing
SSgt	13004024	Kempowicz, John J. Jr.	506	Allen	21 Jul 1944	Interred in USA

Rank	ASN	Name	Sqdn.	Pilot	Dat of Loss	Cemetary Location
2 Lt	0-766282	Kenner, James D. Jr.	67	Green	29 Jul 1944	Interred in USA
TSgt	38102848	Kennon, Daniel	67	O'Neill	11 Dec 1943	Interred in USA
1 Lt	0-661636	Kennon, Wyatt S.	67	Roach	14 May 1943	AR B20-2
1 Lt	0-720263	Ketchum, Jack B.	66	Ketchum	13 Jun 1945	Interred in USA
2 Lt	0-681117	King, James L.	68	Bell	24 Feb 1944	Interred in USA
SSgt	31166867	Kirkey, Vernon O.	68	Corwine	28 Jan 1945	Interred in USA
Sgt	32836806	Kiser, Willard	68	Bledsoe	28 Dec 1944	Interred in USA
SSgt	39303276	Klingler, Roy L.	67	Brown	14 May 1943	CA Wall of Missing
SSgt	37276328	Klose, Kenneth A.	506	Fouts	22 Mar 1943	NE Wall of Missing
SSgt	15019186	Koehler, Harold F.	68	Sweigart	29 Apr 1944	AR B40-56
Capt	0-794428	Konstand, Gus	68	Konstand	28 Dec 1944	LO B20-23
SSgt	07024614	Kosch, Emil M.	506	Whitlock	16 Aug 1943	Interred in USA
TSgt	33338303	Krauss, Charles E.	66	Trolese	26 Nov 1943	Interred in USA
Sgt	32934067	Kraynik, Daniel J.	68	Hobbs	02 Dec 1944	Interred in USA
TSgt	110 10544	Kreissig, Oscar (66th Sqdn)	67	Blaine	08 Iviar 1943	NO D-21-34
TSgt	37116421	Kretzer, Harold	66	Winaer	01 Aug 1943	CA Wall of Missing
Sgt	16067220	Krutsch, Henry	68	Norsen	03 Feb 1943	Interred in USA
TSgt	16004932	Kushinski, Edward W.	68	Bonnet	11 Jul 1944	CA Wall of Missing
Capt	0-727351	La Fleur, Robert A.	68	Garrett	02 Jul 1943	NA Wall of Missing
Sgt	18202589	Lambert, Leonard P. Jr.	68	Hovens	21 Apr 1944	CA C-5-17
1 Lt	0-677785	Landahl, Howard K.	506	Landahl	29 Jun 1944	AR B-28-11
SSgt	15104217	Landreth, Calvin F.	67	Roach	14 May 1943	AR D-38-20
Sgt	31143933	Landry, Henry C.	67	Green	29 Jul 1944	Interred in USA
2 Lt	0-744855	Larsen, George N. (67th Sqdn)	506	Johnston	04 Oct 1943	CA Wall of Missing
SSgt	19108009	Larson. John H.	66	Miller	22 Dec 1943	Interred in USA
2 Lt	0-674210	Latimer, Byron H.	67	Dobson	18 Nov 1943	CA Wall of Missing
SSgt	17071305	Laucamp, Robert L.	67	Pinder	29 Jan 1944	Interred in USA
SSgt	36124604	Laurence, Ralph C.	67	Long	16 Feb 1943	CA Wall of Missing
Sgt	34198246	Lawley, Woodrow	67	Oliphant	15 Feb 1943	CA Wall of Missing
SSgt	33244873	Lawyer, Donald A.	66	Harleman	27 Mar 1944	RH Wall of Missing
1 Lt	0-764355	Lehnhausen, Edward C.	68	Lehnliausen	18 Oct 1944	LX B-17-11
Sgt	37068883	Leisinger, William L. Jr.	66	Gentry	0 1 Aug 1943	AR C-12-23
2 Lt	0-709412	Lentz, Herbert B.	67	Green	29 Jul 1944	CA Wall of Missing
Sgt	17047877	Lester, Julian V.	67	O'Neill	11 Dec 1943	Interred in USA
SSgt	19186283	Le Vake, John W.	68	Sweigert	29 Apr 1944	Interred in USA
TSgt	37224192	Leverich, William F.	68	Bohnisch	05 Feb 1944	NO B10-11
SSgt	33185548	Lewis, Carl R.	67	Roach	14 May 1943	Interred in USA
SSgt	33577302	Lewis, James E. Jr.	67	Goodwin	14 Jan 1944	Interred in USA
2 Lt	0-807917	Liddell, James M.	66	Decker	20 Feb 1944	Interred in USA
TSgt	38047888	Light, Edwin C.	66	Gentry	01 Aug 1943	Interred in USA
Sgt	17035867	Lilley, Robert F.	68	Du Bard	06 Dec 1942	AR Wall of Missing
SSgt	36012770	Lindau, Edward W.	506	Fouts	22 Mar 1943	NE Wall of Missing
2 Lt	0-662346	Lippert, Rexford W.	66	McPhillamey	26 Feb 1943	Interred in USA
TSgt	16041884	Littell, Clyde	67	Oliphant	15 Feb 1943	AR Wall of Missing
1 Lt	0-1996114	Loflin, William E.	68	Konstand	28 Dec 1944	LO E34-36
Sgt	35564011	Logan, Donald J.	67	Mayes	08 Apr 1944	Interred in USA
1 Lt	0-438007	Long, J.B.	67	Long	16 Feb 1943	CA Wall of Missing
SSgt	37722472	Lopez, Charles R.	67	Bakalo	18 Oct 1944	Interred in USA
TSgt	18135755	Lopez, Victor A.	68	Altemus	08 Apr 1944	NE Wall of Missing
F/O	T-126827	Lough, Robert L.	68	Corwine	28 Jan 1945	AR D16-13
SSgt	37138610	Lund, Hilmer G.	66	Key	20 Dec 1942	Interred in USA
SSgt	35372611	Lundstrom, John V.	66	Almlic	13 Nov 1943	NE A8-30
1 Lt	0-789480	Lunenfeld, Raymond C.	68	Sullivan	27 Jan 1943	Interred in USA
Sgt	39328109	Lytle, Leslie L.	67	Clarey	27 Apr 1944	NO B-5-17
Major	0-22367	MacDonald, Donald W.	67	Cullen	15 Feb 1943	Interred in USA
SSgt	17151925	Mace, Glenn E. Jr.	68	Corwine	28 Jan 1945	Interred in USA
1 Lt	0-662351	Mackev, John L.	67	Cullen	15 Feb 1943	NO D-22-33
Sgt	11041425	Maiko, Andrew	66	Billings	16 Feb 1943	CA Wall of Missing
SSgt	15062923	Malone, Hugh J.	66	Scrivner	01 Aug 1943	Interred in USA
SSgt	34335159	Maloy, Aubrey J.	506	Bolin	02 Feb 1944	Interred in USA
2 Lt	0-750204	Maneval, Weldon ft.	08	Starring	21 Jan 19414	Interred in USA
SSgt	18000247	Mansfield, Joe	67	Bronstein	01 Oct 1943	FL Wall of Missing
2 Lt	0-749680	Marcouiller, Gordon L.	66	Trolese	26 Nov 1943	AR D13-7
SSgt	32536008	Markus, Edward R.	66	Trolese	26 Nov 1943	AR A37-15
SSgt	18029077	Marquez, Gabriel A.	67	Warne	22 Mar 1943	Interred in USA
SSgt	13038809	Maruszewski, Frank A.	67	Smith	16 Aug 1943	Interred in USA
TSgt	38511707	Maschmeyer, Gene E.	506	Bentcliff	30 Oct 1944	Interred in USA
SSgt	32635601	Masci, Peter J. Jr.	67	Fish	22 Feb 1944	CA Wall of Missing
1 Lt	0-735418	Mathisen, Gary M.	08	Mathisen	21 Jan 1944	Interred in USA
2 Lt	0-685340	Mauk, Charles N.	66	Fols(rn	07 Mai 1944	CA A-1-5
SSgt	15102491	May, Gordon L.	67	Fish	22 Feb J944	CA Wall of Missing
2 Lt	0-726923	Mayen, Thomas C.	67	Blaine	08 Mar 1943	Interred in USA
2 Lt	0-742181	Mayes, Robert A.	67	Mayes	08 Apr 1944	Interred in USA
1 Lt	0-800011	Maynard, George H.	66	Maynard	29 Jan 1944	Interred in USA

Rank	ASN	Name	Sqdn.	Pilot	Dat of Loss	Cemetary Location
Capt	0-442977	Mazure, Louis A.	66	Mazure	05 Jun 1944	AR Wall of Missing
Sgt	11017929	McArthur, Earl R.	67	Green	29 Jul 1944	CA Wall of Missing
SSgt	13023200	McArtor, John L.	66	Billings	16 Feb 1943	CA Wall of Missing
SSgt	34665208	McBryde, William H.	506	Bayless	02 Dec 1944	Interred in USA
SSgt	36303257	McCabe, Ernest G.	67	Smith	16 Aug 1943	Interred in USA
SSgt	13038391	McCandless, Donald G.	68	Bonnet	11 Jul 1944	AR Wall of Missing
2 Lt	0-728009	McCloud, Merwin K.	66	Billings	16 Feb 1943	CA Wall of Missing
Capt	0-418136	McCoy, Bill	66	McCoy	20 Feb 1943	Interred in USA
SSgt	12165291	McCoy, Richard J.	506	Rawson	20 Feb 1944	NE L-14-16
1 Lt	0-1102377	McCracken, John Jr.	66	Rogers	04 Dec 1944	LO A11-39
SSgt	17056134	McCrady, Leo V. Jr.	68	Jansen	14 May 1943	CA E4-91
2 Lt	0-719113	McDaris, Frederick F.	506	Jacobs	08 Aug 1944	Interred in USA
1 Lt	0-748729	McGeary, Meredyth F.	506	Albert	18 Mar 1944	Interred in USA
SSgt	16039337	McGinnis, Donald C.	67	Long	16 Feb 1943	CA Wall of Missing
2 Lt	0-817721	McGuire, Thomas J.	506	McGuire	12 Aug 1944	Interred in USA
Pvt	?	McJunkins, Rudolph	66	Frawley	18 May 1942	Interred in USA
1 Lt	0-693866	McKenna, James P.	66	McKenna	06 Aug 1944	Interred in USA
SSgt	31155162	McKenna, Raymond H.	68	Barry	08 Apr 1944	Interred in USA
SSgt	18061219	McKinsey, Thomas E.	67	Cullen	15 Feb 1943	AR Wall of Missing
1 Lt	0-728012	McLeod, Stanley W.	66	Adams	26 Feb 1943	AR B-33-10
SSgt	11047450	McMackin, Charles G.	68	Houston	01 Aug 1943	FL Wall of Missing
SSgt	34442753	McWhorter, Lamer	68	Sweigart	29 Apr 1944	AR B-36-56
Sgt	31020279	Mears, William G.	68	Du Bard	06 Dec 1942	AR Wall of Missing
TSgt	37282895	Mears, William J.	506	Swanson	14 May 1943	Interred in USA
SSgt	16070123	Mercer, George W.	66	Bridges	01 Oct 1943	LO G6-1
SSgt	10601009	Merrigan, John	68	Hughes	18 Nov 1943	CA B-5-58
SSgt	33355549	Meskinis, Joseph M.	67	Wahler	08 Apr 1944	CA C-6-55
SSgt	35305177	Mickey, James D.	68	Altemus	08 Apr 1944	Interred in USA
Sgt	18037185	Mickey, Marvin R.	66	Scrivner	01 Aug 1943	Interred in USA
SSgt	31158071	Milillo, Antonio	68	Bell	24 Feb 1944	AR A-24-16
2 Lt	0-818724	Miller, Arthur L.	66	Richardson	08 Apr 1944	Interred in USA
FIO	T-60679	Miller, Kent F.	66	Miller	22 Dec 1943	Interred in USA
SSgt	37133211	Millhousen, George R.	67	Brown	14 May 1943	NE Wall of Missing
2 Lt	0-676093	Mills, John D.	67	Hager	16 Aug 1943	Interred in USA
SSgt	13092560	Millward, Warren F.	66	Hobson	01 Oct 1943	Interred in USA
TSgt	17037191	Mindelsohn, Joseph	67	Goodwin	14 Jan 1944	NO B-7-42
Capt	0-728013	Mitchell, Edward R. (68 Sqdn?)	67	Mitchell	18 Nov 1943	CA Wall of Missing
2 Lt	0-734485	Monahan, Eugene R.	68	Peterson	02 Jul 1943	Interred in USA
SSgt	39841223	Monteleone, Edward G.	506	Albert	18 Mar 1944	LO K15-29
1 Lt	0-727249	Moore, Kenneth H.	68	Cargile	27 Jan 1943	NE Wall of Missing
TSgt	34407173	Moore, Robert L.	506	Bayless	02 Dec 1944	Interred in USA
1 Lt	0-679201	Moriarty, Clifford F.	66	Talbott	15 Mar 1944	Interred in USA
SSgt	20108691	Morin, Joseph E.	68	Bohnisch	05 Feb 1944	NO E20-27
SSgt	17066897	Morse, Kenneth R.	66	McPhillarney	26 Feb 1943	Interred in USA
2 Lt	0-768169	Mortensen, Douglas W.	67	Green	29 Jul 1944	CA E3-93
1 Lt	0-793744	Moss, Benjamin M.	66	Gentry	01 Aug 1943	Interred in USA
SSgt	18188771	Muirhead, Edgar P.	67	Scarborough	16 Mar 1944	Interred in USA
Sgt	31104988	Murach, Stanley Jr.	506	Sprinkle	08 Apr 1944	AR A-31-19
2 Lt	0-801142	Murphy, William T.	67	Houle	18 Nov 1943	CA Wall of Missing
1 Lt	0-677848	Musgrave, Forest M.	66	Musgrave	08 May 1944	CA F-2-13
2 Lt	0-801384	Must, John A.	67	Stamos	04 Oct 1943	CA Wall of Missing
SSgt	18166363	Myers, Billie B.	67	Mitchell	18 Nov 1943	CA Wall of Missing
SSgt	18170066	Myers, Rudy S. Jr.	68	Cary	11 Feb 1944	Interred in USA
SSgt	37263649	Naber, Julius V.	68	Sweigart	29 Apr 1944	AR B24-13
Sgt	15324363	Nalipa, Stanley G.	68	Weaver	07 Jul 1944	AR A37-1
SSgt	37438712	Nappier, Vernon D.	66	Richardson	08 Apr 1944	Interred in USA
SSgt	36851997	Nash, Travis E.	506	Brown	05 Apr 1945	NE F21-19
SSgt	38558214	Natkin, Albert L.	66	Ketchum	13 Jun 1945	CA G4-160
2 Lt	0-730577	Navas, Frank	506	Fouts	22 Mar 1943	NE Wall of Missing
SSgt	35052331	Navish, Kenneth C.	67	Tomer	24 May 1944	Interred in USA
Sgt	31360823	Nedder, Sarkice T.	506	Chandler	24 Mar 1945	Interred in USA
SSgt	36378877	Nelson, Arthur L.	68	Hovey	13 Jan 1944	CA C3-79
2 Lt	0-728017	Nelson, Duane E.	68	Sullivan	27 Jan 1943	NE F-16-26
2 Lt	0-678381	Nesbit, Alden C.	67	Scarborough	16 Mar 1944	Interred in USA
2 Lt	0-755738	Neutze, Robert E. Jr.	506	Sprinkle	08 Apr 1944	Interred in USA
Sgt	31254221	Newton, Roger J.	67	Mayes	08 Apr 1944	Interred in USA
1 Lt	0-676493	Nielson, Thomas W.	66	Maynard	29 Jan 1944	Interred in USA
SSgt	35307431	Niznok, Steve	68	Peterson	02 Jul 1943	Interred in USA
Sgt	35544549	Nome, Albert A.	68	Sweigart	29 Apr 1944	AR A-32-32
TSgt	16020714	Nordquist, Richard K.	506	Fouts	22 Mar 1943	CA Wall of Missing
TSgt	14060975	Nored, George L.	67	Blaine	08 Mar 1943	AR Wall of Missing
1 Lt	0-747876	Norquist, John E.	66	Maynard	29 Jan 1944	Interred in USA
TSgt	35326545	Nowak, Andrew B.	66	Decker	20 Feb 1944	Interred in USA
F/O	T-65165	O'Donnell, Hugh X.	506	Chandler	24 Mar 1945	Interred in USA

Rank	*ASN*	*Name*	*Sqdn.*	*Pilot*	*Dat of Loss*	*Cemetary Location*
SSgt	12158116	O'Donnell, Louis J.	66	Maynard	29 Jan 1944	Interred in USA
SSgt	32436174	O'Hara, Henry H.	67	Mitchell	18 Nov 1943	CA Wall of Missing
SSgt	13104794	O'Neal, Charles E.	67	Mayes	08 Apr 1944	Interred in USA
1 Lt	0-798225	O'Neill, Richard F.	67	O'Neill	11 Dec 1943	AR A25-15
1 Lt	0-740893	Oakley, Warren W.	66	Oakley	22 Dec 1943	Interred in USA
TSgt	32736724	Ogilvie, Robert B. Jr.	67	Crandell	24 Mar 1945	Interred in USA
TSgt	13135813	Ohler, Bernard A.	68	Bohnisch	05 Feb 1944	Interred in USA
1 Lt	0-397270	Oliphant, Rufus A. Jr.	67	Oliphant	15 Feb 1943	CA Wall of Missing
1 Lt	0-819153	Oliver, George H. Jr.	68	Konstand	2R Dec 1944	L D15-14
1 Lt	0-730588	Olson, Stanley F.	506	Olson	01 Oct 1943	FL Wall of Missing
2 Lt	0-698138	Orbach, Norris F.	66	Richardson	08 Apr 1944	Interred in USA
2 Lt	0-678132	Osburn, Richard R.	67	Mitchell	18 Nov 1943	CA Wall of Missing
SSgt	06569189	Ostenson, Jack N.	68	Mathisen	21 Jan 1944	NO Wall of Missing
SSgt	36236878	Ottman, Harry L.	68	Sullivan	27 Jan 1943	Interred in USA
1 Lt	0-730291	Palmer, Frederick H.	66	Winger	01 Aug 1943	Interred in USA
TSgt	31129150	Palys, Joseph E.	67	Goodwin	14 Jan 1944	Interred in USA
2 Lt	0-743260	Papadopulos, John G.	66	Curelli	16 Aug 1943	Interred in USA
1 Lt	0-699237	Parker, George J.	68	Konstand	28 Dec 1944	LO D33-34
SSgt	11045788	Parker, Stephen E. Jr.	67	Long	16 Feb 1943	CA Wall of Missing
Sgt	33586746	Parker, Victor	506	Eberhardt	29 Jul 1944	CA Wall of Missing
SSgt	39537767	Passantino, Thomas J. Jr.	506	Bayless	02 Dec 1944	Interred in USA
2 Lt	0-678758	Passavant, Frank A.	66	Miller	22 Dec 1943	Interred in USA
TSgt	13151627	Patterson, Russell W.	66	Maynard	29 Jan 1944	Interred in USA
SSgt	12155754	Paxton, William A. Jr.	67	Pinder	29 Jan 1944	AR A-12-10
1 Lt	0-689636	Pedersen, Nels W.	506	Landahl	29 Jun 1944	LO C10-79
TSgt	35497759	Permar, Everett E.	66	Almlie	13 Nov 1943	NE Wall of Missing
Sgt	14130256	Pest, David	506	Johnston	04 Oct 1943	NE Wall of Missing
2 Lt	0-806899	Peterson, Clifford C.	68	Hovey	13 Jan 1944	Interred in USA
SSgt	36609092	Peterson, Ray 0.	67	Houle	18 Nov 1943	CA Wall of Missing
1 Lt	0-421662	Peterson, Robert E.	68	Peterson	02 Jul 1943	Interred in USA
TSgt	34268115.	Pharis, Charles W.	68	Peterson	02 Jul 1943	Interred in USA
2 Lt	0-747138	Phelps, John E.	67	Goodwin	14 Jan 1944	Interred in USA
SSgt	32612831	Phillips, Allen W.	67	Clarey	27 Apr 1944	AR C14-32
Capt	0-421129	Phillips, Chester L. Jr.	67	Phillips	14 May 1943	AR D12-2
SSgt	18063461	Phillips, Edward W.	67	Phillips	14 May 1943	AR A35-28
Sgt	19011888	Phillips, Elvin L.	66	Winger	01 Aug 1943	CA Wall of Missing
1 Lt	0-662366	Phillips, Philip P.	66	Scrivner	01 Aug 1943	Interred in USA
F/O	T-125025	Phillips, Robert L.	68	Dayball	18 Oct 1944	HC E12-22
SSgt	39117546	Pierson, Glen C.	68	Sullivan	27 Jan 1943	Interred in USA
SSgt	35316138	Pilch, Stanley Jr.	66	Miller	22 Dec 1943	Interred in USA
2 Lt	0-735107	Pimentel, Robert E.	67	Hager	16 Aug 1943	Interred in USA
2 Lt	0-688396	Plaszcykowski, Edward M.	67	Mayes	08 Apr 1944	Interred in USA
SSgt	11052136	Playford, Joseph E.	68	Mathisen	21 Jan 1944	NO B10-3
1 Lt	0-720346	Podojil, Robert J.	66	Podojil	19 Mar 1945	Interred in USA
Sgt	15097510	Pohlmeyer, Robert L.	66	Richardson	08 Apr 1944	AR C5-47
Sgt	35672481	Pollmann, Edward C.	68	Hovey	13 Jan 1944	CA F3-17
1 Lt	0-789500	Poole, William A.	68	Cramer	15 Feb 1943	Interred in USA
SSgt	34366534	Poole, Elmer H.	67	Houle	18 Nov 1943	CA Wall of Missing
TSgt	11042360	Porter, Donald C.	66	Maynard	29 Jan 1944	Interred in USA
SSgt	37212157	Porter, James M.	67	Henderson	01 Oct 1943	Interred in USA
TSgt	16109394	Post, Herbert F.	67	Bateman	16 Aug 1943	NA Wall of Missing
2 Lt	0-736345	Potter, Joseph H. Jr.	67	Griffin	17 Jul 1943	SR H8-13
SSgt	33675477	Povich, George	68	Konstand	28 Dec 1944	LO B31-26
Sgt	20733281	Pownall, Otis H.	66	Richardson	08 Apr 1944	AR B43-20
SSgt	33289063	Prekopie, Michael L.	67	Bronstein	01 Oct 1943	Interred in USA
Capt	0-398584	Price, Clyde E.	67	Price	08 Mar 1943	AR C33-2
TSgt	12034269	Price, George B.	67	Phillips	14 May 1943	NE Wall of Missing
2 Lt	0-700389	Prince, Bertis R.	67	Tomer	25 May 1944	Interred in USA
1 Lt	0-793166	Propst, Halbert W.	67	Bateman	16 Aug 1943	NA Wall of Missing
2 Lt	0-686492	Purdue, Paul F.	66	Folsom	07 Mar 1944	Interred in USA
SSgt	18218358	Rabb, Harold M.	68	Steinke	07 Jul 1944	AR A28-4
SSgt	35317454	Radu, Charles	506	Sprinkle	08 Apr 1944	AR D23-14
SSgt	35338599	Railing, Alton S.	66	Trolese	26 Nov 1943	Interred in USA
SSgt	35255507	Ramsey, Ivan W.	67	Henderson	01 Oct 1943	FL Wall of Missing
SSgt	31269979	Raniello, John V.	506	Eberhardt	29 Jul 1944	CA Wall of Missing
TSgt	17042564	Raspotnik, Leonard L. (506th)	66	Lasco	01 Aug 1943	Interred in USA
1 Lt	0-661659	Rawls, Malcolm	67	Warne	22 Mar 1943	AR A-39-35
SSgt	34280331	Ray, Thomas C.	66	Trolese	26 Nov 1943	AR D- 18-20
SSgt	34194483	Reasons, John W.	67	Johnson	18 Nov 1943	CA Wall of Missing
SSgt	17033225	Reedy, Wilbur R.	66	Spelts	21 Jan 1944	NO B-11-17
SSgt	13046428	Reeves, Clarence D.	68	Sobotka	21 Jan 1944	NO A-14-42
1 Lt	0-755597	Reeves, Robert H.	506	Westcott	29 Jun 1944	Interred in USA
TSgt	06860263	Reichenbach, Theodore H.	66	Podojil	19 Mar 1945	NE N-21-3
1 Lt	0-747318	Rhodes, Carl E.	67	Clarey	27 Apr 1944	NO B-1-25

Rank	ASN	Name	Sqdn.	Pilot	Dat of Loss	Cemetary Location
2 Lt	0-807052	Rhodes, Lewis W.	68	Starring	21 Jan 1944	CA Wall of Missing
TSgt	39276079	Rich, Fred A.	68	Steinke	07 Jul 1944	AR D-37-16
1 Lt	0-752904	Richardson, Paul	506	Scudday	27 Jun 1944	EP B-32-8
2 Lt	0-687496	Richardson, William M.	66	Richardson	08 Apr 1944	Interred in USA
TSgt	32143092	Riche, Wilson A.	68	Whitaker	01 Oct 1943	Interred in USA
TSgt	16028870	Riefen, Herman	66	Ketchum	13 Jun 1945	CA D2-26
SSgt	32414057	Rieger, Martin A.	67	Clarey	27 Apr 1944	Interred in USA
SSgt	35669582	Ries, Robert P.	506	Scudday	27 Jun 1944	EP B33-8
1 Lt	0-719431	Ritter, Frederick M. Jr.	66	Podojil	19 Mar 1945	Interred in USA
Sgt	35292580	Rizzo, Anthony F.	68	Du Bard	06 Dec 1942	AR Wall of Missing
SSgt	17147154	Roach, James E.	67	Crandell	24 Mar 1945	Interred in USA
2 Lt	0-2015143	Robak, Richard J.	66	Ketchum	13 Jun 1945	Interred in USA
Sgt	35369184	Robbins, Robert E.	68	Hovey	13 Jan 1944	CA F- 1-108
1 Lt	0-688402	Roberts, Gilman N.	68	Sweigart	29 Apr 1944	AR A41-31
SSgt	12171724	Robinson, Frederick A.	66	Almlie	13 Nov 1943	NE Wall of Missing
SSgt	15330702	Robison, Jack C.	67	Pinder	29 Jan 1944	Interred in USA
2 Lt	0-684197	Rodgers, Harold R.	66	Spelts	21 Jan 1944	NO A-11-42
2 Lt	0-727264	Roetto, Lawrence J.	67	Blaine	08 Mar 1943	Interred in USA
Sgt	37235533	Rogers, Fred B.	67	Fish	22 Feb 1944	CA Wall of Missing
TSgt	14023217	Romeo, Santo	506	Tucker	27 Jun 1944	Interred in USA
SSgt	14158075	Roop, Eugene W.N.	506	Money	11 Apr 1944	Interred in USA
SSgt	31145138	Rosenstein, Jacob	66	Bridges	01 Oct 1943	Interred in USA
2 Lt	0-797402	Rossi, Walter Jr.	66	Curelli	16 Aug 1943	Interred in USA
TSgt	18070094	Russell, Eldo A.	506	Fouts	22 Mar 1943	NE Wall of Missing
2 Lt	0-812315	Russell, James F.	67	Mayes	08 Apr 1944	Interred in USA
SSgt	37224426	Russell, Lloyd E.	67	Johnson	18 Nov 1943	CA Wall of Missing
2 Lt	0-797076	Russell, Robert P.	67	Mayes	08 Apr 1944	Interred in USA
2 Lt	0-734982	Saenger, Lester E.	66	Irby	11 Oct 1943	Interred in USA
Sgt	11045878	Salvo, Alberto O.	66	McPhillamey	26 Feb 1943	Interred in USA
2 Lt	0-700988	Sanders, James E.	67	Tomer	25 May 1944	NO C21-43
Pvt	?	Sanneman, Herman R.	66	Frawley	18 May 1942	Interred in USA
SSgt	20631208	Satterfield, Channing N.	66	Scrivner	01 Aug 1943	Interred in USA
2 Lt	0-730624	Scarborough, John I.	67	Scarborough	16 Mar 1944	CA D6-39
Sgt	20317133	Schappert, Thomas F.	66	Scrivner	01 Aug 1943	Interred in USA
TSgt	39092894	Schettler, William J.	67	Weaver	01 Aug1943	AR A- 12-3
2 Lt	0-684807	Schexnayder, Joseph L.	66	Almlie	13 Nov 1943	NE Wall of Missing
SSgt	32529251	Schiess, Charles F.	68	Landahl	29 Jun 1944	Interred in USA
SSgt	35224546	Schmitz, Norbert J.	66	Podojil	19 Mar 1945	LO A29-40
SSgt	39826757	Schoer, Walter B.	68	Houston	01 Aug 1943	AR C- 11-6
2 Lt.	0-682125	Schuyler, Robert E.	506	Sprinkle	08 Apr 1944	NE Wall of Missing
1 Lt	0-733360	Schwab, Harold W.	506	Bolin	02 Feb 1944	Interred in USA
Sgt	39468984	Scott, Layton W.	68	Almoina	28 Jan 1945	CA B2-18
2 Lt	0-2066052	Scott, Wayne S.	68	Corwine	28 Jan 1945	Interred in USA
2 Lt	0-796608	Scott, William	68	Houston	01 Aug 1943	FL Wall of Missing
2 Lt	0-733106	Scriven, Dale R.	66	Lasco	01 Aug 1943	Interred in USA
1 Lt	0-728030	Scrivner, Thomas E.	66	Scrivner	01 Aug 1943	AR D10-38
1 Lt	0-682906	Scudday, Bernie L.	506	Scudday	27 Jun 1944	Interred in USA
2 Lt	0-663420	Seaman, Robert H.	506	Fouts	22 Mar 1943	NE Wall of Missing
2 Lt	0-678476	Seiler, Walter J.	66	Almlie	13 Nov 1943	Interred in USA
TSgt	35420784	Semons, Earl N.	66	Heskett	26 Nov 1943	Interred in USA
TSgt	12044639	Sevick, Stephen F.	68	Houston	01 Aug 1943	Interred in USA
TSgt	33187932	Shaeffer, Clair P.	68	Sobotka	21 Jan 1944	AR Wall of Missing
SSgt	35354093	Shafer, Raymond C.	66	Curelli	16 Aug 1943	Interred in USA
2 Lt	0-678477	Shaffer, Donald E.	66	Miller	22 Dec 1943	Interred in USA
1 Lt	0-700998	Shambarger, Walter B.	68	Weaver	07 Jul 1944	AR D11-28
Capt	0-661667	Shaw, Charles M.	67	O'Neill	11 Dec 1943	AR A41-50
Sgt	37046013	Shea, John J.	68	Dayball	18 Oct 1944	Interred in USA
SSgt	12124435	Sheehan, William J.	66	Miller	22 Dec 1943	AR C- 10-42
TSgt	11116435	Sheldon, Stanley W.	66	McKenna	06 Aug 1944	NE Wall of Missing
2 Lt	0-401892	Sheridan, Charles M.	67	Fish	22 Feb 1944	CA Wall of Missing
SSgt	39261528	Sherwood, Lawrence J.	67	Green	29 Jul 1944	CA Wall of Missing
Sgt	35339045	Short, Emerson D.	506	Johnston	04 Oct 1943	NE Wall of Missing
Sgt	33442877	Shultz, Robert E.	506	Rawson	20 Feb 1944	Interred in USA
Sgt	31284222	Sicard, Edward P.	68	Dayball	18 Oct 1944	Interred in USA
Sgt	17165143	Siecke, Eldon D.	66	Richardson	08 Apr 1944	Interred in USA
2 Lt	0-678397	Siegel, Louis	67	Johnson	18 Nov 1943	CA Wall of Missing
SSgt	17175511	Siegert, Paul C.	67	Mayes	08 Apr 1944	Interred in USA
Sgt	37109907	Sivertsen, Kenneth C.	66	McCoy	20 Feb 1943	CA D3-44
2 Lt	0-736038	Singer, Paul S.	506	Austin	16 Aug 1943	SR J- 12-62
MSgt	13038405	Smith, Allen D.	66	McCoy	20 Feb 1943	Interred in USA
SSgt	14165246	Smith, Charles R.	67	Bateman	16 Aug 1943	SR Wall of Missing
Sgt	39094553	Smith, Donald M.	68	Du Bard	06 Dec 1942	AR Wall of Missing
SSgt	35370944	Smith, Harry G.	68	Peterson	02 Jul 1943	Interred in USA
2 Lt	0-813456	Smith, Joseph R. Jr.	506	Sprinkle	08 Apr 1944	NE Wall of Missing

Rank	ASN	Name	Sqdn.	Pilot	Dat of Loss	Cemetary Location
Sgt	33452262	Smith, Malcolm R.	68	Dayball	18 Oct 1944	Interred in USA
SSgt	31311918	Smith, Louis R	66	Zweig	11 Jul 1944	Interred in USA
SSgt	35456291	Smith, Nick B.	68	Shannon	16 Aug 1943	FL E1-37
SSgt	17020692	Smith, Robert F.	66	Oakley	22 Dec 1943	Interred in USA
MSgt	13027651	Smith, Robert M.	68	Whitaker	01 Oct 1943	AR B44-53
F/O	T-126546	Smith, Thomas P.	68	Hobbs	02 Dec 1944	Interred in USA
2 Lt	0-805997	Smith, William L.	66	Spelts	21 Jan 1944	AR Wall of Missing
TSgt	17032555	Snell, Dalton R.	67	Price	08 Mar 1943	Interred in USA
SSgt	34435403	Snider, Edwon R.	67	Johnson	18 Nov 1943	CA Wall of Missing
Sgt	37219104	Snow, Clarence W.	68	Hovey	13 Jan 1944	Interred in USA
1 Lt	0-799486	Sobotka, Frank W. Jr.	68	Sobotka	21 Jan 1944	AR Wall of Missing
TSgt	32436994	Sofferman, Abe	67	Pinder	29 Jan 1944	Interred in USA
2 Lt	0-886976	Southern, William A.	68	Steinke	07 Jul 1944	AR D9-37
2 Lt	0-679676	Sowers, Richard J.	68	Hovey	13 Jan 1944	Interred in USA
SSgt	37136575	Spears, Milford L.	68	Houston	01 Aug 1943	Interred in USA
Sgt	16063102	Speir, Robert J.	66	Rogers	04 Dec 1944	Interred in USA
2 Lt	0-680326	Spelts, Martin E.	66	Spelts	21 Jan 1944	AR Wall of Missing
1 Lt	0-777858	Spencer, Jack H. (156th Repl Co)	66	Ketchum	13 Jun 1945	Interred in USA
2 Lt	0-678399	Spink, Harold W.	68	Bohnisch	05 Feb 1944	Interred in USA
SSgt	34303915	Spivey, Joseph B. Jr.	66	Lasco	01 Aug 1943	Interred in USA
SSgt	34598241	Springs, Charles E.	506	Sprinkle	08 Aug 1944	Interred in USA
2 Lt	0-808172	Staib, Henry T.	67	Fish	22 Feb 1944	CA Wall of Missing
TSgt	17152057	Stammer, James C.	66	Ketchum	13 Jun 19451	Interred in USA
1 Lt	0-730646	Stamos, Robert G.	506	Money	11 Apr 1944	Interred in USA
TSgt	39453890	Staples, Robert L.	68	Landahl	29 Jun 1944	Interred in USA
F/O	T-190606	Starr, Charles L.	67	Reinhart	01 Aug 1943	Interred in USA
SSgt	13031489	Starr, Henry P.	66	Ledford	30 Sep 1944	AR B18-6
1 Lt	0-743121	Starring, Alfred A.	68	Staffing	21 Jan 1944	Interred in USA
1 Lt	0-668816	Steadham, Roy J.	68	Altemus	08 Apr 1944	NE Wall of Missing
Sgt	19170304	Steele, Arthur M.	68	Starring	21 Jan 1944	NO B22-5
SSgt	39204852	Steinke, Arthur A.	68	Dayball	18 Oct 1944	Interred in USA
1 Lt	0-807537	Steinke, Donald H.	68	Steinke	07 Jul 1944	Interred in USA
SSgt	12239759	Steinmiller, Wilbert R.	68	Corwine	28 Jan 1945	AR D4-5
Sgt	18187261	Stell, Charles E.	68	Bledsoe	28 Dec 1944	Interred in USA
2 Lt	0-667449	Stenborn, Harry W.	66	Lasco	01 Aug 1943	AR B24-4
SSgt	13169810	Stephanovic, Reuben J.	68	Konstand	28 Dec 1944	LO D30-41
TSgt	18074552	Stephens, Raymond C.	67	Long	16 Feb 1943	CA Wall of Missing
TSgt	33133951	Steptoe, Thomas E. Jr.	67	Roach	14 May 1943	AR B20-1
TSgt	16105797	Stern, Jerome J.	67	Bakalo	18 Oct 1944	Interred in USA
SSgt	32478604	Stevenson, Joe A.	67	Bateman	16 Aug 1943	NA Wall of Missing
SSgt	39090749	Stewart, Edwin M.	506	Whitlock	16 Aug 1943	Interred in USA
SSgt	38148621	Stewart, Verne C.	68	Cargile	27 Jan 1943	AR D2-49
Sgt	16097147	Stickel, Robert J.	67	Scarborough	07 Mar 1944	Interred in USA
2 Lt	0-734393	Stigora, Joseph H.	67	Houle	18 Nov 1943	CA Wall of Missing
SSgt	17108124	Stoffel, Glenn C.	506	Maynor	20 Dec 1943	NE Wall of Missing
SSgt	13074162	Strait, Ralph E.	506	Bolin	02 Feb 1944	CA D1-75
SSgt	32734072	Strally, Samuel R.	66	Zweig	11 Jul 1944	Interred in USA
2 Lt	0-679687	Stubbs, Alvin E.	67	Pinder	29 Jan 1944	Interred in USA
SSgt	37161475	Sufka, Edward	67	Blaine	08 Mar 1943	Interred in USA
SSgt	35562810	Sullivan, Kenneth E.	68	Bell	24 Feb 1944	Interred in USA
1 Lt	0-204058	Sullivan, Maxwell W. Jr.	68	Sullivan	27 Jan 1943	NE P22-9
TSgt	35457629	Sullivan, Wilfred C.	67	Johnson	18 Nov 1943	CA Wall of Missing
TSgt	06979809	Suskind, Saul	68	Cargile	27 Jan 1943	NE M22-6
2 Lt	0-728034	Swanson, Clark E.	68	Erwin	03 Jan 1943	Interred in USA
1 Lt	0-733113	Swensson, Berthel	67	Carpenter	01 Oct 1943	AR D37-21
SSgt	16133615	Swetlik, William M.	67	Fish	22 Feb 1944	CA Wall of Missing
Sgt	36113560	Szabo, Paul A. Jr.	67	Fish	22 Feb 1944	CA Wall of Missing
2 Lt	0-736908	Tabor, James A.	68	Peterson	02 Jul 1943	Interred in USA
2 Lt	0-?	Tate, Augustus H.	66	Frawley	18 May 1942	Interred in USA
TSgt	18062096	Taylor, Oran J.	68	Garrett	02 Jul 1943	NA Wall of Missing
Sgt	39196030	Taylor, Russell G.	68	Hovens	21 Apr 1944	Interred in USA
1 Lt	0-728767	Tenney, Ross A.	67	Roach	14 May 1943	Interred in USA
SSgt	16072477	Tenosky, Andy J.	68	Garrett	02 Jul 1943	NA Wall of Missing
SSgt	37281321	Terwey, Alphonse J.	68	Jones	16 Dec 1943	CA A-1-36
Sgt	35520803	Testa, Arthur F.	68	Hovey	13 Jan 1944	CA C-2-79
2 Lt	0-701346	Thielen, Charles M. (448th BG)	66	Zweig	11 Jul 1944	NO 1-24-26
SSgt	16038586	Thompson, Edward J.	506	Westcott	29 Jun 1944	LO D-36-35
Sgt	37211941	Thurman, Homer A.	67	Tomer	25 May 1944	NO C-2-6
Sgt	38101171	Tiller, Homer M.	68	Sweigart	29 Apr 1944	AR D- 11-41
Sgt	12092338	Timme, Arthur C.	66	Oakley	22 Dec 1943	Interred in USA
2 Lt	0-556131	Titus, Dudley G.	506	McGuire	12 Aug 1944	NO G-26-25
1 Lt	0-752794	Toepel, Arthur C.	506	Westcott	29 Jun 1944	LO K17-12
2 Lt	0-693433	Tomer, Frank J.	67	Tomer	25 May 1944	NO B-11-25
SSgt	39542241	Towning, John L.	66	Almlie	13 Nov 1943	Interred in USA

Rank	ASN	Name	Sqdn.	Pilot	Dat of Loss	Cemetary Location
1 Lt	0-670670	Townsend, Raymond H. Jr.	68	Townsend	08 Apr 1944	NE Wall of Missing
2 Lt	0-736049	Travis, William C. Jr.	67	Bateman	16 Aug 1943	FL Wall of Missing
1 Lt	0-743297	Trolese, Alexander	66	Trolese	26 Nov 1943	AR A36-54
LtCol	0-399733	Turnbull, John I. (HQ)	67	Bakalo	18 Oct 1944	Interred in USA
2 Lt	0-738948	Turrou, Victor T.	66	Curelli	16 Aug 1943	SR J2-62
SSgt	17155940	Tyler, Leo M.	68	Mathisen	21 Jan 1944	Interred in USA
SSgt	32385827	Van Cleef, Arthur A.	68	Cargile	27 Jan 1943	NE Wall of Missing
SSgt	37144043	Van Oyen, Harold D.	68	Powell	14 May 1943	Interred in USA
TSgt	32551956	Ventura, Anthony J.	506	Scudday	27 Jun 1944	Interred in USA
TSgt	13030085	Vogt, Robert K.	66	Adams	26 Feb 1943	Interred in USA
Sgt	38263445	Voorhies, Henry H.	67	Dobson	18 Nov 1943	CA Wall of Missing
TSgt	14135751	Walker, Joseph H.	68	Corwine	28 Jan 1945	Interred in USA
Sgt	13056108	Wapensky, Russell A.	506	Rawson	20 Feb 1944	AR D21-17
2 Lt	0-2045032	Ward, Edwin M. Jr.	68	Townsend	08 Apr 1944	Interred in USA
TSgt	34107345	Ward, Joe F.	68	Houston	01 Aug 1943	Interred in USA
2 Lt	0-716788	Ward, Kenneth P.	506	Jacobs	08 Aug 1944	Interred in USA
Sgt	?	Warley, Arlo V.	66	Frawley	18 May 1942	Interred in USA
Capt	0-404099	Warne, Gideon W.	67	Warne	22 Mar 1943	NE Wall of Missing
SSgt	13078765	Warren, Lester D.	506	Scudday	27 Jun 1944	Interred in USA
SSgt	37290897	Warvick, Isley B.	67	Henderson	01 Oct 1943	Interred in USA
SSgt	35401274	Weaver, Lewis R.	67	Oakley	22 Dec 1943	Interred in USA
Sgt	18053822	Weems, Manuel H.	68	With 389th BG	29 Aug 1943	Interred in USA
2 Lt	0-674819	Weiner, Stanley	68	Hovey	13 Jan 1944	Interred in USA
SSgt	32828525	Weinman, Edward 1.	68	Corwine	28 Jan 1945	AR B23-16
TSgt	12033349	Weiser, Samuel S.	67	Cullen	15 Feb 1943	Interred in USA
2 Lt	0-2065203	Wellman, Harrison W. IV	68	Bledsoe	22 Dec 1944	CA F6-129
Sgt	11015413	Welsh, William F.	66	Adams	26 Feb 1943	Interred in USA
SSgt	06150461	Wenke, Raymond G.	68	Townsend	08 Apr 1944	Interred in USA
TSgt	32765359	Wernicki, Edward A.	506	Money	11 Apr 1944	NE P-10-5
SSgt	32432466	Wessman, Helge E.	506	Still	07 Oct 1944	NE F-17-8
SSgt	35917694	West, John W.	66	Podojil	19 Mar 1945	Interred in USA
1 Lt	0-808918	Westcott, Gerald S,	506	Westcott	29 Jun 1944	Interred in USA
SSgt	16162293	Whalen, Jack V.	506	Jacobs	08 Aug 1944	Interred in USA
1 Lt	0-675979	Wheatly, Harold J.	506	Money	11 Apr 1944	Interred in USA
1 Lt	0-885920	Whitaker, Coleman S.	68	Whitaker	01 Oct 1943	LO C17-3
Sgt	11027878	White, Benjamin F. Jr.	67	Blaine	08 Mar 1943	NO B10-41
SSgt	39247916	Wieser, Jerry H.	506	Fouts	22 Mar 1943	NE Wall of Missing
1 Lt	0-729393	Wilborn, Everett W. Jr.	67	Phillips	14 May 1943	Interred in USA
2 Lt	0-728042	Wilkes, Charles E.	67	Oliphant	15 Feb 1943	AR Wall of Missing
Capt	0-426964	Wilkinson, Oscar H.	68	Cargile	27 Jan 1943	NE 08-10
SSgt	36451793	Williams, Charles E.	68	Smith	29 May 1944	CA E4-19
SSgt	18037070	Williams, Don J.	67	Blaine	08 Mar 1943	Interred in USA
TSgt	12031124	Williams, Richard H.	66	Hobson	01 Oct 1943	LO G3-24
SSgt	18037355	Williams, Truitt H.	68	Diehl	01 Aug 1943	NA D-1-8
F/O	T-74	Wilson, Edward R.	506	Whitlock	16 Aug 1943	Interred in USA
SSgt	14124998	Wilson, James L.	506	Bolin	02 Feb 1944	Interred in USA
TSgt	12060904	Wilson, Stanley	66	Gentry	01 Aug 1943	Interred in USA
Sgt	34431710	Winfree, Julian E. Jr.	506	Rawson	20 Feb 1944	Interred in USA
1 Lt	0-662848	Winger, George W.	66	Winger	01 Aug 1943	FL Wall of Missing
SSgt	37135114	Wise, Solomon 1.	68	Cargile	27 Jan 1943	NE Wall of Missing
2 Lt	0-701359	Witkin, Leonard	68	Lehnhausen	18 Oct 1944	Interred in USA
TSat	36233230	Wolf, Frederick T.	506	Swanson	14 May 1943	AR D-10-8
SSgt	13119193	Wood, Fred D. Jr,	66	Harleman	27 Mar 1944	RH Wail of Missing
Sgt	18113166	Wood, Hal N.	68	Hovens	21 Apr 1944	Interred in USA
Sgt	18015826	Wood, Thomas M.	66	Lasco	01 Aug 1943	Interred in USA
TSgt	37374038	Woods, Howard C.	67	Hager	16 Aug 1943	Interred in USA
Sgt	35036742	Woolfe, Chester R.	68	With 389th BG	27 Aug 1943	BR F15-3
2 Lt	0-683521	Worth, Woodrow N.	67	O'Neill	I I Dec 1943	Interred in USA
SSgt	35474099	Wright, Raymond E.	66	Trolese	26 Nov 1943	AR C15-4
1 Lt	0-675462	Wulff, Orville L.	506	Bolin	02 Feb 1944	Interred in USA
TSgt	13116002	Wycheck, Joseph E.	506	Scudday	27 Jun 1944	EP A21-28
TSgt	20364881	Yeatts, Roy J.	67	Carpenter	01 Oct 1943	AR C29-13
SSgt	36068208	Yoakum, Arthur M.	68	Peterson	02 Jul 1943	Interred in USA
SSgt	12024064	Yocco, Dominic P.	68	Wilson	07 Jul 1944	Interred in USA
2 Lt	0-734863	Young, Robert E.	66	Scrivner	01 Aug 1943	Interred in USA
Sgt	36743059	Young, William C.	68	Lelmhausen	18 Oct 1944	Interred in USA
Sgt	33498702	Youse, Charles M.	67	Clarey	27 Apr 1944	Interred in USA
TSgt	31140518	Yurick, Chester W.	506	Bolin	02 Feb 1944	CA F3-4
2 Lt	0-698812	Zajicek, James L.	68	Hovens	21 Apr 1944	Interred in USA
SSgt	31169351	Zdonick, Michael P.	68	Jones	16 Dec 1943	CA E0-38
SSgt	17129592	Ziegler, Norbert J.	67	Bakalo	18 Oct 1944	HC F-1-31
SSgt	17029368	Zimmer, Floyd H.	66	Billings	16 Feb 1943	CA Wall of Missing
SSgt	36529756	Zoller, Harper F. Jr.	66	Curelli	16 Aug 1943	Interred in USA
1 Lt	0-728529	Zwicker, Henry R.	67	Henderson	01 Oct 1943	Interred in USA

NOTES

NOTES

NOTES

NOTES

NOTES

NOTES

Index